Handbook of
Clinical Sociology

Handbook of Clinical Sociology

EDITED BY

HOWARD M. REBACH
University of Maryland, Eastern Shore
Princess Anne, Maryland

AND

JOHN G. BRUHN
University of Texas Medical Branch
Galveston, Texas

Plenum Press • New York and London

Library of Congress Cataloging-in-Publication Data

Handbook of clinical sociology / edited by Howard M. Rebach and John
G. Bruhn.
     p.   cm.
   Includes bibliographical references.
   Includes index.
     ISBN 0-306-43559-4 (cloth with stamping). -- ISBN 0-306-43579-9
(paperbound)
     1. Clinical sociology--Handbooks, manuals, etc.   I. Rebach,
Howard M.   II. Bruhn, John G., 1934-
     [DNLM: 1. Social Medicine. 2. Sociology, Medical.   WA 31 H2355]
HM73.H315 1990
301--dc20
DNLM/DLC   90-7998
for Library of Congress   CIP

---

10 9 8 7 6 5 4 3

© 1991 Plenum Press, New York
A Division of Plenum Publishing Corporation
233 Spring Street, New York, N.Y. 10013

All rights reserved

Printed in the United States of America

To Louis Wirth, Saul Alinsky, John Glass, Alfred McClung Lee, Sojourner Truth, "Mother" Jones, and Jane Addams — all pioneers whose vision and dedication to social change and humanistic values have led to the creation and reemergence of clinical sociology.

We also dedicate this volume to the contributors and our other colleagues who labor in the vineyards.

Contributors

Rae Banks Adams, Department of Sociology, Abilene Christian University, Abilene, Texas 79699

Adrianne Bank, Graduate School of Education, University of California, Los Angeles, California 90024.

Janet Mancini Billson, Department of Sociology and Women's Studies, Rhode Island College, Providence, Rhode Island 02908

Clifford M. Black, School of Community Service, University of North Texas, Denton, Texas 76203

David W. Britt, Department of Sociology, Wayne State University, Detroit, Michigan 48202

John G. Bruhn, School of Allied Health Sciences, The University of Texas Medical Branch, Galveston, Texas 77550-2782

Nathan Church, Department of Counseling and Health Sciences, Western Washington University, Bellingham, Washington 98225

Estelle Disch, Department of Sociology, University of Massachusetts, Boston, Massachusetts 02125-3393

Richard Enos, Center for Public Service, School of Community Service, University of North Texas, Denton, Texas 76203

Jack Ferguson, University of Windsor, Harper Hospital, Detroit, Michigan 48201

Tamara Ferguson, Lafayette Clinic, Harper Hospital, Detroit, Michigan 48201

Jan M. Fritz, Department of Sociology, California State University, San Bernardino, California 92407-2397

John E. Holman, Institute of Criminal Justice, School of Community Service, University of North Texas, Denton, Texas 76203

David J. Kallen, Department of Pediatrics and Human Development, Michigan State University, East Lansing, Michigan 48824

Alfred McClung Lee, Brooklyn College, City University of New York, Brooklyn, New York 11210, and Drew University, Madison, New Jersey 07940

Elliot D. Luby, Wayne State University School of Medicine, Harper Hospital, Detroit, Michigan 48201

Julia A. Mayo, Department of Psychiatry, St. Vincent's Hospital and Medical Center, New York, New York 10011

John S. Miller, College of Arts, Humanities, and Social Sciences, University of Arkansas at Little Rock, Little Rock, Arkansas 72204

James F. Quinn, Institute of Criminal Justice, School of Community Service, University of North Texas, Denton, Texas 76203

Howard M. Rebach, Department of Social Sciences, University of Maryland, Eastern Shore, Princess Anne, Maryland 21853

Lance W. Roberts, Department of Sociology, University of Manitoba, Winnipeg, Manitoba, Canada R3T 2N2

Bruce Saunders, College of Education, University of Washington, Seattle, Washington 98195, and Clinical Sociology Associates, Seattle, Washington 98115

Arthur B. Shostak, Department of Psychology and Sociology, Drexel University, Philadelphia, Pennsylvania 19104

Yvonne M. Vissing, Family Research Laboratory, University of New Hampshire, Durham, New Hampshire 03824, and Department of Pediatrics, Boston City Hospital, Boston, Massachusetts 02118

David W. Watts, College of Arts and Sciences, Southeastern Louisiana University, Hammond, Louisiana 70402

Nina B. Wright, High Risk Youth Prevention, San Marcos, Texas 78666

Foreword

This book is a most welcome addition to the growing literature on sociological practice. There is a wealth of wisdom and experience reflected in these chapters as well as a wide variety of examples of sociology in action.

Clinical sociology, in its broadest sense, is the application of a sociological perspective to facilitate change. Its practitioners are primarily change agents rather than scholars or researchers, and work with a client, be that an individual, family, group, organization, or community.

The reappearance and growth of clinical sociology during the past decade is the realization of a vision of mine, born in the 1960s and 1970s out of my anger and frustration—first as a graduate student and then as a professor—that sociologists, unlike their psychological brethren, did not practice what they preached. Persons trained in other disciplines were practicing clinical sociology, and those few sociologists who did kept it a secret.

The Clinical Sociology Association, which I cofounded in 1978, had its beginnings at a roundtable I led at the American Sociological Association meetings in New York in 1976. I had just concluded four years as the only sociologist on the faculty of the California School of Professional Psychology in Los Angeles teaching graduate clinical psychology students how to do sociology. I saw sociology giving up by default a role in change efforts that necessitate the consideration of social systems. Social workers, psychologists, political scientists, gerontologists, criminologists, marriage and family counselors, to name a few, have eagerly gone where we had failed to tread. Practitioners in these fields, as social systems change agents, have carved a niche, often protecting themselves with licensing laws and other restrictions that make entry by sociologists difficult. Thus we are latecomers in a crowded field.

Another problem facing the sociological practitioner is the invisibility of sociology. If you ask the average citizen what a sociologist is, you will do well if you get a distinction from socialist or social worker. Anything beyond that is gravy! All too many of us hide our identities as sociologists. My own recent experience as manager of a community service program for juvenile offenders is an example. As a nonacademic sociologist, I often do not reveal my background, training, and degree. I was socialized to believe that "real" sociologists become scholars and researchers and that working in the community is for social workers.

Yet clinical sociology can only flourish if its practitioners do good work, identify themselves as sociologists and their work as sociological, and disseminate what they do to a larger public. Until recently, practitioners have not written much about what they do, probably because they do not have the time, opportunities, and incentives that academics have for getting published. Hopefully, this will change as the field matures.

I always have marveled at Kurt Lewin's wonderful dictum, "There is nothing so practical as a good theory," which is equally valid turned around: "There is nothing so theoretical as a good practice." Lewin also believed that the best way to understand something is to try to change it. Theory and practice are two sides of the same coin. Good practice is informed and guided by theory; it is a creative process involving feelings, intuition, risk taking, and problem solving, as so many of the chapters in this book amply illustrate. Jan Fritz's carefully detailed and fascinating resurrection of the long and all but forgotten history of clinical sociology certainly gives a precedent for sociologists to be more involved as practitioners.

In my own community, I am seeing the late Saul Alinsky's brilliant theories and strategies for community organization come alive as a newly formed community group in the San Fernando Valley tackles graffiti, crime, and other problems of a suburban area in transition. My own consulting experience with problems of morale in a corporation credit department led to the discovery of how an alcoholic manager, and a codependent assistant, can affect an entire work group in a highly dysfunctional manner: an example of seeing the systemic consequences of individual behavior.

There are limits to individual treatment. Society increasingly recognizes that powerlessness, homelessness, and drug abuse, for example, are not simply the individual derelictions of deviants but are also symptoms of a disordered social system. Our society is facing unprecedented problems in health care, environmental pollution, a changing work force, and an aging population to name a few current conditions that have profound sociological aspects to their amelioration.

Clinical sociology, despite its name, is not limited to healing the sick, as the range of work described in this book clearly indicates. I am glad to see a chapter on public policy—on the nuts and bolts of making an impact at the societal level. Organizational consulting offers a made-to-order opportunity for clinical sociologists to help solve problems when firms with different cultures merge, or when corporations become multinational or attempt to integrate different ethnic groups in their work force. Clinical sociologists seek to understand the social dynamics of the situation and intervene with this in mind.

Clinical sociology in the eyes of its proponents is guided by humanistic values, a prizing of community, collaboration, concern for others, for the environment, for helping people to realize their potential in the social settings in which they find themselves.

Finally, handbooks such as this one, by the nature of their titles, hard covers, and cost, are usually only found on the shelves of professors and libraries. That would be a shame with this book. It should be available to both introductory and advanced students, scholars, policymakers, and practitioners in allied fields.

Wang-Yang-Ming, a sixteenth-century Chinese philosopher, wrote, "Knowledge is a beginning of practice; doing is the completion of knowing. . . . Those who to the very end of life fail to practice also fail to understand." Thus clinical sociology is a contemporary embodiment of an ancient truth.

JOHN F. GLASS

Studio City, California

Preface

This book is an outgrowth of the reemergence of clinical sociology as a formally organized subdiscipline. In the late 1970s, a group of sociologists met and formed the Clinical Sociology Association. This organization was formed outside the mainstream of sociology, largely because these individuals were actively engaged in intervention and social change but did not find mainstream sociology supportive of their efforts. However, these individuals felt the need to establish a community of interest and share information. They also felt that, by organizing, they could increase awareness of sociological practice and be a catalyst for further developing the discipline.

We feel that, after a decade, it is appropriate to assess our present status and suggest directions for its further development and encourage sociologists and allied disciplines to join in the progress of clinical sociology and sociological practice. Therefore, we submit this book with samples of contributions from clinical sociologists over the past decade.

OBJECTIVES

In our selection of topics and chapters, we were guided by three principle objectives: (1) to present a representative selection of current practice activities and issues; (2) to present a broad spectrum of the field; and (3) to expose readers to a variety of perspectives, general practice concerns, the practice of clinical sociology in specific settings, the work of clinical sociologists with special populations, and to examine issues of identity and future directions of clinical sociology.

The contributors to this volume are themselves actively engaged in the application of sociological knowledge, methods, and theory to active intervention. They work as sociologists. Their contributions draw heavily on their own work in illustrating clinical sociology; therefore, the *Handbook* provides a resource and a guide for sociologists and others on how people have done clinical sociology.

ORGANIZATION

The book is organized around practice concerns, specific settings, and special populations as frameworks. In addition, we have attempted to cover the social spectrum from the individual to small groups, organizations, and community settings. The parts in this book are organized as follows:

Part I outlines the definition and history of clinical sociology.

Part II contains chapters that outline the common concerns of sociological practitioners.

Part III portrays the practice of clinical sociology in several specific settings.

Part IV describes the work of clinical sociologists in mental health settings and with ethnic minorities, women, the elderly, and substance abusers.

The *Handbook* is intended for persons in a number of fields who are related to the practice of clinical sociology. We hope the book will be useful to three target audiences. First, to upper-level undergraduate and beginning graduate students, we offer it as an introduction to clinical sociology and a resource for career decisions. Second, to our sociological colleagues, we offer it in hope that they will appreciate a reemergence of the historic role of sociologists as working for positive social change. We also offer the book to those who wish to develop courses and curricula in clinical sociology, to sociology students, and to others who can benefit from seeing sociology in action. Third, we offer the *Handbook* to our colleagues in other clinical disciplines, who explore tried and untried strategies to seek solutions to social problems. Finally, to all our readers, our intent was to make this a practical handbook.

We are grateful to Paula L. Levine for her expertise in editing numerous drafts of manuscripts and in the reading of proofs.

HOWARD REBACH
JOHN G. BRUHN

Contents

PART II GENERAL PRACTICE CONCERNS

Chapter 3 • Assessment in Clinical Sociology 33

Bruce Saunders

Chapter 4 • Intervention in Clinical Sociology 49

Howard M. Rebach

Chapter 5 • Program Evaluation and Clinical Sociology 65

Adrianne Bank

Chapter 6 • Communication and Relationships with Clients 81

Howard M. Rebach

Chapter 7 • Ethics in Clinical Sociology 99

John G. Bruhn

Chapter 8 • The Effects of Social Change on Clinical Practice 125

Nathan Church

PART III   CLINICAL SOCIOLOGY IN SPECIFIC SETTINGS

Chapter 9 • Clinical Sociology with Individuals and Families 143

Lance W. Roberts

Chapter 10 • Public Policies and Clinical Sociology 165

Alfred McClung Lee

Chapter 11 • The Clinical Sociologist in Medical Settings 181

Yvonne Vissing and David J. Kallen

Chapter 12 • Health Promotion and Clinical Sociology 197

John G. Bruhn

Chapter 13 • Mental Health and Clinical Sociology 217

Tamara Ferguson, Jack Ferguson, and Elliot D. Luby

Chapter 14 • Clinical Sociology in the Criminal Justice System 233

Clifford M. Black, Richard Enos, John E. Holman, and James F. Quinn

PART I

THE REEMERGING FIELD OF CLINICAL SOCIOLOGY

CHAPTER 1

Clinical Sociology

Defining the Field

HOWARD REBACH AND JOHN BRUHN

INTRODUCTION

It is a challenging task to place a definition on a term like *clinical sociology*. Definitions by their nature contain a historical component. They also develop subcultural components as members of a social system communicate and share meanings for a term. Definitions also take on the subjective meanings of actors who use the term. With the term clinical sociology, as with many other concepts, there is also the pragmatic approach; we can observe the contexts in which the concept is applied and abstract the commonalities. The contributors to this volume engage in a variety of professional activities that stem from their professional training and identities as sociologists. Their work as well as historical definitions and our subjective meanings provide a body of data from which to derive some definitional statements about clinical sociology.

The purpose of this introductory chapter is to define the field of clinical sociology. Periodic attempts at such definition are useful for any field. As an exercise in "collective introspection," it can tell us where we are at a given juncture. It is not a complete definition.

A variety of social forces led to the conjunction of the terms *clinical* and *sociology*. Among them was the vision of some that, to justify itself, sociology must serve the needs of the people.[1] That is, sociology must go beyond the theoretical to provide knowledge applicable to real human problems. The application of theory addresses the scientific concern; application is the crucial test of theory.

HOWARD REBACH • Department of Social Science, University of Maryland Eastern Shore, Princess Anne, Maryland 21853.   JOHN BRUHN • School of Allied Health Sciences, University of Texas Medical Branch, Galveston, Texas 77550-2782.

TOWARD A DEFINITION

In moving toward a contemporary definition, it is well to examine some historical commentators. Wirth[2] held that the term *clinical* had come to connote the "case method," rather than pathology. The term clinical sociology, for Wirth, was "a convenient label for those insights, methods of approach, and techniques which the science of sociology can contribute to the understanding and treatment of persons whose behavior or personality problems bring them under the care of clinics for study and treatment." Wirth added that three main features characterized a clinical approach: Attention is focused on a case, a real problem; professionals cooperate, each contributing their special knowledge and insights, and "whatever may be the theoretical interests of the participants, clinical procedure has an immediate, therapeutic aim, and includes, therefore, not merely a study of the 'case' but the formulation of a program of adjustment or treatment." Finally, in his seminal article, Wirth stressed the need for the interplay of theory and practice: "the social sciences have no better way of testing their hypotheses and establishing their theories than by the patient accumulation and assimilation of the cases that actual human experience offers."[2]

Wirth's setting for work was a child guidance clinic. Though Wirth saw clinical sociology as bringing in a cultural approach and highlighting the effects of social roles and statuses on behavior, the application was toward the individual. Dunham's approach to specifying the field was similar.[3] He wrote that "clinical sociology consists basically of the analysis of one human personality as a social unit" and how "social experiences that emerge from the person's involvement with etiological structure, historical events, interpersonal relations, and cultural patterns" are represented in the person's personality. For Dunham, "the central concern . . . is always to obtain an exploration of the influence of these variables in accounting for the self image, role style, behavior pattern, and psychic orientation of a person who is part of a larger social system." The central issue, Dunham said, was the study of the problem personality. Thus, whereas Dunham included macro- and mesolevel issues, the focus was the individual.

In 1982, Freedman[4] identified nine definitional statements. From his informal content analysis, Freedman abstracted the following list of defining themes:
Clinical sociology is:

1. Practice oriented
2. Focuses on case studies
3. Works with individuals, groups, organizations, and communities
4. Diagnostic
5. Change oriented
6. Humanistic
7. Tries to comprehend the societal factors that restrict the individual from being effective
8. Can move beyond the client's formulation of the problem to consider other factors that affect functioning, especially broad social trends

9. Uses insights derived from immersion in the critical sociological tradition; uses sociological imagination
10. Leads to behavior change and growth
11. Tends to have a liberal/cynical or radical ideological cast

Although Freedman concluded that these factors do not create an approach that is *uniquely* sociological—it can be an approach taken by anyone—it is *distinctively* sociological.

DISTINCTIVENESS OF THE SOCIOLOGICAL APPROACH

Freedman's "uniqueness" criterion is a very stringent requirement. No claim is made that clinical sociological practice is unique. However, there are elements of the sociological approach to intervention, as characterized by clinical sociology, that are distinctive. We briefly summarize them here under the subheadings (1) perspective, (2) theory, and (3) methods.

The Sociological Perspective

The sociological perspective begins with the view that membership in human social groupings is the most pervasive characteristic of human beings. Moreover, a group is more than the sum of its parts. Something new is created in the formation and existence of a social grouping that cannot be understood by analysis, no matter how careful or rigorous, of the individual components.

Humans are unique in that people assign meaning to themselves, and to events, objects, and other people and determine their conduct on the basis of the meanings assigned. Meanings assigned and actions taken are shaped and constrained by group membership. The process of becoming and remaining members of social groups structures how people understand and relate to their worlds. Beliefs, values, expectations, and the like that are the basis for conduct emerge from people's interaction with their social environment. Thus, in the sociological view, behavior is largely learned and is an expression of cultural membership.

In specific contexts, actors' behaviors are expressions of role performance within context as the actors have come to understand their roles. The roles emerge from the group, belong to the group, and actors are taught their roles in interaction within context. These views see the "cause" for conduct as emerging from social arrangements rather than from invisible and unknowable "forces." Thus, Straus[5] held that, in analysis of a case, clinical sociologists direct their attention to contexts and conduct within them rather than to causes or hidden determinants. This view is consistent with the scientific outlook of sociology itself that emphasizes an empirical approach: All that can be observed is behavior and its consequences. Recourse to unverifiable phenomena, such a intrapsychic dynamics, has no place in clinical sociological work.

The views expressed here should not be seen as a restatement of social determinism. Individual actors, in enacting their roles in interaction with others, give shape and structure to the social group. There is a dynamic, dialectical relationship between individuals and social groups. As Berger and Luckman[6] have expressed, reality is negotiated as people interact; they shape and are shaped by group process.

These features of the sociological perspective shape and guide clinical sociology's view of human beings and helps define the subfield. This view asserts that humans are not passive responders to situations, but actively, creatively construct and reconstruct themselves and reality and negotiate an understanding of reality in interaction with others in situations. The individual reconstructs experience, forms an internal representation that guides action. Actors also plan; they construct symbolic future realities designed to achieve preferred outcomes. Conduct results from a choice from among the constructed futures. Though potentially limitless, these constructions are constrained by the actor's culture, by norms and values of the social group, by existing social reality, and by the actor's prior learnings. This view implies that, at any given moment, the actors in a situation attempt to adapt to the situation the best they can. And they are marshaling whatever resources they have to accomplish the task. The sociological model of humans also concludes that it is not the actual situation that structures people's conduct but their definition of the situation and their definition of self with respect to the situation.

This model of humans suggests a way to view "problems" to be addressed by the clinical sociological approach. Voelkl and Colburn[7] wrote that "problems are interpreted as being created by the social organization of human relationships." That is, problems are analyzed and addressed as social problems. But, as Dunham and others pointed out, concern is not exclusively with pathology or abnormality. Rather, it is a broader examination of the social circumstances of a case with the recognition that problematic situations for people—for individuals, groups, and larger social aggregates—arise out of social processes, often judged as "normal" by members of social systems who also take these social processes for granted to the extent that they are unaware of their causal influence on the problematic situation.

The contemporary sociological perspective also calls attention to the "social spectrum," the recognition of the many levels of social action from the dyadic relationship—a mother and child, two close friends, a worker and supervisor, and so forth—to whole societies and to humankind. The levels are characterized as micro-, meso-, and macrosociological. It is not simply the recognition of levels that is important but the understanding that a complex interaction exists among them. Mills's[8] notion that "history intrudes in our biographies" is relevant here. The structure and patterns of families, work groups, formal and informal organizations as well as the motives and actions of individual members respond to local and situational forces as well as social, political, economic and geographic forces at work during the epoch in which they exist.

Straus[9] emphasized that clinical sociological work was active intervention "at any or all levels of social organization," from micro- to macrolevels. Straus[10] added that one distinctive aspect of the sociological approach was analysis of the *interplay* of levels in a given case, regardless of the scope of the client social system. Clinical sociologists work with individuals, with families and small groups, with government, corporate, and community organizations, and even larger social aggregates and systems. However, regardless of the scope of the social system being analyzed, a distinctive feature of the clinical sociological approach is recognition of the interaction of levels. That is, when working with clients at the microlevel, meso- and macrolevel factors—their group memberships and larger social and historical forces—are part of the analysis. When working with large social systems, attention to actions of and effects on smaller systems and individuals remains.

Finally, the sociological perspective reflects a dialectic between science and humanism. Although the scientific method is emphasized within the discipline of sociology, it is meant to be science in the service of humanistic values. These values attempt to promote social organization that permits individual autonomy and self-determination. Healthy, supportive, nondestructive social environments produce healthy, creative people.

In sum, then, clinical sociology is defined, in part, by the sociological perspective that forms the basis for its application as an approach to intervention.

Theory

Clinical sociology also benefits from the theoretical development within sociology. Indeed, as Johnson[11] noted, "Sociological theory is a major part of the knowledge base needed by sociological practitioners, including both applied and clinical sociologists." Johnson went on to assert that the role of theory "is to provide models of social behavior that will facilitate the identification of human and organizational problems and suggest possible strategies for solution." In Johnson's view, these models help provide understanding of the actions and patterns of human social life that actors may take as "normal" but that may produce problems for them. For our purposes here, sociological theory may be broadly divided into functionalist, conflict, and microinteractionist perspectives.[12] Although this it not the place to review theory in detail or to reiterate Johnson's excellent paper, it may be useful to simply mention their relevance to clinical practice.

Structural Functionalism

Functionalist theory views social structure as a system, a set of functionally interrelated elements such that the action of any element impinges on the other elements and the system as a whole. It calls attention to systemic levels: The system under analysis is composed of subsystems, sub-subsystems, and so forth and may receive input from and provide output to higher system levels—the suprasystem(s). In the dialectic between stability and change, functionalism emphasizes those social arrangements that lend stability and constancy to social organization. Thus social structures are seen to exist because they contribute to the continued integration and equilibrium of a social system.

For the clinical sociologist, functionalism suggests the interconnectedness of social structures and social life in general. It provides a caution against the confusion of system levels while emphasizing their interdependence. Functionalism also provides the powerful tool of functional analysis. In assessing a case, the question is not only what are the problem behaviors, but what function do they serve and for whom. That is, analysis seeks those things that maintain the problematic situation. Analysis includes both manifest and latent functions and dysfunctions with the recognition that what may be functional for some is dysfunctional for others, who, perhaps are less powerful and of lower status. Finally, functionalist concepts such as equilibrium and boundary maintenance alert clinical workers to issues of boundaries of social groups and structures and processes that maintain problems and resist change.

The Conflict Perspective

Where functionalists see conflict as an aberration, conflict theorists see conflict as a normal social process. Conflict theories emphasize change rather than stability. Conflict theorists argue that most social systems are characterized by inequality and that dominance processes are a feature of most social systems. Those in dominant positions use their resources to maintain their status. Conflict or competition among differing groups over scarce resources within a social system is the engine that drives social change. What stability exists within social systems is seen as a temporary state based on the ability of some to control resources (e.g., power, wealth, etc.) to dominate actual or potential antagonistic groups. But even such dominant groups must accommodate the less dominant groups in some way lest conflict escalates to the point of upsetting the system. Thus intergroup conflict or actions taken by a group to maintain its dominance ultimately bring about change.

In the analysis of specific cases, conflict theories alert clinical sociologists to examine real or potential sources of conflict, to issues of inequality in the distribution of resources, of power and status within social systems, and to the things that produce problems stemming from alienation of members. Conflict theories direct attention toward analysis of dominance processes that exist within social systems. These may be explicit through the exercise of social controls or implicit through methods of training and socialization that get nondominant members to accept their status and the treatment they receive. Dominance processes can range from coercion and means–ends control to diversionary tactics. Assessments may include the contradictions within the system such as between values for free expression and the wish of some to censor expressions they deem harmful. The assessment may also ask how the terms of conflict are defined by participants and what are the conflict structures.

Understanding the conflict perspective may apply in helping communities obtain more adequate services from governments, in issues involving workers and management, in consumer issues, or any situation involving overt conflict among groups. Interventions may have the goal of helping an organization to establish methods of conflict management within their system. Or the intervention may be to assist residents of a community to organize in a conflict structure capable of representing their interests to a municipal government. Or perhaps the intervention may involve mediation between opposing interests helping them restructure the terms of conflict or arbitrating their differences.

The Interactionist Perspective

The symbolic interaction perspective applies primarily to the microsociological level. It emphasizes the development of mutual adaptation and shared meaning through interaction. One of the critical issues is how an individual comes to define self through interaction with others. Other issues concern how and to what extent interactants come to define situations and to share meaning. The concern here is the successful negotiation of a shared reality and ways of behaving with respect to each other and the situation.

Assessments in a case include clarifying who the key actors are and the nature of their interaction, the extent to which they share meanings, and how they define selves with respect to others in the social network. As Straus[8] pointed out, the goal of intervention may be to bring about change in members' definition of the situation.

This brief review was not meant to be a definitive treatment of the role of sociological theory in the work of clinical sociology. The purpose has been to suggest that sociological theory is an intellectual base that helps define clinical sociology and guides the thinking and work of clinical sociologists. By the same token, the array of methods drawn from sociology are also part of what defines clinical sociology.

Sociological Methods

One goal of a clinical sociologist is to come to understand the functioning of the social system and the social relationships within it. The array of research and analytic methods of scientific sociology is among the tools of clinical sociologists. As stated, our purpose here is to simply outline rather than provide definitive treatment. For our purposes, we can divide research methods into quantitative and qualitative methods.

Quantitative methods involve careful operational definition of what is to be measured and the construction or use of valid scales or indexes that indicate the extent or amount of some variable of interest. For example, in a work setting, indexes of worker alienation or group cohesion may provide useful information for assessments, and changes in the value of these variables may chart the progress of an intervention. In other settings, sampling techniques and survey methods can be used for many purposes, such as needs assessments, to discover people's attitudes toward or awareness of issues, proposals, services, and so forth, or to evaluate the success of programs. Well-developed methods of statistical analyses of such data are available. The use of the data gathering and analytical techniques can be a rich source of information about a given social system that can help direct problem definition and design of intervention.

In addition, the examination of recorded data that may be part of the institutional memory and general procedures of an organization may provide useful social indicators for assessing a problem and for tracking the course of an intervention. In a work setting, things like sales figures, accident rates, absenteeism, and the like may be used. Census data, police data, juvenile court data, employment figures, or any other of the mass of data routinely collected by various organizations and government units may provide unobtrusive quantitative data on relevant social indicators.

Not all interests of a clinical sociologist are quantifiable, and not all social systems to be studied are large enough to warrant survey techniques. For these case studies, an array of qualitative techniques provide rich insights to and understandings of the fabric and texture of social life. These techniques include the various forms of observation, in-depth interviews with key respondents, content analyses of messages, and even historical analysis. Qualitative methods are particularly useful in clinical work. They provide the worker with the opportunity to develop a feel for the realities of everyday life within a client's social system. Babbie[13] characterized these methods as "probing social life in its natural habitat," (p. 246) which allows the worker to pick up "nuances of attitudes and behavior" (p. 244) and to understand them within their setting. Babbie also noted that qualitative research methods provide the opportunity to observe social processes over time. These methods are particularly useful for clinical sociologists who work in microlevel contexts, but even for those who work with larger social systems, the combination of qualitative methods and quantitative methods can provide both depth understanding and rigor.

In sum then, clinical sociology is partly defined by its roots in scientific sociology. The perspectives, theories, and research methods of sociology form the major underpinnings. In addition, the research findings in sociology and other social sciences add points of departure. These all provide ways of thinking and analytical tools to which clinical sociologists add reflection and creativity in designing interventions to achieve clinical goals.

ROLES FOR CLINICAL SOCIOLOGISTS

Roles taken on by clinical sociologists give another clue to the definition of an emerging field. The following discussion of such roles is meant to be illustrative rather than definitive or exhaustive. It allows readers to draw some conclusions based on the activities of those engaged in the work of sociological intervention who call themselves clinical sociologists.

Organizational Consultant/Organizational Development

Organizations of many types are frequently confronted by problems that require sociological expertise and intervention. Issues internal to organizations, such as power and authority, communication, and resources distribution and use, are examples. Organizations also confront social and technological changes in their environments requiring them to seek help to adapt creatively. Interorganizational problems also emerge. Articles in this volume by Britt, Vissing and Kallen, and others elaborate on these themes. As intervention agents, clinical sociologists, applying sociological methods, theory, and knowledge can supply research, policy recommendations, and work with organizations to solve problems.

Social Impact Assessment

Social impact assessment has become a part of the general environmental impact statements that are often required in the planning and decision making for resource development. Preister and Kent[14] discussed the role of clinical sociologists in assessing and managing the social and cultural effects of resource development. Social impact management requires the assessment but continues as an "ongoing decision making process designed to identify, evaluate, respond to, and monitor the public issues arising from major industrial and government activities." Preister and Kent argued that the clinical sociologist's role includes both assessment and management of social impacts and they express the view that

> clinical sociologists are best suited to address the profound shift in our society from a vertical (power elite based) to a horizontal (community based) decision making system. Once outside the influence of the vertical system, one can see that clinical sociology emphasizes the ecological process working with rhythms and multilevels of interaction. The ecological focus replaces the mechanistic and hierarchical focus of past sociological concentration. We have assembled many of the tools needed to understand and function in this new horizontal age. Social impact management represents a statement on how our tools are used and offers a model for intervention at the community and organizational levels.

Community Organization

Local community groups also often need expert help in bringing about positive change to improve conditions for local residents. Work with such groups is almost a natural role for clinical sociologists. Glass[15] saw community organizer Saul Alinsky as a pioneer clinical sociologist. For Alinsky, community organization meant getting indigenous, local people involved in change rather than agencies superimposed on the community. It also meant "understanding . . . the fashion in which a local community functions within the larger social organism" and that attention must be directed "toward those larger socioeconomic issues which converge upon that scene to create the plight of the area."[16]

Anderson[17] developed a well-articulated theory applying interorganizational theory to the process of change at the community level. Referring to community development as "planned change," Anderson noted that not only must community members come together, they must work with various agencies and institutions to achieve their goals. Anderson's work, like the early work of Alinsky, exemplifies roles for clinical sociologists in community organization and community development.

Mediation/Conflict Resolution

Some clinical sociologists have become involved in mediation and conflict resolution. One such role was enacted as an adjunct to the judicial system where parties to a dispute get involved in dispute resolution mediation as an alternative to litigation. Other forms of conflict resolution, not associated with the courts, also occupy clinical sociologists. Miller's chapter in this volume discusses and elaborates on this theme.

Program Development/Program Evaluation

Clinical sociologists have also been involved in the development and evaluation of various programs designed to solve human problems and better meet people's needs. As an example of program development, Abbott and Blake[18] described "the 'Street Youth Employment Program,' a program designed by sociological practitioners to intervene in the lives of homeless street youth." Program development and program evaluation are interrelated. The latter feeds evaluative information back into the program for additional program development (See chapter by Bank).

Counselor/Sociotherapy

One role that many clinical sociologists are engaged in is that of counselor or "sociotherapist." This includes work with troubled individuals, families, groups, or couples. Though similar in form to the work of social workers, psychologists, psychotherapists, or family counselors, the work is guided by sociological principles. It recognizes that personal problems and problems of conduct have a social base, that problems result from adaptations to a given social context and the patterns of interaction within them, that actors' social relations, social contexts, and definitions of situations may provide a basis for problems, that roles and statuses and definitions placed on actors by others may also result in their getting "stuck" and not having adaptive strategies for becoming unstuck. Articles in this volume by Roberts, Mayo, Adams, and Billson address issues on this microlevel of sociological intervention.

Teacher/Trainer

Some clinical sociologists enact teaching roles as a way of facilitating social change in communities, organizations, and even for interested individuals. Providing people with action-usable information and training can be an important way of empowering people to be able to solve their own problems.

Ventimiglia[19] gave an example of applying his earlier research on disability and divorce to interventions with couples where one member was afflicted with multiple sclerosis. In regard to a teaching function, Ventimiglia described how dissemination of information on coping, role performances, exchange, and the like was a useful basis for intervention in helping people cope and adapt.

Similarly, Lavender[20] described a role for clinical sociologists as sex educators that recognizes societal factors in sexual behavior and sexual dysfunction. Citing the work of Masters and Johnson, Lavender noted that 8 or 9 out of 10 cases of sexual dysfunction "are caused by psychosocial factors—including psychological, interpersonal, environmental, and cultural factors." Lavender also noted that "even when sexual dysfunctions manifest themselves as psychological problems, the origins frequently are based in societal values, expectations, etc." Lavender described his own role as a clinical sociologist enacting a teaching role as sex educator providing sociologically based information so that "knowledge and understanding can help protect people from sexual dysfunction."

Broker

Brokering is not a new role for clinical sociologists, especially those involved in criminology, marriage and family counseling, and organizational development. A new aspect of this role, however, can involve brokering health information to enhance health care resources to facilitate change in the health behavior of individuals and families, to help ameliorate intraorganizational or interagency problems that affect the availability or quality of health care, or to assist in social planning among governmental bodies. Health brokering is appropriate for the clinical sociologist who is concerned with problems of health and disease that are not fragmented by nosology or disease labels. In addition, brokering conveys an active, innovative role for the clinical sociologist in health promotion and community health planning (Bruhn[21]).

Advocate

Clinical sociologists usually perform the roles of inquirer and implementor. Advocacy involves the clinical sociologist as an "external analyzer." That is, one concerned about how individuals, groups, organizations relate to each other to accomplish mutual goals or to solve problems. Advocacy requires that clinical sociologists "take a position" and make their values and beliefs known to others. Advocacy may be an uncomfortable role initially and be seen as antithetical to a sociologist's training. However, a clinical sociologist can offer ideas, observations, and advice that may facilitate changes that are not readily apparent to the nonsociologist. Advocacy can be a positive role, but it involves risk taking and taking a position of leadership. Clinical sociologists may feel most comfortable when they act as advocates for their clients as opposed to the broader role of advocacy that surrounds social issues and problems that, in turn, involves them in political and special interest groups. Nonetheless, the role of advocate need not be an exclusive role. Indeed, there is an advantage in blending advocacy with other related roles lest the clinical sociologist become too involved in the process rather than guiding change.

Group Facilitator

The clinical sociologist is a master teacher of group relations and group dynamics. Issues surrounding roles, status, power, and leadership are common in all groups and are usually key in unraveling the bases for group conflict as well as understanding group cohesion. Family therapy is an example where a clinical sociologist can assist family members in understanding their relationships to each other as a step toward solving whatever issue keeps them from functioning as an effective family. Clinical sociologists can be useful facilitators in many types of problem-centered groups and in groups concerned with planning, goal and agenda setting, and mutual aid or self-help groups.

CONCLUSION

The work of clinical sociology has the goal of planned positive social change on a case-by-case basis. The clinical sociologist recognizes that human problems are rooted in social life and applies the methods of scientific sociology to examine and analyze a case. But clinical sociological work is not a chair-bound activity. The sociologist goes where necessary and works within the client social system to develop data. Based on data accumulated for the task, the worker and client come together to define the problem for work and to agree on the programmatic steps to be taken.

Another key feature of clinical sociology is an active role as a social change agent. The clinical sociologist, working with an interdisciplinary team or working alone, is an active intervention agent, guiding the client system toward the desired change.

Clinical sociologists offer services to clients and client systems across the social spectrum, from microlevel work with individuals, groups, couples, or families, to work with larger social systems. Regardless of the level of work, analysis of and attention to the interplay of levels remains a key feature of the sociological approach. This includes recognition of the role of social and historical trends in the understanding, definition, and solution of problems.

Finally, clinical sociology retains a humanistic base. It respects clients' autonomy and rights and maintains the goal of assisting clients to improve the quality of their lives within their social systems.

The contributions to this volume reflect the diversity of activities and settings of contemporary clinical sociology. We see this diversity not as chaotic but as a healthy sign of a vigorous, growing, dynamic field approaching its adolescence. Like an adolescent, it has not completely defined itself nor established a rigid identity. As the chapters that follow show, clinical sociology is more a perspective than a set of theory groups and structured methodologies. It has no rigid theoretical lines, nor does it have a set of generalizable techniques to apply across cases. It demands instead a careful analysis of each case, and guided by sociological theory and knowledge, it calls for creative selection of the loci of intervention and creative development of activities designed to interact with the social context of a social problem to bring about change.

REFERENCES

1. Lee, A. McClung. (1988). *Sociology for people: Toward a caring profession.* Syracuse: Syracuse University Press.
2. Wirth, L. (1931). Sociology and clinical procedure. *The American Journal of Sociology, 37,* 49–66. Reprinted in *Clinical Sociology Review,* (1982) *1,* 7–22.

3. Dunham, H. W. (1982). Clinical sociology: Its nature and function. *Clinical Sociology Review, 1*, 23–33.

4. Freedman, J. A. (1982). Clinical sociology: What it is and what it isn't—A perspective. *Clinical Sociology Review, 1*, 34–49.

5. Straus, R. A. (1987). The theoretical base of clinical sociology: Root metaphors and key principles. *Clinical Sociology Review, 5*, 65–82.

6. Berger, P. L., & Lackmann, T. (1966). *The social construction of reality*. Garden City, New York: Doubleday & Company.

7. Voelkl, G. M., & Colburn, K. (1984). The clinical sociologist as family therapist: Utilizing the strategic communication approach. *Clinical Sociology Review, 2*, 64–77.

8. Mills, C. W. (1959). *The sociological imagination*. New York: Oxford University Press.

9. Straus, R. A. (1982). Clinical sociology on the one-to-one level: A social behavioral approach to counseling. *Clinical Sociology Review, 1*, 59–74.

10. Straus, R. A. (1984). Changing the definition of the situation: Toward a theory of sociological intervention. *Clinical Sociology Review, 2*, 51–63.

11. Johnson, D. P. (1986). Using sociology to analyze human and organizational problems. A humanistic perspective to link theory and practice. *Clinical Sociology Review, 4*, 57–70.

12. Collins, R. (1985). *Three sociological traditions*. New York: Oxford University Press.

13. Babbie, E. (1983). *The practice of social research* (3rd ed.). Belmont, CA: Wadsworth Publishing Company.

14. Preister, K., & Kent, J. A. (1984). Clinical sociological perspectives on social impacts: From assessment to management. *Clinical Sociology Review, 2*, 120–132.

15. Glass, J. F. (1984). Saul Alinsky in retrospect. *Clinical Sociology Review, 2*, 35–38.

16. Alinsky, S. D. (1984). Community analysis and organization. *The American Journal of Sociology, 46*, 797–808. Reprinted (1984) in *Clinical Sociology Review, 2*, 25–34.

17. Anderson, R. C. (1986). An interorganizational approach to the explanation of community development activities. *Clinical Sociology Review, 4*, 71–90.

18. Abbott, M. L., & Blake, G. F. (1988). An intervention model for homeless youth. *Clinical Sociology Review, 6*, 148–158.

19. Ventimiglia, J. (1986). Helping couples with neurological disabilities: A job description for clinical sociologists. *Clinical Sociology Review, 4*, 123–139.

20. Lavender, A. D. (1985). Societal influences on sexual dysfunctions: Clinical sociologist as sex educator. *Clinical Sociology Review, 3*, 129–142.

21. Bruhn, J. G. (1987). The clinical sociologist as a health broker. *Clinical Sociology Review, 5*, 168–179.

CHAPTER 2

The Emergence of American Clinical Sociology

JAN M. FRITZ

When sociology emerged as a discipline in the United States after the Civil War and Reconstruction, the nation was struggling with issues of democracy and social justice. The era of Jim Crow was upon us, blacks were being lynched,* women were still without the vote, and there was rural and urban poverty. Farmers and workers in the late 1800s could see the centralization of economic and political power in the hands of limited groups of people. Frustration led to public protests and the development of reform organizations. In this environment, it is not surprising to find that many of the early sociologists were interested in solving or at least reducing the pressing social problems confronting their communities.

The early publications and titles of academic courses reflect at least two basic approaches to the field. There were those sociologists who wished only to provide information and analysis, but there were others who also wanted to develop a "practical" sociology. These applied and clinical sociologists often were scholar–practitioners, combining a scientific approach with practical application.

An adequate history of American sociology** would need to trace both the development of science as well as the development of practical sociology. Too often the latter has been presented as if it were, by its nature, unscientific. Some also have

---

* This is not to say that only blacks were being lynched. According to Martin,[87] there have been at least 4,736 lynchings between 1882 and 1962, and about 70% of the victims were black. The 1890s, the period in which American sociology was developing, "saw the heaviest toll—154.1 lynchings annually."
** Much of the history of sociology that has been published has been the history of social thought and the history of the development of empirical sociology. The history of sociological practice also needs to be integrated with these other approaches. This new history would need to underscore how science, humanism, and practice often have been combined.

JAN M. FRITZ • Department of Sociology, California State University, San Bernardino, California 92407-2397.

incorrectly treated practical sociology as if it were only an interest of the earliest sociologists—or the students—and an interest that needed to be left behind. This limited approach has resulted in a history of the field that is inaccurate.

Even those chroniclers who have included some information about practical sociology often have done so in ways that have diminished the importance of the area. Howard Odum,[1] for instance, in his history of American sociology, referred to several practitioners as " 'promising sociologists' " but said they had chosen to work in "borderline sociology." Labeling practical sociology as *borderline* or *non-academic* encourages the view that sociological practice is peripheral to the discipline.

This chapter follows the emergence of clinical sociology, one of the areas of sociological practice. Clinical sociology is defined here as the creation of new systems as well as the intervention in existing systems for purposes of assessment and/or change. Clinical sociologists are humanistic scientists who are multi-disciplinary in approach. They engage in planned social change efforts by focusing on one system level (e.g., interpersonal, community, international) but integrate levels of focus in their work and do so from a sociological frame of reference.

This chapter will help to show that the history of American clinical sociology is lengthy, important, and central to the discipline. First, it provides new information about some of the earliest courses in clinical sociology and then traces the history of the term *clinical sociology* in publications.

THE FIRST COURSES IN CLINICAL SOCIOLOGY

There has been general agreement that some of the early American sociologists had interests that could be characterized as *clinical*. It had been assumed, however, that even those academics who were clinically oriented had not actually taught courses in clinical sociology. We now know that is not the case. A number of courses had clinical components, but there also were courses actually called *clinical sociology*.

The earliest known proposal was not for just a course in clinical sociology but for a whole department. The proposal was put forward by Milton C. Winternitz (1885–1959), a physician who was dean of the Yale School of Medicine from 1920 through 1935.[2] At least as early as 1929, Winternitz[3,4] began to develop plans to establish a department of clinical sociology within the medical school. He wanted each medical student to have a chance to analyze cases based on a medical specialty as well as a specialty in clinical sociology.

Winternitz vigorously sought funding from the Rosenwald Fund for his proposed program but, in the end, he was unable to carry out his plans. He did note, however, the success of a course in the medical school's section on public health that was "modeled directly after the outlined plan for clinical sociology."[5,6]

The first known courses called *clinical sociology* were taught at the University of Chicago by Ernest W. Burgess (1886–1966). Burgess, a graduate of the university who joined the faculty in 1919, is considered to be one of the second generation of sociologists who taught there. He was a central figure in the department until his retirement in 1951. During his career, Burgess was president of the American

Sociological Association, the Sociological Research Association, the National Conference on Family Relations, and the Gerontology Society.

Burgess first taught the clinical sociology course in 1928 and then offered it twice in 1929. During these years, the course was considered to be "special" and did not appear in the course catalog. As a regular course, clinical sociology was offered a total of five times by Burgess from 1931 through 1933. The course remained in the catalog for the next several years but was not taught after 1933.

In 1929 Burgess[7] wrote that "the time has now been reached when it will be profitable for biology, psychology, psychiatry and sociology to collaborate in the setting up of laboratories for personality study. . . ." This suggested that perhaps Burgess focused his clinical sociology course on issues of personality and criminal behavior.

The university catalogs did not include a description of that course, but it always was listed only under the social pathology grouping. All courses in this section dealt with topics such as criminality, punishment, criminal law, organized crime, and personal disorganization.

Because information about the course content was unavailable, some students enrolled in the clinical sociology courses were contacted.[8] One of them, Joseph Symons,[9] now an 83-year-old sociologist from Utah, was a graduate student at the University of Chicago from 1932 through 1936. In the fall of 1933, he was enrolled in Sociology 473 (clinical sociology) with E. W. Burgess as the instructor. He remembers the course and even still has his class notes.*

According to Symons's notes, Burgess said that clinical sociology "denotes an interest in pathological cases" and focuses on "social interaction and cultural conditioning." The main concepts that were used in the course were identified as "ecological, social interaction, cultural conditioning, fundamental wishes, personality types and social types." During the course of the term, students were expected to use provided forms to analyze personalities and to conduct a case study.

The course was taught for two hours one night a week, and each session began with a "discussion of certain written materials." The required reading included E. A. Bjorkman's[10,11] *Gates of Life* and *The Soul of a Child* as well as C. R. Shaw's[12,13] *The Natural History of a Delinquent Career* and *The Jack-Roller*, "a delinquent boy's own story." Also on the reading list were J. Black's[14] *You Can't Win*, an account of Black's life as a professional thief, and Jane Hillyer's[15] *Reluctantly Told*, the fascinating story of the author's mental breakdown.

Of particular interest, Symons's notes indicate that in 1933 Burgess stressed the importance of sociologists in child guidance work. The notes state "there are three types of children's clinics in the U.S." These were distinguished by leadership: "psychiatrists at head; psychologists at head; sociologists at head."

When the clinical sociology course was first offered, several students were placed in child guidance clinics. Clarence E. Glick,[16,17] for instance, now an 83-year-old sociologist from Hawaii, took the clinical sociology course each time it was offered in the 1920s. Burgess arranged for Glick to be the staff sociologist at the

* I am indebted to Joseph Symons for sharing his course materials. I appreciate his taking the time to help with this project.

Lower North Side Child Guidance Clinic and another class member, Leonard Cottrell, was the clinical sociologist at the South Side Child Guidance Clinic.*

Tulane University in Louisiana is believed to be the second institution to have offered a course in clinical sociology. Louis Wirth (1897–1952), a full-time faculty member and director of the New Orleans Child Guidance Clinic,[18] was scheduled to teach the course in the spring of 1930.

Wirth was unable to teach that course because he accepted a one-year Social Science Research Council Fellowship to work in Europe from February 1930 to January 1931. The clinical sociology course was taught in his absence, but university files do not identify the professor who took Wirth's place.

According to the *Tulane University Bulletins* (1928–1929),[19] the course was a "clinical demonstration of behavior problems and practice in social therapy through staff conferences and field work in a child guidance center." The course was entered in the school catalog as part of the sociology, social work, and graduate school listings.

When Wirth returned to the United States in 1931, he joined the faculty at the University of Chicago. In the spring of 1932, he taught a "minor" course in clinical sociology at the University of Chicago. This course was not listed in the course catalog but was recorded in the *Instructors' Reports*.[20] University records offer no descriptive information about this course, and none of the 18 students who enrolled in it could provide information.**

By 1932 Wirth appears to have dropped his involvement with child guidance clinics. Anna Hyman,[21] a staff member of the New Orleans Child Guidance Clinic, wrote Wirth to tell him that the New Orleans clinic was closing because of a lack of funds. She asked Wirth if he knew of any job possibilities. In his letter of June 17, Wirth[22] indicated he had "been somewhat out of touch with clinical work recently."

During the 1953–1954 academic year, Alvin W. Gouldner (1920–1980) was teaching in the Department of Sociology and Anthropology at Antioch College, a progressive school in Ohio. Before joining the faculty, Gouldner had been a university teacher for four years and then had worked for one year as a consultant to Standard Oil of New Jersey.

At Antioch, Gouldner offered a course titled "Foundations of Clinical Sociology." The course was taught at the highest undergraduate level, and enrolled students were expected to have successfully completed the department's course in

---

* Glick's role at the Lower North Side Child Guidance Clinic was to be part of the diagnostic team for the case load of "problem" boys, though Glick says the psychiatrist in charge of the clinic barely tolerated the young sociologist who had been made a colleague. Glick interviewed each boy about his "social world" and interviewed relevant community members about each boy's situation. Glick was a team member for analysis and diagnosis and, at times, also was an intervenor. Glick says the goal of the center was to "help get the boy on the right track."

Glick says he remembers little of the course that he thinks was a tutorial. He took the paid job in the center because Burgess offered it "as a way to be able to stay in school." After he left the center, Glick said he did not think about continuing with that kind of work because "it wasn't my specialty."

** Alexanderene Liston Fischer,[88] now a 90-year-old retired teacher from Michigan, remembered taking part in the course but had no information about content. She also said she "would have loved to have been a sociologist but at that time they weren't getting much pay."

social pathology. The archives at the school have very little information about the course, but there is the description that appeared in the *Antioch College Bulletin*:[23]

> A sociological counterpart to clinical psychology, with the group as the unit of diagnosis and therapy. Emphasis on developing skills useful in the diagnosis and therapy of group tensions. Principles of functional analysis, group dynamics, and organizational and small group analysis examined and applied to case histories. Representative research in the area assessed.

There have been a number of contemporary courses in clinical sociology, many of which are described in two 1980s publications.[24,25] Now we know these "new" courses are part of a 60-year tradition.

THE APPEARANCE OF THE LABEL *CLINICAL SOCIOLOGY*

The Sociological Practice Association (SPA), founded in 1978 as the Clinical Sociology Association, has had a substantial impact on the publication of materials about clinical sociology. In recognition of this influence, publications will be discussed within two periods—before and after 1978.

When a discussion of "clinical sociology" or the "clinical" approach began to appear during the first period of publication (1930 to 1977), the authors often used the terms with slightly different meanings. Many were unaware of the clinical work by other sociologists, and some even felt they were independently inventing a new direction for the field.

The 1970s began a new period of publication. Now many of those involved in the area were communicating frequently. Some agreements were beginning to be reached about basic definitions, information was reviewed by other sociological practitioners before publication, and a foundation was laid for synthesis and growth in a number of the specialty areas.

Presentations about the field of clinical sociology—labeled as such—began at professional sociology meetings during the 1970s. By the late 1970s, presentations and training sessions as well as publications appeared with regularity.

Pre-SPA Publications: 1930–1977

The first linking of the words *clinical* and *sociology* in print was in 1930—and in rather unlikely places. Milton C. Winternitz, a pathologist and dean of the Yale University Medical School, wanted to establish a department of clinical sociology. After working on this idea at least as early as 1929, he wrote about it in a report to the president of the school. The report was published in the *Bulletin* of Yale University.[4] Later that same year a speech was published that Winternitz had given at the dedication of the University of Chicago's new social science building. It too mentioned clinical sociology.[3]

Abraham Flexner,[26] a prominent critic of medical education and director of the Institute for Advanced Study at Princeton, also mentioned clinical sociology in 1930. Flexner, writing in his *Universities: American, English, German*, did not approve of the Institute of Human Relations that Winternitz was establishing at Yale. In the pages of criticism devoted to the institute, Flexner briefly mentions clinical sociology: "Only one apparent novelty is proposed: a professor of clinical sociology."

Winternitz[5,27-31] continued to write about the value of clinical sociology until his last report as a dean was filed in 1936. One of his most forceful statements in support of the field was the very contemporary-sounding one that appeared in his 1930–1931 annual report[29]:

> The field for clinical sociology does not seem by any means to be confined to medicine. Within the year it has become more and more evident that a similar development may well be the means of bringing about aid so sorely needed to change the basis of court action in relation to crime. . . .
>
> Not only in medicine and in law, but probably in many other fields of activity, the broad preparation of the clinical sociologist is essential. . . .

The first discussion of clinical sociology written by a sociologist appeared in 1931. That was the year Louis Wirth's[32] "Clinical Sociology" appeared in *The American Journal of Sociology*. Wirth wrote at length about the possibility of sociologists working in child development clinics, though he did not specifically mention his own clinical work in New Orleans. In this article he said, "It may not be an exaggeration of the facts to speak of the genesis of a new division of sociology in the form of clinical sociology."

Wirth[33] also wrote a career development pamphlet that same year which stated:

> The various activities that have grown up around child-guidance clinics, penal and correctional institutions, the courts, police systems, and similar facilities designed to deal with problems of misconduct have increasingly turned to sociologists to become members of their professional staffs.

Wirth "urged [sociology students] to become specialists in one of the major divisions of sociology, such as social psychology, urban sociology . . . or clinical sociology."

In 1934 Saul Alinsky,[34] a staff sociologist* and member of the classification board of the Illinois State Penitentiary, published his article, "A Sociological Technique in Clinical Criminology" in the *Proceedings of the Sixty-Fourth Annual Congress of the American Prison Association*. Alinsky eventually was recognized nationally for his work as a community organizer. According to Reitzes and Reitzes,[35] Alinsky's early work in corrections "led to a focus on community as the unit for investigating crime and on community organizations as a means of crime prevention."

In 1935 Charles Winslow,[36] a friend of the retiring Dean Winternitz of the Yale School of Medicine, said the following about clinical sociology in an address to the Association of Yale Alumni in Medicine: "The depression made it for the moment impossible to realize Dean Winternitz' splendid ideal of a University department of Clinical Sociology." The address was published that same year by the Yale University Press.

In 1941 Walter Webster Argow's article, "The Practical Application of Sociology," appeared in the *American Sociological Review*. Argow[37] noted that Giddings, Wirth, and Fairchild had offered "a program of an 'applied' or 'clinical' sociology."

---

* Alinsky received his undergraduate degree from the University of Chicago in 1930 and, according to the university registrar, took two years of graduate work in sociology. His courses included Burgess's 1931 clinical sociology course.

In 1944 the first formal definition of clinical sociology appeared in H. P. Fairchild's *Dictionary of Sociology*. The author of that definition, Alfred McClung Lee,[38] is known now as one of the founders of the Society for the Study of Social Problems, the Association for Humanist Sociology, and the Sociological Practice Association. (Lee later used the word *clinical* in two article titles—"Analysis of Propaganda: A Clinical Summary"[39] in 1945, and "The Clinical Study of Society,"[40] in 1955.)

Also appearing in 1944 was "An Approach to Clinical Sociology," an article in *Sociology and Social Research*. The author, Edward C. McDonagh,[41] had read Lee's definition of clinical sociology but had not seen Wirth's 1931 article.[42] McDonagh[41] proposed establishing social research clinics that had "a group way of studying and solving problems."

In 1946 George Edmund Haynes's "Clinical Methods in Interracial and Intercultural Relations" appeared in *The Journal of Educational Sociology*.[43] Haynes, the first black to receive a Ph.D. from Columbia University, was a co-founder of the National Urban League (1910) and the first black to hold a U.S-government subcabinet post.[44] His 1946 article was written while he was executive secretary of the Department of Race Relations at the Federal Council of the Churches of Christ in America. It discussed the department's urban clinics that were designed to deal with interracial tensions and conflicts by developing limited, concrete programs of action.

In 1949 David Ulrich's "A Clinical Method in Applied Social Science" appeared in *Philosophy of Science's* symposium on applied social research in policy formation. Ulrich[45] suggested a "combined research-consulting operation of seeking out management and employee interests and stimulating their participation in the development of a plan which will fit their needs and which they can regard as their own."

Three articles appeared in the 1950s, in addition to the one written in 1955 by Lee.[40] Alvin Gouldner's article, "Explorations in Applied Social Science,"[46] was published in 1956 in *Social Problems* and is reprinted in a 1965 book[47] he edited with S. M. Miller.* In this essay he examined the differences between engineering and clinical sociology. Gouldner was interested in the development of a clinical sociology in which clinicians made "their own independent identification of [a] group's problems." In 1957 Marie Kargman's "The Clinical Use of Social System Theory in Marriage Counseling"[48] appeared, and James Schellenberg discussed clinical sociology in his article, "Divisions of General Sociology," in the *American Sociological Review*.[49]

A number of publications in the 1960s mentioned clinical sociology. In 1963 "Problems of Interpretation in Clinical Sociology" by James Taylor and William Catton, Jr., appeared in *Sociological Inquiry*.[50] That same year, an article on clinical sociology by van Bockstaele, Barrot, and Magny appeared in a French journal.[51]

In 1964 H. Warren Dunham published a chapter section, "Clinical Sociology and Personality Vulnerability," in *Anomie and Deviant Behavior*.[52] Dunham wrote that the field of clinical sociology must be developed in order to have adequate

---

* The first section of Gouldner and Miller's 1965 book was entitled "A Clinical Approach" and the second was "Practitioners and Clients."

explanations of deviancy. And in 1965 Frederick Lighthall and Richard Diedrich[53] discussed the school psychologist's research as an example of "what can only be called clinical sociology."

In 1966 there were two publications. Julia Mayo[54] discussed the transition from psychiatric caseworker to clinical sociologist in an article in the *Archives of General Psychiatry*, and Alfred McClung Lee[55] published a chapter called "The Challenge of the 'Clinic' " in his *Multivalent Man*. In that chapter Lee identified three ways for social scientists to be "clinical":

> (1) through critical discussions with practical observers of spontaneous social behavior in problematic situations, (2) through scientific utilization of available clinical data, and (3) through participation directly in clinical situations.

Lee wrote that these three approaches "as well as the more usual sorts" were basic to his whole book.

Patterns in Human Interaction: An Introduction to Clinical Sociology, written by Henry Lennard and Arnold Bernstein,[56] appeared in 1969. The authors wrote that their "application of research methodology and sociology theory to the data of the 'clinical' situation and to subject matter traditionally falling within the fields of psychiatry and clinical psychology seemed to us to deserve a new characterization, to which the term clinical sociology seems ideally suited."

In 1973 Alfred McClung Lee's *Toward Humanist Sociology* was published.[57] In the section titled "Clinical Sociologists in American Conflicts," Lee discussed a laboratory confrontation method for "conflict abatement or conflict transformation."

Finally, in 1977, the 1975 *Current Sociology* issue on sociotechnics appeared.[58] The volume had been edited by Adam Podgorecki, a founder of the sociotechnics movement in Poland.[59] The first section of the *Current Sociology* volume was about social engineering. Here Podgorecki outlined "three possible models of socio-technique"—the classical model of social engineering, the clinical model of social engineering (as described by Gouldner),* and the interventionist model.

Podgorecki's annotated bibliography in the volume stated the following about Gouldner and Miller's *Applied Sociology* (1965):

> One of the basic books in the field of social engineering. A new approach toward applied sociology is proposed: a clinical one—which tries to overcome the prejudices, misunder-standings, and limitations of the sponsor.

Post-SPA Publications: 1978–1988

The Clinical Sociology Association was formed in San Francisco in 1978. The aims at that time were to provide a network for practitioners, to attract and maintain clinicians as members in sociology organizations, and to actively support humanist

---

* Adam Podgorecki was a founder and then became the facilitator of the sociotechnics movement ("social engineering or social architecture") in Poland during the 1960s. He knew of Gouldner's work, and in his diary on November 13, 1975, he wrote the following: "Gouldner is my acquaintance, not my friend. Not a very close acquaintance, just a reasonably good one. He was a professor in Amsterdam where he spent four years with his family. He is one of the best sociologists in the world, the author of many books and also the creator of the idea of clinical social engineering."[59]

clinical sociology. Additionally, many of the founding members wanted the organization to act as a pressure group to encourage the American Sociological Association to recognize and support sociological practice.

Over the years, publications have been a very high priority for the Clinical Sociology Association and its successor, the Sociological Practice Association. Individuals were encouraged to publish in different arenas and identify their work as clinical sociology. The association also opened publication avenues for members by publishing their materials directly or sponsoring their development.

Albion Small, the founding editor of *The American Journal of Sociology*, had recognized the value of controlling his journal and identifying it with the University of Chicago. In a similar way, the leaders of the Clinical Sociology Association/Sociological Practice Association launched, supported, and controlled many of the publications that fostered the development of clinical sociology. Most of the publications that stressed the connection between a specialized area of practice and the broad field of clinical sociology were written by association members.

In 1978 Hugh Gardner[60] published an article about clinical sociology in the magazine *Human Behavior*, and Charlotte Green Schwartz's article on teaching, "Clinical Sociology—Qualitative Sociology as Practice in Everyday Life," appeared in the *New England Sociologist*.[61]

In 1979 Billy Franklin[62] published an article on the history of the field, Roger Straus wrote about clinical sociology as "An idea whose time had come . . . again,"[90] and Estelle Disch[63] wrote about sociological psychotherapy. Also that year, a special issue of the *American Behavioral Scientist*, edited by Roger Straus,[64] was devoted to clinical sociology, and Longman published the book, *Clinical Sociology*, by Barry Glassner and Jonathan Freedman.[65]

In 1980 articles appeared by L. Alex Swan[66] on the emergence of the field, Drukker and VerHaaren[67] on consulting, and Black and Enos[68] on counseling. In 1981 Harry Cohen's book on theory and clinical sociology was published by Iowa State University Press.[69]

The Clinical Sociology Association* began its publication program with a newsletter, now called *The Practicing Sociologist*, in 1978 and published an annual journal, the *Clinical Sociology Review*, beginning in 1982. In 1985 the association sponsored the volume, *Using Sociology: An Introduction from the Clinical Perspective*, edited by Roger Straus[70] and, in cooperation with the American Sociological Association, two volumes were published on courses and programs in clinical sociology.[24,25]

Most recently, the association has acquired *Sociological Practice* and has begun publishing this journal annually as a theme issue. The first SPA-sponsored issue, edited by Jan Fritz and Elizabeth Clark,[71] reviews the history and development of clinical and applied sociology. The second issue, edited by Alvin Lackey, is on community.[91]

Other publications that appeared in the 1980s included two books with clinical sociology in the title—*The Practice of Clinical Sociology and Sociotherapy*, by L. Alex Swan (1984),[72] and *The Clinical Sociology Handbook*, by Jan Fritz (1985).[73] Two books by Alfred McClung Lee—the 1986 (second edition) of *Sociology for Whom?*[74]

---

* This section, because of space limitations, unfortunately does not specifically name most of the articles and chapters that have appeared in association-sponsored publications.

and the 1988 *Sociology for People*[75]—mention the Clinical Sociology Association/ Sociological Practice Association. In his 1988 book, Lee writes that the association was one of three that "helped to broaden the opportunities by the younger and nonconforming sociologists . . . [and does] a great deal to keep sociology relevant and vital. . . ."

Among the articles mentioning clinical sociology that appeared in the 1980s were Alfred McClung Lee's "The Long Struggle to Make Sociology Useful" (1982)[76] and "Steps Taken toward Liberating Sociologists" (1988).[77] Also published during that period were Joseph Fichter's (1984) "Sociology for Our Times," his 1983 presidential address to the Southern Sociological Society,[78] and "The Progress of Practice" (1986), by Clifford Black and John Holman.[79] A 1987 series of articles on clinical sociology also appeared in the journal *Free Inquiry in Creative Sociology*.

CONCLUSION

Research during the past decade has revealed a great deal about the history of American clinical sociology. But only about five years ago did sociologists begin to recognize the range of publications specifically referring to the clinical approach, and it is less than two years since we discovered information about some of the earliest clinical sociology courses. We now know enough, however, to realize that the commonly perceived history of American sociology is inaccurate because it has not included and valued the history of clinical sociology.

The history of clinical sociology is also inaccurate because it is not complete. Just like some of the chroniclers of the general history of sociology, most of the focus has been on universities considered to be elite and prestigious. We have not provided enough information about sociologists who have worked in practice settings or at a number of the "other" colleges and universities. This kind of work can be more difficult for several reasons: Archival materials often are not readily available; such research may be less appreciated within the sociological community; and this work can be costly to undertake. But we need to undertake this research if we wish to understand the real history of the discipline.

We also need to expand the history in several other ways. Much of the clinical work that has been undertaken has not necessarily been called *clinical*.* We need to integrate, for instance, the kinds of activities showcased by Arthur Shostak in his 1966 *Sociology in Action: Case Studies in Social Problems and Directed Social Change*.[80] This integration work is just beginning to be undertaken.[44,81–84]

Additionally, we need to include international developments. Information is available, for instance, about practice activities in Poland, the Netherlands, Can-

---

* Many of the early Europeans and Africans who are considered to be founders or precursors of the field of sociology were not known primarily as sociologists during their lifetime. We also might expect that many of those we identify as early clinical sociologists did not apply that label to themselves. This probably is particularly true for those who were primarily practitioners—especially those working outside of medical settings—rather than those who were primarily academic sociologists.

ada, and England. As part of this initiative, we need to identify and conduct research on the practitioner movements as well as the individual women and men who have been scholar–practitioners in the developing as well as the economically developed countries.

The experience of Dean Milton Winternitz at Yale[2] as well as the analyses of John Stanfield[85] and Jonathan Turner and Stephen Turner[86] remind us of the importance of the resource base in allowing the development and even "encouraging" the direction of a program or a discipline. As always, we need to pay attention to our resources to retain the field's value orientation, support essential services (e.g., clinical training, publication, opportunity development, networking) and influence the larger sociology associations, graduate programs, and labor markets. One of our strongest resources can be a more accurate history of the general field of sociology.

REFERENCES

1. Odum, H. W. (1951). *American sociology: The story of sociology in the United States through 1950.* New York: Longmans, Green and Company.
2. Fritz, J. M. (1989). Dean Winternitz, clinical sociology and the Julius Rosenwald Fund. *Clinical Sociology Review, VII.*
3. Winternitz, M. C. (1930). Medicine as a social science. In L. D. White (Ed.), *The new social science* (pp. 40–45). Chicago: University of Chicago Press.
4. Winternitz, M. C. (1930). Report of the School of Medicine to the president of Yale University, 1928–29. *Bulletin of Yale University.*
5. Winternitz, M. C. (1931). Report of the School of Medicine to the president of Yale University, 1929–30. *Bulletin of Yale University.*
6. Winternitz, M. C. (1931). Notes on clinical sociology. Yale University Archives. School of Medicine, Records of Dean. YRG-27-A-5-9. Box 112, Folder 2604.
7. Burgess, E. W. (1929). *Personality and the social group.* Chicago: University of Chicago Press. Reprinted in 1969 by Books for Libraries Press in Freeport, New York.
8. *Instructor's Reports* (1928–38). University of Chicago, Office of the Recorder. University of Chicago, Department of Special Collections.
9. Symons, J. (1933). Student notes from sociology 473 (clinical sociology), University of Chicago.
10. Bjorkman, E. A. (1922). *The soul of a child.* New York: A. A. Knopf.
11. Bjorkman, E. A. (1923). *Gates of life.* New York: A. A. Knopf.
12. Shaw, Clifford. (1931). *The natural history of a delinquent career.* Chicago: University of Chicago Press.
13. Shaw, Clifford. (1930). *The jack-roller, a delinquent boy's own story.* Chicago: University of Chicago Press.
14. Black, J. (1926). *You can't win.* New York: Burt.
15. Hillyer, J. (1926). *Reluctantly told.* New York: The Macmillan Company.
16. Glick, C. E. (1989). Telephone interview. January 19.
17. Glick, C. E. (1989). Letter to J. M. Fritz. March 24.
18. "Head of Tulane child guidance clinic arrives" (1929). Newspaper article (September 18) in the *Tulane Scraps,* a university scrapbook. Volume 17. Archives, Tulane University Library.
19. Clinical sociology course description. *Tulane University Bulletins,* 1928–29.
20. Clinical sociology course listing. *Instructors' Reports* (1932). University of Chicago, Office of the Recorder. University of Chicago, Department of Special Collections.
21. Hyman, Anna. (1932). Letter to Louis Wirth. June 7. Louis Wirth Collection. Box XXVIII, Folder 11. University of Chicago, Department of Special Collections.

22. Wirth, Louis. (1932). Letter to Anna Hyman. June 17. Louis Wirth Collection. Box XXVII, Folder 11. University of Chicago, Department of Special Collections.

23. Foundations of clinical sociology. Course description. *Antioch College Bulletin* (1953).

24. Clark, Elizabeth, & Fritz, Jan. (Eds.). (1984). *Clinical sociology courses: Syllabi, exercises and annotated bibliography*. Washington, DC: American Sociological Association Teaching Resources Center.

25. Fritz, Jan, & Clark, Elizabeth. (Eds.). (1986). *The clinical sociology resource book*. Washington, DC: American Sociological Association Resources Center.

26. Flexner, Abraham. (1930). *Universities: American, English, German*. New York: Oxford University Press.

27. Winternitz, M. C. (1930). *Practical study of social relations: Plan for graduate department of clinical sociology at Yale*. Report. 10 pp. Yale University Archives, School of Medicine, Records of Dean. YRG-27-A-5-9. Box 174, Folder 3608.

28. Winternitz, M. C. (1931). *Clinical sociology at Yale*. Report. 7 pp. Yale University Archives, School of Medicine, Records of Dean. YRG-27-A-5-9. Box 112, Folder 2604.

29. Winternitz, M. C. (1932). Clinical sociology. Pp. 50–51 in report of the dean of the School of Medicine, 1930–1931. *Bulletin* of Yale University. New Haven.

30. Winternitz, M. C. (1935). Report of the dean of the School of Medicine to the university president, 1933–34. *Bulletin* of Yale University. New Haven.

31. Winternitz, M. C. (1936). Report of the dean of the School of Medicine to the university president, 1934–35. *Bulletin* of Yale University. New Haven.

32. Wirth, L. (1931). Clinical sociology. *American Journal of Sociology, 37*, 49–66.

33. Wirth, L. (1931). *Sociology: Vocations for those interested in it*. Pamphlet. Vocational Guidance Series, No. 1. Chicago: University of Chicago. Louis Wirth Collection, University of Chicago, Department of Special Collections. Box LVI, Folder 6.

34. Alinsky, S. (1934). A sociological technique in clinical criminology. *Proceedings of the Sixty-Fourth Annual Congress of the American Prison Association*, 167–78.

35. Reitzes, D. C., & Reitzes, D. C. (1982). Saul D. Alinsky: A neglected but promising resource. *The American Sociologist, 17*(February), 47–56.

36. Winslow, C. E. A. (1935). *Dean Winternitz & the Yale School of Medicine*. Address delivered before the Association of Yale Alumni in Medicine on June 17, 1935. New Haven: Yale University Press.

37. Argow, W. W. (1941). The practical application of sociology. *American Sociological Review, 6/1* (February), 37–44.

38. Lee, A. M. (1944). Sociology, clinical. In H. P. Fairchild (Ed.), *Dictionary of sociology* (p. 303). New York: Philosophical Library.

39. Lee, A. M. (1945). The analysis of propaganda: A clinical summary. *The American Journal of Sociology, 41/2* (September), 126–35.

40. Lee, A. M. (1955). The clinical study of society. *American Sociological Review, 20/6* (December), 648–653.

41. McDonagh, E. C. (1944). An approach to clinical sociology. *Sociology and Social Research, 27/5* (May–June), 376–383. Reprinted in the 1986 *Clinical Sociology Review*.

42. Fritz, J. M. (1986). History of clinical sociology: The initial contributions of Edward McDonagh and Marie Kargman. *Clinical Sociology Review, IV*, 11–13.

43. Haynes, G. E. (1946). Clinical methods in interracial and intercultural relations. *The Journal of Educational Sociology, 19/5* (January). Reprinted in the 1988 issue of the *Clinical Sociology Review, VI*, 51–58.

44. Hunter, H. M. (1988). The clinical sociology of George Edmund Haynes (1880–1960). *Clinical Sociology Review, VI*, 42–50.

45. Ulrich, D. (1949). A clinical method in applied social science. *Philosophy of Science, XVI/3* (July), 243–249.

46. Gouldner, A. (1956). Explorations in applied social science. *Social Problems, III/3* (January), 169–181. Reprinted pp. 5–22 in A. Gouldner and S. M. Miller (Eds.), *Applied sociology*. New York: Free Press, 1965.

47. Gouldner, A., & Miller, S. M. (Eds.). (1965). *Applied sociology*. New York: Free Press.

48. Kargman, M. W. (1957). The clinical use of social system theory in marriage counseling. *Marriage and Family Living, XIX/3* (August), 263–269. Reprinted in the 1986 issue of the *Clinical Sociology Review, IV*, 19–29.
49. Schellenberg, J. A. (1957). Divisions of general sociology. *American Sociological Review, 22/6*, (December), 660–63.
50. Taylor, J. B., & Catton, Jr., W. R. (1963). Problems of interpretation in clinical sociology. *Sociological Inquiry, XXXIII* (Winter), 34–44.
51. van Bockstaele, J., van Bockstaele, M., Barrot, C., & Magny, C. (1963). Travaux de sociologie clinique. [Work in clinical sociology: An investigation of several conditions of socioanalytic intervention.] *L'Anee Sociologique.* Paris: Presses Universitaires de France.
52. Dunham, H. W. (1964). Anomie and mental disorder. In M. B. Clinard (Ed.), *Anomie and deviant behavior* (pp. 128–157). New York: Free Press of Glencoe.
53. Lighthall, F. F., & Diedrich, R. (1965). The school psychologist, the teacher, and research: Willing and reluctant cooperation. *Psychology in the Schools, 2/2* (April), 106–110.
54. Mayo, J. (1966). What is the 'social' in social psychiatry? *Archives of General Psychiatry, 14*, 449–455.
55. Lee, A. M. (1966). *Multivalent man.* New York: George Braziller.
56. Lennard, H. L., & Bernstein, A. (1969). *Patterns in human interaction.* San Francisco: Jossey-Bass Inc.
57. Lee, A. M. (1973). *Toward humanist sociology.* Englewood Cliffs, NJ: Prentice-Hall.
58. Podgorecki, A. (Ed.). (1977). Sociotechnics: A trend report and bibliography. *Current Sociology, XXIII:1* (1975). The Hague: Mouton.
59. Podgorecki, A. (1986). *A story of a Polish thinker.* Translated by Margaret Watson. Koln: Verlag für Gesellschaftsarchitektur.
60. Gardner, H. (1978). Some "real" doctoring for sick societies. *Human Behavior*, September, 68–69.
61. Schwartz, C. G. (1978). Clinical sociology—qualitative sociology as practice in everyday life. *New England Sociologist, 1/1* (Fall), 4–12.
62. Franklin, B. (1979). Clinical sociology: The sociologist as practitioner. *Psychology, A Quarterly Journal of Human Behavior, 16/3* (Fall), 51–56.
63. Disch, E. (1979). Integration in a two-career person: Sociological psychotherapy and psychological sociology. *New England Sociologist, 1/2* (Spring), 13–19.
64. Straus, R. (Ed.). (1979). Special issue on clinical sociology. *American Behavioral Scientist, 22/4* (March/April).
65. Glassner, B., & Freedman, J. (1979). *Clinical sociology.* New York: Longman.
66. Swan, L. A. (1980). Clinical sociologists: Coming out of the closet. *Mid-Atlantic Review of Sociology, 1* (Spring), 89–98.
67. Drukker, E. L., & Verhaaren, F. (1980). Paradoxen in het organisatie—adviesproces [Paradoxical intervening processes in consulting.] *Tijdschrift voor Agologie, 9* (Sept./Okt.), 361–380.
68. Black, C. M., & Enos, R. (1980). Sociological precedents and contributions to the understanding and facilitation of individual behavioral change: The case for counseling sociology. *Journal of Sociology and Social Welfare, 7/5* (September), 648–664.
69. Cohen, H. (1981). *Connections: Understanding social relationships.* Ames: Iowa State University Press.
70. Straus, R. (Ed.). (1985). *Using sociology: An introduction from a clinical perspective.* New York: General Hall.
71. Fritz, J. M., & Clark, E. J. (Eds.). (1989). *Sociological practice: The development of clinical and applied sociology, VII.*
72. Swan, L. A. (1984). *The practice of clinical sociology and sociotherapy.* Cambridge, MA: Schenkman.
73. Fritz, J. M. (1985). *The clinical sociology handbook.* New York: Garland.
74. Lee, A. M. (1986). *Sociology for whom?* (2nd. ed.). Syracuse, NY: Syracuse University Press.
75. Lee, A. M. (1988). *Sociology for people: Toward a caring profession.* Syracuse: Syracuse University Press.
76. Lee, A. M. (1982). The long struggle to make sociology useful. *Public Relations Journal, 38/7* (July), 8–11.
77. Lee, A. M. (1988). Steps taken toward liberating sociologists. *Critical Sociology, 15/2* (Summer), 43–59.
78. Fichter, J. H. (1984). Sociology for our times. *Social Forces, 62/3* (March), 573–584.

79. Black, C. M., & Holman, J. E. (1986). The progress of practice. *Sociological Practice, 6/1* (Fall), 9–30.
80. Shostak, A. B. (Ed.). (1966). *Sociology in action: Case studies in social problems and directed social change.* Homewood, IL: Dorsey.
81. Fritz, J. M. (1987). The history of clinical sociology: The Whyte line. *Clinical Sociology Review, V,* 13–16.
82. Fritz, J. M. (1988). W. E. B. Du Bois, Scholar-Practitioner. *The Practicing Sociologist,* Fall/Winter.
83. Fritz, J. M. (1988). The history of clinical sociology: Charles Gomillion, educator-community activist. *Clinical Sociology Review, VI,* 13–21.
84. Fritz, J. M. (1989). The history of clinical sociology. *Sociological Practice, VII,* 72–95.
85. Stanfield, J. (1985). *Philanthropy and Jim Crow in American social science.* Westport, CT: Greenwood Press.
86. Turner, J. H., & Turner, S. P. (1989). *The impossible science: An institutional history of American sociology.* Unpublished draft manuscript.
87. Martin, R. E. (1987). Lynching. *The Encyclopedia Americana, 17,* 884–885.
88. Fischer, A. L. (1988). Telephone interview. November 1.
89. Gordon, J. B. (1989). Notes on the history of clinical sociology at Yale. *Clinical Sociology Review, VII.*
90. Straus, R. (1979). Clinical sociology: An idea whose time has come . . . again. *Sociological Practice.* 1/3 (Fall), 21–43.
91. Lackey, A. (Ed.) (1990). *Sociological Practice: Community. VIII.*

PART II

GENERAL PRACTICE CONCERNS

CHAPTER 3

Assessment in Clinical Sociology

BRUCE SAUNDERS

INTRODUCTION

This chapter tells how to organize and conduct assessments of any problem in clinical sociology: what questions you should ask, what information to gather, decision points, and cautions. The chapter focuses on problems associated with individuals and formal organizations, but many of the principles given here are generalizable to other fields of clinical sociology.

Assessment may be defined as the set of activities undertaken to formally analyze clients' problems and judge their character and significance. Assessments provide information used to design workable interventions that resolve or manage clients' problems. The assessment process is more than a mechanical application of techniques to discover what is "wrong." Sociological imagination and the will to tease out and wrestle with the realities of the client's social world are necessary skills. Assessments cannot be done at a distance from the client's setting. The clinician, like the ethnographer, needs to be in the client's world, observing, analyzing, taking meticulous notes, looking for clues and sensitizing ideas (Blumer,[1] Glaser & Strauss,[2] Greer,[3] Lofland[4]).

Assessments in clinical sociology are "sociological," and findings are based on the same kind of effort that establishes claims in mainstream sociology. Scientific reasoning, hypothetical thinking, and hypothesis testing, attention to the rules of data gathering and analysis, avoidance of *post hoc* analyses, methodical planning of clinical work, and associating findings with accepted theory and literature keep clinical sociology from becoming fakery. Assessment has a recursive nature: At each stage, results of earlier inquiries are used to plan the next stage of the investigation. The clinician learns what has been tried before by other practitioners in comparable situations and what the client himself has tried. He consciously and explicitly documents his reasoning about the nature of the clinical problem and is prepared

BRUCE SAUNDERS • College of Education, University of Washington, Seattle, Washington 98195, and Clinical Sociology Associates, Seattle, Washington 98115.

to show clients or colleagues the logic behind the assessment and the evidence that compels conclusions.

In the assessment, the clinician and client work together to build a jointly constructed knowledge base (Berger & Luckmann[5]) that consists of both empirically confirmable propositions and interpretive understandings (which do not have a literal, confirmable nature). Interpretive propositions are nonconsensual views that have a tentative, suspendable character and may be overturned prospectively or retrospectively by new discoveries or by changes in the ways actors (clinicians, clients, and others) interpret their knowledge (Garfinkel,[6] Wilson[7]). Interpretive propositions are not generalizable and have little relevance in analytic/empirical sciences. They are, however, fundamental in interpretive/hermeneutic disciplines like clinical sociology (Habermas[8]). Ultimately, what warrants findings from an assessment is not their generality but how much they contribute to the discovery of an intervention acceptable to the client.

THE LOGIC OF CLINICAL ASSESSMENT

A logically planned assessment involves several steps. The first step is to learn everything possibly relevant about the client and the setting by using the client as an informant, field methods to thoroughly explore the problem's setting, and library research to fill in missing background. Background research is essential if you are not intimately familiar with the milieu you are exploring.

To discover what is wrong, the clinician engages in "hypothetical thinking." Reasoning from what is known about the client, the problem, and the setting, and drawing upon clinical experience, comparative knowledge of similar settings, and general knowledge of sociology, the clinician generates testable hypotheses about the causes of the problem and proposes simple, meaningful ways to test likely candidates. Hypotheses must be couched so they are rooted in sociological theory and findings and anchored in the "facts" of the client's world.

Hypotheses generated about what is wrong should have two additional properties. They must be disconfirmable (and a clinician needs to be able to say explicitly what information would confirm or disconfirm each hypothesis). And hypotheses must be comparative in nature. Each hypothesis should imply that a real situation comparable to the client's exists in which one or at most only a few elements are different. In that other setting, the client's problem is found not to occur. The inference (and our hypothesis) is that those changed elements are the "cause" of the client's problem (Andreski,[9] Wenkert[10]).

Clinical hypotheses must be testable, but they need not be tested rigorously in a formal way. A major part of clinical judgment is the capacity to correctly propose and discard hypotheses about what may be wrong on the basis of small indicators and clues. As ideas about what is wrong are tested and abandoned, the clinician's knowledge of the problem grows, the investigation narrows and becomes more pointed, and the clinician is left with a few intransigent hypotheses. This is the time to begin thinking about possible interventions that are consistent with the hypothesis (hypotheses) you cannot reject. Be wary, however, of single-factor explanations of what is "wrong." Clinical problems are typically ramified and complex, and single-factor explanations of what is "wrong" oversimplify and trivialize the problem.

ANALYTICAL ASSESSMENT PHASES

Assessment is an ongoing seamless activity, but several phases of the process can be analytically described. *Preliminary screening* centers on assessing whether to accept the client and the presented problem. The *intake* phase focuses on gathering enough information to clarify the problem, get clear about the work to be done, and estimate resources and time needed to complete the project. In the *exploratory* phase (from Blumer's[1] term, *exploration*), the clinician gathers data; generates, tests, and winnows hypotheses; and tries to establish concretely what is wrong. Once the nature of the problem is understood, an *assessment of possible interventions* follows. The assessment process concludes with two final phases, *assessment of the outcomes of intervention*, and *summatory assessment*, or the final summing up that brings closure to the clinical act.

Preliminary Screening

Preliminary screening of potential clients is the first step of the assessment process. Let us suppose the client is an individual who comes for help with a personal problem. The central issue is whether to accept this person as a client. Usually, this decision must be made on the basis of what can be learned in a brief interview. One decision rule is never get in front of your knowledge base. There are gray areas, but many clients should be referred to another practitioner: a physician, psychotherapist, policeman, attorney, or priest. Clinical sociology is an appropriate specialty when clients' problems are interactional or rooted in role performance difficulties (Banton[11]), spring from group or cultural conflicts, stem from ignorance of the "rules" of the client's setting, have to do with organizational dynamics and functioning, or flow from the interaction of persons with institutions.

Preliminary assessment is the time to spot obvious red flags. Are any of the following issues present: unacceptable legal liability or other legal problems, substance abuse, addiction, depression or other mental illnesses, suicidal tendencies, a crime, child abuse, an untreated medical condition? Will any local mandatory reporting laws be triggered? Is the problem inherently unmanageable? Too large? What are prospects for finding a solution acceptable to the client? Are the resources and commitment of the client sufficient to carry the project through? Does the client have unreasonable expectations? Is the client likely to be cooperative?

Intake Assessment Survey

Once a client is accepted, the next phase of assessment begins—a detailed intake survey. The goal of the survey is to clarify the nature of the problem with the client and determine the boundaries of the work to be done. You must establish with the client what is sensitive or off limits in the investigation and what will signal completion of the work.

The problem the client brings you is the "identified problem." Frequently, the identified problem is inchoate or contains contradictory elements. Occasionally, the identified problem is not even "real." The structuring formula for clinical sociology demands that clients present a "problem" to be solved and thus forces clients to have "problems." Inherent in this formula is the possibility that clients will invent problems to form or continue an association with you. Clinical workers may unintentionally create, cause, or perpetuate clients' problems. Thus at every stage of the investigation, we need to assess whether "the problem" is iatrogenic, and we have somehow become responsible for it.

As you sort out the problem with the client, you should be building a relationship with him or her. If the client's expectations for you are not met, he or she may quit, leaving the project a failure. Giving information and analyses usually is not enough to resolve a problem. The client will expect support and encouragement from you. Your relationship with the client should be constructed deliberately and consciously with the intent of making the relationship a major tool for the assessment and clinical work you must do.

Once a problem is understood and a feasible intervention is found, you need to know whether the client will be able to make the intervention work. Many clients who come to us are stuck because of unresolved therapy issues and cannot be moved without a great deal of help. These persons may need more help than most clinical sociologists can supply.

If you are lucky, your clients will only have unmet learning needs, which are easy to deal with. The majority of interventions require teaching or explaining something to the client. You need to assess what should be taught and how best to teach it. Adult educators have developed methods for determining the learning styles of different types of people and assessing learning needs (Brookfield[12]). It pays clinical sociologists to master these skills (Knowles,[13] Long,[14] Knox[15]). The teaching function is an important element in the clinical sociologist's role, but students learning clinical work are seldom taught how to teach. Technologies for assessing learning needs and teaching adults (singly and in groups) are well developed in adult education (Freire,[16] Mezirow[17]), as are methods for assessing problems that stem from developmental problems (Brim & Kagan,[18] Gould,[19] Havighurst,[20] Levinson,[21] Lowenthal,[22] Smelser[23]), and critical events in persons' lives (Brim,[24] Freire,[16] Mezirow,[17] Smelser,[23] Sheehy[25]).

There is much we need to learn from the preliminary assessment. How long has the problem been going on? Who are the significant players on centerstage, and who is behind the scenes? Who gives advice to the client, and what is the advice? What ethical problems will we run into? This is also the moment to probe the client's motives and see whether problems are hidden here. The client is likely to have layers of unexpressed agendas, and unless these are teased out, assessed, and factored in, the client may never be satisfied with the work we do.

Negotiating a formal agreement is a major goal of the intake survey. At a minimum, the agreement we strike with our clients should include definite understandings about (1) reporting processes (to whom, when, and in what detail shall progress reports be made); (2) goals or objectives of the project, framed so it is clear to all parties what the product of the work will be; (3) an overall plan for the work that is sufficiently detailed that both you and the client understand, in detail, the steps you will take; (4) a timeline for the project; (5) an assessment of potential risks, including the risk that the project will not succeed; and (6) an estimate of the cost of the work. The client must decide whether to accept your help and work with you on the problem, and the client needs a great deal of information that only you can supply to assess whether he or she wants to go ahead with the project. If the client does decide to go ahead, the two of you ought to agree on terms by which the work can be halted before the project is finished. You should build into the project plan clear decision points at which you or the client may assess the state of the project and decide whether to continue or abandon the effort.

Exploratory Assessment

In the exploratory phase of assessment, the main concern is a quest for sensitizing ideas (Blumer[1]) and insights into the problem that will lead to testable hypotheses about what is wrong. A useful initial strategy is to adopt the pose of "the stranger," a person who comes to the setting with little foreknowledge of what he or she will encounter (Schuetz[26]).

Suppose the presented problem is the "poor peer relations" of an adolescent boy. What analytical categories are needed to shape and guide an assessment of this problem? Should the clinician begin with family expectations for the boy; the mechanics of acceptance and popularity in the boy's circle; teachers' and other children's perceptions and appraisals of him; or should one determine whether his peer relations are satisfactory from the boy's point of view? Is the boy's role strain real; a normal stage of adolescence? The clinician cannot explore every facet of the client's problem. A parsimonious narrowing of the investigation to elements that will speedily point to an effective intervention from the client's perspective is necessary, but what are the relevant elements? The clinician cannot be certain what is relevant at this stage of exploration, so an informed guess is made, the problem is tentatively conceptualized, possibly relevant analytical categories are proposed, and the clinician begins the exploratory assessment by seeking confirmation he is on the right track.

The development of a conceptual framework for the problem is a recursive process in which analytical elements are modified or abandoned as new insights emerge and the clinician's understanding of the client's problem expands. Exploratory assessment can take many directions. In your initial choice of paradigm and analytical categories, be sure to cast a wide enough net. Maximize the probability the investigation will pin down the problem. This suggests a thorough and detailed investigation, even if you are sure at the outset you know what is wrong. Following are checklists of problem areas that turn up often in assessments of individuals, organizations, and persons in relationships. The checklists are abbreviated and heuristic and are not meant to be practical guides for organizing real exploratory assessments. They are maps of domains where answers to problems are likely to be found. As a practical matter, no clinician would work through these lists, category by category, checking each item.

Checklist for Exploratory Assessment of Persons

If the client is an individual, assessment quickly centers on facts of the person's social life. Get the main facts quickly (education, occupation, income, marital status, religion, age, criminal and health statuses), then fill in the details. One technique for profiling a person's social life is to do a life history (Dollard[27]). Map out elements of the client's role and status sets, past and present, and discover the identities of significant role partners. What are the formative events? Who are the significant others? What is the quality of their relationship with him? (McCall[28]) To confirm your emerging sense of your client's life, follow the client through several days of ordinary activity. Live in the world with the client and see the world as he experiences it. Meet the important actors in his life.

Get a clear understanding of the client's cultural background and assess the ways it both supports and undermines the client's present life. Learn how the client was socialized and by whom. Assess whether the client's primary and secondary socialization is appropriate preparation for his or her current statuses (Becker & Strauss,[29] Brim,[24] Goslin[30]). Determine whether the client has any unusual experiences that are dysfunctional for his or her present life (e.g., prison stays, school failures, in-patient mental treatment, service in Vietnam (Levy[31]), loss of a child). Look for contradictions between the client's background and present way of life. Has the client failed to make an expectable status transition, at all or on time (Marini[32]). Examine the client's natal and present family structure (McLanahan,[33] Mare[34]). Be sensitive to the special, disorienting problems of immigrants, upwardly mobile (Blau[35]) people, and others whose lives have taken them across class, national, or other boundaries.

Assess the consistency and appropriateness of your client's myths, moral structures, and normative systems and see whether these facilitate or inhibit adaptation to his milieu. Inquire about your client's heroes, the situations he fears, the persons he pities. Analyze how your client handles responsibility and failure: Does he make excuses, scapegoat, deny, blame, keep trying? Check for signs that your client is a deeply religious person, or true believer of some ilk (Hoffer[36]) or a person who has trouble compromising his principles and beliefs. Be especially concerned about such persons if assessment reveals they are isolates and not socially embedded in a network of sympathetic others who give them appropriate role support.

The object of this phase of the exploratory inquiry is to gain the clearest possible understanding of how clients interact with their social world. What patterns can be discerned in their relations with others? Are they aloof, or do they function well with others? Is their behavior consistent and goal oriented? Are their expectations for role partners fair and clearly communicated? Do they give and receive pleasure, or are they anhedonic? Are their emotions in character and appropriately managed? (Blum,[37] Cartwright,[38] Foote,[39] Mills,[40] Denzin[41]) Examine patterns of exchange (Blau[42]) in your client's role relations and see whether these are equitable and fulfilling. Assess the client's role enactments. Do these suggest confidence, enthusiasm, trust, competence? Study the client's presented self (Goffman[43]), presentation of self, his persona, manners, ways of treating others. Is he attractive? (Clifford,[44] Webster & Driskell[45]) Likeable, pleasant, desirable? What behaviors does he elicit from others? Assess whether other persons in the client's setting pose problems the client cannot resolve. See how selfish and how dependent on others your client is. Examine the division of labor in your client's milieu and see whether your client has an inappropriate share. Either too much or too little is significant. Examine the cultural capital (Bourdieu[46]) available to your client and assess whether it is sufficient for the role work he must perform.

Identify sources of conflict in the setting and link these with persons who maintain the conflict. Identify your client's friends and enemies, look for hidden allies and persons who are eager to give more role support. Check to see how efficiently the client performs required role duties. Disorganized, scattered, slow moving, unwilling people create problems for themselves. If your client is in a position where he must master one or more new roles, assess the availability and quality of coaches (Strauss[47]) or mentors. Do persons in the setting facilitate or impede your client's role learning? Are the other actors in the client's setting good role partners? Is their role behavior toward the client appropriate? Who in the setting might be tapped to provide additional role support and encouragement (McCall[28])? Assess your client's available resources, his economic, intellectual, social, moral, emotional, and interpersonal capital. Are these adequate for his situation? Assess his structural position and life chances. Is he poorly educated (Collins[48]), locked in a dead-end job track, impoverished, chronically ill or moribund, less successful than the norm for his cohort, past the age when he can marry or have children?

Assess the client's memberships and social participation and determine whether these are consistent with the client's primary statuses. Determine whether the client has any significant subcultural memberships (Arnold[49]) and assess whether subcultural memberships play any part in the presented problem. Assess whether cohort effects are implicated in the client's problem. Be sensitive to the client's occupation, especially if it poses any traps for workers in that field. Be especially watchful of workers in "dirty" occupations—persons whose clients are ambivalent about the services they receive (e.g., prison guards, vice squad cops, dentists, teachers, undertakers) (Hughes[50]). "Dirty" workers are always short of role support and experience much more stress than other workers (Kahn[51]). Evaluate the client's social type and the social types of significant role partners (Klapp,[52] Strong[53]). Recognize that the study of situated social types is particularly relevant to assessment because it gives insight into the "axes of life" or collective problems that like-situated persons in bounded communities must struggle to resolve (Clemmer,[54] Strong,[53] Sykes[55]).

Look for evidence that some person or agency has escalated your client to a deviant status (Lofland[56]) or is trying to "cool him out" (Clark[57]). Some persons (the young, the very old, the mentally ill, the handicapped, the retarded, immigrants, the poor, members of some minority communities) are vulnerable to escalation attempts from official agencies and private persons. Look for labeling in your client's milieu. Search for imputations of deviance (Rubington & Weinberg[58]).

Check whether your client is an "outlaw," a person such as a bohemian, a communist, an eccentric, an iconoclast, or a substance abuser, whose sentiments or behavior puts him at odds with conventional norms (Liebow,[59] Polsky[60]).

Be sensitive to hidden handicaps your client may not have revealed that impact his or her ability to meet normal role expectations. Look for evidence of deviance disavowal (Davis[61]), or "passing" (Goffman[62]). Never assume that your client is functionally literate or numerate, whatever his station or accomplishments. Assess whether your client has a demeaning social stigma (handicap, medical problem, mental illness, retardation, illiteracy) and what strategies he uses to cope with it. Watch out for clients who are good at "passing" and who may try to hide their stigma from you (Goffman[62]).

If your client is a professional person or has roots considerably removed from your own, expect the person's real self to be masked (Strauss[47]). Look for opportunities to get "backstage" in the client's life and ways to penetrate his fronts (Corwin[63]). Map out the client's role system and look for ambivalence, role strain, contradictions, unresolved role conflicts, and indications of role overload (Gross[64]). Distinguish his role commitments from role attachments (McCall[28]) and look for roles to which the client is committed but not attached (e.g., prisoner, student (for some children), sick person, poor person, the elderly, the moribund). Check for role failures (Saunders[65]), roles in which role support is missing or inadequate (McCall & Simmons[66]), and inappropriate role identities and orientations to particular roles. Assess whether the client has experienced assaults on cherished role identities. See if the client has failed to achieve or preserve a desired status. Assess whether all of the client's major statuses are "crystallized" (Lensky[67]).

Look for indications that the client may be an alienated person (Keniston,[68] Seeman,[69] Schacht,[70] Sykes[71]). Investigate the client's goal set, aspirations, and social connectedness for signs of anomia. Does the client have meaningful direction and purpose? Useful things to do? Associates and friends? Assess whether your client has adequate power for the roles he possesses or wishes to assume. Check whether at least a few roles in the client's role set regularly produce gratifying role support. If the client is grieving, do not fail to notice this. Gauge the client's stress. Know and look for signs of common untreated medical problems, alcoholism, depression, psychotic disorganization, obvious personality disorders (e.g., narcissistic, obsessive, antisocial, hysteric, borderline personality types) (American Psychiatric Association[72]).

Assess whether any significant developmental problems are present (Brim,[24] Levinson,[21] Lowenthal,[22] Smelser[23]). Clinical sociologists who work with individuals should know the child and adult development literatures and be able to recognize and distinguish normal and gross developmental problems (Piaget[73]). Do not confuse normal development problems with "real" problems. Most development problems experienced by "normals" tend to take care of themselves and do not require intervention beyond reassuring the client.

As you get deeply into the exploratory assessment, watch for signs that the client's attitudes or behavior are the cause of his problem. A good indication that the locus of the problem is within the client is a steadily worsening relationship with him. If he has trouble with others, he will have trouble with you. Some warning signs are denial of access, unwillingness to confirm or disconfirm your hypotheses and interpretations, attempts to control, choke off, or misdirect the exploratory assessment, impatience, uncooperativeness, and attacking or belittling you or clinical sociology. A client who is not on your side is a handful. In some cases, the best thing to do is cut your losses and run. Be on the lookout for the two most intractable and frustrating types of clients: the persistently stupid (Dexter[74]) and the persistently evil clients. If you are losing ground with a client, if the situation is getting muddier and your confusion is mounting, if you feel frustrated or revulsed and cannot seem to get the investigation moving, consider the hypothesis that your client does not want his problem solved but is using you for some private purpose. Some clients are professional groupies, some come to you seeking only intimacy or closeness, some want consolation or comfort from the clinician they have hired. Be sensitive to these behaviors and recognize them for what they are: therapy issues that should be dealt with by qualified psychotherapists.

Checklist for Assessing Organizations

When the client is an organization rather than an individual or a small interacting group of persons, exploratory assessment takes longer, requires considerably more resources, and is inherently more complex. No single person "speaks" for an organization, and in the field setting there are numerous interpretations and differing perspectives concerning the organization's character, problems, and functioning. Complex organizations are cauldrons that brew diverse and contradictory opinions, evaluations, and interpretations.

When assessing organizations, the first caution is do not attempt to "average," merge, or reconcile discordant opinions. Never set yourself up as a judge of who is "right" and never attempt to construct your own "true" picture of the organization (Kapsis & Saunders[75]). Clinical sociologists do not have privileged frames of reference. Rather than bog down in the impossible minutia of sorting out who is right and who is wrong, plan to see each divergent opinion as an opportunity to learn more about the life of the organization, as another route into its complexity. Each set of truths leads to a different community of actors with distinctive interests to defend.

Not every aspect of organizational life is elusive. Some phenomena have broad consensual support (usually empirical phenomena) and can be said to be "robust" in the sense that most persons will confirm their existence. To search for robust phenomena, use the strategy of "triangulation" (Denzin[41]): A phenomenon is robust if it can be confirmed by more than one analytical means. In your exploratory assessment, plan to survey crucial documents: policy manuals, business plans, budgets, mission statements, tables of organization. Spend time in the setting with members observing what they do and how they interrelate. Ask differently placed informants to talk about the organization and follow the leads they provide.

At the beginning, tease out respondents' views of the organization's structure and dynamics. Note critical and evaluative judgments. Record memories of formative events in the organization's history. Check whether like-situated persons (floor nurses, typists, skip tracers, middle managers, library aides, deacons) have consistent views of the organization. Contrast the table of organization with the information members give you about seats of power. Look for offices that lack power to do necessary work. Hunt for gross inequities and violations of common norms (either structural or isolated) and see whether these are associated with categories of resentful persons. Pay attention to distributive justice in the organization. Look at patterns of social relations within the organization and see whether categories of persons are persistently mistreated.

Look for consensus-building and consensus-destroying processes. Study the pace of change within the organization. See whether it is measured and realistic or whether the organization is constantly in a state of unsettling ferment. Assess whether management styles breed hostility, suspicions, mistrust, or institutionalized conflicts. Examine the adequacy of the organization's internal communications and managers' knowledge of the state of the organization. Look for opportunities for sabotage and for evidence sabotage is occurring. Hunt for evidence of low commitment of organization members, cynicism, or indifference and try to spot structural reasons for their low dedication. Check whether official norms are the norms governing actual practice. Assess the organization's culture and see whether it helps members to flourish or inhibits them.

Assess whether the organization is insufficiently or overbureaucratized. Are the organization's routines rational and integrated, and are they attended to by members? Look for unmet staff training and development needs. Check the organization's planning and agendas. See whether the organization has clear goals and coherent plans to achieve them. Estimate the consensus for these goals. Inquire whether the goals are perceived as legitimate by members. Assess whether the goal set is rationalized or whether there are inconsistent elements. Check the clarity and consistency of the organization's mission statement and see whether the organization's policy structure matches its mission.

Examine characteristic ways the organization conducts its business. Look for deleterious effects of its practices on insiders and outsiders. Assess the organization's reputation in its milieu. Assess the quality of present leadership. See how much key members of the organization know of its purposes and history. Assess whether managers have good comparative knowledge of how similar and successful organizations are structured and function. Check for management problems and poor management performance or incompetence. Assess leaders' problem-spotting and problem-solving skills. See whether most members know how to do their jobs. Are there obstacles that need to be removed before some members can do their work? Look at decision making. Is it centralized or decentralized? Is the organization's knowledge base adequate for decisions that must be made? Do members have adequate access to the organization's knowledge? Explore the organization's internal politics. Look for structural opportunities to use interstitial (Sanford[76]) or illegitimate means to reach approved goals. Identify categories of persons who use these means for their own ends.

What problems (recognized or not) does the external environment present? Assess how well the organization is doing with its strategic planning. Check the adaptiveness of the organization and fruitfulness of present and past directions. See how flexible the organization is, how readily it recognizes a need for change, and whether it is able to transform itself when it must adapt. Assess whether the organization makes efficient use of its resources. Examine personnel policies. Assess machinery for recruitment and replacement of members. Scrutinize the performance review system and study whether evaluations of members are used to improve job or role performance. If the organization is profit making, assess its business plan and its profitability. Assess the work the organization actually accomplishes and the suitability of available machinery for allocating and accomplishing the work. Assess whether the organization demeans its members or clients. See whether the organization's moral elements (norms, values, ideologies) are in agreement with the organization's official myths. Assess whether decision processes are decisive and decisions carried out effectively. Check whether the total roster of role duties is rationalized or whether there is overlap or gaps in work assignments.

If the organization is a volunteer organization, look for signs of burnout among leaders. See if the organization's leaders have become entrenched or have turned the organization into a private empire. Check whether the pool from which volunteers are drawn is sufficiently large to sustain the organization. Assess whether the interests and goals of leaders have diverged significantly from those of the member community (Friedson[77]). Assess personnel policies and practices, recruitment, selection, and training of new members. Recognize that in voluntary organizations, where disgruntled members vote with their feet, the rules are quite different than in organizations that hire members. Study how well members are inducted into their roles (both new members and old members into new roles).

If the client organization is a public agency that must put its major policies or plans before a hostile or critical public, check whether the organization has become stalemated by "elite pluralism"—a condition in which many interest groups have sufficient power to veto proposed changes but in which no coalition has enough power to force a change on everyone else. If the presented problem centers on management of change in any client organization, assess obstacles that stand in the way of change. Assess the process that must be negotiated to create change. Discover human resources that can be mobilized to build support for proposals. Assess how skillfully managers deal with coalition politics.

If the client organization is part of a large network of interconnected organizations, trace how the system functions as a whole (Beder,[78] Neal[79]). How much autonomy does each member organization have and in what domains? Where does the power lie, and how does power sharing take place? How is interorganizational communication handled? What information is communicated, to whom, and when? What is the nature of the network of personal contacts that links member organizations? What formal and informal rules govern interpersonal contacts? How much does the parent organization understand about the local setting and its requirements? How are goals and priorities established for the whole network of members? If the parent organization has a supervisory role, what are the mechanics and limits of supervision? How does decision making and ratification of decisions occur? What is the cultural ethos of the intertied organizations? If the organization is a public agency, what are the material political considerations? Hidden problem areas can sometimes be teased out by asking members to tell some of their "war stories" about interorganizational coordination.

Partial Checklist for Assessing Relationships among Persons

If the presented problem centers on persons in relationship to one another (couples, partnerships, neighbors, families, congregations, work groups, etc.), exploratory analysis should focus on the relationship's history, the quality of affect between members, patterns of interaction, reciprocity of mutual expectations, exchange patterns, expressed satisfactions, equity within the relationship, imputations from relationship members and others, contextual demands and constraints, economic constraints, role competence of interactants, moral and normative frameworks brought to the relationship by actors and frameworks they jointly construct, role-taking ability and capacity of actors to take the perspective of others (Turner,[80] Turner,[81] Wilson[7]), presence of machinery for negotiating conflicts and grievances, satisfactoriness of mutual role support, actors' self-knowledge and knowledge of how to conduct their relationship, and the degree to which actors' other involvements spill over into the relationship.

Assessment of Possible Interventions

If you have assiduously done your exploratory investigation, been careful in your choice of paradigms and analytical categories, done comparative analyses and hypothesis testing as you went along, you will reach a point where you are confident you know the nature of the problem and have ideas about what should be done. If you have worked the problem and do not yet know what to propose, you probably have not learned enough about the setting. If the problem is real, it is there to be found.

As you begin to think about interventions, search for "weak links" in the complex dynamical systems you have explored. Complicated dynamical systems have points of instability, critical places where a small push can have large consequences. The trick is to find these weak points and use them to modify the system's behavior. A different kind of weak link, which presents opportunities for intervention with adults and children, are the cusps of developmental phases, during which individuals are ready to grapple with particular tasks. The experience of development affords teachable moments, and if the teachable moment is to be captured, it must be coincidental with developmental tasks required of participants (Havighurst[20]).

When choosing an intervention from a set of several possible candidates, select a "minimally disruptive" intervention. Assess the "costs" of possible interventions. Gauge the anticipated effects of a proposed intervention on other persons in the client's world. Ethically the clinician may not solve the client's problem by creating trouble for someone else. Be sure to assess the extent to which a possible intervention is grounded in results from the exploratory assessment, comparative data, and sociological theory. Be certain that you have not missed a simpler hypothesis about what is wrong that points to a more trivial intervention.

While assessing candidate interventions, try to anticipate unexpected and unwanted effects of proposed interventions (Argyris[82]). Check to be sure that a candidate intervention is fitted to all of your client's characteristics. The intervention must fit the client as a whole person and the setting in its entirety. And always check that the benefits of the intervention will outweigh its costs. When you have settled on a candidate intervention, assess how to teach the client to enact the intervention, using data from the intake assessment. Consider ways to explain your reasoning to the client and sell him on the proposed intervention. Assess what must be done to carry out the intervention. Outline the steps that must be taken and lead the client through these. Give the client a written explanation of what you want done and why. Explain the results you expect from the intervention and how long it will take before the client should see them. Be sure that you and the client agree, at this point, on the nature of the intervention and what can be expected of it.

Assess the enthusiasm of the client for the intervention and his willingness to put it in place. Once he accepts it, do whatever teaching is necessary to begin the intervention and monitor how the intervention is carried out. Note ways the client's enactment departs from your plan. If the intervention has been in place for the necessary time and the results are disappointing, assess why the intervention failed and plan a new round of assessment and intervention. If the intervention is not a success, go back to basics again.

Summatory Assessment

And now we come to the final phase of assessment, summatory assessment or moving toward closure. Here we write our final case notes and assess what has been learned from the clinical episode. What were our mistakes? What bright ideas did we have? What new techniques or strategies did we devise? What were our disappointments? Did we make any serendipitous discoveries? How satisfactory to us and to our client were the outcomes of the case?

We are now ready for the last two steps of the assessment process. We should have a final, exit interview with the client and ask him to evaluate the clinical episode as a whole. The criticisms of clients can be devastating and humbling, but they are invaluable for what they teach us about how we conduct our clinical practice. If the work has been long under way, it is good to terminate the relationship with the client with a small ceremony of farewell, an informal dinner perhaps, or a drink. When the client is discharged, there is one remaining chore, and that is to reflect on the case, to distill what we have learned from it, and, if we have made some important gains, to communicate what we have learned to our colleagues.

REFERENCES

1. Blumer, H. (1969). *Symbolic interactionism: Perspective and method.* Englewood Cliffs, NJ: Prentice-Hall.
2. Glaser, B., & Strauss, A. (1967). *The discovery of grounded theory.* Chicago: Aldine.
3. Greer, S. (1969). *The logic of social inquiry.* Chicago: Aldine.
4. Lofland, J. (1971). *Analyzing social settings: A guide to qualitative observations and analysis.* Belmont, CA: Wadsworth.
5. Berger, P. L., & Luckmann, T. (1966). *The social construction of reality.* Garden City, NY: Doubleday.
6. Garfinkel, H. (1967). *Studies in ethnomethodology.* Englewood Cliffs, NJ: Prentice-Hall.
7. Wilson, T. P. (1970). Conceptions of interaction and forms of sociological explanation. *American Sociological Review, 35*(4), 697–710.
8. Habermas, J. (1971). *Knowledge and human interests.* Boston: Beacon Press.

11. Banton, M. (1965). *Roles: An introduction to the study of social relations*. London: Tavistock.
12. Brookfield, S. (1983). *Adult learners, adult education, and the community*. New York: Teachers College Press.
13. Knowles, M. S. (1975). *Self-directed learning: A guide for learners and teachers*. New York: Association Press.
14. Long, H. B. (1983). *Adult learning: Research and practice*. New York: Cambridge.
15. Knox, A. B. (1977). *Adult development and learning*. San Francisco: Jossey-Bass.
16. Freire, P. (1970). *Pedagogy of the oppressed*. New York: Herder & Herder.
17. Mezirow, Jack. (1978). Perspective transformation. *Adult Education, 28*, 100–110.
18. Brim, O. G., & Kagan, J. (Eds.). (1980). *Constancy and change in human development*. Cambridge: Harvard University Press.
19. Gould, R. L. (1978). *Transformations: Growth and change in adult life*. New York: Simon & Schuster.
20. Havighurst, R. J. (1952). *Developmental tasks and education*. New York: David McKay.
21. Levinson, D., Darrow, C. N., Klein, E. B., Levinson, M. H. & McKee, B. (1978). *The seasons of a man's life*. New York: Knopf.
22. Lowenthal, M. F., Thurnher, M., & Chiriboga, D. (1975). *Four stages of life*. San Francisco: Jossey-Bass.
23. Smelser, N. J. & Erikson, E. H. (Eds.). (1980). *Themes of work and love in adulthood*. Cambridge: Harvard University Press.
24. Brim, O. G. (1966). Socialization through the life-cycle. In O. G. Brim, Jr., & S. Wheeler (Eds.). *Socialization after childhood* (pp. 1–49). New York: Wiley.
25. Sheehy, G. (1976). *Passages: Predictable crises of adult life*. New York: E. P. Dutton.
26. Schuetz, A. (1944). The stranger: An essay in social psychology. *American Journal of Sociology, 49*, 499–507.
27. Dollard, J. (1949). *Criteria for the life history*. New York: Peter Smith.
28. McCall, G. J. (1970). The social organization of relationships. In G. J. McCall, M. M. McCall, N. K. Denzin, G. D. Suttles, & S. B. Kurth (Eds.), *Social relationships* (pp. 3–34). Chicago: Aldine.
29. Becker, H. S., & Strauss, A. (1956). Careers, personality and adult socialization. *American Journal of Sociology, 62*, 253–63.
30. Goslin, D. A. (Ed.). (1969). *Handbook of socialization theory and research*. Rand McNally.
31. Levy, C. J. (1971). ARVN as faggots: Inverted warfare in Vietnam. *Transaction, 8*, 18–27.
32. Marini, M. M. (1984). The order of events in the transition to adulthood. *Sociology of Education, 57*(2), 63–84.
33. McLanahan, S. (1985). Family structure and the reproduction of poverty. *American Journal of Sociology, 90*(4), 873–901.
34. Mare, R. D., Winship, C., & Kubitschek, W. N. (1984). The transition from youth to adult: Understanding the age pattern of employment. *American Journal of Sociology, 90*(2), 326–358.
35. Blau, P. M. (1956). Social mobility and interpersonal relations. *American Sociological Review, 21*, 290–295.
36. Hoffer, E. (1951). *The true believer*. New York: Harper.
37. Blum, A., & McHugh, P. (1971). The social ascription of motives. *American Sociological Review, 36*, 98–109.
38. Cartwright, D. (1952). Emotional dimensions of group life. In M. L. Reymert (Ed.), *Feelings and emotions* (pp. 439–47). New York: McGraw-Hill.
39. Foote, N. N. (1951). Identification as the basis for a theory of motivation. *American Sociological Review, 16*, 14–21.
40. Mills, C. W. (1940). Situated actions and vocabularies of motive. *American Sociological Review, 5*, 904–913.
41. Denzin, N. (1970). *The research act*. Chicago: Aldine.
42. Blau, P. M. (1964). *Power and exchange in social life*. New York: Wiley.
43. Goffman, E. (1959). *The presentation of self in everyday life*. Garden City, NJ: Anchor.
44. Clifford, M. M., & Walster, E. (1973). The effects of physical attractiveness on teacher expectations. *Sociology of Education, 46*, 48–58.
45. Webster, M., & Driskell, J. E. (1983). Beauty as status. *American Journal of Sociology, 89*(1), 140–165.
46. Bourdieu, P., & Passeron, J. (1977). *Reproduction in education, society, and culture*. Beverly Hills: Sage.
47. Strauss, A. (1959). *Mirrors and masks*. New York: Free Press.

48. Collins, R. (1979). *The credential society*. New York: Academic Press.

49. Arnold, D. O. (1970). *The sociology of subcultures*. Berkeley: Glendessary Press.

50. Hughes, E. C. (1964). Good people and dirty work. In H. S. Becker (Ed.), *The other side: Perspectives on deviance* (pp. 23–36). New York: Free Press.

51. Kahn, R. L., Wolfe, D. M., Quinn, R. P., Snoek, J. D., & Rosenthal, R. A. (1964). *Organizational stress: Studies in role conflict and ambiguity*. New York: Wiley.

52. Klapp, O. (1962). *Heroes, villains, and fools*. Englewood Cliffs, NJ: Prentice-Hall.

53. Strong, S. M. (1943). Social types in a minority group: Formulation of a method. *American Journal of Sociology, 48*, 563–73.

54. Clemmner, D. (1958). *The prison community*. New York: Holt, Rinehart.

55. Sykes, G. (1958). *The society of captives: A study of a maximum security prison*. Princeton: Princeton University Press.

56. Lofland, J. (1969). *Deviance and identity*. Englewood Cliffs, NJ: Prentice-Hall.

57. Clark, B. (1960). The 'cooling-out' function in higher education. *American Journal of Sociology, 65*, 569–76.

58. Rubington, E., & Weinberg, M. S. (1973). The social deviant. In E. Rubington & M. S. Weinberg (Eds.), *Deviance: The interactionist perspective* (pp. 1–10). New York: Macmillan.

59. Liebow, E. (1967). *Tally's corner*. Boston: Little, Brown.

60. Polsky, N. (1969). *Hustlers, beats, and others*. New York: Doubleday Anchor.

61. Davis, F. (1964). Deviance disavowal: The management of strained interaction by the visibly handicapped. In H. S. Becker (Ed.), *The other side: Perspectives on deviance* (pp. 119–137). New York: Free Press.

62. Goffman, E. (1963). *Stigma: Notes on the management of spoiled identity*. Englewood Cliffs, NJ: Prentice-Hall.

63. Corwin, R. G., Taves, M., & Haas, J. E. (1960). Social requirements for occupational success: Internalized norms and friendship. *Social Forces, 39*, 135–40.

64. Gross, N., Mason, W. S., & McEachern, W. (1958). *Explorations in role analysis*. New York: Wiley.

65. Saunders, B. (1975). *Analysis of role failure*. Unpublished PhD dissertation. Berkeley: University of California.

66. McCall, G. J., & Simmons, J. L. (1966) *Identities and interactions*. New York: Free Press.

67. Lensky, G. E. (1954). Status crystallization: A non-vertical dimension of social status. *American Sociological Review, 19*, 405–413.

68. Keniston, K. (1963). *The uncommitted: Alienated youth in American society*. New York: Dell.

69. Seeman, M. (1959). On the meaning of alienation. *American Sociological Review, 24*, 783–790.

70. Schacht, R. (1971). *Alienation*. New York: Doubleday Anchor.

71. Sykes, G. (Ed.). (1964). *Alienation* (Vols. 1 & 2). New York: George Braziller.

72. American Psychiatric Association. (1987). *Diagnostic and statistical manual of mental disorders* (3rd ed. rv.). Washington, DC: American Psychiatric Association.

73. Piaget, J. (1972). Intellectual evolution from adolescence to adulthood. *Human Development, 15*, 1–12.

74. Dexter, L. A. (1964). On the politics and sociology of stupidity in our society. In H. S. Becker (Ed.), *The other side: Perspectives on deviance* (pp. 37–49). New York: Free Press.

75. Kapsis, R., Saunders, B., Smith, J., & Takagi, P. (1970). *The reconstruction of a riot: A case study of community tensions and civil disorder*. Brandeis University: Lemberg Center for the Study of Violence.

76. Sanford, Mark. (1970). *Making do in graduate school*. Unpublished PhD dissertation. Berkeley: University of California.

77. Friedson, E., & Rhea, B. (1963). Processes of control in a company of equals. *Social Problems, 11*, 119–31.

78. Beder, H. (Ed.). (1984). *Realizing the potential of interorganizational cooperation*. San Francisco: Jossey-Bass.

79. Neal, D. C. (1988). *Consortia and interinstitutional cooperation*. New York: Macmillan.

80. Turner, R. (1956). Role taking, role standpoint, and reference group behavior. *American Journal of Sociology, 61*, 316–28.

81. Turner, R. (1962). Role-taking: Process versus conformity. In Rose, R. M. *Human behavior and social process*. Boston: Houghton Mifflin.

82. Argyris, C. (1973). *Intervention theory and method: A behavioral science view*. Reading, MA: Addison-Wesley.

CHAPTER 4

Intervention in Clinical Sociology

HOWARD REBACH

INTRODUCTION

The most basic attribute that sets the subdiscipline of clinical sociology apart is that of intervention; the clinical sociologist is an active change agent. It is not possible, at this stage of development, to present a concise and comprehensive model of clinical sociological intervention. Intervention in clinical sociology is not just the mechanistic application of a set of techniques that automatically follow from a problem label. The problem of trying to characterize intervention in clinical sociology is also exacerbated by the diversity of clinical sociology. Therefore, rather than offer specific interventions for specific problems, this brief chapter will outline general considerations for developing interventions: First this chapter will briefly consider the nature of intervention in clinical sociology, then turn to several "guiding themes" of intervention, and close with some consideration of intervention targets.

THE DIVERSITY AND UNITY OF INTERVENTION IN CLINICAL SOCIOLOGY

One way to characterize the diversity of clinical sociology is by a three dimensional matrix of clients, settings, and activities.[1] The term *clients* refers to those persons on whose behalf intervention is conducted. They may be the actual persons who seek a clinical sociologist or other members of their social networks. (Deciding "who" your client is can sometimes be a knotty problem.)

The term *settings* refers to the various social and physical settings in which work takes place. These may include the consultant's office, a school, a business or government agency, a community, and so forth. Finally, the term *activities* refers to

HOWARD REBACH • Department of Social Science, University of Maryland Eastern Shore, Princess Anne, Maryland 21853.

those things that the clinical sociologist does, alone or in concert with members of an interdisciplinary team, in working toward solutions to identified problems.

Clients span a broad range including individuals, groups, and families, organizations, communities, governmental units, and political subdivisions—counties, states, regional agencies. Settings are as diverse as the social world, and activities are bound only by the creative imagination of the clinical sociologist. Straus[2] described a "social behavioral" approach in working with individuals and gave examples of work with obese persons. Church[3] and Voelkl and Colburn[4] have described work with couples and families. Kallen[5] described an intervention on behalf of a hospital developing a treatment component for sick and injured adolescents that included work with an interdisciplinary team. The intervention involved changes in the physical setting, had an educational component for staff, and restructured hospital routines and staff behavior. Jones[6] worked with designers, planners, architects, and consumer groups in the design of buildings. Anderson and Rouse[7] and Sengstock[8] reported clinical sociological interventions with spousal abuse. Jacques[9] reported macrolevel intervention with the British National Health Service, and Bennello[10] worked nationally and regionally helping to organize and develop worker-managed businesses.

The multiparadigmatic nature of sociology adds another element of diversity. Clinical sociologists may choose an interactionist, social constructionist, critical, or conflict perspective. Others may be more eclectic, choosing a perspective that best fits the circumstances of the case. Straus,[11] for instance, expressed the view that "whatever . . . theoretical orientation [is] brought to bear on the problem," eclecticism occurs in practice. Straus argued that theory may help clarify the empirical circumstances, but intervention is about results. The important criterion for intervention is that desired changes take place. Swann[12] discussed what he called "grounded encounter therapy," a form of sociotherapy. Swann's approach was also eclectic; that is, the theories and approaches to intervention activities emerge from interaction with clients. For both Swann and Straus, intervention programs are unique to the specific clients as they see their social context. Thus Swann noted, "The same problem may have a different context for different clients and hence would be treated differently."

Clinical sociological intervention may take place on many levels—the micro, the meso, or the macro. This means that interventions may be on behalf of individuals, families, work units, or community groups, organizational, or governmental units. Despite its diversity, intervention is unified by the fact that sociology is the fundamental corpus of knowledge that illuminates clinical sociologists' understanding and approach to cases. This body of knowledge directs our attention to social interaction and social arrangements as the basis of problems and targets for change. Our general understanding of sociology informs us of the relationship between social structures and individual action and that the individual cannot be understood apart from the social context. Even when work is on a microlevel with individuals or families (sociotherapy), we are aware that the isolated individual is a fiction, convenient for some purposes, but a fiction nonetheless. Individuals are tied into social networks that form a system that influences action. Action, in turn, is an expression of culture, the culture of the interacting individuals, their subcultures, and the larger cultural context.

GUIDING THEMES

Because sociology is the knowledge base of clinical sociology, several "guiding themes" are relevant to intervention.

Science

Sociology prompts us to apply the scientific method. Choosing intervention activities is a creative activity, almost an artistic endeavor. The problematic situation in a given case is filled with uncertainties and complex interconnections, some of which are unknown and, perhaps, unknowable. The reality of a case is without structure. Single cases are characterized by uniqueness and uncertainty. Imposing structure on reality is a human endeavor. Application of the *methods* of science, the process of scientific investigation, is one way to impose such structure.

Intervention in a single case is not a scientific activity, but it is illuminated by science in at least two ways. First, sociological findings may channel creative thinking for the analysis of a problem and design of an intervention program. For example, findings that children have major health problems following their parents' divorce[13] and that mothers' reports of children's health are associated with marital status and ethnicity, together with other demographic factors,[14] could inform the development of a plan for health services within a community, a basis for activism nationally, or the basis for work with an individual child or mother and child.

Although scientific findings may support the development of intervention programs, the scientific method guides all clinical sociological work. The various steps in the clinical process use the methods of sociology to aid in investigation and conceptualization of the problem and aid in developing an operational definition of the problem and of the change to take place. These are "structure-promoting" activities. The scientific method also prompts continuing evaluation of an intervention program. Program design in a specific case is essentially the formulation of a hypothesis: Given the problem as defined, the social context of the problem, and available assessment data, the worker hypothesizes that the proposed program will lead to a desired outcome. The implementation of the program is subjected to continuous testing to support or disconfirm this hypothesis. In short, work with clients is data-driven.

Intervention as Process

Intervention is a process, not an event. Moreover, it is a social process. The intervention agent interacts with members of a client system, over time, to achieve objectives set through negotiation between clients and the agent. Just as "the problem" is not an event—it developed over time—its amelioration is a process that occurs over time. As a process, intervention can be thought of as including strategic steps: (1) assessment; (2) program design; (3) program implementation; and (4) program evaluation.

The assessment phase includes those activities designed to gather data leading to a definition of the problem, an understanding of who the relevant actors are, what systems are involved, what needs to be changed, and what can be changed. Program design is the development of an action plan to achieve the goals of intervention. It includes a statement of who will do what, when, and where. Program implementation turns the plan into action. Finally, evaluation determines the efficacy of the plan.

These phases are presented here as discrete steps. In reality, they are not discrete. For example, assessment is a process that continues throughout the course of intervention. As you work on a case, you become increasingly familiar with the circumstances and the client system. Experienced clinical workers find that they often get new insights. In addition, as the clinical situation or the relationship with the client changes, the client may present information previously withheld—for a variety of clinical reasons—that alters the clinical picture. For example, after several weeks of work with a depressed adolescent who had made at least two known suicidal gestures, the client revealed to the author that, on several occasions, she had been sexually abused by an uncle. She reported she had privately wished the man dead—and he had died shortly thereafter. The girl subsequently harbored a sense of guilt at having "caused" the man's death, which affected her interaction with significant others and seemed partially to explain interaction with age-mates that resulted, among other things, in problematic self-conception. The presentation of these facts significantly altered the clinical picture and subsequent work.

There is an important feedback loop in this intervention schema—the loop between program design, implementation, and evaluation. Appropriate evaluation is as essential to intervention as all other steps, but it is the most frequently neglected. It cannot be stressed too strongly that the evaluation step must be built into all intervention plans and must be an ongoing activity that occurs in conjunction with program implementation. The program is designed to alter the value of certain critical variables or indicators. The program should be carefully monitored to see if the critical indicators show improvement, no change, or decline. Improvement indicates the program may be working. If continuing evaluation shows no change, worsening, or undesirable side effects, reassessment and redesign should be undertaken, and necessary program changes implemented, and evaluation should continue. To reiterate a point made earlier, ongoing evaluation is the application of the scientific method to intervention.

Intervention as a Humanistic Pursuit

Though guided by the methods of science, intervention in clinical sociology is also guided by humanistic values. Professional help is sought to redress an existing or potential disequilibrium between the client and the environment stemming from attempts to cope with and adapt to the environment. Clients seek professional helpers because they are confronted by problems they cannot solve with their own resources. Their inability to solve their own problems causes distress for them, for others within the social system, or for the social system itself. Help is sought because the client or client system is "stuck" and has no strategies for becoming unstuck, for choosing new outcomes or new courses of action to achieve existing goals. Previously learned and acquired strategies for handling and adapting to circumstances do not achieve desired outcomes, and this failure to achieve such outcomes has become problematic.

The humanistic view recognizes the voluntary nature of action and that people are active constructors of their lives, themselves, and their situations. We take in the materials of experience and actively construct our understanding of them as we represent reality to ourselves. But it is not a solitary process. Our social structures constrain us. Reality is negotiated in interaction with others within the situation. Though the individual actor actively constructs reality, that reality can only be fashioned from the materials at hand. At any given moment, each actor in a situation is choosing behaviors based on his or her own construction of events and self, and each actor's present adaptation is the best it can be. The actor is striving for autonomy, self-determination, and desired outcomes. Maladaptive behaviors develop through the same types of processes that produce more adaptive behaviors: interaction and learning by group members within a sociocultural context.

All this implies a particular orientation to intervention. It implies a "working-with" rather than a "doing-to" or a "doing-for" approach to intervention. The clinician's role is to assist the client(s) to add constructive choices to their repertoire of action. Ultimately, the clients or members of client systems will choose their own courses of action. This clinical orientation calls for respect for clients' autonomy, ability to learn, their unique—often idiosyncratic—ways of learning, and ability and right to control their own destiny within the systems in which they choose to operate. It requires recognition of the fact that clients are capable of solving problems and reconstructing reality in appropriate ways as options open up for them. Finally, it requires recognition that the clinician does not stigmatize the client for having a problem and the clinician does not blame the client for the existence of the problem. It sees the genesis of "problems" in the clients' attempts to cope with their surroundings and the demands that those surroundings place on them. Such an orientation acknowledges the role played by normal developmental processes and by social systems in which people exist.

For example, many contemporary observers decry the fact that illiteracy is on the rise in the United States. The literacy level, even of undergraduate college students, has been found wanting. One analysis blames the youth for lack of motivation and failure to learn. An alternative analysis suggests that social systems have failed these youth; the schools, their families, the mass media, and their communities have failed to find effective methods for teaching literacy and/or have failed to promote the skills and values that promote literacy. These social systems, in turn, respond to social, political, and economic realities and priorities. The recognition that systems shape maladaptive actions of individuals and social units, as they shape adaptive behaviors, will enable the clinical sociologist to adopt the most helpful orientation to clients—the recognition that clients are competent, capable, autonomy-seeking partners in the clinical enterprise.

Intervention in clinical sociology is what Gutknecht[15] called a "client centered collaborative effort which includes sensitivity to cultural traditions of client groups and awareness of the ways in which the structural embeddedness of interlocking problems affects . . . behavior and structures." Gutknecht emphasized that collaboration should lead to "development of an ongoing learning system" and the "need for clients to participate in the formulation of their own questions and devise their own answers."

Although Gutknecht's remarks referred to the organizational setting, it is important to note that they apply, as well, to all levels of intervention. The clinical sociologist does not assume an authoritative role to adjust persons to systems but rather works with people so that their systems meet their needs and they develop their own problem-solving capacities. The partnership mode objectifies the problem. It is not something that you, the client, has and that the clinical helper will cure you of. Rather, the problem becomes something to which you, the client, and the clinical helper will combine their resources and talents to find constructive alternatives.

The Goal of Intervention Is Behavior Change

It must be understood that the goal of intervention is behavior change. No matter at what level the intervention takes place, and no matter what the problem situation, for change to occur, significant actors and role occupants must alter their actions and interactions within relevant contexts. This means that the specific actors and contexts must be carefully and accurately defined. It also means—and this is critical—that problematic behaviors and the new behaviors must also be operationally defined. Program design must very carefully specify the indicators that will show whether movement toward intervention goals is occurring.

This is the major way that intervention in clinical sociology differs from other forms of intervention: The emphasis is on *observable*, measurable changes in overt action. The focus is *not* on unobservable intrapsychic events or hidden causes, nor is the goal some vague specification of enhanced functioning or the restoration of equilibrium. The work must proceed with clear operational definition of desired outcomes. The work must also proceed with careful monitoring of indicators specified *a priori*. If these do not show movement, reassessment and redesign take place.

Though a clinical sociologist may privately use terms like *empowerment, role strain,* and *marginality,* these are shorthand or summary phrases. They may be helpful in understanding a case, but, as Voelkl and Colburn[4] pointed out, these terms must be translated to specific interactional behaviors within the client system. They are not solvable problems.

The clinical sociologist is aware that application of a label does not lead to application of a generic set of techniques. For the clinical sociologist, there are no sets of techniques mechanistically applied. The intervention agent must have reflective and adaptive capacities. The clinical sociologist constantly monitors events and creatively adapts intervention steps to interact with changing conditions, unstable conditions, and changing goals. The sociocultural contexts are sources of environmental disturbances that require program adaptation.

Intervention steps consider the sociocultural contexts and the specific patterns of action within context. As Swann[12] observed,

> For example, what we know about family violence should not necessarily be the knowledge used in treating a case of family violence. The knowledge to be applied comes from the process of discovery about the problem and its context.

Though behavioral change is the goal, cognitive events are not totally ignored. In his many writings on clinical sociological intervention, Straus[16] directed our attention to the need to change the clients' operational definitions of the situation "since they form the basis upon which conduct will be constructed by human actors." Straus noted, however, that sociological interventions "are more concerned with the manifestations . . . in patterns of conduct and joint conduct being enacted by the individuals, groups, and/or systems under scrutiny." Although cognitive events may underlie action, behavioral change can result in cognitive change and vice versa. Thus, for Straus, the *operational* definition of the situation is found in patterns of action of an individual or groups of persons in small and large social systems. Ultimately, even internal socially constructed realities manifest themselves in behavior and, ultimately, it is behavior that must change if problem solving is to take place.

Problems Addressed as Social Problems

Problems are conceptualized as being created by social organization and as social problems regardless of the level of the presenting problem. The most disordered behavior of an individual has its social dimension. The actions of a 9-year-old boy, assessed as having an attention deficit disorder with hyperactivity may engage in actions unacceptable to others in his role set. His behavior would not be problematic had others (more powerful than he) not defined his behavior as a problem. Moreover, his actions have consequences for others in his social settings. Though this boy may receive medication to deal with a biological base of his behavior, the social dimension also demands attention. For medication to be effective, his family must carry out the medical regimen. His earlier behavior patterns may have caused him to receive a label within family, peer, and school social systems that may continue to define him in a certain way and place expectations on him that support continuation of disruptive actions. Role relationships may need attention. It is not uncommon for the parents of such children to have lost control; the child comes to have the power to control family patterns. Thus intervention may need to find ways to reestablish (or establish) the status of the parent as the legitimate authority. This means that parents and others may have to alter their actions toward the boy as a way of changing his actions. A central feature of sociological intervention is the focus on interactive behaviors and role relationships.

Barriers to Change

Because change—becoming unstuck—is the goal, the clinical sociologist needs to analyze why client systems do not change. The issues are knowledge, skill, and motivation in order of increasing difficulty where the success of intervention is concerned. That is, clients may be stuck for lack of knowledge about the existence of constructive alternatives. They may not be aware of changing conditions requiring new adaptive strategies. The value of the provision of useful information as a component of intervention cannot be overlooked.

Clients may lack the skill to make options into real alternatives to their present course of action. Program activities may include education, training, role rehearsal, incorporation of new kinds of roles, and the like that increase the pool of skills that allow for adaptive change.

With knowledge and skills, however, the clients or members of a client system may not be motivated to make the changes previously identified as necessary to interact effectively with their environment. Change carries an element of risk and unpredictability. The nice thing about the way you have always done things is that they are familiar and you can predict the outcome, even if that outcome does not maximize your rewards. Change, or a change-oriented intervention, may produce serious disequilibrium within the client system and spark efforts to restore that equilibrium. Thus, when an individual starts to change his/her actions, members of the person's role set may exert pressures against change. They typically have related to the person in a specific way and may not be prepared to change their familiar and habitual interaction pattern.

Assessment should also try to uncover any actors who benefit from the problematic situation and their relative power to sabotage change efforts. Even by inaction, certain actors in key roles may disrupt attempts to bring about change. In some cases, these actors are opinion leaders or legitimizers. In other cases, legitimizers and decision makers, such as managers, may be all for change, and resistance comes from workers who may be threatened by change or whose superior knowledge of actual conditions creates a very rational resistance to proposed changes. To be effective as a change agent, the clinical sociologist must consider all elements of a system.

Other aspects that detract from clients' motivation to change need to be considered in program planning. The program steps and the changes must be consistent with clients' conception of self (individual or corporate), their moral and ethical standards, their sociocultural norms and practices, and the like. The situation gets more complex when these elements are, themselves, at the root of the problem. For example, in work with an individual, the conception of self may be extremely negative. In family work, a spouse's conception of his or her role may be problematic. Brisbane and Stuart[17] reported how subcultural norms of keeping things that go on in the home, in the home, conflicted with several black woman's participation in a group for black women with alcoholic parents. This conflict caused them to withdraw from the self-help group that was designed to deal with the many problems faced by adults reared by alcoholic parents.

Loci of Intervention: Targets for Change

Program design is an exercise in the practical and the workable, not the ideal. Limitations of resources—time, energy, money, personnel, and so forth—must be taken into account. Existing social, political, economic, and physical constraints must also be taken into account. Careful analysis is necessary to determine the "loci of intervention." The clinical sociologist must be aware of what can be changed and not waste time and resources and create frustration attacking things that cannot be changed, given the resources—time, money, people, power, and the like—available for the work.

One approach is to think in terms of linear causal trains: Antecedent conditions → response → consequences. That is, some set of circumstances may bring about a specific set of maladaptive responses on the part of a client system. The actions of one system—individual, group or institution—may be found to reliably elicit a specific patterned action on the part of another system. This interaction may produce an outcome that is functional for one or both systems involved, but the train of events may prove maladaptive in some way. Change efforts may attempt to alter any or all of these situations. Assessment needs to point the way to the part(s) of the chain where change can take place.

For example, Britt[18] worked with a company that made cooling systems. The company found that overhead costs were rising. The company's practice was to ship the systems to the customer, but upon arrival, the systems did not work on site. Customer complaints were handled by a customer relations unit of the company that would schedule engineers and technicians to go to the site and make the necessary adjustments. It was this latter response that created unacceptable excessive cost to the company. Customer complaints never got back to the production department or the shipping department. The change was to have customer complaints go directly to production. Production and shipping later coordinated to modify procedures and equipment that significantly reduced the rate of failure of systems to work when they arrived at the customer's location.

Initially, the company's response to the situation was the first target of change; that is, changing the routing of customer complaints. This led, later, to changes in the antecedent conditions, the production and shipping of systems to customers. In turn, these changes led to more positive outcomes—the company saved a substantial sum of money and probably prevented damage to its reputation.

A change in the antecedent conditions may produce a new response leading to new outcomes. Where preconditions cannot be changed, perhaps responses can be altered, or intervention can alter the situation so changes can occur in the response that lead to more positive outcomes than the habitual response pattern.

Intervention in clinical sociology takes cognizance of many levels, and intervention may take place across levels. Work with an individual, couple, or family, may also involve schools, the workplace, the community, and so forth. Work with large organizations may involve work with the role relationships within specific groups, the relationships between groups within an organization, and work with individual role occupants. Freedman[19] emphasized this concern for levels when he noted that, when working with individuals, we need to be aware of the broader issues of social structures and "when working on broader issues of social change, you have to keep in mind the effect on the individual." Gutknecht,[15] in discussing organizational development, also argued that an intervention takes place across levels within a social system. He noted that "clinical sociology infuses organizational development with more flexible techniques of integrating micro and macro approaches to social and organizational change."

In my own work with a 9-year-old boy whose violent behavior was defined as a problem at home, at school, and in the neighborhood, it was necessary to work with him, others in his role set, and other systems. Work included attempting to empower his mother, a single parent with two other children, to bring his behavior under her control. It was also necessary to work with teachers, other school staff, and the schoolbus driver to help the boy reduce the perceived threats and frustrations that appeared to prompt his actions. The work also included a session with his math class where the boy, his classmates, the teacher, and I talked about appropriate behaviors and responses to situations. With the help of the teacher and the other students, we enacted role-play situations that included both inappropriate and appropriate actions. The repeated role plays allowed us to shape the behavior of the boy, the other children, and even the teacher. Follow-up suggested that the intervention was working.

Clinical sociological intervention, as Freedman pointed out, may have to "move beyond the clients' formulation of the problem to consider other factors that affect functioning, especially broad social trends. Whyte[20] also suggested questioning the clients' formulations, the "standard model." Referring to organizations, Whyte cautioned that the client may conceptualize the problem as "the standard model is not working well." Those who accept the standard model, however, tend to normative thinking. They "assume that it would work well if only they could recruit better people for leadership positions, provide better training for supervisors and develop better means for monitoring activities and punishing people who are not doing what they are supposed to do."

APPROACHES TO INTERVENTION

Approaches to intervention will be profoundly influenced by the practice setting of the clinical sociologist. My own setting is an outpatient community mental health clinic. Cases are individuals, couples, and families with occasional work on behalf of schools and nursing homes. Other clinical sociologists specialize with larger social systems. In an earlier attempt to impose some structure on the diversity of interventions in clinical sociology, Straus[16] defined levels of intervention as occurring with persons, groups including families, organizations, and worlds. By organizations, he meant such structures as "corporations and associations, communities and governments." "World" or "social world" he adopted from Lofland[21] to describe more or less organized fields of endeavor. These are referred to in phrases like "the academic world," "the business world," and so forth. They describe a type of subculture of "norms, values, folkways, mores, language, and technology differentiating its participants from members of other social worlds."

This typology suggested, for Straus, targets of intervention. Where the client is an individual, the target is the individual's behavior, both intra- and interpersonal. Where a group is the social system of concern, Straus suggested that the target was role relationships. For organizations, the target Straus suggested was "the institutionalized patterns of relations between groups rather than the role relations within the group" and "routinized patterns of social relations" that constitute social organization of larger-scale social systems. Finally, interventions in a "social world targets the culture, mainly the nonmaterial aspects of culture."

To Straus's typology, it is worth adding that intervention in clinical sociology may address several social system levels. Thus the intervention agent may need to consider intergroup relations, role relationships within groups, and individual conduct and role performance, all in the same case.

The clinical-sociologist-as-change-agent enacts a role as teacher and guide after the assessment is complete and the goals of the work are contracted for. In work with individuals, with individual conduct the target, the task is resocialization, what Fein[22] described as "role problems," helping individuals "change dysfunctional social roles into more satisfying ones."

For example, adult children of alcoholics were often "parentalized" in their families of origin. They often had to take on role responsibilities that were beyond their years and experience and had to cope with situations with little guidance and few effective strategies. In addition, their experience provided little security, and they learned not to trust because the alcoholic parent often made promises subsequently not kept. Adult children of alcoholics often remain stuck in earlier role performances. They often display continued inability to trust others, have difficulty with relationships, especially close relationships such as marriage, and continue the parentalized role by generally taking responsibility for and trying to direct the actions of others. These are often two sources of disappointment and distress. A third source of distress is that adult children of alcoholics are often perfectionistic, stemming from their earlier belief that if only they had tried harder and been better, things would have turned out differently. These patterns interfere with their performance of a variety of social roles, spouse, worker, parent, and so forth.

As Fein[22] noted, these roles and ways of enacting them are at the core of identity. Fein cited Stryker who referred to "transsituational roles" to describe roles not tied to specific social settings. Performance of these roles becomes part of a person's definition of self—roles such as family hero, scapegoat—and therefore, part of their behavioral repertoire across social settings.

An example of such a case was Will, a 32-year-old white, married male, with a 4-year-old daughter. Will, himself, had been an alcoholic for about 5 years. Four years earlier, he stopped drinking on his own, without treatment. At the time of intake, he was in a partnership with two others in a building contracting business that was quite successful after 3 years of operation. Will came alone to the first session and listed several problems: He could not trust anyone; he and his wife were in constant conflict with each other, especially over child rearing; he was embroiled in trying to straighten out the lives of his four younger siblings, all adults now, and he was concerned that he "couldn't feel anything," including remorse over his father's recent death. Though it had not occurred for several years, Will's earlier conflicts with his wife had included physical abuse.

Assessment revealed, among other things, Will's father's history of alcoholism, the father's consistent denigration of Will, telling Will he was worthless and stupid, the father's abuse of the mother, Will's attempts to win his father's approval (though failing no matter how hard he tried), and Will's taking on a quasi-parental role in helping to raise his younger siblings and supporting/protecting the mother.

Resocialization as an intervention strategy includes, for me, work with the individual and with significant others—for example, spouse or present partner, parents, and so on. Selection of others depends on the case. For example, with a child or adolescent, parents, sibs, teachers, friends, or classmates may be included. With Will, work included individual sessions and sessions with him and his wife. In the individual sessions, we carefully went over his earlier socialization experiences with instruction on how these early role performances manifested themselves in present conduct. His present predicament was demystified as Will learned how his prior socialization and role models shaped his present definition of self and his adult role performances. Because roles are negotiated in interaction, work in sessions with his wife included instruction in spousal communication, including how to conduct conflict, instruction on joint parenting, and instruction and homework designed to facilitate a more egalitarian role relationship with his spouse and changes in role relationships with his now-adult siblings. Methods included role playing, role reversal, and modeling by me. Resocialization also included referral to Adult Children of Alcoholics (ACOA), a self-help group. The purpose of the referral to the group was to help Will and his wife develop a supportive network of others who understood the problem and could help them develop coping strategies. Though presented here in brief, the case illustrates work on at least two levels—individual and group—and the instructional role of a clinical sociologist in resocialization as well as in helping the clients find supportive networks.

Intervention with groups and families often involves role relationships. Attention should be paid to power structures, communication structures, and the nature and organization of family systems and subsystems. An example was the case of Sheila Roberts. The local school asked for help with this 12-year-old girl whose actions disrupted the entire elementary school. Upon arrival at school, Sheila began screaming and refusing to attend class. School personnel—teachers, principals, guidance counselors, and school nurse—all attempted to mollify the girl and get her to attend class. Eventually, in despair, the girl's mother was usually called. Mrs. Roberts was asked to take the girl home and keep her there for a few days.

At intake, the problem was identified as the girl's concern that "something terrible" would happen to her mother, and she wanted to be with her mother and be assured of Mom's safety. At intake, it was also learned that, at 12 years old, the girl admitted to weighing 210 pounds (which was an underestimate by 20 pounds). She admitted that she was teased unmercifully by her classmates, a situation she said she could no longer take and wished to avoid.

The antecedent conditions include the interactions between the girl and her classmates, the school's requirements for attendance, and specific requirements for performance of the student role—going to class, doing work, and the like. The child's response was to engage in actions designed to escape/avoid the punishing situation, and, by and large, her actions got the outcome she wanted: The school suspended her, her family allowed her to stay home for as long as they could, and they permitted her to stay home from school whenever she wished. This sequence, however, was seen as maladaptive by both school personnel and the mother. The girl may suffer educational and developmental deficits that affect her life chances, and county laws governing school attendance could lead to serious consequences for the parents.

Assessment revealed that Sheila's father had little positive to say about school in general, about Sheila's school, or about the staff at the school. The father, weighed 350 pounds, doted on Sheila, though he was autocratic toward his wife and Sheila's older sister. He issued commands to his wife and older daughter but made no demands on Sheila and supported her every move, especially with regard to school. As a result, Sheila became the dominant figure around which the family structure revolved—she achieved this status with the father's collusion. At the time the case was referred, however, the father was disturbed by Sheila's actions, although he mistrusted the school and doubted their ability (as well as mine) to deal with his daughter or with the problem.

Intervention in this case called for instructing Sheila's parents about the present structure of their family and about methods of regaining control—of restoring what some family therapists call "the executive subsystem," empowering the parents to gain control of Sheila and her behavior and to end the disruption her behavior was causing.

Multiple interventions are indicated here. Obviously, one issue is the girl's weight, which may later prove unhealthy for her. However, the conditions of school are set as an antecedent. Though the system offers some home teaching in cases such as severe illness, they see it as a temporary measure, and their resources for this are limited. In any event, that is not indicated here because home teaching would not solve the problem—it would be the ultimate reward to Sheila for her actions. However, it may be possible to alter the reactions of her peers and to change the response of school staff and parents. By these interventions, it may also be possible to change the girl's reaction to school.

This case required work with Sheila, her school, and her family. Resocialization of Sheila was part of the work with this family as well as helping the family restructure role relationships. In addition, work included intergroup relationships in negotiating between the family and school personnel who were also implicated in the problem. Altering role relationships within the family and altering the relationship of the family to the school also had the effect of resocializing Sheila and contributed to a solution of this problem.

These cases have illustrated some themes for sociological intervention. One is that sociological work often must cross levels. Lippitt[23] called this "the challenge of multi-system thinking, i.e., to integrate data about the client at the level of individual, group, and organizational dynamics, and interactions with the environment."

A second theme is the role of sociologist as teacher in helping clients resolve problems. The humanistic approach of clinical sociology asserts that people will and can solve their own problems and that work with clients should leave them with enhanced problem-solving skills. Thus, the instructional role of sociologist-as-helper pays attention to this humanistic view. Rather than taking responsibility from clients, doing *for* them, this role helps them learn to do for themselves as they learn alternative strategies.

At the level of larger social systems, such as organizations, Lippitt's[23] analysis of work with organizations also showed a preponderance of teaching roles for sociological consultants as well as the role of group facilitator in brainstorming and other group problem-solving sessions. The sociologist's role is not only providing the instruction for change; as Lippitt noted, providing organizational clients with insight about and guidance through the change process also facilitates constructive change.

Readers are directed to Lippitt's excellent article for more detailed considera-tion of work in organizations and themes of problems. However, Lippitt provided some generic interactions used across contexts and they are worth quoting here at length:

1. *Entry client involvement.* In almost all client situations, I find it important to design "what it would be like if I worked with you" situations that involve a sample of participative experiences.
2. *Generating an inside–outside team.* Another effort in all situations is to discover one or two inside staff persons who are interested in teaming up, want to get the benefits of the professional development opportunity of learning from the outsiders, and can get sanction and support from their managers to spend part of their time as members of the project team.
3. *Developing ad hoc work teams.* [This involves groups] of two to eight to put energy and creativity into development priorities.
4. *Providing training in having productive meetings.* In every situation, one of the great wastes is the tolerating of unproductive meetings. Brief training sessions on the designing and leading of effective meetings provides a quantum leap in the quality of work.
5. *Introducing process interventions into task work.* I use a number of tools to help client groups look at how well we are doing and how can we improve our ways of working with each other.
6. *Using tryout and rehearsal techniques.* Many times a client team needs help in preparing for presentations and recommendations. The most helpful tool is a "reality practice" rehearsal with feedback and repractice. A repertoire of role-playing and simulation skills is an important part of the repertoire of every consultant. (Lippitt[23])

Trial runs, pilot projects, or demonstration projects may be added to this list. They may be expanded in scope following an evaluation. However, it is often the case that unrealistic amounts of resources are expended on a trial run or pilot project. On the microlevel, the clinician may carefully walk a client through a situation, providing lots of support and guidance. At the organizational or govern-mental level, a team of experts, heavily invested in the success of the enterprise, may show a great deal of success in interacting with a problem situation. But a caveat is necessary here: The program should be sufficiently robust that the client or client system can be reasonably expected to make it work on his or her own in everyday life with the usual resources and members of his or her role-set.

CONCLUSION

Clinical sociology is not a chair-bound activity. The clinical sociologist must "go where the action is." In assessment, the clinical sociologist must go to relevant social environments and observe functioning of client systems. As a change agent, the clinical sociologist must again be on hand to instruct and guide actors in making the changes they desire. The work helps client systems change networks, add roles, strengthen relationships, deal with interactional difficulty and with socially constructed reality.

Intervention in clinical sociology is guided by humanistic values, by sociological knowledge and theory, and by the application of the scientific method that involves continuing evaluation of the progress of intervention and creative adaptation of the client situation. Each case presents a unique challenge to be approached with creativity and care. And the work calls for imposing structure on the materials of a single case, to understand the case; setting the problem for work; and creatively devising strategies that will interact with the problematic situation to bring about desired changes.

However, the clinical sociologist's task is not completed when the client's specific problem is solved. The task of the change agent is to leave the client system not only with the specific problem solution but with enhanced problem-solving abilities to ensure that the positive changes will last beyond the term of the clinical work. Not only must the clinical sociologist bring about a specific change, but it is also necessary that intervention plans include establishing structures that prevent regression and facilitate continued adaptation and change as needed by the social system.

REFERENCES

1. Sundberg, N. D., Tyler, L. E., & Taplin, J. R. (1973). *Clinical psychology: Expanding horizons.* Englewood Cliffs, NJ: Prentice-Hall.
2. Straus, Roger. (1982). Clinical sociology on the one-to-one level: A social-behavioral approach to counseling. *Clinical Sociology Review, 1*, 59–74.
3. Church, Nathan. (1985). Sociotherapy with marital couples: Incorporating dramaturgical and social constructionist elements of marital interaction. *Clinical Sociology Review, 3*, 116–128.
4. Voelkl, G. M., & Colburn, K. (1984). The clinical sociologist as family therapist: Utilizing the strategic communication approach. *Clinical Sociology Review, 2*, 64–77.
5. Kallen, David. (1984). Clinical sociology and adolescent medicine: The design of a program. *Clinical Sociology Review, 2*, 78–93.
6. Jones, Bernie. (1984). Doing sociology with the design professions. *Clinical Sociology Review, 2*, 109–119.
7. Anderson, C., & Rouse, L. (1988). Intervention in cases of woman battering: An application of symbolic interaction and critical theory. *Clinical Sociology Review, 6*, 134–144.
8. Sengstock, Mary. (1987). Sociological strategies for developing community resources: Services for abused wives as an example. *Clinical Sociology Review, 5*, 132–144.
9. Jacques, Elliott. (1982). The method od social analysis in social change and social research. *Clinical Sociology Review, 1*, 50–58.
10. Benello, C. George. (1982). Clinical sociology in the service of social change: The experience of developing worker management. *Clinical Sociology Review, 1*, 93–114.
11. Straus, Roger. (1987). The theoretical base of clinical sociology: Root metaphors and key principles. *Clinical Sociology Review, 5*, 65–82.
12. Swann, L. Alex. (1988). Grounded encounter therapy: Its characteristics and process. *Clinical Sociology Review, 6*, 76–87.
13. Guidubaldi, J., & Cleminshaw, H. (1985). Divorce, family health, and child adjustment. *Family Relations, 34*, 35–41.

14. Angel, R., & Woroby, J. L. (1988). Single motherhood and children's health. *Journal of Health and Social Behavior, 29,* 38–52.
15. Gutknecht, Douglas B. (1984). Organizational development: An assessment with implications for clinical sociology. *Clinical Sociology Review, 2,* 94–108.
16. Straus, Roger. (1984). Changing the definition of the situation: Toward a theory of sociological intervention. *Clinical Sociology Review, 2,* 51–63.
17. Brisbane, F. L., & Stuart, B. L. (1985). A self-help model for working with black women of alcoholic parents. *Alcoholism Treatment Quarterly, 2,* 199–219.
18. Britt, David. Personal communication, 1989.
19. Freedman, Jonathan. (1982). Clinical sociology: What it is and what it isn't—A perspective. *Clinical Sociology Review, 1,* 34–49.
20. Whyte, William Foote. (1982). Social inventions for solving human problems. 1981 presidential address. *American Sociological Review, 47,* 1–13. Reprinted in *Clinical Sociology Review, 5,* 45–64.
21. Lofland, John. (1976). *Doing social life.* New York: Wiley-Interscience.
22. Fein, M. L. (1988). Resocialization: A neglected paradigm. *Clinical Sociology Review, 6,* 88–100.
23. Lippitt, Ronald. (1985). Six problem-solving contexts for intervention decision making. *Clinical Sociology Review, 3,* 39–49.

CHAPTER 5

Program Evaluation and Clinical Sociology

Adrianne Bank

Chapters with straightforward titles such as this often start out with straightforward definitions of terms. I rarely find such definitions helpful. They are either common sense and therefore unnecessary or very technical and therefore counterintuitive.

But it is important to have a shared understanding between writer and reader of what is being discussed. So, as a program evaluator with most of my experience in educational and nonprofit settings, I want to indicate in broad strokes what program evaluation has come to mean over the years to those evaluators involved with social and educational programs. This is preferable to attempting any kind of definition because, at this point in the development of program evaluation, with all its diversity, it may not be possible to find one that would be acceptable to most program evaluators.

Why should clinical sociologists be interested in learning something about the complexities of program evaluation? Why should the terms in the title be linked? At least four possibilities come to mind. Clinical sociologists may want to know about program evaluation so that they can ask and answer evaluative questions about their own work, so that they can do program evaluations in organizations, so they can hire others to evaluate projects in which they are involved, or so they can protect themselves against program evaluations that are inappropriate or misguided.

In lieu of a definition, then, the introductory section will provide some background on the nature of programs and on program evaluation. In the following sections, four of the many models of program evaluation will be discussed. Then a utilization-focused perspective will be proposed as the criterion by which an evaluation model can be selected to fit a particular situation. Finally, some of the issues involved in planning and conducting an evaluation will be outlined.

ADRIANNE BANK • Graduate School of Education, University of California, Los Angeles, Los Angeles, California 90024.

INTRODUCTION

Programs come in many shapes and sizes. The term *program*, especially in education and the social services, usually refers to a funded activity that has specific structural components: stated goals and objectives, defined activities in relation to target populations, staff and resources to perform those activities, and a specified duration. Many funding agencies now include an evaluation plan as a required component.

The term *program*, however, is elastic enough to describe many types of interventions. For example, a single practitioner working with one individual or with small groups of clients in relatively open-ended fashion to improve their functioning in a particular manner may be thought of as a program. Or, at the other end of the spectrum, a large-scale, multiyear, multi-million-dollar operation involving the delivery of services by many experts to thousands of clients may also be regarded as a program. And the term *program* need not refer only to service delivery activities but extends to other activities such as training, technical assistance, and consultation.

Whatever their scope or duration, programs of interest to clinical sociologists are likely to deal with many different topics. For example, a recent issue of *New Directions for Program Evaluation*,[1] a publication of the American Evaluation Association discusses the evaluation of programs in such diverse areas as welfare, low-income housing assistance, juvenile delinquency, and mental health. A brief glance at the table of contents of the journal *Evaluation and Program Planning*[2] for 1987 reveals that evaluation issues are analyzed in relation to medical students' patient-interviewing skills, energy conservation educational efforts, family planning programs, and the success of volunteer efforts.

The word *evaluation*, like the word *program*, refers to a catchall and imprecisely defined set of activities. In daily life, we evaluate all the time: we evaluate whether we like the individual we have just met, whether we want steak or fish for dinner, or whether a new job offer is better than our current work. More formally, we know about being evaluated through receiving grades in school, scores on admission tests, or going through personnel evaluations to justify getting our merit increase.

Whatever their particular purpose, an evaluation usually involves making judgments based on evidence and using some criteria or standard to justify those judgments. In most ordinary situations, we make these judgments quickly and intuitively rather than deliberately. Our evidence may be anecdotal and accidental rather than intentionally assembled; and our standards may be private and implicit rather than public and explicit.

Program evaluation, as discussed in this chapter, deals with these same issues of judgment, evidence, and standards and how they might clarify aspects of programs with which clinical sociologists may be involved. However, in contrast to personal evaluations, program evaluators should identify what the judgments will be about, what evidence will be collected, and what standards will be used to assess the evidence.

Program evaluation, viewed as a set of methodologies for inquiring about how social and educational programs work, is a relatively new field, less than 40 years old. Its growth has paralleled the growth of such programs themselves and was fueled by the rapid expansion of federal funding for them during the 1960s and early 1970s. Thus, program evaluation was invented as a way to satisfy the need of policymakers to discover how best to create programs to resolve complex social issues. So academic departments at colleges and universities were encouraged to devise methods for doing such program evaluations. Professors and soft-money researchers tried out their ideas as they became consultants either for government funding agencies or for the recipients of such funds.

At the present time, even though it has become an established academic discipline—and there are courses in program evaluation taught within departments such as education, sociology, public health, mental health, public policy, and management—the practice of program evaluation is still somewhat eclectic and still changing. Currently it draws for its orientations, philosophies, methodologies, and practitioners from many disciplines, among them sociology, anthropology, economics, political science, and statistics.

Its deepest roots, however, remain in the theory and design of social science research, and the constant struggle of those who do program evaluation is to free their work from the inappropriate encumbrances of research methodology. For example, during the early years of program evaluation, the method of first preference seemed to be that of experimental or quasi-experimental design. This design preference predisposed evaluators to ask the question that the methodology was intended to answer, namely does the "treatment" work better than "no treatment"? Other potentially more useful evaluative questions were thereby obscured and often not even raised to attention.

The intent of most individuals doing social science research, whatever their field, is to discover knowledge, test theories, and make generalizations that hold across unique situations. As social science researchers began to apply their research orientations in the new field of program evaluation they discovered for themselves that this work, although it seems like research in many ways, is quite different from research.

It differs from research in terms of its initial conceptualization and in terms of its conduct and outcomes. While research is aimed at generalizable conclusions, program evaluation is aimed at situation-specific decisions. While research asks questions to produce the theory in which to ground action, evaluation asks questions about an existing set of organized actions in order to produce answers that have immediate practical implications. While research tries to be context-independent, program evaluations are always context-dependent.

At the same time that program evaluators have been learning that their new craft must sometimes part company with its research forebears and that evaluation requires unique skills and sensitivities, program directors and others involved with interventions have been learning that evaluation activities can be positive rather than negative experiences. The threat from evaluation felt by many program directors in the early days of program evaluation was due to a number of factors. First, most associations with the word *evaluation* itself tend to be aversive—fault finding, critical, harsh, and demoralizing rather than as positive, helpful, and instructive. These ordinary everyday connotations tended to spill over into professional activities.

Furthermore, as program evaluation activities got under way, most evaluators got their assignments from funders—either government agencies or foundations—who wanted to find out whether a program was "any good," whether there was "waste, fraud, and abuse," whether a program should be refunded or defunded. Thus, in the beginning, there was a built-in adversarial relationship between program evaluators working for those who held the purse strings and program managers who wanted to see their programs survive.

However, within the past 15 years, various distinctions have been incorporated into the repertoire of program evaluators making it possible for them to use their skills in support of program improvement. Program evaluators now consult as often for program administrators as they do for program funders. They can and do function as program advocates as frequently as they work as program adversaries.

One of the most important and critical distinctions allowing this to happen is that made by Michael Scriven between summative and formative evaluation.[3] Summative evaluation answers questions about the worth and merit of a program or intervention. As we have noted, these summative, or summary, inquiries were where program evaluations got their start. The audience was external to the program, the evaluator was external to the program, and the important factors to be examined were results and costs. The evaluation provided data for decisions relating to program survival. By contrast, formative evaluation answers questions about program operations, implementation, and outcomes for the purpose of "forming" the program or helping it improve. The audiences for formative evaluations are usually internal to the program; the evaluator may be external or internal; the important factors to be examined are processes and problems; the decisions relate to program improvement.

In the wake of this distinction, new thinking about how to maximize the utility of evaluative information for those running a program has emerged. Now evaluations can be designed to meet the information needs not only of program funders but also of program planners, managers, consultants, trainers, and even of program participants, clients, and service recipients. Thus, today, program evaluations are conducted in order to satisfy many different purposes and to meet many different needs. How to deal with the two notions with which evaluation is usually concerned—judgment and standards—differs from situation to situation, as do the techniques for collecting and analyzing the data to be used as evidence. Earlier simplistic views of program evaluation have given way to more complex current understandings.

For example, the early summative view was that evaluations were primarily for judging whether a program was good or bad. The current view, applicable in either summative or formative situations, is that a program evaluation can help with any of the following: determining needs, setting program goals, contributing to program planning, increasing understanding about program operations, trouble shooting, providing evidence and making judgments about program effectiveness, efficiency, and impact, and comparing like programs with one another.

The early summative view was that evaluations were primarily for finding out what was wrong with a program. The current view is that a program evaluation can and should identify program strengths as well as areas needing attention, describe how and why a program works as well as how it might be improved.

An early view was that there was one right way to do an "objective scientific" evaluation. Currently, most evaluators believe there are many ways to do useful evaluations. The field has come to acknowledge that evaluations require both science and craft. Evaluations vary in methodology according to who the evaluator is, why the evaluation is being done, and what political or financial constraints are operating. Evaluations these days often include as evidence perceptions, attitudes, and opinions as well as overt or measurable behaviors.

FOUR MODELS OF PROGRAM EVALUATION

The variety of orientations and techniques available to program evaluators in doing their work makes the field confusing to those who believe that evaluations are shelf items—standardized and ready to be applied to any program. Rather, evaluations are customized, each tailored to fit the characteristics of a given situation. The criteria by which to select among evaluation models will be discussed later. Four models commonly used to evaluate the types of interventions familiar to clinical sociologists will be presented here. These are the objectives-based model, the decision-oriented model, the naturalistic inquiry model, and the expert model.

The Objectives-Based Model

One of the earliest evaluation models, and the one that still commands the loyalty of many evaluators, is known as the objectives-based model. Used by Ralph Tyler[4] in his famous 8-year study of American education and subsequently applied to the evaluation of many social programs, this model asks the simple evaluative question, "To what extent have the goals of the program been attained?" In order to answer this evaluative question, program staff and evaluator must reach agreement as to the general goals of the program and also on the specific observable outcomes expected in the target population if the program were to be counted as successful. Then the evaluator develops or selects measurement devices that accurately document client behaviors or outcomes. At the end of the program, or at points during the program, the measures are administered to samples of the target population. The discrepancy between the hoped-for outcomes, as stated in the form of objectives, and the actual outcomes, as measured by assessment instruments, provides the answer to the evaluative question and directs attention to program objectives not being achieved.

For many years, it was an accepted truism that an evaluation could only be carried out if program goals were stated in clear, specific, and measurable terms. A great deal of energy was expended by evaluators in arguing among themselves about the level of detail at which goals should be stated, about who should participate in the process, about how the selection of goals should be justified, and about the means to establish priorities among goals. Similar amounts of attention were paid to creating the valid and reliable measurement instruments required by this evaluation model: tests, interviews, observations, logs, journals, records such as attendance sheets, and phone logs.

Although the objectives-based model was frequently used by evaluators employed by funding agencies to assess the extent to which a program or organization was attaining its objectives, it was also used by evaluators employed by managers interested in improving their organization's functioning through self-evaluation. For example, an evaluator might help initiate a top-down, deductive process to bring goals, activities, and outcomes in line with one another. Key individuals in an organization, meeting with evaluators, would examine their own mission statement to make sure that the organization's stated goals were unambiguous and easily understood. The staff in each department would then set program goals consistent with the mission statement and framed in terms of desired client outcomes. Then the evaluator would set up and pilot data-collection systems to amass evidence about the actual impact of services on clients. The next step would be to work with program staff to design the study: select the sample, find a comparison group if appropriate, determine the schedule, and collect the data. Finally, the evaluator would analyze the data, report them back to the agency, and discuss their implications with program and policy staff.

Such evaluative work with entire organizations or with smaller programs often have beneficial effects. It may stimulate administrators to invite many individuals, previously ignored, into a discussion of goals and objectives. For example, in education, the thrust for objectives-based evaluations encouraged school district administrators to involve parents and teachers in setting educational priorities. This came to be seen as an essential preliminary to undertaking the expensive process of developing the tests to measure the extent to which children were achieving specified objectives.

Another beneficial outcome of the objectives-based evaluation model was that it forced many individuals in the social services arena to shift their program-planning focus from emphasis on what they themselves would do to an emphasis on what their clients would become able to do. Many foundations and other funding sources now routinely examine proposals to determine if program goals are stated in terms of observable and measurable client outcomes rather than on staff intentions. They often require in their evaluation designs a comparison between individuals who have participated in a program and those who have not.

In spite of the simplicity of the objectives-based evaluation model, in spite of its salutary effects in forcing clear thinking about goal statements, and in spite of its helpfulness in emphasizing programmatic consistency between the intents, measures, and outcomes of programs, it is easy to raise a number of objections to this approach.

The goals of institutions and programs usually cannot be reduced only to those involving client outcomes. Organizations need to position themselves in relation to other organizations, to present a face to the public, to compete for funds, to maintain their work force, in short, to satisfy multiple audiences. The explicit client-outcome goals that evaluators may goad program directors into affirming may be far from the informal understandings that guide people's everyday work. The evaluative question about the extent to which the program is achieving its goals may, in some circumstances, be irrelevant or misleading, particularly if the emphasis is placed exclusively on client outcomes.

A second simplistic aspect of an objectives-based evaluation model is the assumption that the relationships between goals and outcomes can be easily found with the proper measuring devices. In some cases, such relationships can indeed be easily established. For example, programs funded to build appropriate housing for the elderly can show the number of completed buildings that meet all the pre-specifications.

In other cases, however, outcomes may be delayed or small or specific to particular subgroups in the target population. They may be hard to find or to attribute to the intervention being evaluated. For example, a Big Brother program may have a difficult time ascertaining what is its impact on the children it serves separate from the effects of school, peers, neighborhood and other adults. Sub-stance abuse prevention programs may not be able to demonstrate that they have achieved their announced goal of an overall reductions in the use of drugs or alcohol in a target population, but they may be able to find evidence of success on a related but unstated goal—that of increased awareness of risk—perhaps a precur-sor for reduced use—among some types of individuals.

Because objectives-based evaluations are tied to stated objectives and because stated objectives may be more accurate reflections of hopes rather than of achiev-able realities, objectives-based evaluations may misestimate the effectiveness of programs designed to deal with complex and long-standing social problems. The additional difficulties of designing sensitive and valid instrumentation to measure complex outcomes need not be detailed here; nor the ambiguities of inferring cause-and-effect relationships from small samples and single programs.

Another difficulty sometimes associated with objectives-based evaluations is that of the paucity of data from which to make inferences about program improve-ment. Because the focus of this form of evaluation is on gathering evidence as to the presence or absence of expected outcomes in a defined population, there is rela-tively little attention paid to gathering evidence about why a program may or may not be working.

The Decision-Oriented Model

A second model of evaluation has been developed to help program managers answer questions of concern to them: "Which aspects of our program are working well, which are not, and why?" Although this approach—geared to providing managers with evaluative assistance in looking at their own programs—is called a model, it actually entails several different evaluation techniques each of which has a different purpose. The discussion draws on the vocabulary used by Daniel Stuffle-beam in laying out his Context, Input, Process and Product (CIPP) evaluation model.[5]

Basic to understanding this evaluation model is an understanding of its assumptions about program development. Programs are assumed to be discrete entities that have a life cycle that starts with planning, proceeds to implementation, and then moves to fine tuning. Although Stufflebeam and others recognize that not all programs emerge in sequenced stages, and that, in reality, implementation may come before goal statements, or that fine tuning may happen as early as in the first month of operations, they key their evaluation techniques to the decision making that they believe occurs within each stage.

They assert that, early in the conceptualization of a program, decisions must be made about which audience is to be served, which problems are to be solved, and which needs are to be met. These decisions determine the goals and objectives of the program. *Context evaluation* looks at these decisions and how they were made. For example, an evaluator called in to assist with context evaluation might help a program do a needs assessment to document the existence, intensity, and importance of the need that the program addresses or the problem it wants to resolve. The evaluator might do this by assembling expert opinions, by surveys of the target population, by analysis of existing statistics or in a number of other ways.

An evaluator asked to assist a program in the next stage would be doing *input evaluation*. Programs structure their activities by deploying staff, by amassing resources, and by designing and sequencing activities. An input evaluation might collect information that would be useful to managers in deciding what to do by inventorying available resources, by assembling comparable cost figures, by analyzing failed and exemplary programs, or by reviewing the literature in the field.

After a program has been conceptualized and organized, things start to happen. People carry out activities, perform tasks, do jobs. *Process evaluation* is a set of techniques with which evaluators look at various aspects of program implementation. For example, at a very simple level, a process evaluator might ask social workers to log their telephone conversations so as to make intake procedures in a social agency more efficient and more humane at the same time. Or the evaluator might look at the interactions of staff assigned to each of several related operations and ask questions about how they coordinate their efforts, communicate with one another, and resolve conflicts when they occur. Or the evaluator might simply observe and interview staff to find out problem areas and "hot spots" that need management attention.

The fourth stage of a program is program outcomes or products. *Product evaluation* focuses on these outcomes. An evaluator assisting a program to look at what it has accomplished might encourage the examination of a range of outcomes. Not only might managers want to assess the results associated with the program's stated goals (as they would in the objectives-based evaluation model), but they might also want to document positive and negative unanticipated outcomes. For example, a program to employ neighborhood aides in a school may not produce the expected higher test scores for students but may instead have the unexpected and positive effect of reducing local unemployment or of increasing feelings of self-esteem in community members.

The CIPP evaluation model—the acronym formed from the initial letters of the evaluation stages, context, input, process, and product—can be used in two ways. First, evaluators may use it concurrently with program development. In this way, evaluators would provide information to managers as they make decisions about their program. Most of the examples given illustrate this use. However, this form of evaluation may also be used retrospectively. An evaluator might be hired by an outside group or agency to discover the comprehensiveness and quality of thinking that went into the decisions made by program staff at each stage of their deliberations.

The decision-oriented evaluation model is flexible and adaptable to the questions that managers or administrators are confronted with in the course of their work. It helps them, or their funders, to identify problem areas in many areas of program functioning. Instead of confining the focus of evaluative activities to the match between objectives and outcomes as in the previously discussed model, decision-oriented evaluations broaden the scope of concern to include all aspects of program startup, functioning and, effectiveness.

Clearly the decision-oriented model is a more comprehensive view of evaluation than is the objectives-based model. Nevertheless, it, too, is limited because it looks primarily to those issues about which decision makers make decisions. Because it views evaluation activities as providing assistance to managers or those to whom managers are accountable, it overlooks many other aspects of program functioning. In order to broaden further their understanding of what was really going on during the course of a program or an intervention, many evaluators moved, in the mid-1970s, to naturalistic inquiry, as a way to capture the complex motivations and behaviors of the many individuals involved.

The Naturalistic Inquiry Model

Like the decision-oriented model, the naturalistic inquiry model is not a single model but many techniques that share a common orientation. The progenitors of each evaluation technique are individualistic, each stressing a different aspect of the evaluative enterprise. However, all of the proponents of naturalistic inquiry reject an input–outcome point of view and instead welcome evaluation techniques that take into account the totality and complexity of human endeavors. They advocate multiple sources of data—subjective and objective, qualitative and quantitative, attitudes, opinions, values, and behaviors. They reject preplanned and sequenced evaluation efforts in favor of emergent efforts shaped by the issues that arise as people engage in the experience.

Naturalistic evaluators place themselves within an interpretive phenomenological epistomology as opposed to the more traditional positivist approach assumed by those evaluators using an objectives-based or a decision-oriented approach. Naturalistic evaluators are interested in finding out about what is going on and what meaning people assign to what is going on. The naturalistic evaluator changes roles as the evaluation proceeds: first a learner, later an interpreter, then finally a teacher. Program participants also change roles. They start out as informants, then become cointerpreters with the evaluator, and, finally, they become learners in order to understand the program in new ways. They also become problem solvers so that they, along with the evaluator, can figure out what to do next to improve the program.

The naturalistic evaluator, as a consultant, may work in a number of ways: reading background documents, "hanging out," talking with key informants, watching carefully. Some naturalistic evaluators bring with them theoretical frameworks from other disciplines such as anthropology, sociology, organizational development, social psychology, and use these to organize their work.

Within the field of education, Robert Stake[6] has sketched out many ideas for what he calls responsive evaluation. Responsive evaluations "respond" to the reactions, concerns, and issues of people involved in the program. These people he calls stakeholders. The evaluator is likely to report data to these stakeholders in the form of case studies, testimonials, stories, and anecdotes. Recommendations are likely to start with feedback to various groups of stakeholders; from their responses and suggestions, the responsive evaluator will, at the end of the evaluation, put forth suggestions rather than directives.

Michael Patton[7] has outlined some steps for doing naturalistic evaluation. But there is no requisite prescription for what to do first. Usually, however, an initial task for naturalistic evaluators is to talk with the variety of people connected with the program in order to understand the scope of the program and to identify the "stakeholders" to the evaluation—all those individuals affected by the program or by the evaluation. These may include funders, managers, staff, clients and their families, media, competing or cooperating agencies, and community groups. Stakeholders, either individually or as members of groups, may range from important to peripheral in their relationship to the program. Although the evaluator considers all views important, he or she is likely to spend more time in interviews and observations with those stakeholders whose influence or attitudes importantly affect the program.

Because the naturalistic evaluator's job starts out being loosely defined, usually in terms of a helping, problem-solving or program improvement consultative relationship, the evaluator's next task, after he or she understands who are the players, is to help the organization or program focus the evaluation questions. This means identifying those concerns, issues, or problems that need clarification or resolution.

This process is likely to be time consuming. Different stakeholders will have different views on what the "hot spots" are within the organization. For example, funders may want to know why results are so slow in coming. Managers may want to know why costs are so high. Staff may want to know why they are not consulted when policy changes are being considered. Clients might want quicker service. The community might want more publicity.

Focusing the evaluation by agreeing on the major questions to be answered occurs through protracted discussion between the evaluator and selected stakeholders. This interaction is part of the learning process for both the evaluator and program stakeholders. As the evaluative task becomes clearer, the role of the evaluator becomes more defined. At some point, after both the client group and the evaluator understand the purpose, the procedures and the desired outcomes for the evaluation effort, an agreement is reached between them. This may be informal but more often is written and signed by both parties.

At the next stage of the work, the evaluator synthesizes information obtained from many sources and offers back to the stakeholders question options that they may then revise and modify. These questions form the framework for the remainder of the evaluation activities.

The next task of the evaluator is to decide on the kinds of information needed to answer the evaluation questions. Here again the evaluator works with stakeholders to ascertain what is credible for them. Do statistics or stories convince them? Are case histories more compelling than survey data? Are expert judgments more or less plausible than client preferences? The interactive process continues with the evaluator framing the data collection possibilities and the stakeholders reacting and responding from their points of view.

Data collection occupies a large percentage of the total time available for any evaluation. Whether the data is collected by questionnaire, personal interviews, observations, examination of existing records, or the creation of new ones, there are many technical decisions that must be made to insure the accuracy and credibility of the information to be collected. These are the tools that all evaluators, even naturalistic evaluators, have in common.

When doing a naturalistic evaluation, the evaluator provides feedback to various stakeholder groups as the information is collected and analyzed. This process continues and advances the mutual learning. When the evaluator moves from data analysis to recommendations or when the evaluator presents suggestions or scenarios or portrayals to stakeholders in concluding the work, there should be very few surprises. Both parties will have worked together to devise new understandings of the program.

Naturalistic evaluation depends very heavily on the personal abilities and talents of the evaluator. In addition to conceptual skills in formulating the evaluation questions and technical skills in data collection and analysis, the naturalistic evaluator needs good communication skills—in listening and in speaking and in writing. He or she also needs good interpersonal skills in order to fully understand the concerns of stakeholders.

Naturalistic evaluation can provide a rich look at program complexities. New insights and new theories can emerge from the productive interraction between evaluators and program stakeholders. But the weaknesses of naturalistic evaluation are inherent in its strengths. Because it is person-dependent and in some measure, subjective, it may be badly done by incompetent individuals. There are no built-in safeguards for program administrators when contracting with naturalistic evaluators except through checking out their reputation and previous work. Clarification of the integrity, professionalism, and biases of the evaluator should happen in lengthy interviews with program managers before consultative arrangements are finalized. There are no assurances, apart from faith in the evaluator and in the process, that the relevant program issues will be addressed and that problems will be resolved. Naturalistic evaluation relies for its success on the judgment and standards of the evaluator as these interact with the evidence supplied by the people and the activities of a particular program.

By contrast, the fourth evaluation model described relies on the experience and standards of experts who may not acquire intimate familiarity with the details of a specific program but who are acquainted with the entire field.

The Expert Model

Expert judgment, either by individuals or by groups, is a traditional method of evaluation not necessarily dependent on the acquisition of program-specific data. Experts who presumably are familiar with like situations can quickly size up a particular instance and make comments about it. Program evaluators have used a variety of formats to do evaluations using experts.

Accreditation procedures, originally developed to find out whether institutions meet an agreed-upon set of standards, use a combination of checklists, self-study, and peer review. Checklists call for information, explanation, and description assembled by in-house self-study teams. Peer reviews, usually done through examination of these checklists and other written materials as well as through site visits, supplement and certify the self-study reports. Then, either the site visitors or independent panels look at all the evidence and make a determination about compliance with standards. Such accreditation procedures have been modified for use with programs. They are relatively inexpensive and easy to do once the checklists have been assembled and the site visit teams trained.

A second procedure for bringing expertise to bear on program evaluations calls on testimony from experts and witnesses within a courtroom-type setting. Called adversary evaluation,[8] the proceedings are set up like a court trial. The issues to be discussed are defined in advance. Evidence is presented as to the success or failure of the program, cross-examination explores the credibility and truthfulness of the witness, and then a judge and jury hand down a verdict.

A third procedure for using experts is called the convening process.[9] One way to organize this is as follows: Expert consultants are assembled for a several day workshop and asked to help resolve a problem faced by an organization or a program. They are provided with background information, pertinent documents, and the names of program personnel who could enlighten them further. They are divided into small teams that visit the project site for interviews or observations. The teams reconvene and, in a large group setting, discuss their findings, look for discrepancies, raise questions, and decide on the additional information they need. The second day is spent in small- and large-group data analysis and the formulation of recommendations.

The simplest evaluation procedure using expert opinion is to call in a single individual who, like a literary or theatre critic, reviews the program using whatever private criteria he or she prefers and makes judgments. This last use of expertise does not fall within the usually accepted limits of contemporary program evaluation that requires publicly stated criteria for collecting evidence and making judgments.

A UTILIZATION-FOCUSED PERSPECTIVE

How can we make sense of all these different perspectives on program evaluation and choose the method most appropriate to a particular situation? How do we evaluate the evaluations?

As the field of program evaluation changes and matures, new professional standards have been formulated to upgrade practice and guide practitioners in making choices. In 1981, a joint committee on standards for educational evaluation identified 30 separate standards for evaluation and divided them into four groups.[10] These included (1) utility standards, (2) feasibility standards, (3) proprietary standards, and (4) accuracy standards. After protracted discussion among the participants, the standards were arranged in the order given rather in reverse order.

The ordering of the standards with utility as the first priority represented a substantial shift for the evaluation community and an explicit recognition of the distinction between research studies and evaluative studies. The joint committee, after protracted debate, asserted that evaluations first must "serve the practical information needs of a given audience." The accuracy standards, which are intended to insure that an evaluation will "reveal and convey traditionally adequate information about the features of the object being studied that determine its worth or merit" are important. However, they do not take precedence—as they might in a basic research study—over the needs of a specific audience for information that they themselves can use.

The priority reflected in this ordering of standards represents a new commitment on the part of the educational evaluation community to provide services that clients see as useful rather than to create technically correct measures and reports that may not provide direction for action. A utilization-focused approach to evaluation, in contrast to an approach more closely linked to the methodology of basic research, should help ensure that future evaluation reports will not sit, unread, on administrators' bookshelves.

The philosophical roots of this emphasis on utility or utilization lie in the traditions of pragmatism. Pragmatists focus on practical problems and on reducing the uncertainty about what actions to take concerning them. Evaluation, in this view, is seen to have instrumental use as a tool to reduce uncertainty and to guide decision making. In addition, utilization-focused evaluation is seen as having an educational use: It enlarges the perspectives of those engaged in programs or interventions. Finally, utilization-focused evaluators recognize the symbolic or persuasive uses that evaluations can have. Conducting an evaluation may be regarded as evidence that a program or institution is concerned about implementation and outcomes, wants to improve its own performance or effectiveness, and is change oriented and self-renewing.

ISSUES IN PLANNING AND CONDUCTING EVALUATIONS

Every institution, program, or intervention need not be evaluated. Evaluations cost money, money that might be better spent delivering services or hiring staff or consultants with substantive or process skills in, for example, fund raising or public relations. Evaluations also cost time—of staff, of clients, of board members—both in preparing for and in participating in an evaluation. Time represents an opportunity cost that sometimes might be better devoted directly to program improvement rather than to evaluation. Furthermore, evaluations performed too early in the life of a program may be misleading and damaging. This final section suggests several issues to be considered by both client and evaluator as they discuss evaluating a program or intervention.

Should We Evaluate?

When considering whether or not to do an evaluation it is important to decide whether an evaluation is likely to benefit the program in either instrumental, conceptual, or symbolic ways. Questions to be asked and answered include: Who needs the evaluation? Will the evaluation reduce uncertainty? Is this a time in the life of the program when evaluative information can be used? Is there willingness on the part of leaders and other stakeholders to engage in evaluation? Are there sufficient resources to support not only the evaluation itself but also the changes that should follow as a consequence of the evaluation?

Who Should Evaluate?

Having decided to plan and conduct an evaluation, the next issue is whether to use an external evaluator, an internal evaluator, or a combination of both. In some cases, particularly when summative evaluation is called for, an external evaluator is legally required and clearly preferable. An external evaluator is unlikely to have a vested interest in the program and will be seen as impartial and therefore credible to outside groups. External evaluators bring with them fresh perspectives and may be able to see solutions where insiders can only see problems. On the other hand, external evaluators may be unfamiliar with the territory and need time to get acquainted. Appropriate ones for the job at hand may be hard to find.

Internal evaluators, particularly for formative, improvement-oriented evaluations, come with inside knowledge. They may be able to spot organizational needs quickly. It is likely that they can assemble instruments and collect data with a minimum of trouble and provide continuing feedback to managers. A team approach where an external and internal evaluator define their responsibilities so as to capitalize on their assets and minimize costs to the program may also be desirable.

Locating the pool of possible external evaluators and then selecting the most appropriate one for the job at hand is a critical step in mounting an evaluation. As noted in the preceding sections, all evaluators come with their own perspectives and competencies. They have preconceptions, preferences, and biases. They are more comfortable with some evaluation models than with others. The key question is not, "Which is the best evaluator?" but "Which evaluator is the best fit with our program and its need for evaluation?"

What Should Be Evaluated?

The scope of the evaluation is determined in part by the questions that various stakeholders want answered. If the evaluation is being done in response to funding agency directives for documenting program implementation or program outcomes, then these may dictate the questions to be answered. If the evaluation is being done to provide managers and administrators with more information for decision making, then these concerns may drive the evaluation. If there are internal problems or divisive interpersonal relationships, then these may become the focus of the evaluation. The selection of evaluation questions to be answered depend upon considerations of urgency and centrality. High priority should be given to answering those questions that many stakeholders agree are of immediate importance and central to program functioning.

However important the evaluation questions are, the scope of the evaluative effort is, in practice, limited by the resources that can be committed to the evaluation. What is the budget required for the evaluation? How long should it last? How much time should be invested? There are only a few rules of thumb available for guidance. Federally sponsored evaluations have in the past set aside between 2% and 4% of program funds for evaluation. Evaluators can provide in their preliminary proposals an estimate of their time and evaluation costs. These should be negotiated between client and consultant.

How Should the Evaluation Be Done?

The negotiation with the evaluation consultant that begins before he or she is employed is the beginning of a process that continues through the life of the evaluation. The selection of an evaluation model is helpful in shaping the evaluation, but the details of sample selection, instrument development, and instrument administration shape it further. Every one of these details is important to a productive outcome and needs to be discussed rather than assumed. Each of these small decisions should be made with the end of the evaluation in view. What effect will doing things this way rather than that way have on the usability and credibility of the evaluation in the eyes of those who must take action on evaluation findings? The evaluator is usually the expert on evaluation design, but the program administrators are usually the experts on the political and social context in which the program operates. Together they should reach agreement on the best way to go.

How to Deal with Evaluation Findings?

There are many ways for evaluators to work with program people to inform them of the evaluation findings. It used to be that only a formal written report would be issued at the end of the evaluation. This written report may have been the first as well as the last word back to program personnel about the evaluator's interpretation of tests, surveys, interviews, and observations. In current practice, it is customary for evaluators and their clients to keep in closer touch. Evaluators may transmit their findings informally through conversations or at meetings. Or, more formally, they may make progress reports to groups of stakeholders designated in advance.

Feedback from evaluators to program personnel is a critical part of the utilization perspective. Badly handled feedback can damage all the good will and negotiated agreements made up to that point. A successful feedback technique used by many evaluators is to provide a discussion draft of the final report to stakeholders for their reaction. The evaluator listens to the reactions—ranging from editing corrections to substantive disagreements—and decides whether to incorporate them into the final report. If the evaluator chooses not to modify the draft, some channel should be found to permit the disagreements to enter the record.

This procedure is open to the charge of collusion between evaluator and stakeholders. Indeed, the evaluator must take care not to water down negative findings in order to propitiate stakeholders with whom a constructive relationship has been developed. However, if the evaluator has a sensitive ear for language, there are ways of handling critical material without sacrificing integrity. The decision about whether to use this technique depends upon many factors, among them the audience for the evaluation, whether the evaluation is formative or summative, and the likely effect the report will have on the program. Whatever techniques are adopted, all arrangements for progress reports and final reports should have been negotiated between client and evaluator at the outset of the evaluation, not at the end of the process.

After the Evaluation, Then What?

There is some controversy within the evaluation community as to how far the evaluator should go beyond the presentation of findings. Some evaluators take the position that they should simply present the data and let the decision makers draw their own conclusions. Others prefer to indicate directions or scenarios that seem to be implied by the data. A third group feels that those commissioning the evaluation want definitive recommendations from the evaluator even though, after debate within the agency, these recommendations may be rejected in whole or in part.

There is yet another professional discussion occupying the evaluation community. It has to do with the extent to which the evaluator becomes, after the completion of the evaluation, a change agent, actively intervening in the program or organization to see that the recommendations are implemented. Some evaluators feel that once the evaluation report is filed, their job is over. They regard it as a real or potential conflict of interest to stay involved with the organization as an "implementation coach." Others feel just the opposite: Because they already know so much about how the organization functions, they believe that it is their responsibility to provide guidance, timelines, and budgets for program change. They see the evaluation as the beginning of a change process, and they feel themselves both responsible and capable of assisting the process to its conclusion. These differences of opinion among evaluators make it important that this final aspect of the relationship between client and evaluator be anticipated, discussed, and resolved before the evaluation begins.

REFERENCES

1. *Lessons from selected programs and policy areas* (No. 37, Spring, 1988), New Directions for Program Evaluation, a publication of the American Evaluation Association, San Francisco: Jossey-Bass.
2. *Evaluation and program planning* (Vol. 10, No. 1, 1987). New York: Pergamon Press.
3. Scriven, M. (1973). The methodology of evaluation. In B. R. Worthen & J. R. Sanders (Eds.), *Educational evaluation: Theory and practice.* (pp. 68–75) Belmont, CA: Wadsworth.
4. Tyler, R. W. (1942). General statement on evaluation. *Journal of Educational Research, 35*, 492–501.
5. Stufflebeam, D. L. (1983). The CIPP Model for program evaluation. In G. F. Madaus, M. Scriven, & D. L. Stufflebeam (Eds.), *Evaluation viewpoints on educational and human services evaluation.* (pp. 120–131) Boston: Kluwer-Nijoff.
6. Stake, R. E. (1967). The countenance of education evaluation. *Teachers College Record, 68.*
7. Patton, M. (1980). *Qualitative evaluation methods.* Beverly Hills: Sage.
8. Wolf, R. L. (1979). The use of judicial evaluation methods in the formulation of educational policy. *Educational Evaluation and Policy Analysis, 1*(3), 19–28.
9. Gold, N. (1984). *The convening process.* Unpublished manuscript.
10. Joint committee on standards of educational evaluation (1981). *Standards for evaluation of educational programs, projects and materials.* New York: McGraw-Hill.

CHAPTER 6

Communication and Relationships with Clients

HOWARD REBACH

INTRODUCTION

Clinical sociologists practice at many levels across the social spectrum. They use a variety of theoretical perspectives and apply techniques germane to the setting of practice, the assessed problem, and the client system. The structuring formula common to all clinical sociologists—and to all the helping professions—is that a client comes seeking help. People expect professionals to have special knowledge, procedures, and techniques. The success of specific techniques, however, is related to the quality of one's relationship with clients. The purpose of this chapter is to discuss the nontechnical issues of clinical work,[1] the client–professional relationship.

Forming positive relationships with clients is as much art as science. It involves coming to the encounter with certain mind sets, a few techniques, the ability to "read" people, and the flexibility to adapt interaction in response to others' behavior. As Schon[2] observes, "The unique case calls for an art of practice which 'might be taught if it were constant and known, but it is not constant.'" For Schon, the art of practice calls for "reflection in action," the adroit selection of behaviors based on the dynamics of the relationship and on what the client presents from moment to moment. No amount of instruction in how to draw, how to use light and shadow, how to use color will produce a Degas or Monet. But these and other mundane skills may be necessary when artists apply their creativity. So it is with the art of practice.

Relationships emerge from interaction. Your communication skills and how you "use yourself" often determine the course of interaction and the developing relationship. This chapter will consider communication and the development of relationships between clients/members of a client system and clinical workers.

HOWARD REBACH • Department of Social Sciences, University of Maryland, Eastern Shore, Princess Anne, Maryland 21853.

Because my own practice is at a community mental health clinic and my work is with individuals, families, and small groups, this chapter is biased toward sociological practice on the microlevel, but at any level, you must eventually meet face-to-face with identifiable role occupants, gain trust and cooperation, and form a productive working relationship.

A note on terminology is relevant here. I use the term *client* to refer to the person or group that hires you. The term *client system* refers more broadly to the client and others within the client's social network. This could mean family members, coworkers, adversaries, employees, services providers, or anyone else that you might interact with as part of your work with a case. For simplicity, the term *client* will be used to imply both.

The importance of the relationship with clients cannot be overstated. Your ability to conduct a valid and useful assessment and design and implement an intervention program depends on how willing clients and members of a client system are to trust you and work cooperatively with you. People may have to reveal embarrassing or threatening facts and feelings or expose their vulnerability in the face of powerful norms that stress adequacy or even perfection. You may need to ask them to expose their deeply held—and often hidden—feelings or question their definitions of self. The course of the work will depend on your ability to develop an effective working relationship with clients.

ON RELATIONSHIPS, GENERALLY

Relationships between people are emergent and come to be rule governed. Factors that influence interaction and the development of relationships can be identified, but emergent phenomena cannot be completely predicted from knowledge of the context, sociocultural background, or characteristics of interactants. The possibilities for the emergent structure are infinite. Communication is both an expression of culture and a creator of it. Although social roles, statuses, context and purpose of interaction as well as normative social behavior act as constraints, a relationship emerges as participants communicate, process information from transactions, and *adapt* in context. The emergent relationship and its rules are the result of a specific kind of negotiation among interactants.

When strangers meet, Person (defined here as the one who initiates interaction) presents self to Other.[3] This presentation is influenced by Person's history, self-conception, and definition of the situation—Person's role definition, status vis-à-vis Other, purpose for the interaction, context in which interaction takes place, and so forth.

In the normal course of everyday life, Other, conforming to a normative social contract, generally accepts Person's presentation of self and also offers a presentation of self. Both try to manage the impression the other forms. Usually, they collude in each other's impression management. As interaction continues, the different selves try to adjust to each other. They continue to "train" each other on how they are to be seen and treated.

Training is conducted outside the awareness of the participants; most of the time, the interactants are not aware they are training and being trained. Training is carried in the messages each gives in response to messages received from others. As Bateson argued, "the relationship *is* the exchange of. . . messages."[4] Interactants set and try to maintain personal boundaries as they respond to others.[5]

As mutual training continues, the relationship is a source of information that is fed back. Each person adapts, reads the feedback, adjusts some more, and so forth. Interactants adopt specific roles in interaction, define other(s), self, situation, as they interpret messages. The process is dynamic, not static. An actor's definition of the situation is not fixed but continually adapts to the flow of feedback. Over time, the relationship develops patterns and norms and becomes governed by implicit rules. The training is a form of negotiation. As each trains the others, they are negotiating their relationship. Actions that Person directs to Other are accepted, modified, or rejected. Actions that are accepted are likely to be repeated and become a feature of the relationship. Repetition of unacceptable behaviors may undermine the relationship, perhaps to the point where one of the interactants withdraws from the relationship.

Continued interaction is a product of joint willingness to continue, which is contingent on rewards stemming from continuing. A person cannot determine if the interaction has potential rewards unless a definition can be placed on the situation. The person processes information in attempting to determine what the outcomes—rewards or costs—are for self.

THE CLINICAL RELATIONSHIP

What is generally true is true of clinical relationships. They emerge from interaction, develop patterns and rules, and are constrained by context and purpose. Clients enter the encounter searching for structure and assume the existence of an objective reality that can be shared.[6] They will attempt to train you to perceive them and treat them in ways that are familiar to them or the ways they prefer to be seen and treated. And they will assess the likelihood of rewards from interaction.

Beyond these similarities, the relationship between a clinical sociologist and a member or members of a client system is *not* an ordinary social relationship. You are there to develop a special kind of relationship—a helping relationship. Unfortunately it is not possible to provide a precise, invariant operational definition of that relationship, nor is it possible to specify an invariant set of behaviors. Clients and settings are unique. The key is how you adapt your communication in context; the difficult task is to create a close yet professional relationship. The relationship you get is the one you ask for, both overtly and unconsciously, as the client perceives your communication behaviors and assigns meaning to them.

The time spent with the client must be used to construct a working relationship, an understanding of the problematic situation, define objectives, and attempt to move toward them. Understanding the situation requires understanding *with* and understanding *about*. The former refers to understanding clients' models of reality from their perspective. Like a good ethnographer, you must attempt to understand their cognitive world, discover their modes of cognition and perception,[7] and learn "those features of objects and events which they regard as significant for defining concepts, formulating propositions, and making decisions."[8] People will have their own ways of understanding their reality and their own ways of constructing and accounting for the problematic situation.

You must understand and accept their reality without defining it as objective reality. You must also retain an analytic perspective, to interact with Other in terms of your world, the world of analytic concepts.

You must also bring to the situation the awareness that your behaviors contribute to the structure and quality of the relationship. You must present conditions that communicate the uniqueness of clients' relationship with you. You must communicate your interest in them, that you are trustworthy, and that you can be helpful.

Presenting Conditions

Evidence from a variety of sources suggests that the client–clinician relationship be defined as status equals, mutually engaged in problem solving. Humanistic values remind us to respect clients' rights to self-determination. Your role is not to tell clients what to do but to help them expand their range of choices so they can cope more effectively with their environment. Although your background and training may make an appropriate course of action seem obvious, clients may be unable to use it because it is not yet included in their model of reality. Their social reality (e.g., class, gender, organization membership, ethnicity, culture, etc.) may make your "solution" unacceptable or inaccessible.

From this perspective, then, the client–clinician relationship is seen as a working partnership among role occupants who are status equals. Carl Rogers[9] characterizes the approach as "client centered," an orientation that respects others' significance, worth, and dignity as human beings. Rogers wrote:

> Do we tend to treat individuals as persons of worth, or do we subtly devaluate them by our attitudes and behavior? Is our philosophy one in which respect for the individual is uppermost? Do we respect his capacity and his right to self-direction, or do we basically believe that his life would be best guided by us? To what extent do we have a need and desire to dominate others? Are we willing for the individual to select and choose his own values, or are our actions guided by the conviction (usually unspoken) that he would be happiest if he permitted us to select for him, his values and standards, and goals?" (p. 20)

Rogers's approach, often stereotyped as "nondirective," does not imply *laissez-faire*. Passivity could communicate lack of interest, indifference, or rejection and does not indicate to the person that you care or that you believe the person to be worthwhile. But Rogers's approach suggests that practitioners, in whatever setting, show concern, respect, genuineness, accurate empathy, and nonjudgmental regard. These do not produce change, as such, but they set the conditions for progress.[10]

Studies of professional–client interaction in medical settings found that the "affective component of the physician's communication [was] a major feature in patients' evaluations."[11] The affective component included directing behavior toward the person rather than the "case," allowing adequate time, and showing interest. Buller and Buller[11] compared what they called an *affiliative style* to a *controlling* one. An affiliative style included behaviors that communicated friendliness, empathy, warmth, genuineness, candor, honesty, a desire to help, and a nonjudgmental attitude. A controlling style was one that communicated control over the interaction with obvious power differences. Buller and Buller found a high correlation between patients' evaluations of physicians' communication and their satisfaction with health care services. Greater satisfaction was associated with the affiliative style.

Studies of psychotherapy find that the relationship climate between the therapist and client is associated with progress and satisfaction.[12] A facilitative climate is one in which the therapist genuinely tries to understand what the client tries to say, is accepting, interested, nurturing and egalitarian, and shows respect.

Saltzman *et al.*[13] studied the relationship aspects in the initial stages of psychotherapy. Compared to those who showed their dissatisfaction by dropping out, remainers expressed feelings of (1) being respected as human beings, (2) being understood and understanding what the clinician tried to convey, (3) being able openly to express feelings and receive an open reaction, (4) confidence in the clinician's competence and commitment to help as long as needed, (5) uniqueness of the relationship and the response they received, (6) being involved in a relationship that they thought about between meetings, and (7) coming to grips with problems and making progress. Therapists' reactions also made a difference. Data showed that for clients who remained, therapists felt able to (1) accept and respect the client as the client is, (2) understand what the client tries to convey and is understood by the client, (3) express self and communicate openly, (4) have a sense of concern for and participation with the client, (5) be involved in an ongoing relationship that was anticipated between meetings, and (6) acknowledge emotional reactions generally and toward the client in particular.

Data also showed that these relationship aspects were positively correlated with clients' and therapists' assessments of client improvement and problem resolution. These results indicate the importance of the interpretations clients/members of client systems place on the messages they receive.

Communication

The most basic, axiomatic statement stresses the impossibility of *not* communicating. Given the presence of another person, "you cannot NOT communicate."[14] The presence of an observer creates the possibility that the observer will assign meaning to your behavior. You may not *intend* to send a message, but you have no control over whether or not someone interprets your behavior. You also have no direct control over *what* meaning the observer assigns. Each observer applies a personal model of reality to interpret messages. Your intentions are not a necessary component of the meanings that an observer assigns to your actions.

As people and as clients and clinicians, we make behaviors available for interpretation on many levels. The most obvious are the language symbols that we use, but language is just one band that carries potential meaning. Paralinguistic cues— stress, intonation, speech rate and pitch, vocabulary, and so on—and nonverbal cues also influence interpretations. Eye contact, hand and facial gestures, gross body movements, and postures are examples. A person's use of time, space, and context also has potential message value to an observer.

Messages are not always consonant across modalities. For instance, consider the total message of a parent who tries to discipline and elicit obedience from a child but conducts the entire transaction while smiling, barely looking at the child, and never moving from a slouched position in an easy chair. The words may admonish, but the other behaviors seem to give the child tacit permission to ignore what has been said.

Though communication occurs whether we intend to send messages or not, we also operate on our environment by intentionally encoding messages, most often verbal messages. The purpose of such messages is to elicit a more or less predetermined response from the audience member(s). Perhaps a second axiom of communication is to note that each message carries at least two kinds of information: content and relationship information.[14] The content aspect is defined as the semantic meaning and the response you, as message source, want from the receiver. The relationship aspect of messages contains information about who you think you are and how you see your relationship to the other person. Most often, the content aspect is carried in the words.

Relationship information is usually carried through paralinguistic and nonverbal behaviors. Epstein[15] reported that higher status interactants initiate more touching than lower status people. Women show more facial display of feelings and smile and look at interacting partners more than men do. Men and higher status people take more personal space and are more likely to interrupt and "over top" (talk while other is talking). Men are especially prone to over top when talking to a woman or a child. Social characteristics such as class, race, ethnicity, age, occupation, and sex as well as context cues—the topic, roles of interactants, purpose of interaction—influence communication behaviors.

For clinical workers, tuning in to nonverbals is an important part of establishing effective relationships. Nonverbal messages may be a clue to inner states.[15] Early workers indicated that nonverbal cues may reflect actors' adaptation to the situation and communicate information about their reactions to their interacting partner.[16,17] Those who seek approval use more eye contact as they search for cues to structure behavior. People also avert gaze during nonfluency and when they are dealing with complex or more intimate material. There is also less looking at a disliked person.[18-20]

The point of this recitation is to alert beginners and even experienced clinical workers to the range of elements that have potential message value for workers and clients. Effective communication, getting the response you want, requires carefully observing your receivers and adapting your communication behaviors on the basis of the feedback you receive.

Preparing for Communication

One way to achieve effective communication is to prepare for it. The most basic step in preparing for communication is to take stock of yourself. Have a good look at your own attitudes, biases, prejudices, and blind spots that may act as barriers.

Are there certain kinds of people, situations, topics, or problems that you do not care to deal with or that make you feel uncomfortable? For example, how do you feel about authority and hierarchical structures? Do you automatically identify with one side or the other? Do you see all lower status members as downtrodden and oppressed and all authority as exploitative? Or do you see higher status members as invariably right and lower status members as recalcitrant? Are there certain political, social, or economic stances that arouse your impatience or hostility? Do you grow impatient or get frustrated when certain religious or moral positions are introduced? Are you prone to moralize? Do you grow impatient with people who question you or who do not immediately understand you? Do you shy away from or get irritated when people are hostile, dependent, or passive? Do you need to talk constantly or at least when there is a brief lapse in the conversation? Do you have mannerisms that call attention to themselves or are distracting? Absentmindedly shaking a foot, picking at nails, or fiddling with a pen are physical examples. Verbal examples include excessive use of jargon or verbalizations such as "yeah, hunh" uttered repeatedly after every phrase or sentence of the other person. Learning about yourself can be very useful, but it is not easy. Monitoring yourself can be helpful. Working with a trusted colleague can also be helpful if you take the time to debrief each other's actions and can be open and candid with each other. Role playing and videotaping can also help you learn a great deal about your own interactive behavior.

Another way of preparing for communication is to pay attention to the physical surroundings, which should provide privacy and be free of distractions including telephone calls, interruptions, and people milling about. The environment should help communicate that the person is important, has your undivided attention, and that this is a safe place to speak without fear of being overheard. Each individual clinical sociologist may have to decide on role props, trappings of status and expertise, and questions of furnishings and their placement. Various combinations communicate different things. For example, meeting with people while you sit behind a big imposing desk in an equally imposing chair while they sit in smaller, ordinary chairs in front of the desk places a barrier between you and may imply status differences. No desk between you and similar chairs for all creates a more open and egalitarian, partnership feeling. Gathering around a conference table, communication can be influenced by the shape of the table and where the various actors sit. The choices you make will depend on the tone you wish to set.

If your client is an organization, you should learn something about the organization and its culture, its purpose and goals, and status structure. Organizations often develop a specialized language that differentiates insiders and outsiders. Businesses, police departments, schools, health care providers all develop shorthand terms. Learning the jargon facilitates communication. On the other hand, it is probably not a good idea to adopt street patois or adolescent slang in hopes of gaining acceptance if it will appear phony.

Anticipating the needs of clients is another way of preparing for communication. If you are aware of special needs—an interpreter for non-English-speakers or for hearing-handicapped persons—you can make provision for such needs. One general need of most clients beginning a relationship with helping professionals is the need for structure and role clarity. You must be prepared to provide structuring information.

In some settings, particularly in microlevel practice, the professional may have the higher status role. In other settings, status relationships may be less clear. In organizations, for example, the professional may have to work with people who define their own status as higher due to their position in the organization's hierarchy. It may also be the case that the professional is seen as an unwelcome intrusion or even a threat. You must be prepared to deal with authority issues, hostility, and resistance.

Initial Meetings

Initially it may be best to be less task oriented and more person oriented.[21] Introductions are obviously a part of openings. A warm-up period may be appropriate. Some sensitivity to clients and setting is also a good rule. Too easy familiarity and automatic (or nonreciprocal) use of first names may be inappropriate or offensive, indicating lack of respect. Warm-up periods of informal conversation can be useful in establishing rapport, especially in certain cultural groups such as Hispanics, Asians, and Native-Americans[22] or with adolescents or nonvoluntary clients. A warm-up period provides clients with an opportunity to "size you up" and begin to get an idea of what kind of person you are. Sometimes it may be appropriate to provide information about yourself such as background, expertise, auspices, and objectives. At other times, warm-up may be unnecessary. Clients may be anxious to begin telling you their stories and will be annoyed by what they might interpret as triviality. Again, sensitivity to clients and setting is the rule.

It is often useful, in initial meetings, to anticipate uncertainty and purposefully negotiate structure. Reassurances of confidentiality and clarification of the need for a partnership relationship may be a start. From there, you work toward structure as you and the client negotiate a line of action.[23] For example, with a new client it may be useful to describe that, together, you will need to conduct an assessment of the problem situation and negotiate a concrete definition of it. This opens the way for negotiating the responsibilities of each party.

When problems have been defined and agreed upon, discussion of intervention options brings clients and workers to a choice point. Given a clearer understanding of the problem, statement of objectives, potential steps to achieve the goal, and the array of consequences, the client may decide to terminate. The program may have effects the client is not willing to accept; the client may not be willing to expend the resources necessary; or the client may not be prepared to take the steps needed for change. If no acceptable alternatives are available, the client may decide to accept the present level of the problem as preferable to change. You have choices also. There may be agreement on the nature of the problem, its history, causes, manifestations, and functions but disagreement on what steps to take. If the steps chosen by the client are not compatible with your skills or values, admission of this and further negotiation may be necessary. Termination or referral may also be the only appropriate step. Having decided to go on, program planning and contracting follows.

As assessment and establishing a relationship with clients begins, you need to answer two important questions: Should you take the case? If you do, can you form an effective working alliance with this client? You must determine if the problem meshes with your skills and legal limitations. Not all problems are within our purview. Often we can be most constructive by referring the case to a more appropriate source of help.

Second, ask yourself, do you *want* to take the case? You need not take every case that is within your expertise. Certain types of cases may bore you. Others may take too much of your time and emotional energy or conflict with your values. The decision to take a case is a commitment. Half-hearted commitment is worse than not taking the case. It deprives the client of the chance to work with someone who will make the necessary commitment to the work. A poorly motivated helper is not a help.

If you choose not to take the case, it is your obligation to make an appropriate referral. Your assessment centers on the goal of determining what is the best referral for this client. Making the referral should be an active task. It is not enough, in my view, to say, "You should see a ———," and terminate the relationship. In discussion with the client, you can identify a specific resource. This can include making telephone calls with the client present and even scheduling an appointment between the client and the referral source. You can help the client learn how to get access to the referral source and develop strategies for accessing and overcoming barriers to effective use of the referral. In some cases, your most important intervention will be to connect a client with resources.

One final note on referrals. Your obligation extends to a follow-up to see if the client was able to use the referral, did use it, and how effective the referral was. This communicates to both the client and the services network your continuing concern. It also provides you with information to guide future referrals.

The second question was whether you can form an effective working alliance with this client. Can you relate to this client system in a way that will allow you to understand and value the people involved? Do your biases and personal preferences provide significant barriers? Is there something about this particular client that you dislike? Is there something about this client, organization, or this problem that engages your own history in ways that will make you ineffective? Things like the background, language, gender, racial, ethnic, or subcultural membership may make it difficult for you to understand and form an alliance with the client. The issue turns on whether or not you and your client can understand each other and whether you can take an involved, yet objective approach.

Approaching Clients

Clinical sociologists must learn about a problem to help alleviate it. Members of the client system have an understanding of the problem and models of reality to aid understanding. These models are rich and rational and support inferences that meet needs and facilitate action. This conceptual structure includes the causes and consequences of the problem. Your task is to learn about the conceptual structure by getting into the clients' models. It is a problem of communication between

Expert and Other who will not necessarily share meaning for concepts nor have the same way of organizing information. Clients have different sets of information, which differ in structure because of different understandings of links between facts. The Expert has more and different linkages. Evans *et al.*[24] saw the problem as the absence of shared vocabularies and shared meaning. Even when similar terms are used, their semantic content may differ.

The challenge is to determine the meaning of terms the client uses and the phenomena that words label. Another common problem is the professional's use of terms that have come to summarize (for the professional) a complex set of concepts and actions (e.g., "socialization"). Clients are unlikely to probe for clarification of terms. You need to learn their language and teach them yours.

Special attention should be given to clients' labels for the problem that signify observations, subjective experiences, and other relevant information. Labels also affect ongoing adaptation to and understandings of the problem. You need to pay close attention to language and help clients unpack the cognitive content of the labels.

Open Listening

As clients begin to tell their story, active listening and empathic communication furthers rapport. Be open to whatever they present. They will talk about whatever you will listen to, so be careful and selective about what you choose to reinforce. You will get the story best if you let clients tell it in their own way. Start where the client is. The work is a process, not an event; do *not* jump to solutions. Attend to clients' concerns and emotions. Their agenda—they have one—comes first. Listen to their questions without trivializing them. Questions contain concerns. Answer them openly. By so doing you model openness and indicate your concern and your respect that you have no secrets and no hidden agendas. Be alert to cues, especially nonverbal and paralinguistic cues already discussed, that express their feelings. There may be authority issues, ambivalence about help seeking and change, or negative or hostile feelings. Respond to these cues. It does no good to ignore them. Reach behind negative feelings by openly acknowledging them and try to see what prompts them. Be alert to cues about client motivation and expectations. These help you understand what they want and allow you to say what you can do and how you can help.[22]

Reach for strengths also. The temptation is to focus on dysfunctions, but noting strengths can help you and the client mobilize resources. Finally, be aware that people often speak in global terms and metaphors. Your task is to help them reach a concrete problem definition that can be operationalized and made the target of work.

Active Listening

An important communication skill for establishing effective working relationships is active listening. This includes such skills as "minimal prompts," paraphrasing, empathic responses, questioning, and summarizing.

Minimal prompts.   Minimal prompts are a set of verbal and nonverbal acts that indicate that you are following what is said but do not disturb the flow. Verbally, minimal prompts can be an occasional "uh huh," or "yes" or "I see." Nonverbal indicators that you are following are also important. Forward lean is a nonverbal indication of attention. Appropriate eye contact and head nods also indicate that you are interested and are following. They also provide the speaker with reinforcement.

Paraphrasing.   Paraphrasing, restating in your own words your understanding of what has just been said, also indicates following and interest. You must be careful not to put words in the clients' mouths and to avoid interpretations, especially those derived from your preconceptions. By paraphrasing, you provide an opportunity for the client to give you feedback, correcting and extending your understanding. It also furthers the relationship by indicating your active involvement.

Questioning.   Asking questions is a part of any interview but be careful that you are not cross-examining or interrogating. Open-ended questions are most useful. Generic open-ended questions such as "Can you clarify that for me?" or "Can you tell me more about?" invite the client to elaborate a topic. Closed-ended questions are best used sparingly and only when you need a specific bit of information. Generally, they limit talk production. You might ask the closed-ended question, "Do you like working here?" Such a question usually elicits a one or two word response. The open-ended question, "How do you feel about working here?" is more likely to elicit more material and exploration of the employee's attitude toward the job.

Questions that begin with *How* or *What* or *Could* are usually more useful than *Why* questions.[25] For example, the employee might indicate low satisfaction with his job. The question, "Why don't you like your job?", puts him on the defensive and implies a judgment. He may not know why. Or it may not be as simple as like–dislike. The question, "What is it about working here that you find unsatisfactory?", invites him to continue and may elicit elaboration of his attitude.

Empathic responding.   Perhaps the most important skill and often the most difficult, especially for beginners, is reaching for feelings. Be alert and sensitive to underlying or overtly expressed feelings. Nonverbal behaviors often express feelings. Do not be afraid to reach for them. Use your own experiences with people and yourself. If you observe anger or tension or some other nonverbal display, you can reach for it by saying something like "You seem very tense right now. Can you tell me what you're tense about?" This lets the client know that you are tuned in. It also focuses the interview on the here and now and may aid you and the client deal with feelings surrounding the interview or your relationship.

Verbal productions also have a feeling component. An employee may say, "I've been working here for 20 years. I work hard and try hard and what's it get me? Nothing!" The best reflections of feelings are focused. A generic statement such as "I see you are upset" is too diffuse. It recognizes a feeling but not its object. A more directed response might be, "You feel you're not appreciated, that you never get recognition for the things you have contributed." A useful form is to label the feeling and use a well-formed sentence with an object such as "You ——— about ———." A response to the employee might be "you're angry about never getting any recognition for what you have done for the company." As with paraphrasing, the client can revise and correct your interpretation.

Some Cautions.   Generally, people will talk about what they think others will listen to or want to hear. Be careful about what you reinforce. You may direct the person away from material that is central. It is possible, especially for beginners, to become enthralled with the soap-opera-like qualities of accounts that you might forget your role and lead the person into ever more involved telling of stories that may not be germane.

Do not parrot. The person says, "I am really angry." To reflect feelings by saying, "You're angry," is likely to elicit "that's what I just said [stupid]." Avoid overuse of contrived lines like "I hear you saying." Also avoid making interpretations and judgments of the person's private logic and ways of constructing reality. Finally, do not mind-read. If you can make an interpretation, paraphrase, or empathic response, check it out with the person to get feedback on your accuracy.

Listen for Sensory Language.   Neuro Linguistic Programming[26,27] advocates listening for people's sensory language as an aid to getting into clients' models. The theory asserts that people organize experience with information received through the senses. Sensory experience is mapped into language. Though we are capable of representing reality with all our senses, we differ as to which is the most highly valued—either visual, auditory, or kinesthetic (feelings and physical sensations). We reveal this with the sensory words we use, called *predicates* which are verbs, adverbs, and adjectives. You can determine a person's most valued representational system by listening to these predicates. For example, the person who says things like, "I see myself as unappreciated around here," or "my view is. . . ." or, to take one of Grinder and Bandler's[27] examples (p. 10), "The dazzling woman watched the silver car streak past the glittering display" is using terms that denote visual senses as the preferred mode. An alternate utterance such as "I feel I am not appreciated around here" denotes kinesthetic senses.

Grinder & Bandler advocate matching predicates or sensory words when interacting with clients or members of a client system. They offer the following example (p. 15):

> *Meaning*: Describe more of your present experience to me.
> *Kinesthetic*: Put me in touch with what you are feeling at this point in time.
> *Visual*: Show me a clear picture of what you see at this point in time.
> *Auditory*: Tell me in more detail what you are saying at this point in time.

Note the use of specific sensory terms in each example. By discovering the person's preferred mode, you can understand more about how the person organizes his or her model of reality. By matching predicates you can facilitate clearer, more direct communication and facilitate trust building. Grinder and Bandler describe this as follows:

> Suppose we have a client who has a kinesthetic representational system. First we listen to his experience, then we check out our understanding of what he says (his model of the world) and phrase our questions—in fact structure all of our communication with him—with kinesthetic predicates. . . . [I]f we communicate with predicates that are kinesthetic, it will be easier for him both to understand our communication and to know [in this case to *feel*] that we understand him. . . . [T]o allow our clients to understand our communication with greater ease is the basis and beginning of trust. (p. 14)

Bandler and Grinder[26] have provided strategies for helping people chunk down problems. Like the symbolic interaction perspective, they also note that we construct internal representations of reality. People get into trouble "not because the world is not rich enough to allow them to satisfy their needs, but because their representation of the world is impoverished" (p. 45). Models are impoverished because the person deletes, distorts, or generalizes in ways that impoverish his or her understanding of his or her world. The task is to understand his or her representation and help him or her reframe and/or elaborate his or her model of reality to add constructive choices to his or her behavior. People display their models of reality through their verbal productions.

Internal representations give rise to utterances, but they may be incomplete. The statements "we cannot communicate" or "I am anxious all the time" are incomplete. They are not well formed. Something has been deleted. By asking the questions "What is it you cannot communicate *about*?" or "what are you anxious *about*?" you invite the person to supply the missing piece. Or you and the person may discover his or her model of reality is incomplete in the same way that the utterance is incomplete.

An exchange like the following may also illustrate the idea of well formedness.

PERSON: We can't communicate.

YOU: [recognizing that this is not well formed] What is it that you cannot communicate about?

The person may be able to identify some specific topic that leads to further exploration, or he or she may respond (more typical):

PERSON: Everything.

You don't get frustrated, but you continue:

YOU: Can you tell me just one specific thing you have difficulty communicating about?

The idea here is to help the person go from vague, global utterance to specific areas that are problematic. You cannot simply repair communication, but you might help people communicate about something specific to identifiable others.

You can also challenge deletions that impoverish with leading questions that invite the person to explore an expanded model of reality. Perhaps having discovered what/who the person cannot communicate about/with, you ask: "What stops you from speaking to X about Y?" or "What would happen if you spoke to X about Y?"

Other utterances display distortions of reality. Listen for generalizations, presuppositions, and semantic ill-formedness that impoverish the person's model of reality and limit choices. An example of semantic ill-formedness might be an expression like, "They never made me feel valued or part of the team." This is a distortion that attributes control of one's reality to others and gives them responsibility for one's feelings and well-being. These formulations should be rejected.

The basic strategy for working with people involves listening carefully to the forms of utterances as well as to the content. Utterances that are not well formed provide clues to the problem and to ways of helping. More detailed elaboration of Bandler and Grinder's communication strategies for helping people is beyond the scope of this chapter. Interested readers would do well to study *The Structure of Magic*.

In sum then, effective communication with clients involves careful listening and responding. This section has tried to sketch briefly some skills that have proven useful. We turn now to some further cautions.

BARRIERS, BREAKDOWNS, AND PROBLEMS

Many things can interfere with communication. You must avoid the "like-me" assumption often characteristic of everyday interaction. In a medical setting, McElroy and Jezewski[28] found that miscommunication occurred when staff assumed that patients' lifestyles were similar to their own. This included class differences, household composition, daily routines, marital status, and so forth. Ignoring economic differences, making poor assumptions about patients' knowledge and abilities, and failure to follow through by providing adequate information and clarification also contributed to communication breakdown and thus, poor outcomes.

Hepworth and Larson[22] offered a laundry list of things that inhibit effective communication and relationship building:

CONTENT
1. Moralizing
2. Advising and giving suggestions
3. Judging, criticizing, blaming
4. Persuading, giving logical arguments, lecturing, arguing
5. Analyzing, diagnosing, making glib dogmatic interpretations
6. Sympathizing, consoling, excusing
7. Sarcasm and inappropriate humor
8. Threatening, warning

PROCESS
9. Using questions inappropriately: too many closed-ended questions, stacking questions, questions that have hidden agendas
10. Interrupting inappropriately or excessively
11. Dominating interaction
12. Fostering social interaction
13. Infrequent responding

14. Parroting or overusing phrases and cliches ("you know")
15. Dwelling on remote past
16. Inappropriate self-disclosure

Creating a defensive climate also inhibits.[29] A defensive climate may be created by evaluation, control, superiority, certainty, by ordering, warning, preaching, advising, lecturing, judging, ridiculing, diagnosing, praising. These things cause persons to focus on how they appear to you, how to appear favorable in their own and others' eyes, and how to dominate, win, impress, and escape, avoid, or reduce real or anticipated punishment.

Client Training Clinician

In ordinary social interaction, actors train each other. When you interact with clients, be aware that their communication behaviors will represent their habitual ways of interacting. This can be a trap for the unwary who automatically react to clients' presentations. Research by Heller, Myers, and Kline[30] demonstrated that clients' actions can evoke personal reactions from therapists. In their study, trained actors posing as clients confronted counselors with one of four conditions: friendliness or hostility, dominance or dependence. Results from the clinical interviews showed that client dominance evoked interviewer dependence, whereas client dependence evoked interviewer dominance; client hostility evoked interviewer hostility, whereas client friendliness evoked interviewer friendliness. These counselors appeared to react as though this was ordinary social contact, not a clinical encounter. These results suggest that clinicians be alert to a tendency to be drawn into the clients' patterns rather than adapting to clients' presentations. You are not offering a clinical relationship when you allow your judgments of clients to structure your reactions.

Being drawn into the existing patterns goes beyond the interview setting discussed by Heller *et al.* Although it is important for the clinician to learn clients' vision of reality and how clients define themselves, the clinician must avoid being trained to accept clients' versions of reality with their problematic features.

As Snow and Anderson[31] asserted, the drive for a sense of self-worth is basic, though achievement depends on roles that are differentially distributed in social systems. To avoid stigma, people engage in identity work, "the range of activities to create, present, and sustain personal identities congruent with and supportive of self concept." Thus clients and members of a client system present "accounts" consistent with their identity work. Although you must accept the persons, you must understand that the accounts they present are geared to have you accept their versions of reality. Accepting persons, however, is not the same as accepting their versions of reality.

An individual is part of ongoing social networks, which include the person's significant others and those with the power to influence the person's conduct. You enter and become part of an ongoing social system to learn about and help the system change. Your entry creates new relationships and alters existing ones, and the social structure changes.

An ongoing group develops a "culture," sets of norms, rules for interaction, and characteristic ways that members communicate and relate with each other. Members share meaning about the objects and events in their world and, in particular, about the nature of the problematic situation and its causes. Overall, the system, though perhaps characterized by dysfunctional elements, has a stable equilibrium of which the dysfunction may be a necessary part. The organization of families with an alcoholic member that continues to support the alcoholic behavior is but one of many well-known examples.

The entry of the clinical sociologist, even if invited, is a threat to the system's equilibrium. The clinician, as a new entrant into the system, needs to be wary of being drawn into the culture of the group. There will be powerful attempts to influence you to share the socially constructed reality. Various members of the client system may present accounts of conduct in hopes that you will accept and validate their definitions of the situation. Families, groups, and organizations will similarly attempt to socialize you into seeing things the way they do. In addition, social systems ordinarily have set communication and relationship patterns that will be upset as change occurs. These patterns will work against change, and you should be alert to these.

Finally, how members of a client system communicate with you is important assessment data. People's characteristic behaviors are thoroughly internalized, and they usually occur outside the actor's awareness. Even when they are on their "best behavior," possibly because of your presence, people will have difficulty keeping their habitual communication behaviors masked for long. Observation of their communication patterns may provide useful clues to the problem situation. Use your own reactions as a source of hypotheses. If, in interaction with a person or in a group, you feel angry, or helpless, or calm, or defiant, or happy, others who are part of the group or who interact with the individual may also have the same response. Do not automatically assume this but treat it as a hypothesis to be checked by assessing how others react to the group's or person's communicative behaviors.

CONCLUSION

Communicating and forming effective working relationships with clients requires self-awareness and attention to communication skills, as well as the flexibility to adapt communication in context to others. It is the art and craft of professional practice. There are few rules or guidelines, but successful practice cannot be achieved without being able to form effective relationships.

REFERENCES

1. Parloff, M. B. (1986). Frank's "common elements" in psychotherapy: Nonspecific factors and placebos. *American Journal of Orthopsychiatry, 56*, 521–530.
2. Schon, D. E. (1983). *The reflective practitioner.* New York: Basic Books.
3. Goffman, E. (1959). *The presentation of self in everyday life.* Garden City, NY: Doubleday.
4. Bateson, G. (1972). *Steps to an ecology of mind.* New York: Ballantine.

5. Vuchinich, S. (1984). Sequencing and social structure in family conflict. *Social Psychology Quarterly, 47*, 217–234.
6. Gurevitch, Z. D. (1988). The other side of dialogue: On making the other strange and the experience of otherness. *American Journal of Sociology, 93*, 1179–1199.
7. Lindesmith, A. R., Strauss, A. L., & Denzin, N. K. (1988). *Social psychology* (6th ed.). Englewood Cliffs, NJ: Prentice-Hall.
8. Frake, C. (1962). Cultural ecology and ethnology. *American Anthropologist, 64*, 53–59.
9. Rogers, C. (1951). *Client centered therapy.* New York: Houghton Mifflin.
10. Wexler, D. A., & Butler, J. M. (1976). Therapist modification of client expressiveness in client-centered therapy. *Journal of Consulting and Clinical Psychology, 44*, 261–265.
11. Buller, M. K., & Buller, D. P. (1987). Physician's communication style and patient satisfaction. *Journal of Health and Social Behavior, 28*, 375–388.
12. Lorr, M. (1964). Client perceptions of therapists: A study of the therapeutic relation. *Journal of Consulting Psychology, 28*, 146–149.
13. Saltzman, C., Luertgert, M. J., Roth, C. H., Creaser, J., & Howard, L. (1976). Formation of a therapeutic relationship: Experiences during the initial phase of psychotherapy as predictors of treatment duration and outcome. *Journal of Consulting and Clinical Psychology, 44*, 546–555.
14. Watzlawick, P., Beavin, J. H., & Jackson, D. D. (1968). *Pragmatics of human communication.* New York: W. W. Norton.
15. Epstein, C. F. (1986). Symbolic segregation: Similarities and differences in the language and non-verbal communication of women and men. *Sociological forum, 1*, 27–49.
16. Argyle, M. (1969). *Social interaction.* New York: Atherton Press.
17. Mehrabian, A. (1972). *Nonverbal communication.* Chicago: Aldine-Atherton.
18. Kendon, S. (1967). Some functions of gaze direction in social interaction. *Acta Psychologica, 26*, 22–63.
19. Exline, R. V., & Winters, L. C. (1965). Affective relations and mutual gaze in dyads. In S. Tomkins & C. Izzard (Eds.), *Affect, cognition, and personality.* New York: Springer.
20. Exline, R. V. (1969). The effects of cognitive difficulty and cognitive style upon eye to eye contact in interviews. Unpublished paper reported in M. Argyle, *Social interaction.* New York: Atherton Press.
21. Shulman, L. (1984). *The skills of helping individuals and groups.* Itasca, IL: F. E. Peacock Publishers.
22. Hepworth, D. H., & Larsen, J. A. (1986). *Direct social work practice: Theory and skills.* Chicago: The Dorsey Press.
23. Blumer, H. (1962). Society as symbolic interaction. In A. Rose (Ed.), *Human behavior and social processes* (pp. 179–192). Boston: Houghton Mifflin.
24. Evans, D. A., Block, M. R., Steinberg, E. R., & Penrose, A. M. (1986). Frames and heuristics in doctor-patient discourse. *Social Science and Medicine, 22*, 1027–1036.
25. Ivey, A. E., & Gluckstern, N. B. (1974). *Basic attending skills: Participant manual.* North Amherst, MA: Microtraining Associates, Inc.
26. Bandler, R., & Grinder, J. (1975). *The structure of magic I.* Palo Alto, CA: Science and Behavior Books, Inc.
27. Grinder, J., & Bandler, R. (1976). *The structure of magic II.* Palo Alto, CA: Science and Behavior Books, Inc.
28. McElroy, A., & Jezewski, M. A. (1986). Boundaries and breakdowns: Applying Agar's concept of ethnography to observations in a pediatric clinic. *Human Organizations, 45*, 202–211.
29. Cline, R., & Johnson, B. McD. (1976). The verbal stare: Focus on attention in conversation. *Communication Monographs, 43*, 1–10.
30. Heller, K., Myers, R. A., & Kline, L. V. (1963). Interviewer behavior as a function of standardized client roles. *Journal of Consulting Psychology, 27*, 117–122.
31. Snow, D. A., & Anderson, L. (1987). Identity work among the homeless: The verbal construction and avowal of personal identities. *American Journal of Sociology, 92*, 1336–1371.

CHAPTER 7

Ethics in Clinical Sociology

JOHN G. BRUHN

This chapter considers issues and problems that raise questions about good and bad human conduct. Ethics is the study of what constitutes good and bad human conduct, including related actions and values. Ethics is concerned with questions of right and wrong, of duty and obligation, of moral responsibility. Occasionally, the term *ethics* is used interchangeably with *morals*. Although this usage is acceptable, it is more accurate to restrict the terms *moral* and *morality* to the conduct itself and to use *ethics* and *ethical* to delineate the study of moral conduct or the code a person follows. We will focus on ethical issues in the practice of clinical sociology and the variety of contexts in which clinical sociologists practice.

ETHICAL IDEALS AND BEHAVIOR

Most of our personal and professional attitudes stem from a handful of values. How do professional values arise? Why does one professional advocate patient rights at great personal expense, whereas another opts for quiet autonomy? There are four main sources from which we derive our values: experience, culture, science, and religion.

Our values are shaped by experience. Those who have felt the sting of discrimination may become champions of fair and just treatment. Health professionals who have been patients themselves can become highly sensitized to patients' rights. The values we hold as individuals and as groups are inseparable from the continual changing experiences of our lives. Much of our experience is vicarious; we learn by watching and listening to other people. What others have experienced or are experiencing are powerful influences in ordering our personal values.

Each of us has a value system that is unique. Nonetheless, our individual values originate from the core values of our culture. Some social scientists have suggested that these core values reflect a particular culture's orientation to five recurring

JOHN G. BRUHN • School of Allied Health Sciences, University of Texas Medical Branch, Galveston, Texas 77550-2782.

human problems: human nature, the environment, time, activity, and human relationships.[1] Our culture offers a variety of positions on these issues that can affect one's practice as a clinician. For example, ignoring a person's feelings of privacy or being insensitive to his or her religious beliefs, not being considerate of a person's reservations about confidentiality and informed consent, or disagreeing about how much of a person's welfare check should be allocated to health care, can affect the type of relationship that can be established between a client and helper.

Our culture values time highly, for example, not wasting time, being on time, and so forth. Therefore, clients who may be chronically late for appointments, miss appointments without canceling, show up for an appointment on the wrong day, often elicit the frustration and anger of helpers who equate time with money. In addition, some clients may find it difficult to project their activities into the future and hence seem overly concerned with their present life situation. This may create problems for helpers who take a long-range, preventive attitude.

Our culture also influences the way we interact with others. Competition is highly valued among many health professionals because competition has been necessary in their own professional advancement. Therefore, clients who may lack initiative, seem overly dependent, or express hopelessness and despair may lead helpers to expend less effort in helping them, for in their view, such clients lack the necessary motivation.

Discovering what, in fact, we do value is an important exercise. The values clarification approach can assist professionals and clients alike in dealing with an array of attitudes and emotions. Values clarification can help to identify conflict areas; isolate, evaluate, and choose alternatives; and set goals. Values clarification alone is inadequate to help us determine what to value or how to behave. It does not provide a basis for value selection or for moral choice. Values clarification does, however, *describe* the value process. It is useful in illuminating what we actually do value and, thus, can help to initiate a critical analysis of those values.

The process of "helping" involves confronting one's values. Often there is a gap between what patients or clients value and what the helper views as important, or there is a direct clash between clients' goals and practitioners' values and culture. Clinical sociologists need to have a good understanding of their own values before they can understand the value systems of others. Hoff has pointed out that it is important for the helper to "attempt to understand" the patient or client and "to make the patient or client feel understood."[2] This entails removing barriers to communication such as unwarranted assumptions and double messages that are value driven. We have personal and professional codes of ethics that spell out certain limits or boundaries for what constitutes acceptable and unacceptable behavior. The codes of ethics of professional organizations establish the norms by which the behavior of its members will be judged. In this sense, codes of ethics set out "ideal behavior," which all subscribers should aspire to emulate.

MODELS OF A HELPING RELATIONSHIP

A relationship involves the joint participation between two social entities, such as two persons, a person and a group, or a person and an organization. A relationship involves some degree of interaction over an extended period of time. The interaction is mutually based in that each participant takes the other's behavior into account. However, this mutuality does not necessarily imply cooperation. Relationships can be classified as formal or personal. Formal helping relationships present several challenges. One is the establishment of trust between helper and client. Trust is established by technical proficiency and interpersonal sensitivity and concern. Once trust is established, the second challenge is to elicit relevant information. A third challenge is to understand the information (verbal and nonverbal) a patient or client is giving. A fourth challenge is to explain the treatment or the intervention and negotiate with the patient or client how he or she will work with the helper in achieving a satisfactory outcome. The degree to which these four challenges are met will determine the "power" of the relationship. Indeed, the quality of the relationship is directly related to patient or client satisfaction.[3]

Szasz and Hollender have proposed three basic models of the relationship between a patient and a physician.[4] They are applicable to relationships between clinical sociologists and their patients or clients. The *active–passive* model is one in which the helper establishes the format, content, and outcome of the interaction, and the patient or client responds to the cues and provides the information requested by the helper. A second model is that of *guidance cooperation* in which the helper facilitates or guides the interaction and the patient or client cooperatively follows along. In this model, the helper is less directive and less active. A third model is that of *mutual participation*. This is the ideal type of interaction in which both helper and patient or client work together to achieve a mutually satisfactory outcome.

ROLES AND NORMS

The central issue in the professional–client relationship is the allocation of responsibility and authority in decision making. Ethical models are, in effect, models of different distributions of authority and responsibility in decision making. The professional–client relationship can be viewed as one in which the client has the most authority and responsibility. The professional is the client's employee, as in the case of a consultant or advocate, or the relationship can vary from one in which the professional and client are equals, as in a partnership, to one in which the professional, in different degrees, has the primary role, such as in counseling and therapy. Bayles has described the obligations of professionals to clients in these different situations.[5]

The appropriate ethical conception of the professional–client relationship is one that allows clients freedom to determine how their lives are affected by their ability to make decisions. As clients have less knowledge about the subject matter for which the professional is engaged, the professional must assume more responsibility for formulating plans, presenting their advantages and disadvantages, and making recommendations. A professional's responsibilities to the client increase as a client's knowledge and capacity to understand lessen.[5]

The models of the client role and the professional–client relationship examined so far focus on the traditional dyadic relationship. Although this might be the most common pattern of interaction, there are a variety of service delivery systems that reflect different models of the professional–client relationship. These include the team approach.[6] The clinical sociologist working in universities, large hospitals, neighborhood health centers, or health maintenance organizations will be most familiar with this approach.

Ducanis and Golin[7] note several positive effects of the team approach. The patient's or client's welfare rests with a number of professionals, decreasing the client's dependence on any one of them and lessening the individual professional's personal responsibility for the client. Clients may be given more responsibility for their own care and be expected to play a more active role in decision making. When the value of client self-determination is the primary consideration in clinical decisions, the ethical principle of autonomy is predominate. The principle of autonomy requires respect for the freedom of self-determination of those affected directly by a decision. The exercise of personal autonomy involves two levels: (1) agency, the freedom to decide among all the options available, and (2) action, the freedom to carry out the course of action that is chosen. Freedom of action is protected by formal consent requirements. Client agency allows clients to participate fully and freely in determinations about their care. This entails access to information about one's condition and options, as well as freedom from coercion.[8]

It is sometimes assumed that the team approach will more likely involve the client's family and extended social network. However, sometimes, in exchanging the collective wisdom of team members, the client's feelings are forgotten. This can be the case, for example, when considering the institutionalization of a client or patient. On the other hand, regard for autonomy can produce clearly different judgments among team members. For example, a client may have committed a crime, or may be pursuing a lifestyle that is illegal, or may not be assuming social and financial responsibility for a large number of illegitimate children, and the client's primary helper may differ with other team members about the client's disposition and what is the best disposition for the community and society at large.

The team approach connotes active participation by both client and helper, enhances client's self-respect and increases motivation. More recently, legislation has specified the participation of clients and family members in treatment and educational planning. For example, individualized written rehabilitation programs require the signature of the client receiving services from state–federal rehabilitation programs. Similarly, Public Law 94-142 requires parental approval of a child's individualized educational program if the child is receiving special education services.

The idea that clients can serve as comanagers in treatment and rehabilitation is not new. Psychotherapists and counselors have traditionally tended to emphasize the need to develop a therapeutic relationship in which the client assumes a major responsibility for treatment and plays an active role. Family therapy and group therapy also reflect departures from the asymmetrical dyad. Reichman refers to comanagement as a "teaching relationship" between professional and client.[9] For the team member, the more active role of the client may be a mixed blessing. The client's participation in team meetings may call for adjustments that may be difficult for some members, team interactions may become more formal, inhibited, and reports abbreviated. In some cases, team conferences may become a formality with the real decisions made outside of the team meeting.

It is sometimes assumed that the quality of care may be better and the prevention of problems more effective with an interdisciplinary team. It should be emphasized that whatever the role of a particular client vis-à-vis the professionals on the team, the client remains the major focus of the team's efforts. The problems presented by the client define what the team is to do and who is to do it. The client is the reason for the existence of the team. There are several examples where clinical sociologists can work with other team members (or disciplines), such as family systems therapy, family network therapy, system consultation, patient or client education groups, consultation with natural helping networks and self-help groups.[10]

CULTURAL SENSITIVITIES

William James quoted a carpenter friend as having said, "There is very little difference between one man and another, but what little there is, is very important." Some helpers come from environments that are too predictable and have life experiences that are too limited to have the ability to understand and empathize with persons whose backgrounds are different than their own. We like to think, and hope, that through education, cultural narrowness can be broadened, but this is not always true. It is not uncommon to hear professionals complain that ethnic minorities are unresponsive to professional intervention because of their lack of motivation.[11] But it may not be lack of motivation; the professional's advice may be at odds with the client's cultural values and standards. Clinical practitioners need to be prepared to respond to the needs of social, ethnic, and cultural groups whose social, psychological, and behavioral problems are accentuated by economic hardship, discrimination, and environmental stress (e.g., persons with AIDS, drug addicts, sexual deviations, etc.). There is a need to adapt techniques and interventions to be applicable to culturally diverse clients. There is also a need to be aware of different value orientations of clients from different countries. Sensitivities are not limited to culture or ethnicity. Indeed, sex, age, religion, socioeconomic status, political views, lifestyle, and geographic region can all impact on the values, beliefs, and actions of both client and practitioner.[12]

Ethical issues arise with respect to these sensitivities in that most professional codes of ethics propose that individuals have the right to respect and dignity without prejudice, the right to self-direction and self-development, and the right to choice and responsibility.

There have been numerous attempts to define ethical guidelines for cross-cultural situations, but most guidelines remain broad and directed to the preparation of counselors and counseling practice. Helpers like to think they are not biased, yet stereotyped beliefs can affect some of our assumptions, such as those relating to self-disclosure, assertiveness, self-actualization and trust, nonverbal behavior, and directness.[13] With respect to self-disclosure, it cannot be assumed that clients will be ready to talk about intimate personal issues. It cannot be assumed that clients are better off if they behave in assertive ways. An assumption that the individual should become a fully functioning person may not be realistic if such behavior has an impact on significant people in the person's life. Some cultural expressions related to personal space, eye contact, handshaking, time, dress, may be misinterpreted depending upon whether Eastern, Oriental, or Western, Anglo values are applied. In the West, we value directness. Lack of assertiveness that, in the East, might be interpreted as a sign of respect, in the West, could be assumed to indicate lack of interest or motivation.

During a counseling staff meeting, a white, male colleague said to the group: "Based on my years of experience, I've found that I'm color blind. I do the same things to all clients with the same results. This whole business of minority counseling is a camouflage for the real issues. Some counselors just don't have it." Although one would hope that such a statement would be rare, it points out the need for clinical practitioners to be adaptable, sensitive, changing persons.

SELF-DISCLOSURE OF PROFESSIONAL AND CLIENT

Self-disclosure is a social phenomenon that involves four elements: a person, a target, a relationship, and a situation. Self-disclosure is closely related to the purpose and types of professional–client relationships previously discussed. The purpose and types of professional–client relationships will determine the approach to self-disclosure used by the professional and the response by the client. For example, when the purpose of an intervention is to seek general information, the professional will take an active, probing approach toward the client. When the purpose of an intervention is to elicit specific information, a structured approach is often used. When the purpose of an intervention is disclosure, a reflective, reciprocal approach, which is the most likely of these approaches to build rapport, can be used. Client responsiveness to self-disclosure will vary with situations. For example, it has been found that high disclosers are attracted to group therapy situations. Disclosure may also change with changes in life situations and personal development.[13]

Many counselors struggle with the issue of how much self-disclosure to clients is appropriate. Van Hoose and Kottler admit that self-disclosure by the counselor or therapist has many values, but they caution that there is a fine distinction between appropriate, timely self-disclosure and self-disclosure that serves the counselor's own needs.[14] Self-disclosures on the part of the counselor need not be excessive. Facilitative disclosure is hard to learn, but it can enhance the therapeutic process. If some counselors go to the extreme of denying their professional role in order to be seen as friendly and human, some go to the opposite extreme. Professional aloofness may stem from the unrealistic expectations that some counselors have concerning their roles.[11]

Kottler discusses risks to therapists, their vulnerabilities and pressures to perform.[15] He notes that self-disclosure easily can be abused under the guise of being helpful.

Self-disclosure, as an ethical issue, is related to client dependence. Counselors can encourage dependence on the part of their clients for many reasons. Stensrud and Stensrud observe that counseling can be hazardous to health, for it can teach people to be powerless instead of teaching them to trust themselves.[16] Ethical guidelines of the American Association of Counseling and Development warn against creating dependency.

PRIVILEGED COMMUNICATION AND CONFIDENTIALITY

Privileged communication is a legal right, granted to certain professionals, not to testify in a court of law regarding confidential information obtained in their professional relationship. Confidentiality, on the other hand, has most often been described as an ethical decision not to reveal what is learned in the professional relationship.

Confidentiality has an important ethical meaning for counselors. Chase wrote, "The right to privacy is basic not only in maintaining a democracy, but also in preserving human dignity."[17] Counselors always have an ethical obligation to maintain a client's confidentiality unless the client or others are in danger, or unless there is a legal requirement to testify in a court of law. The Ethical Standards of Sociological Practitioners are shown in Appendix A. Clinical sociologists are bound to maintain confidentiality unless their client or others are in danger, or the client or the client's legal representative has given consent for disclosure.[18]

Privileged communication originated in common law through customs and rulings of the court, but it has been expanded through legislative bodies. Common law originally allowed privileged communication in only two relationships: husband–wife and attorney–client. Counselors in a number of states have been granted privileged communication by statutes. In the absence of state legislation, counselors can probably be required to testify in court about information obtained in the counseling relationship.[18] Privileged communication exists for clients, not counselors. Thus clients can waive their rights. Privileged communication developed because of the need for justice and the individual's need for privacy. Some relationships are so valuable that state laws have exempted certain professionals, such as attorneys, priests, physicians, and psychologists, from testifying about those relationships.

MANIPULATION OF BEHAVIOR

Manipulation is also of ethical concern to practitioners of behavior change. The production of change may meet the momentary needs of the client—whether it be an individual, an organization, or a community—yet its long-range consequences and its effects on other units of the system of which this client is a part may be less constructive. Kelman discusses the basic dilemma of freedom of choice as a fundamental value and manipulation of the behavior of others as a violation of their humanity.[19] He examines three roles involving social science knowledge about behavior change, those of the practitioner, the applied researcher, and the basic researcher.

Practitioners must remain alert to the possibility of imposing their own values on clients. Similar situations hold for a group leader or facilitator. Applied group dynamics, human relations skills, or group process sensitivity are designed to involve the group in decision making and to foster individual self-expression, yet possibilities for manipulation abound. A skillful leader or facilitator may be able not only to manipulate the group into making the decision that the facilitator desires but also to create the feeling that this decision reflects the will of the group arrived at through a democratic process. A further problem occurs when the group leader is training others in human relations skills. Typically, group members are members of organizations where they will apply the skills being learned. The group leader, therefore, is, in a sense, improving the group member's ability to manipulate others in the organization the member represents.[19] Kelman sets out three steps to mitigate the manipulative aspects of behavior change. These, in their general form, involve (1) increasing our own and others' active awareness of the manipulative aspects of our work and the ethical ambiguities inherent therein; (2) deliberately building protection against manipulation or resistance to it into the processes we use or study; and (3) setting the enhancement of freedom of choice as a central positive good for our practice and research.[19]

RIGHTS OF CLIENTS AND PRACTITIONERS

Various meanings are attached to a *right*. Thomas Hobbes associated a right with a liberty. In this view, to say that individuals have a right to do something means that they are free to do it. Another meaning of "right" connects it with the force of law. In this view, right is permission to do something that is secured and protected by law. Still other definitions associate right with duty. A duty is something one is obliged to perform. Others associate a right with conditional duty—duty that binds only on the condition that the beneficiary chooses to have it exercised. There is something to recommend in each of these interpretations of the meaning of a right to heath care. These definitions suggest three basic characteristics inherent in the concept of *right*.[20] The first characteristic of a right is that it is permissive of its possessor. For example, patients have a right to be informed about the benefits and risks of a medical procedure, but they are not required to exercise the right. Second, a right implies duty of other individuals. Although patients may or may not demand information about medical procedures, practitioners are required to provide information on request. Third, a right is, or ought to be, protected by society or secured by law to the individual. For example, the patient's right to know about the risks and benefits of a medical procedure is protected by law. Furthermore, moral rights should be protected and respected. This explains the formulation of a bill of rights for patients (See Appendix B).

The issue of rights is important to the sociological practitioner, especially in the roles of counselor, consultant, or mediator where clients may have views of "health" or what constitutes "normal" behavior that are different from those of the practitioner. For example, whereas standard height/weight tables establish the medically acceptable standards for normal weight, the definition of obesity is also a social and cultural definition.

There is always the risk of paternalism and patronizing the client under the guise of being helpful. One unsettled argument about rights has to do with individuals' responsibility for their own health. The evidence that lifestyle significantly effects health is enormous, and factors that increase health and longevity are considered health virtues. Yet, it can be argued that it is not the role of social scientists and health educators to influence people thought to be at risk for certain diseases to change their lifestyles. It is the responsibility of clinical practitioners to give clients facts and information to advise them about their options and the possible consequences for certain behaviors, as well as inform them about the limits of the practitioner's responsibility. Individuals have the power and moral responsibility to maintain their own health and well-being. There are realistic limits to an individual's power to change his or her social and physical environments. Practitioners should help clients understand these limits so that they do not withdraw from their individual responsibility, become hopeless, and attribute their problems to others and "the system."

Client self-determination sometimes conflicts with the helper's professional and social responsibility. This is especially true with problem clients. Problem clients include persons who are or who could be destructive to themselves and/or to others; those who are demanding, clinging, or uncooperative; those who are fulfilling the requirements of probation; and those who use a professional relationship to manipulate the behavior of others and who do not choose to change their personal behavior or social situation. Problem clients often seek or are referred for professional help because they are uncooperative, deviants, or exhibit behaviors that have been regarded as less than ideal, such as having problems with authority figures.

Helpers should do thorough assessment interviews at the first encounter with a potential client, before a contract is agreed upon. One of the purposes of the assessment is to determine whether the client's problem is within the helper's expertise and what the client's stated goals are. The assessment interview can help to screen out clients that may be particular problems for a helper. Certainly, as a professional–client relationship evolves, new or heretofore unexpressed issues may emerge as problems. Helpers must be aware of their limitations, should be ready to admit to the client that they have reached an impasse, and refer the client. Helpers must rely on their intuition and clinical experience in agreeing to work with clients and should not agree to work with clients who will disappoint them.

Helpers need to understand their client so that they can formulate an *optimal* approach to the client. Helpers should be aware that their own personalities influence how they interact with clients, and a particular mix may bring about a conflict, yet, we rarely speak of a "problem therapist or helper." It is apparent that a client who does not fit a helper's expectations is soon regarded as a problem. But the client may have been a problem for others also. A helper's respect for a client's self-determination must be reality based. Not all clients can be helped, and a given helper is not qualified to help all kinds of clients.

SELF-DETERMINATION

Client self-determination is an important practice ethic. When patients or clients put themselves in the hands of practitioners, they expect to receive consideration and judgment aimed at maximizing their health or social institution. The patient's relationship to the professional is largely one of voluntary dependence. As a result, the practitioner has a considerable amount of power. How much power should a practitioner exercise over a client, and how much autonomy can a client expect to retain? A Patient's Bill of Rights (Appendix B) specifically recognizes a patient's right to refuse treatment and to refuse to participate in experimentation. Some might argue that persons receiving placebos stand to benefit from them, but not all placebos are harmless. And, there are social placebos as well as medical ones. Indeed, the therapist's personality and attitude are potent therapeutic agents in the professional–client relationship.

A patient's right to information and autonomy can be interrelated, but this is not always the case. For example, whether or not children should have some control over decisions that affect them is a question of whether children are considered to be self-governing. Similarly, whether or not the poor are capable of exercising free choice depends upon what options are available to them. The institutionalized clients' rights to choose activities depends largely on what activities institutions make available to them. Patient's rights and self-determination, especially when they involve special groups such as children, the elderly, the dying, the poor, and the mentally ill, and how these rights bear on special bioethical issues such as abortion, euthanasia, human experimentation, and the allocation of resources, still are an uncharted field.

NEGOTIATING SOUND CONTRACTS

One of the main advantages of contracts is that they force the clients out of the sick role and require them to assume and specify their responsibility for their own behavior. It has been found, for example, that patients who made compliance contracts dropped out of treatment at a lower rate and maintained treatment goals to a significantly better degree than control patients.

A strategy that works particularly well to increase compliance in children is to have parents participate in establishing a behavioral contract to reinforce compliant behavior. Involving family support may also improve compliance in adult patients when combined with other methods.[22] An advantage of family involvement is that it places the reinforcement of compliance in the patient's immediate environment.

Self-determination is an important aspect of contracting. Contracting is a mutual decision-making process. In trying to contract with difficult clients, it is usually necessary to expand the client system to include family members or significant others. The client sometimes seeks goals that are beyond the expertise or resources of the practitioner. It may not be possible for the client and practitioner to enter into an agreement. Contracting may also be impossible when a client seeks an objective that violates the values of the practitioner. When there is a fundamental clash in values, the practitioner must acknowledge this conflict, inform the client, and if appropriate, give an appropriate referral.[18]

There are problematic situations in contracting that may limit the possibilities of success. Either client or practitioner may enter into a contractual agreement with hidden agendas. For example, a practitioner and client may agree to work on a particular problem they have each identified, whereas, all the time, one of them is hoping to move to some other problem. Another kind of difficulty can arise when there are several persons in the client system and/or the practitioner's system. When agreements are not known to all parties or when they are only partially disclosed, this can result in parties working against each other. Contracting should take place at the onset of a proposed relationship, and all parties should explicitly state their desires and expectations. An important principle in contracting is that conflict should not be avoided, but differences should be identified and negotiated.[21]

Some contract failure is the responsibility of the practitioner. Some practitioners are unable to contract successfully with clients because of their own perceptions of competency. They perceive themselves as having a special professional expertise and do not see any merit in bargaining with a client. These practitioners tend to impose "professional judgment" on a client. A practitioner should use professional skill to facilitate the client's participation in the contract process. A practitioner who contracts successfully is concerned about what responsibilities are shared or divided in carrying out a decision and how the client is involved in the process.

EVALUATION RESEARCH

Clinical sociologists are involved in practice situations that require questioning clients through questionnaires and surveys, direct observation of clients, and experimental manipulation through simulations, role playing, and interventions. Kelman has discussed the ethical issues surrounding these different methods.[23] The two major issues in social research, which have direct implications for participant interests and to which regulation must address itself, are public exposure and impaired capacity for decision making. The risks entailed by public exposure and, hence, the need to regulate the confidentiality of the data are a central concern in research based on questionnaires and tests, in surveys and interview studies, in studies based on records and secondary analysis, and in participant observation studies, as well as in social and organizational experiments. Impairment of participants' capacity for decision making is a central issue in laboratory experiments employing deception, in intrusive field experiments, in structured observation using hidden observers, and in disguised participant observation. The problem may also arise in social and organizational experiments and in questionnaire and test studies if people are led to believe that their participation is required, and in studies based on records and secondary analysis, if the data are used for purposes that clearly diverge from those for which consent was originally granted. Studies using unobtrusive observation of public events, by their nature, do not offer participants the opportunity for informed consent, but Kelman believes that in public situations people give tacit consent to observation of their behavior.

These ethical issues also highlight other practices of interest to clinical sociologists. Participants can be subjected to stressful or degrading experiments in simulations. They may experience a certain degree of discomfort arising from the nature of questions asked when responding to questionnaires, personal interviews, and tests. Invasion of privacy is a potential issue in structured observation, in field experiments, in participant observation, and in studies based on unobtrusive observation. Respondents' control over their self-presentation is also reduced by the use of indirect or projective items in questionnaires and by the dynamics of the interaction process in many interview situations. Similarly, there are a variety of ways in which participants' choices may be restricted, especially when they are excluded from the process of selecting options, in studies of secondary analysis, and in participant observation studies.

Clinical sociologists share many of the problems faced by other practitioners, such as physicians and clergy.[24] The only values that are supposed to influence a clinical practitioner are truth, objectivity, and the open distribution of knowledge.[25] Social control, with respect to the harmful effects of social research, must be exercised through the public policy process. In debating these issues, the potential harms of social research have to be seen in the context of other societal processes that contribute to the erosion of trust, invasion of privacy, spread of manipulation, and perpetuation of inequity.[23]

THE CLINICAL SOCIOLOGIST AS AN EXPERT WITNESS

Sociologists and clinical sociologists are not commonly called upon to testify in court. Even Thornton and Voight point out, "testifying in court immediately comes to mind as the most frequent consulting activity of criminologists. . . yet, the small amount of research on this subject suggests that most academic criminologists have never served in this capacity."[26] Depending on the jurisdiction of a case and the idiosyncrasies of judges and attorneys, the process of becoming qualified as an expert witness is quite variable. In general, admissibility of expert testimony requires that the court decide whether or not expert testimony can assist in understanding the evidence, and the court must determine if the expert witness is qualified to give the testimony sought. Witnesses can be qualified as experts based on special knowledge, skill, experience, education, or a combination of these factors. If one becomes qualified as an expert witness, rules of evidence must be followed in presenting testimony. Rules vary from state to state and in federal courts. There are no standards for clinical sociologists as expert witnesses, so the standards of the American Psychological Association were adapted by the author for clinical sociologists (See Appendixes C and D).

Attorneys often pick experts who are not the most qualified but who will support their client's case and perhaps conceal the case's weaknesses. The result may be a battle of experts. One area in which court-appointed experts are used extensively is in juvenile court. This is particularly true of judges who follow a social service philosophy rather than a legal philosophy. The expert gives testimony, in reality to the judge, on the key historical and contemporary elements of the case under question. In most cases, the expert witness must give a deposition. The way in which information from an expert witness is used may present moral or ethical dilemmas for the clinical sociologist. These concerns must be dealt with on an individual basis, given the circumstances of each case. Indeed, the clinical sociologist may want to resolve these dilemmas before accepting a job as an expert witness.

PROFESSIONAL ACCOUNTABILITY

Although there are many possible impediments to being an effective clinical sociologist, maintaining currency in skills and knowledge is of great importance. Professional competence is monitored through the credentialing process of a professional organization. Most professional organizations, especially those involving clinical knowledge and skills, require members to keep current in their professions by proving attendance at a minimum number of continuing education activities over a specified period of time. Keeping current is an ethical responsibility practitioners have to both their profession and clients.

The risk of burnout is particularly high for clinical sociologists, other counselors, and human service workers. Unpredictable or ambiguous outcomes, lack of peer support, difficult or large client loads, stress, lack of control over working conditions, unrealistic performance expectations, and other factors can contribute to burnout. Once burnout occurs, there are two possible approaches: change or modify one's environment or change or modify one's own response to the environment. Practitioners, especially those engaged in therapy or counseling, need to take time for themselves and their emotional renewal.

Kottler has noted the hardships of clinical practice and discusses the need for practitioners to engage in creative outlets and personal growth as ways to counteract boredom and burnout.[15] Professional boards, which grant licenses to practitioners, have an obligation to monitor the quality of service provided and the competency of the practitioners. Medical practice laws, for example, mention unethical conduct as grounds for disciplinary proceedings, but there is wide variation in the laws, regulations, and policies. The lack of enumeration of professional incompetence in the laws has long been a weapon of defense attorneys who have used it to acquit practitioners who are their clients. One of the most glaring faults of the whole system of professional accountability is the inadequate reporting of disciplinary procedures. Although it should be the responsibility of each profession to police its own ranks, unless all clinical practitioners work together to improve their methods, professional accountability will remain a highly individual matter. Thus an ethical responsibility of practitioners is to help their discipline police itself.

MALPRACTICE

Malpractice is the opposite of acting in good faith. It is defined as the failure, through ignorance or negligence, to render proper service, resulting in injury or loss to the client. Professional negligence consists of departing from usual practice or not exercising due care. Violations of confidentiality and sexual misconduct have received the greatest attention in the literature as grounds for malpractice suits. In order to be liable, clinical practitioners must violate client confidentiality under those circumstances mandated by ethical guidelines or by state laws. Other frequent causes of malpractice actions against human service professionals include a countersuit for fee collection; abandonment; misrepresenting one's professional training and skills; the failure to refer a client when a person needs intervention that is beyond the practitioner's level of competence; the failure to consult; unethical research practices; failure to keep adequate records; and failure to provide informed consent.[18] In recent cases, counselors have been held liable for damages when poor advice was given. If clients rely on the advice given by a professional and suffer damages as a result, they can initiate civil action. One of the best ways to protect oneself from becoming embroiled in malpractice actions is by taking the preventive measure of acting within the scope of one's competence.

NEW ETHICAL ISSUES

Besides consulting physicians for less serious conditions, patients now consult them for conditions that were previously considered unsuited to medical treatment. Several observers have noted a historical trend toward reclassifying deviant and undesirable forms of behavior as disease, rather than crimes or religious transgressions.[27] Examples of this medicalization of behavior include alcoholism, drug addiction, child abuse, and some forms of impulsive violence. Physicians are also increasingly asked to "treat" physical conditions that are not traditional diseases— baldness, unattractive facial features, breasts that are too large or too small, fatigue, and jet lag. Crawford points out that the movement to enhance and control personal health ("healthism") is a way to mystify and channel discontent, and perhaps deviance, itself, into forms that are basically nonthreatening to the social order.[28] Just as the language of caring or help obscures the unequal power relationships of a therapeutic relationship, so the language of "healthism" and self-care, individual responsibility, and holism obscures the power relations underlying the social production of disease and discontent.[29]

Medicalization makes it possible to relieve many distressing conditions that previously could not be remedied, but it has a paradoxical side effect. It leads people to believe that more and more of their discomforts, infirmities, and impairments are curable. This creates a problem of rising expectations. The lack of cures becomes a failure of the health care system (victim blaming).[30] Studies of obesity and disfigurement illustrate this negative effect of unfulfilled expectations.

The medicalization of everyday life has implications for the practice of clinical sociology. As the norms and values surrounding "health," "wellness," and "normality" change, practitioners will have to reconsider how deviations are defined and assessed.[30] The blurring relationships between health and disease and between normality and abnormality will make it more difficult for practitioners to develop an intervention and attribute its success to a single effect. It will also be difficult for practitioners to deal solely with individual clients without the involvement of members of the client's social system. And it will increase the necessity for practitioners from different disciplines to work together for a given client to solve problems that are increasingly complex and require several different clinical skills.[32] Ethical issues surrounding treatment, intervention, and consultation will increase as consumers' expectations are raised about solutions for their problems and the amount of time, cost, and individual effort it requires to solve them.

APPENDIX A: SOCIOLOGICAL PRACTICE ASSOCIATION: ETHICAL STANDARDS OF SOCIOLOGICAL PRACTITIONERS

Adopted September, 1982; revised August, 1985; revised June, 1987;

Preamble

Clinical and applied sociologists respect the dignity and worth of the individual and honor the protection of fundamental human rights. They are committed to increasing knowledge of human behavior and of peoples' understanding of themselves and others and to the utilization of such knowledge for the promotion of human welfare. While pursuing these endeavors, they make every effort to protect the welfare of those who seek their services or of any human group, or animal(s) that may be the object of study. They use their skills only for purposes consistent with these values and do not knowingly permit their misuse by others. While demanding for themselves freedom of inquiry and communication, clinical and applied sociologists accept the responsibility this freedom requires: competence, objectivity in the application of skills and concern for the best interests of clients, colleagues, and society in general. In the pursuit of these ideals, clinical and applied sociologists subscribe to the following principles: (1) Responsibility, (2) Competence, (3) Moral and Legal Standards, (4) Public Statements, (5) Confidentiality, (6) Welfare of the Student, Client and Research Subject, and (7) Regard for Professionals and Institutions.

Principle 1. Responsibility

In their commitment to the understanding of human behavior, clinical and applied sociologists value objectivity and integrity, and in providing services they maintain the highest standards of their profession. They accept responsibility for the consequences of their work and make every effort to insure that their services are used appropriately. The clinical or applied sociologist is committed to avoid any act or suggestion that would support or advance racism, sexism, or ageism.

   a. *As scientists*, clinical and applied sociologists accept the ultimate responsibility for selecting appropriate areas and methods most relevant to these areas. They plan their research in ways to minimize the possibility that their findings will be misleading. They provide thorough discussion of the limitations of their data and alternative explanations, especially where their work touches on social policy or might be construed to the detriment of persons in specific age, sex, ethnic, socioeconomic or other social groups. In publishing reports of their work, they never suppress disconforming data. Clinical and applied sociologists take credit only for the work they have actually done.

   Clinical and applied sociologists clarify in advance with all appropriate persons

or agencies the expectations for sharing and utilizing research data. They avoid dual relationships which may limit objectivity, whether political or monetary, so that interference with data, human participants, and milieu is kept to a minimum.

b. *As employees* of an institution or agency, clinical and applied sociologists have the responsibility of remaining alert to and attempting to moderate institutional pressures that may distort reports of clinical or applied sociological findings or impede their proper use.

c. *As teachers*, clinical and applied sociologists recognize their primary obligation to help others acquire knowledge and skill. They maintain high standards of scholarship and objectivity by presenting information fully and accurately.

d. *As practitioners*, clinical and applied sociologists know that they bear a heavy social responsibility because their recommendations and professional actions may alter the lives of others. They are alert to personal, social, organizational, financial, or political situations or pressures that might lead to misuse of their influence.

e. *As employers or supervisors*, clinical and applied sociologists provide adequate and timely evaluations to employees, trainees, students, and other whose work they supervise.

Principle 2. Competence

The maintenance of high standards of professional competence is a responsibility shared by all clinical and applied sociologists in the interest of the public and the profession as a whole. Clinical and applied sociologists recognize the boundaries of their competence and the limitations of their techniques and only provide services, use techniques, or offer opinions as professionals that meet recognized standards. Clinical and applied sociologists recognize the boundaries of their competence and the limitations of their techniques and only provide services, use techniques, or offer opinions as professionals that meet recognized standards. Clinical and applied sociologists maintain knowledge of current scientific and professional information related to the services they render.

a. *Teaching.* Clinical and applied sociologists perform their duties on the basis of careful preparation so that their instruction is accurate, current and scholarly.

b. *Professional Development.* Clinical and applied sociologists recognize the need for continuing education and are open to new procedures and changes in expectations and values over time. They recognize differences among people, such as those that may be associated with age, sex, socioeconomic, and ethnic backgrounds. Where relevant, they obtain training, experience, or counsel to assure competent services or research relating to such persons.

c. *Professional Effectiveness.* Clinical and applied sociologists recognize that their effectiveness depends in part upon their ability to maintain effective interpersonal relations, and that aberrations on their part may interfere with their abilities. They refrain from undertaking any activity in which their personal problems are likely to lead to inadequate professional services or harm to a client; or, if engaged in such activity when they become aware of their personal problems, they seek competent professional assistance to determine whether they should suspend, terminate or limit the scope of their professional and/or scientific activities.

Principle 3. Moral and Legal Standards

Clinical and applied sociologists' moral, ethical and legal standards of behavior are a personal matter to the same degree as they are for any other citizen, except as these may compromise the fulfillment of their professional responsibilities, or reduce the trust in clinical or applied sociology or clinical or applied sociologists held by the general public. Regarding their own behavior, clinical and applied sociologists should be aware of the prevailing community standards and the possible impact upon the quality of professional services provided by their conformity to or deviation from these standards.

a. *As teachers*, clinical and applied sociologists are aware of the diverse backgrounds of students and, when dealing with topics that may give offense, treat the material objectively and present it in a manner for which the student is prepared.

b. *As employees*, clinical and applied sociologists refuse to participate in practices inconsistent with legal, moral and ethical standards regarding the treatment of employees or of the public. For example, clinical and applied sociologists will not condone practices that are inhumane or that result in illegal or otherwise unjustifiable discrimination on the basis of race, age, sex, religion, national origin, sexual orientation or disability in hiring, promotion or training.

c. *As practitioners*, clinical and applied sociologists avoid any action that will violate or diminish the legal and civil rights of clients or of others who may be affected by their actions.

d. *Both as practitioners and researchers*, clinical and applied sociologists remain abreast of relevant federal, state, local and agency regulations and Association standards of practice concerning the conduct of their practice or of their research. They are concerned with developing such legal and quasi-legal regulations as best serve the public interest and in changing such existing regulations as are not beneficial to the interest of the public.

Principle 4. Public Statements

Public statements, announcements of services, and promotional activities of clinical and applied sociologists serve the purpose of providing sufficient information to aid the consumer public in making informed judgments and choices. Clinical and applied sociologists represent accurately and completely their professional qualifications, affiliations and functions, as well as those of the institutions or organizations with which they or the statements may be associated. In public statements, providing sociological information or professional opinions or providing information about the availability of sociological products and services, clinical and applied sociologists take full account of the limits and uncertainties of present sociological knowledge and techniques.

a. *Announcement of Professional Services.* Normally, such announcements are limited to name, academic degrees, credentials, address and telephone number and, at the individual practitioner's discretion, an appropriate brief listing of the types of services offered, and fee information. Such statements are descriptive of services provided but not evaluative. They do not claim uniqueness of skills or methods unless determined by acceptable and public scientific evidence.

b. In announcing the availability of clinical and applied sociological services or products, clinical or applied sociologists do not display any affiliations with an organization in a manner that falsely implies the sponsorship or certification of that organization. In particular and for example, clinical and applied sociologists do not offer SPA membership as evidence of qualification. They do not name their employer or professional association unless the services are in fact to be provided by or under the responsible, direct supervision and continuing control of such organizations or agencies.

c. Announcements or training activities give a clear statement of purpose and the nature of the experiences to be provided. The education, training and experience of the clinical or applied sociologists sponsoring such activities are appropriately specified.

d. Clinical and applied sociologists associated with the development or promotion of devices, books or other products offered for commercial sale make every effort to insure that announcements and advertisements are presented in a professional, scientifically acceptable, and factually informative manner.

e. Clinical and applied sociologists do not participate as clinical or applied sociologists for personal gain in commercial announcements recommending to the general public the purchase or use of any proprietary or single-source product or service.

f. Clinical and applied sociologists who interpret the science of sociology or the services of clinical or applied sociologists to the general public accept the obligation to present the material fairly and accurately avoiding misrepresentation through sensationalism, exaggeration or superficiality. Clinical and applied sociologists are guided by the primary obligation to aid the public in forming their own informed judgments, opinions and choices.

g. As teachers, clinical and applied sociologists insure that statements in catalogs and course outlines are accurate and sufficient, particularly in terms of subject matter to be covered, bases for evaluating progress, and nature of course experiences. Announcements or brochures describing workshops, seminars, or other educational programs accurately represent intended audience and eligibility requirements, educational objectives, and nature of the material to be covered, as well as the education, training and experience of the clinical or applied sociologists presenting the programs, and in which clinical services or other professional services are offered as an inducement make clear the nature of the services, as well as the costs and other obligations to be accepted by the human participants in the research.

h. Clinical and applied sociologists accept the obligation to correct others who represent the clinical and applied sociologist's professional qualifications or association with products or services in a manner incompatible with these guidelines.

Principle 5. Confidentiality

Safeguarding information about an individual or group that has been obtained by the clinical or applied sociologist in the course of teaching, practice, or research, is a primary obligation of the sociologist. Such information is not communicated to others unless certain important conditions are met.

a. Information received in confidence is revealed only after most careful deliberation and when there is clear and imminent danger to an individual or to society, and then only to appropriate professional workers or public authorities.

b. Information obtained in clinical or consulting relationships, or evaluative data concerning children, students, employees, and others are discussed only for professional purposes and only with persons clearly concerned with the case. Written and oral reports present only data germane to the purposes of the evaluation and every effort is made to avoid undue invasion of privacy.

c. Confidential materials may be used in classroom teaching and writing only when the identity of the person involved is adequately disguised.

d. The confidentiality of professional communications about individuals is maintained. Only when the originator and other persons involved give their express permission is a confidential professional communication shown to the individual concerned. The clinical or applied sociologist is responsible for informing the client of the limits of the confidentiality.

e. Where research data are being made public, the clinical or applied sociologist assumes responsibility for protecting the privacy of the subjects involved if confidentiality has been promised or called for by the nature of the research.

Principle 6. Welfare of the Student, Client and Research Participant

Clinical and applied sociologists respect the integrity and protect the welfare of the people and groups with whom they work. When there is a conflict of interest between the client and the clinical or applied sociologist's employing institution, clinical and applied sociologists clarify the nature and direction of their loyalties and responsibilities and keep all parties informed of their commitments. Clinical and applied sociologists inform consumers as to the purpose and nature of evaluation, treatment, educational or training procedures and they freely acknowledge that clients, students or participants in research have freedom of choice with regard to participation.

a. Clinical and applied sociologists are continually cognizant of their own needs and of their inherently powerful position vis-à-vis clients, students and research participants, in order to avoid exploiting their trust and dependency. Clinical and applied sociologists make every effort to avoid dual relationships with clients and/or relationships which might impair their professional judgment. Examples of such dual relationships include treating employees, supervisors, close friends or relatives. Special care is taken to insure that clients, students and research participants are not exploited in any manner, e.g., sexually, politically, economically or socially.

b. Where demands of an organization on clinical or applied sociologists go beyond reasonable conditions of employment, clinical and applied sociologists recognize possible conflicts of interest that may arise. When such conflicts occur, clinical and applied sociologists clarify the nature of the conflict and inform all parties of the nature and direction of the loyalties and responsibilities involved.

c. When acting as a supervisor, trainer, researcher, or employer, clinical and applied sociologists accord informed choice, confidentiality, due process, and protection from physical and mental harm to their subordinates in such relationships.

d. Financial arrangements in professional practice are in accord with professional standards that safeguard the best interests of the client and that are clearly understood by the client in advance of billing. Clinical and applied sociologists are responsible for assisting clients in finding needed services in those instances where payment of the usual fee would be a hardship. No commission, rebate, or other form of remuneration may be given or received for referral of clients for professional services, whether by an individual or by an agency. Clinical and applied sociologists willingly contribute a portion of their services to work for which they receive little or no financial return.

e. The clinical or applied sociologist attempts to terminate a clinical or consulting relationship when it is reasonably clear that the consumer is not benefiting from it. Clinical and applied sociologists who find that their services are being used by employers in a way that is not beneficial to the participants or to employees who may be affected, or to significant others, have the responsibility to make their observations known to the parties involved and to propose modification or termination of the engagement.

Principle 7. Relationships with Professionals and Institutions

Clinical and applied sociologists act with due regard for the needs, special competencies and obligations of their colleagues in sociology, other professions, and the institutions or organizations with which they are associated. Special care is taken to insure that colleagues are not exploited in any manner, e.g., sexually, politically, economically, emotionally or socially.

a. Clinical and applied sociologists understand the areas of competence of related professions, and make full use of all the professional, technical, and administrative resources that best serve the interest of consumers. The absence of formal relationships with other professional workers does not relieve clinical or applied sociologists from the responsibility of securing for their clients the best possible professional service, nor does it relieve them from the exercise of foresight, diligence, and tact in obtaining the complimentary or alternative assistance needed by clients.

b. Clinical and applied sociologists respect other professional groups and cooperate with members of such groups.

c. Clinical and applied sociologists who employ or supervise other professionals or professionals in training accept the obligation to facilitate their further professional development by providing suitable working conditions, consultation and experience opportunities.

d. As employees of organizations providing clinical or applied sociological services, or as independent clinical or applied sociologists serving clients in an organizational context, clinical and applied sociologists seek to support the integrity, reputation and proprietary rights of the host organization. When it is judged necessary in a client's interest to question the organization's programs or policies, clinical and applied sociologists attempt to affect change by constructive action within the organization before disclosing confidential information acquired in their professional roles.

e. In the pursuit of research, clinical and applied sociologists give sponsoring agencies, host institutions, and publication channels the same respect and opportunity for giving informed consent that they accord to individual research participants. They are aware of their obligation to future research workers and insure that host institutions are given adequate information about the research and proper acknowledgement of their contributions.

f. Publication credit is assigned to all those who have contributed to a publication in proportion to their contributions. Major contributions of a professional character made by several persons to a common project are recognized by joint authorship, with the researcher or author who made the principle contribution identified and listed first. Minor contributions of a professional character, extensive clerical or similar nonprofessional assistance, and other minor contributions are acknowledged in footnotes or in an introductory statement. Acknowledgement through specific citations is made for unpublished, as well as published material that has directly influenced the research or writing. A clinical or applied sociologist who compiles and edits material of others for publication publishes the material in the name of the originating group, if any, and with his/her own name appearing as chairperson or editor. All contributions are to be acknowledged and named.

Violations. Procedures Governing Alleged Violations of Ethical Standards

When a clinical or applied sociologist, who is a member of the Sociological Practice Association, violates ethical standards, clinical and applied sociologists who know first-hand of such activities should, if possible, attempt to rectify the situation. Failing an informal solution, clinical and applied sociologists bring such unethical activities to the attention of the Chair of the Ethics Committee. The Ethics Committee will consider the matter and the Chair of the Ethics Committee will forward the recommendation of the Committee to the Executive Board of the Sociological Practice Association for disposition.

APPENDIX B. A PATIENT'S BILL OF RIGHTS

The American Hospital Association Board of Trustees' Committee on Health Care for the Disadvantaged developed the Statement on a Patient's Bill of Rights, which was approved by the AHA House of Delegates February 6, 1973.

The American Hospital Association presents a Patient's Bill of Rights with the expectation that observance of these rights will contribute to more effective patient care and greater satisfaction for the patient, his physician, and the hospital organization. Further, the Association presents these rights in the expectation that they will be supported by the hospital on behalf of its patients, as an integral part of the healing process. It is recognized that a personal relationship between the physician and the patient is essential for the provision of proper medical care. The traditional physician–patient relationship takes on a new dimension when care is rendered within an organizational structure. Legal precedent has established that the institution itself also has a responsibility to the patient. It is in recognition of these factors that these rights are affirmed.

1. The patient has the right to considerate and respectful care.
2. The patient has the right to obtain from his physician complete current information concerning his diagnosis, treatment, and prognosis in terms the patient can be reasonably expected to understand. When it is not medically advisable to give such information to the patient, the information should be made available to an appropriate person in his behalf. He has the right to know, by name, the physician responsible for coordinating his care.
3. The patient has the right to receive from his physician information necessary to give informed consent prior to the start of any procedure and/or treatment. Except in emergencies, such information for informed consent should include but not necessarily be limited to the specific procedure and/or treatment, the medically significant risks involved, and the probable duration of incapacitation. Where medically significant alternatives for care or treatment exist, or when the patient requests information concerning medical alternatives, the patient has the right to such information. The patient also has the right to know the name of the person responsible for the procedures and/or treatment.
4. The patient has the right to refuse treatment to the extent permitted by law and to be informed of the medical consequences of his action.
5. The patient has the right to every consideration of his privacy concerning his own medical care program. Case discussion, consultation, examination, and treatment are confidential and should be conducted discreetly. Those not directly involved in his care must have the permission of the patient to be present.

6. The patient has the right to expect that all communications and records pertaining to his care should be treated as confidential.

7. The patient has the right to expect that within its capacity a hospital must make reasonable response to the request of a patient for services. The hospital must make reasonable response to the request of a patient for services. The hospital must provide evaluation, service, and/or referral as indicated by the urgency of the case. When medically permissible, a patient may be transferred to another facility only after he has received complete information and explanation concerning the needs for and alternatives to such a transfer. The institution to which the patient is to be transferred must first have accepted the patient for transfer.

8. The patient has the right to obtain information as to any relationship of his hospital to other health care and educational institutions insofar as his care is concerned. The patient has the right to obtain information as to the existence of any professional relationship among individuals, by name, who are treating him.

9. The patient has the right to be advised if the hospital proposes to engage in or perform human experimentation affecting his care or treatment. The patient has the right to refuse to participate in such research projects.

10. The patient has the right to expect reasonable continuity of care. He has the right to know in advance what appointment times and physicians are available and where. The patient has the right to expect that the hospital will provide a mechanism whereby he is informed by his physician or a delegate of the physician of the patient's continuing health care requirements following discharge.

11. The patient has the right to examine and receive an explanation of his bill regardless of source of payment.

12. The patient has the right to know what hospital rules and regulations apply to his conduct as a patient.

No catalog of rights can guarantee for the patient the kind of treatment he has a right to expect. A hospital has many functions to perform, including the prevention and treatment of disease, the education of both health professionals and patients, and the conduct of clinical research. All these activities must be conducted with an overriding concern for the patient, and, above all, the recognition of his dignity as a human being. Success in achieving this recognition assures success in the defense of the rights of the patient.

APPENDIX C. STANDARDS FOR THE EXPERT WITNESS

The principles regarding expert testimony were reiterated by the U.S. Court of Appeals for the Ninth Circuit in its Amaral decision.[1] The general principles regarding testimony by an expert witness can be summarized as follows:

1. *The Witness Must Be a Qualified Expert.* During qualification, the judge hears a recitation of the proffered expert's education, training, and experience and decides whether the testimony of the witness is to be admitted.

2. *The Testimony Must Be about a Proper Subject Matter.* To qualify, the testimony must present information beyond the knowledge and experience of the average jury panelist. Further, the testimony of the expert must not invade the juror's province by evaluating evidence or witnesses.

3. *The Expert's Testimony Should Be in Accordance with a Generally Accepted Explanatory Theory.* The expert's testimony is expected to meet the test put forth in *Frye v. United States* that the scientific community accepts and agrees about the reliability and

validity of devices or machines that are used to come to conclusions or opinions presented by the expert witness.[2] This principle is seldom applied to the testimony of medical experts or psychologists.[3] This principle may be applied more stringently in the future.

4. *The Probative Value of the Testimony Must Outweigh Its Prejudicial Effect.* Probative value refers to evidence that is important in determining culpability or liability. If the expert's testimony has no relationship to the issue of guilt or innocence or the issues of contention between two parties, it is generally not admissible. The judge must also ensure that the expert's testimony does not unduly or unrealistically prejudice the members of the jury or confuse the issue at hand.

References

[1]*United States v. Amaral*, 488 F.2d 1148 (9th Cir: 1973).
[2]*Frye v. United States*, 293 F. 1013 (D.C. Cir. 1923).
[3]*Coppolino v. State*, 223 So.2d 68 (Fla. App. 1968), *appeals dismissed*, 234 So.2d 120 (Fla. 1969), *cert. denied*, 399 U.S. 927 (1970).

APPENDIX D. COURTROOM STANDARDS AND BEHAVIOR

Given the paucity of specific standards regarding what clinical sociologists should and should not do in the courtroom, the following guidelines, adapted from those provided for psychologists, are proposed:

A. Quality of Work

1. The clinical sociologist should follow the principles and standards for scientific and professional conduct promulgated by the American Sociological Association and the Sociological Practice Association.

2. All procedures utilized by the clinical sociologist in the process of research review, assessment, research, or evaluation preliminary to an appearance as an expert witness should be carefully documented and available for discovery procedures, direct examination, and cross-examination.

3. Before testifying as an expert witness, the clinical sociologist should submit a written report of findings and opinions to the attorney or the court that has retained the clinical sociologist.

4. The quality of work done, the practices and procedures used, and the conclusions reached should follow the usual and customary standards of the profession.

5. The clinical sociologist who gives evidence as an expert witness should be sure that the opinions rendered are consonant with the current research base in the social and behavioral sciences.

6. Opinions and conclusions rendered by the clinical sociologist serving as an expert witness should be supported by a known and generally respected theoretical position.

B. Competence and Decorum

1. The clinical sociologist who serves as an expert witness represents sociology when appearing in court and should conduct himself or herself with such professional skill and style as to bring credit to the science and profession of sociology.

2. The clinical sociologist who represents himself or herself as an expert witness should be prepared to demonstrate education, training, and experience in the avowed area of expertise sufficient to meet the standards of sociology and the requirements of the court.

3. The clinical sociologist as expert witness should be sufficiently familiar with local, state, and federal statutes regarding the role of the expert witness in order to serve that role without confusion or errors of ignorance.

4. The clinical sociologist who serves as an expert witness should be sufficiently familiar with the case law associated with the matter at hand so that the evidence presented by the expert will be appropriate and probative.

5. The clinical sociologist who serves as an expert witness should ensure that sufficient consultation takes place before deposition or trial so that the attorney who has retained the clinical sociologist understands the extent as well as the limits of the expert's findings and opinions.

6. Where clients, patients, or defendants are involved in the matter at hand, the clinical sociologist who is to act as an expert witness should understand, and clearly state to all parties involved, the nature and limitations of privileged communication in the case.

7. When in doubt about any practice or procedure, the clinical sociologist preparing to serve as an expert witness should consult with an attorney and/or an experienced colleague for guidance, within the constraints of professional ethics and privileged communication.

8. When testifying as an expert witness, the clinical sociologist should ensure that nothing in his or her report or testimony infringes on the responsibilities or privileges of the triers of fact by rendering opinions concerning the verdict in the litigation to which the expert testimony is directed.

C. Financial Arrangements

1. The clinical sociologist should never accept a fee contingent upon the outcome of a case.

2. The fee structure and details of reimbursement should be established between the clinical sociologist and the retaining attorney during the initial consultation. The understanding should be in writing between the two parties.

3. All outstanding fees should be paid before the clinical sociologist testifies.

4. Misunderstandings or disagreements about fees should be resolved before proceeding in the case.

5. Clinical sociologists who testify regularly as expert witnesses should devote some portion of their professional time to *pro bona publica* cases.

As clinical sociologists gain experience as expert witnesses in a variety of settings, it is expected that standards will be developed and promulgated. The guidelines above are suggestions, having no special quality or status.

REFERENCES

1. Coleman, J. C. (1974). *Contemporary psychology and effective behavior*. Glenview, IL: Scott, Foresman.
2. Hoff, L. A. (1989). *People in crisis: Understanding and helping* (3rd ed.). Redwood City, CA: Addison-Wesley.

3. Hays, R., & DiMatto, M. R. (1984). Toward a more therapeutic physician–patient relationship. In S. W. Duck (Ed.), *Personal relationships 5: Repairing personal relationships* (pp. 1–20). New York: Academic Press.

4. Szasz, T. S., & Hollender, M. H. (1956). A contribution to the philosophy of medicine: The basic models of the doctor–patient relationship. *Archives of Internal Medicine, 97*, 585–592.

5. Bayles, M. (1981). *Professional ethics*. Belmont, CA: Wadsworth.

6. Wise, H., Beckhard, R., Rubin, I. & Kyte, A. L. (1974). *Making health teams work*. Cambridge, MA: Ballinger.

7. Ducanis, A. J., & Golin, A. K. (1979). *The interdisciplinary health care team*. Rockville, MD: Aspen Systems.

8. Gadow, S. (1980). Medicine, ethics, and the elderly. *The Gerontologist, 20*, 680–685.

9. Reichman, S. (1981). The physician–patient relationship: Expectations and reality. *Bulletin of the New York Academy of Medicine, 57*, 5–12.

10. Pilisuk, M., & Parks, S. H. (1986). *The healing web: Social networks and human survival*. Hanover and London: University Press of New England.

11. Corey, G., Corey, M. S., & Callanan, P. (1988). *Issues and ethics in the helping professions* (3rd ed.). Pacific Grove, CA: Brooks/Cole.

12. Henderson, G. (1979). Toward a helping relationship. In G. Henderson (Ed.), *Understanding and counseling ethnic minorities* (pp. 485–517). Springfield, IL: Charles C Thomas.

13. Chelune, G. J., & Associates (1979). *Self-disclosure*. San Francisco: Jossey-Bass.

14. Van Hoose, W. H., & Kottler, J. A. (1985). *Ethical and legal issues in counseling and psychotherapy* (2nd ed.). San Francisco: Jossey-Bass.

15. Kottler, J. A. (1986). *On being a therapist*. San Francisco: Jossey-Bass.

16. Stensrud, R., & Stensrud, K. (1981). Counseling may be hazardous to your health: How we teach people to feel powerless. *Personnel and Guidance Journal, 59*, 300–304.

17. Chase, C. (1976). Classroom testing and the right to privacy. *Phi Delta Kappan, 58*, 331–332.

18. Hummel, D. L., Talbutt, L. C., & Alexander, M. D. (1985). *Law and ethics in counseling*. New York: Van Nostrand Reinhold.

19. Kelman, H. C. (1982). Manipulation of human behavior: An ethical dilemma. In H. Rubenstein & M. H. Block (Eds.), *Things that matter: Influences of helping relationships* (pp. 89–98). New York: Macmillan.

20. Barry, V. (1982). *Moral aspects of health care*. Belmont, CA: Wadsworth.

21. Seabury, B. A. (1982). Negotiating sound contracts with clients. In H. Rubenstein & M. H. Block (Eds.), *Things that matter: Influences of helping relationships* (pp. 99–106). New York: Macmillan.

22. Levine, D. M., Green, L. W., Dees, S. G., Chwalow, J., Russell, P. & Finlay, J. (1979). Health education for hypertensive patients. *Journal of the American Medical Association, 241*, 1700–1703.

23. Kelman, H. C. (1982). Ethical issues in different social science methods. In T. L. Beauchamp, R. R. Faden, R. J. Wallace, & L. Walters (Eds.), *Ethics issues in social science research* (pp.). Baltimore, MD: Johns Hopkins University Press.

24. Bulmer, M. (1982). *Social research ethics*. New York: Holmes and Meier Publishers.

25. Diener, E., & Crandell, R. (1978). *Ethics in social and behavioral research*. Chicago: University of Chicago Press.

26. Thornton, W. E., & Voight, L. (1988). Roles and ethics of the practicing criminologist. *Clinical Sociology Review, 6*, 113–133.

27. Barsky, A. J. (1988). The paradox of health. *New England Journal of Medicine, 318*, 414–418.

28. Crawford, R. (1980). Healthism and the medicalization of everyday life. *Journal of Health Services, 10*, 365–388.

29. Edelman, M. (1974). The political language of the helping professions. *Politics and Society, 4*, 295–310.

30. Crawford, R. (1977). You are dangerous to your health: The ideology and politics of victim blaming. *Journal of Health Sciences, 7*, 663–680.

31. Bruhn, J. G. (1974). The diagnosis of normality. *Texas Reports on Biology and Medicine, 32*, 241–248.

32. Bruhn, J. G. (1987). The clinical sociologist as a health broker. *Clinical Sociology Review, 5*, 168–179.

CHAPTER 8

The Effects of Social Change on Clinical Practice

NATHAN CHURCH

INTRODUCTION

The issue of social change and clinical practice is more complicated than the title of this chapter would appear to indicate. The issues involved in conceptualizing social change reflect the essential role of sociology in the process of establishing clinical interventions in human behavior at the individual, organizational, and societal levels.

This chapter begins with some of the problems raised by considering any clinical approach within its broader social context. These considerations, it is hoped, will stimulate the reader to think about the serious nature of clinical work and the particular advantages of sociology as a basis for clinical work. In the second section, a procedure for incorporating an awareness of social change into the formulation of an intervention is presented. The final substantive part examines the effects of recent social changes on clinical practice at various levels. The chapter concludes with some remarks about the implications of social change for clinical practice and some suggestions about the future of clinical sociology.

CONCEPTUAL CONSIDERATIONS

Clinical sociology is naturally situated to deal with the role that social change plays in our efforts to intervene successfully in human behavior. This does not mean that all sociological clinicians attend to the issues of social change when they approach a problem. Sometimes they do not. When they do choose to deal with these issues, they are empowered with a perspective that is already sensitized to the dimension of human behavior that is framed for us by the nature of social change.

NATHAN CHURCH • Department of Counseling and Health Sciences, Western Washington University, Bellingham, Washington 98225.

Social change serves as one of the subfields of sociology and has since the nineteenth century when Auguste Comte made the distinction between social statics and social dynamics. Other disciplines involved with clinical endeavors do not typically embrace the issue of social change. This is a serious shortcoming of nonsociological clinical perspectives and shows the critical need for the clinical sociology perspective. The sociological clinician finds it not only interesting but essential to understand why, in the 1950s, you would be hard pressed to find a single case of anorexia nervosa, and yet, by the mid-1970s, you could not find a high school or college campus in the country that was not struggling to deal with a range of eating disorders that included not only anorexia but also bulimia, bulimarexia, and obesity. The sociological understanding of this symptom of social change is essential to the development of effective clinical interventions. To simply accept the existence of newly emerging clinical problems on the microlevel, as do most disciplines that pursue interventions on this level, is to render even a basic understanding of the etiological process of the problem on various levels impossible. It is even possible for clinicians to exacerbate emerging problems by reifying them through labeling and the development of techniques of intervention without first coming to grips with the location or generation of the problem within dynamic social structures.

The broad implications of social change for clinical interventions highlight the necessity to conduct the analysis of any problem on the three essential levels that typically characterize the interrelated foci of sociology: micro-, meso-, and macrolevels of analysis. Other disciplines and perspectives are not naturally predisposed to conduct multilevel analysis. Sociology is uniquely situated to do so (if we can successfully dislodge it from its ivory tower isolationism.) It is critically important that those of us who conduct clinical sociology primarily at the microlevel maintain a high degree of awareness and commitment to the necessity of multilevel analysis lest we simply become "another mental health profession." We must be committed to what C. Wright Mills called the sociological imagination—a vivid awareness of the relationship between personal behavior and the societal context within which it is framed.[1] The sociological clinician not only finds it interesting, but essential, to note that an individual who committed suicide in Detroit was unemployed as a result of the closing, 5 months earlier, of an automobile manufacturing plant. The plant closing is social change at a mesolevel, an aspect of change at the macrolevel, both of which are related to this human's behavior at the microlevel.

The "client" or object of analysis in sociologically oriented clinical work may, and usually does, undergo significant systematic change in a relatively short time and lives within social structures that are constantly undergoing change. Even choosing or being chosen to be a client of a sociological clinician (i.e., hiring a clinical sociologist as an organizational consultant in a manufacturing firm or being an inmate who is assigned to a clinical sociologist) is social change. As that clinical relationship is pursued, there are likely to be further aspects of social change. The formulation of the process, itself, is social change, as are later dimensions of the clinical undertaking. The acquisition of a formal label in such a process may simply hinder or help the process of positive intervention. The labeling of juvenile delinquents is one example of the potential hindrance, and the Hawthorne effect is a good example of the helpful process involved in labeling. The object of intervention can experience change for other reasons that we may be unaware of or over which we may have little or no control. For example, the inmate may become a parolee—not because of any successful intervention on the clinician's part but as a result of prison overcrowding and a court mandate to release a specific percentage of inmates to alleviate the problem. The same inmate may be the subject of derision by peers for having "fraternized with the enemy" by forming a genuine rapport with the clinical sociologist. Likewise, the manufacturing firm may be sold to, or overtaken by, a larger corporation that does not favor the use of social scientists as consultants.

We must accept the fact that intervention, itself, is social change to a degree that may vary considerably depending on how extensive it is and the levels at which it occurs. Interventions at the macro- and mesolevels will have more effect on more behavior than will changes at the microlevel. The many historical examples of the effects of single individuals upon meso- and macrolevel social structures are, typically, the exception rather than the rule.

In addition to the fact that our clinical work will effect specific social change within the particular object(s) we are analyzing, our clinical work will result in distinct social changes at the meso- and macrolevels. The very acts of clinical intervention require various levels of organization. The name *clinical sociologist* is not a stand-alone term; it comes attached to the history and organizational structure of the discipline of sociology and to the movements within it. As we practice our profession as clinical sociologists, we create social change as we create new terms, procedures, organizations, methodologies, journals, books, and everything else that goes along with a professional enterprise within the context of an advanced technological society.

As a culture, we grasp social process and social change quite well when our work involves physical technology, but we have failed to appreciate the dynamics of social technologies that we have and continually produce. Sociologists and anthropologists have developed the concept *culture lag* to highlight the inevitable delay between the introduction of a new technology and the adjustment of the culture to that new technology.

We have not been as sensitive to culture lag when it involves the introduction of new social technologies such as psychotherapy or democratic decision making. Thomas Szasz[2] and others have commented upon the medical model of dealing with some kinds of behaviors and the impact that this has had upon the law and criminal proceedings with regard to competency to stand trial; we are still struggling with this issue and will continue to do so in the foreseeable future.

Another illustrative case is presented by American Christianity and other religions that have yet to resolve the dilemma presented by their support or belief in static moral principles and their apparent belief in, and commitment to, the democratic process. The dilemma is the "obvious" contradiction between the two philosophical systems, especially because the latter is so intricately involved in a dynamic relationship with social change, particularly with respect to the development of law and social bureaucracies.

It is not my desire to demonstrate all of the features of culture lag as it relates to the introduction of these relatively new social technologies but to illustrate the fact that we do not fully appreciate their reality. We must be sensitive to social change as we consider cases. We must also be aware of the fact that we are creating social change as we establish new dimensions of our profession. We create specific social changes through the interventions we devise.

As we create new dimensions of our profession, we must be careful to avoid letting premature concepts find their way into the more static aspects of the social change we are bringing about. Premature clinical concepts, for example, Freud's "unconscious," may set a field back for decades. The seductiveness of such a concept, which may account for a difficult initial conceptualization, may deter the search for more accurate and helpful concepts. Even when more accurate and explanatory concepts are discovered, they must often wait a long while to replace their predecessors. Thus important and helpful concepts in family therapy, for example, codependency and the dynamics of being an adult child of an alcoholic, have been hindered at the developmental and the implementation levels. Some of this process is inevitable; greater awareness and attention by clinical sociologists could result in more progressive and useful intervention than is available in other perspectives and disciplines.

We are engaged in social change. Important ethical questions are raised for sociological practitioners as interventions are implemented. Clinical sociologists are uniquely situated, conceptually, to deal with the reality of effecting change. Merton's concept of *unintended consequences* has become a permanent fixture of the sociological perspective. It has alerted us to the fact that, regardless of what we intend to accomplish with a particular intervention, it may result in a number of unanticipated outcomes. This suggests at least two ethical requirements for the clinical sociologist: (1) commitment to careful observation of the consequences following the implementation of an intervention and (2) commitment to the anticipation of unintended consequences *prior* to the implementation of an intervention. The use of simulation, when possible, and the development of other mechanisms, such as peer review, should enhance our abilities to anticipate the consequences of our interventions, which should then be monitored according to a set of guidelines established for that purpose.

The foregoing are a few of the conceptual considerations that the dynamics of social change imply for clinical sociology. They are not an exhaustive list of those implications, merely an illustration of some of the issues that are involved and a demonstration of the superiority of sociology as a basis for clinical interventions when the process of social change is particularly important. It is hoped that thoughtful clinicians with expertise at the various levels of intervention will give attention to the issues raised here and contribute to a further refinement of the clinical sociological perspective.

CONTEXTUAL DETERMINATION

The first order of business for the clinical sociologist should be the analysis of social changes that have been instrumental in structuring the situation or phenomenon to be dealt with. The clinical sociologist is uniquely trained and sensitized to the social context within which events occur and phenomena exist and should be able to deal with a situation in a fashion that is least likely to participate in self-fulfilling prophecies and cultural myths. It is critical that the clinical sociologist incorporate analysis of social change and social context into the development of an intervention. Otherwise, the clinical sociologist merely becomes another mental health professional, consultant, or policy expert with nothing of particular merit to offer over others in the same area of practice. In the pages that follow, we will look at an example at each level of analysis—micro-, meso-, and macrolevels—to see how the sociological practitioner might go about the process of contextual determination.

Let us suppose that you have been commissioned to work with an adolescent with a drug abuse problem and want to determine the context of your work with this adolescent. You could begin with an assessment of the terms used to define the situation. For example, what is an adolescent? Because it does not take a long trek back into history to determine a time when the term *adolescent* was nonexistent, you can begin to isolate the social changes that resulted in its development and use. As Demos and Demos[3] noted, until 1900, the word was nonexistent in our literature. It is interesting to note that Aries[4] made a similar contribution regarding the concept of childhood as a status. The sociological clinician begins with the understanding of age status as a fluid rather than a static phenomenon. Even the term *adolescent* is insufficient as identification of this individual's age status. Is she/he an early adolescent, middle adolescent, or a late adolescent? As these age status indicators illustrate, something as individual as one's identity is wrapped up in complex features of social change at the macro- and mesolevels of analysis. Even more important to delineate are the critical features of those social changes and how and why they resulted in labels that indicate differences in age status.

In our example, Demos and Demos point to two important changes at the macrolevel: the shifting economic focus from an agrarian society to an industrial one and the interrelated process of urbanization. They also point to two significant changes at the mesolevel: the development of child labor laws and the emergence of the juvenile justice system. All of these changes, they argue, resulted in a displacement of the adolescent from the economic role of an apprenticing agrarian producer. The result, for adolescents, is a loss of meaning for existence, not merely in an emotional sense but also in an economic sense.

This point is easily overlooked by the traditional clinical professions that might respond to this adolescent's drug abuse problem. They try, therapeutically, to induce a sense of meaning, often through the technology of group process and positive peer pressure. Such programs, on the whole, are miserable failures, unable to transmit a genuine sense of meaning or alter the adolescent's position within the macro- and mesolevel structures of society. Adolescents are very preceptive with regard to this reality, even though traditional therapists often label their complaints as "acting out" or "resistance" to therapy. The obvious challenge to the clinical sociologist is to discover concrete ways in which adolescents can locate themselves within the macro- and mesolevel structures in which they exist, ways that adolescents can genuinely identify as meaningful to themselves.

The clinical sociologist would also want to discover what mesolevel structures this and other adolescents have to contend with; what definitions adolescents use to characterize school, police, youth culture phenomena, religion, and so on. It is not enough, and it is less than informative or helpful to observe that one feature of being an adolescent is the experience of "adolescent rebellion." To use W. I. Thomas's[5] concept, the sociologist would want to discover adolescents' "definition of the situation," "the situation" being their perception of the mesolevel structures that they contend with on a regular and concrete basis.

There are other questions to address in analyzing this problem: the socialization experience of this adolescent and how it differs from, or is similar to, that of adolescents who can be identified as living within different or similar cultural, subcultural, religious, racial, or regional groupings; the patterns of socialization that this adolescent's parents have carried forward from their own families of origin; the normative standards, values, and definitions of the situation that this family has established and how they have changed over time; the family's definition of the situation with regard to the adolescent's drug abuse problem; how the family would change if this adolescent's drug problem was resolved. As family therapists, like Jay Haley[6] and Salvador Minuchin,[7] have noted, the behavior of an individual within a family structure may serve some purpose for that family. A change may result in resistance by family members, regardless of their verbal indications of support for change.

The clinical sociologist then must ask some questions regarding the social changes that have resulted in the definition of the adolescent's use of marijuana as a drug abuse problem. One might ask how the adolescent's use of this substance has come to be labeled as a serious problem with the mother's long-term use of vallium and the father's history of dependence on alcohol have not been labeled as such. Is the adolescent's use of marijuana more damaging emotionally, socially, or physically than the parents' use of vallium and alcohol? Adolescents tend to be very keen in their ability to decipher the contradictions that are present in such situations. The clinician must be prepared to grasp and appreciate the reality of those contradictions and to deal with them honestly with the adolescent and the parents.

The clinical sociologist must realistically resolve these complex contextual issues or stand indistinguishable from other mental health professionals. It is hard to envision the merit of yet another brand in the mental health marketplace. If these sociological issues are addressed adequately, however, we should expect interventions that are clearly effective, well-grounded conceptually, and quite readily accepted by other clinicians.

At the mesolevel, let us suppose that, as clinical sociologists, we have been asked to consult with an institution of higher education interested in establishing an effective program for the recruitment of minority students. Before we design an intervention, we must determine the context for the problem. As with our adolescent drug problem, a good place to begin is with an analysis of the social changes that have taken place and how they define the terms we use to describe the problem. We do not have to go very far back into history to find an absence of terms such as *minorities* or *recruitment of students*. As Joyce Ladner[7] and others have pointed out, sociology, itself, has been staffed and directed by the dominant group in our society. It has, in fact, contributed to the problem of racial and ethnic discrimination.

Sociology must be cognizant of itself: a difficult and suspect enterprise under virtually any circumstance. The task of determining the social changes on the macrolevel that have resulted in the terms that we use to frame the problem is one that must be undertaken.

One the mesolevel, we must also look to the social changes within the institution that has established the framework within which the intervention is to be designed and implemented. It is important to consider not just the immediate social changes that have resulted in the desire to accomplish this end at this time, but also, if the intervention is successful, the changes that will be effected within the institution and the academic support and student service capabilities available to meet the demands that an increased minority enrollment would require.

On the microlevel, one must ask how personality dependent the desire for increased minority enrollment is. Does the push for this outcome reflect a change that has been experienced by the president or the board of the institution, or does it reflect a genuine change in the institution itself? What changes will occur in the personal lives of the minority students who enroll? Will they lose their affiliations with their families, friends, and former neighborhoods? Will they experience so much stress, anomie, and alienation in the process that their personal quality of life will suffer significantly?

I have raised these issues to point out how important an assessment of the social changes at all levels is to determining the context of the problem for which clinical sociologists design an intervention.

On the macrolevel, let us suppose that you have been asked by the U.S. State Department to be involved in the formulation of a strategy to reestablish diplomatic relations with Iran. You need to assess the social changes in both countries that have been instrumental in formulating the terms by which we make reference to the problem.

You have to conduct analysis from both the American world view and the Iranian world view. Realistically, you would have to broaden this to include a number of key players in world events, such as the United Nations, the Soviet Union, the other OPEC nations, Israel, and Islamic cultures that are Sunni rather than Shiite. It is critically important to understand the social changes in the United States that motivated our initial relationship with Iran in the modern era, especially with the Shah, and the changes that occurred within Iran that allowed for this initial relationship. To fully appreciate the complexity of the problem, you must understand the broader historical framework of social change within Iran. Then you would have to understand former U.S. policy with regard to Iran and the kind of social change that it induced within the latter. You would also have to be aware of the social change that has occurred since the breaking of diplomatic ties between the two countries.

At the mesolevel, you would have to observe the critical changes that occurred in the international relations organizations or bureaus within both countries and at the various business and economic organizations and the changes that have been important in framing the context of the problem. At the microlevel, you would have to access the changing roles of the various actors and the changing actors in the drama of relations between the two countries.

You would have to anticipate the kind of changes that would be effected within either country, should the strategy be successful. How would this alter perceptions of the arrangement of power within the Middle East? To do otherwise would relegate the clinical sociologist to the anonymous role of policy formulator.

There are many other aspects of change to be analyzed and many aspects involved in determining an adequate model and effective techniques for the resolution of our conflict with Iran. The point of this exercise is to highlight the significance of considering the dynamics of social change as they affect the development, implementation, and evaluation of an intervention to solve problems at the macrolevel of analysis.

In considering examples of problems at the micro-, meso-, and macrolevels of analysis, we have raised more problems than we have solved. This has been the very point of this exercise. Clinical sociology has something unique and valuable to offer at all levels of analysis, partly *because* it recognizes the complexities that *are* involved in these problems. What we have only touched upon here illustrates the complexities involved in the dynamics of social change. There are many issues of similar importance that sociologists are uniquely situated to analyze. One could argue that it is the very same ability of sociologists to appreciate the complexity of the intervention process that accounts for their reticence in getting directly involved with the formulation and implementation of interventions. Individuals who are directly involved in interventions become immersed in sociological issues with which they must, and do, grapple; albeit their grappling comes without the benefits of a sociological perspective and sociological knowledge. This places a heavy burden upon the individual with a sociological perspective to become more fully involved in interventions at all levels of practice.

DETERMINING THE CONTEXT OF ADVANCED TECHNOLOGICAL SOCIETY

In the foregoing examples of specific problems at different levels of analysis, we have focused our attention on the need to determine the particular sociological context for a problem in order to develop an effective intervention for its resolution. We have noted that this contextual determination requires an analysis of the way in which particular social changes have situated the problem, and we have seen how the intervention, itself, must be seen as social change. A set of primary elements of social change sets the ground for any clinical sociology situated within American or any other advanced technological society. What informs a sociologically based intervention approach is not simply the "big picture," which is presented by an awareness of macrolevel phenomena. It is a keen sense of social change and its effect on the interplay between phenomena at the macro-, meso-, and microlevels of analysis. This is where the potential of clinical sociology exists. In order to appreciate this interplay, clinical sociology must sense the way in which social change has situated advanced technological society and the dynamic nature of society as it continues to undergo change on these levels.

What follows is a sample of those elements of social change that have had, are having, and will continue to have a profound influence upon clinical practice. Changes at any level of analysis effect changes, or have implications on, other levels of analysis. However, it is easiest to specify important social changes by the level at which they *primarily* occur.

Macrolevel Changes

Beginning with the publication of Daniel Bell's book, *The Coming of Post-Industrial Society*, in 1973, sociologists and social thinkers have recognized that we have experienced sufficient change on the macrolevel to call the label of industrial society into serious question.[9] What will serve as an adequate label for contemporary society is a question that has remained a topic of discussion and debate since Bell's volume emerged. It may simply indicate that we have to be well within the parameters of an emerging set of social structures for some time before we can identify its central features sufficiently well to come up with a new label. The changes are typically incremental, and a significant mixture of old and new features clouds our ability to make clear distinctions. Until a new label can be applied, we probably are saddled with a number of *post* identifications, such as *post-industrial*, *post-modern*, *post-traditional*, and so forth. In this chapter, the term *advanced technological society* has been used. Although the author is no more committed to this term than to any number of alternatives, the term does highlight a feature of contemporary society that has been suggested throughout the chapter—the predominance of the development of new technologies, physical as well as social, over the past two or three decades. In fact, we have a general expectation of built-in obsolescence in any new technology that is developed. There has also been an attempt, in this chapter, to highlight the significance of changes in social technologies.

In addition to the emergence of a technology-based orientation on the societal level, there have been some key demographic changes. One of these is an emerging pattern, generally referred to as the "graying of America," that draws attention to the fact that, as a result of declining death rates and declining birth rates, our population has become proportionately older. Clinical sociology must be sensitive to this fact because it affects so many aspects of the quality of human life. It represents a fundamental change in the ratio of wage-earning to non-wage-earning individuals within the society. It is also well past the time of adequate planning; we are already experiencing this change. The pressure on the social security system is adequate testimony to this unfortunate fact. It is of little wonder that so many clinical sociologists already work in this area; the need for adequate models and interventions is great.

Family size has shrunk considerably during the last two to three decades. This is related to the changing age composition of the society and to serious complications within an immigrant society. The growth of the existing population is almost at replacement level, yet the population continues to grow significantly due to large-scale immigration. Incoming populations soon outstrip the growth of the existing population due to extensive immigration and the fact that immigrating populations tend to have an initially high birth rate. The social, economic, and racial problems that result are complex, especially in a society in which democratic ideals and freedom are strong inhibitors of rigid and restrictive immigration policies.

In a relatively short time, we have experienced escalating rates of divorce and a growing number of single-parent and step-parent families. This has resulted in the emergence and growth of mediation as a method that is preferable to adversarial models of achieving the dissolution of families. It is, however, far from becoming the norm. We must acknowledge the reality of a growing proportion of women and children whose socioeconomic position has suffered because of an inadequate system of child support. We also must acknowledge the fact that step-families are more likely than intact families to be prone to problems of conflict, instability, and physical and sexual abuse of children.

We have witnessed a phenomenal growth in dual-career marriages. This has resulted in massive economic changes that have, at least in part, fueled a situation in which the presence of two working spouses is no longer a matter of choice but a financial necessity. This has created greater disparity between the purchasing power of families at different income levels, particularly between that of intact families and that of single-parent families. It has also created a child care dilemma for our society.

We have seen an amazingly rapid surge in megalopolitan growth, growth in sunbelt population, and business migration patterns. This has created problems of sizable proportions for our urban areas, particularly in the sunbelt locations where growth has been much more rapid than that of other urban locations. Complex problems involving planning and zoning, air and water pollution, availability of adequate water, and transportation have emerged.

In addition to demographic changes, the role of women has changed dramatically in recent years. Women have made significant advances in educational attainment and advancement into the work force, but they are far from reaching parity with men on almost any indicator. They have gained little in high-paying executive and governmental positions and earn about two-thirds to what their male counterparts earn when performing the same job. Sexual harassment and violence against women show little sign of abating.

Our social world can be described as highly depersonalized and anonymous. This has resulted in a growing privatization that has created a large rift between our private experience and the society within which we live. Levels of political apathy and chemical abuse are high, indicating the severity of the problem.

Sweeping changes in telecommunications technology have taken place in recent years. There appears to be no end in sight for the refinement and development of entirely new technologies in computers, satellite-based communications, and available interactive digital systems, even in the form of touch-tone telephones, software, and related technologies. This has led to an information explosion that is unprecedented in history. It has changed virtually every facet of the workplace and created a new generation of computer illiterates. It has given us the ability to access enormous amounts of data. It has made our money and a lot of other things more an electronic reality than a paper reality. It has introduced some thorny security and privacy issues for all of us.

The techniques by which we survey or poll people have become extremely sophisticated. This is one area that is highly illustrative of culture lag with regard to the introduction of a social technology; for example, the impact this has had and will have on the forecasting of elections is profound. Even before the polls in parts of the country have closed, election outcomes can be projected with a high degree of accuracy. The fact that every political campaign with even a modest budget has an in-house pollster on the payroll raises some serious questions about the current and future state of the selection of our leaders and the resolution of substantive initiatives through a potential form of "high-tech follower-ship." This new technology also poses some difficult ethical and privacy issues for those involved in mass marketing and the measurement of consumer preferences.

Recent decades have seen the phenomenal growth and influence of multinational corporations. It is common knowledge that a host of countries are dwarfed by the output and power of many large multinationals. The implications for international politics have been a topic of considerable discussion by radical social thinkers since the late 1960s, but we still do not have a clear picture of the interrelationships for international politics or economics.

We have been observers of major changes in religion since the late 1960s, when a seemingly inexorable process of secularization suddenly reversed itself. The growth in religious ranks occurred where it was least expected—within fundamentalist religious groups, while many liberal denominations continued to lose strength. Charismatic elements emerged within the most formal and ritualistic religions, such as the Catholic and Episcopal churches, and religious pluralism reached totally unexpected proportions, running the gamut from Eastern religious gurus and swamis of every sort to New Age religious mysticism touting the salutary and spiritual qualities of crystals and pyramids. We are a long distance from an understanding of the basis for these changes in religion or exactly what their impact might be. We did learn, in 1980, that the growth of fundamentalism could fuel a thunderous return of the Republicans to the executive branch of government. We also saw the fundamentalists discover the use of television and, along with it, scandal and "sin."

Although this is admittedly a thumbnail sketch of macrolevel social change, it does give us an idea of the general macrolevel context for clinical sociology without making it the sole topic for a book-length treatise. Even full-length books on macrolevel issues are uniformly thematic, rather than comprehensive, giving us some indication of the enormity of the task.

Mesolevel Changes

This is the area within the contemporary world where most change is currently underway. In the United States, especially, Western society has demonstrated a tenacious grasp on inefficient bureaucratic structures for organizations, agencies, and corporations. As Naisbitt and Aburdene[10] indicate, however, the challenge both for production and the quality of the human work experience is to create new mesolevel structures that demonstrate high levels of efficiency while maintaining human dignity and worth. The Japanese have led the way, at least with regard to efficiency. There is still much to be learned and applied in this area, and clinical sociology is best situated to forge new social technologies here. It may be our greatest hope of making an impact while expanding the perspective and familiarizing society with the advantages of using sociology clinically. It is less than certain, however, that clinical sociologists fully realize the potential here. If we are to be successful in this area, it is critical that we know the context for our practice at the mesolevel as well as the macrolevel. What follows are some of the most obvious aspects of change at the mesolevel of analysis.

We have seen a change in the mentality of those who are in charge of organizations and agencies. Perhaps due to competition with Japan, leaders have focused upon the issue of accountability. Instead of simply assuming that a particular organizational structure or technique is working, they have insisted upon knowing if it is working. There has been a phenomenal growth of what social scientists would call evaluation research. It is likely that needs assessments and simulations studies and the like also will increase.

We have observed the emergence of an era of scientific management. We have seen experimentation with quality circles and worker ownership, respectively, as scientifically generated technologies to devise more effective means of management and employee motivation. The success or failure of different companies or organizations is closely watched as studies or assessments are printed in lay publications as well as in more academic business journals or newspapers.

Decided efforts have attempted to reorganize the structure of the business enterprise through what has been referred to as corporate restructuring. These have often been large-scale efforts involving huge corporate entities rather than small-scale experimental changes. These efforts have been less than scientific in nature and have usually been motivated by the panic or the fear of losing further ground to foreign competitors.

It has become accepted practice for organizations or corporations to provide in-house training programs for their employees. Some firms, like Arthur Anderson (one of the Big Eight accounting firms), have set up veritable in-house colleges. In this process, new group technologies like brainstorming, production, or problem-solving groups are presented to employees as methods to improve production or resolve specific company problems.

The introduction of computerization and robotics has just begun in the United States, although it has been in place in Japan for some time. Although the effects of this change on American business and workers are poorly understood, being pursued with considerable vigor, motivated, many would say, by panic or fear that without it we will lose even more ground to the Japanese.

Although little more than a thumbnail sketch of mesolevel changes has been offered, it is hoped that it will stimulate thinking about clinical practice in this area. Hopefully, it will also help to communicate the importance and potential of clinical sociology at the mesolevel.

Microlevel Changes

One could have started with the microlevel and worked up to the macrolevel in the foregoing analysis of social change. But it would have given the appearance that most of the identified changes emanated from changes that occurred at the microlevel. My position here is one that is distinctly sociological in that it identifies changes at the macro- and mesolevels and the impact that those changes have on life at the microlevel rather than the reverse. Particular individuals sometimes have dramatic effect on the course of social change but only in terms of how much impact they have on the macrolevel and mesolevel social structures that affects the microlevel. One could take an individualistic approach and chronicle the ways that specific individuals' lives have been affected by the course of social change. That is the grist of novels and biographies. To their credit, they give a special flavor to our genuine understanding of social change. Our task here, however, is to look at a few of the crucial changes that have occurred to phenomena that exist primarily at the microlevel. To the careful analyst, they will clearly illustrate the interplay with phenomena on the macro- and mesolevels, but they are presented here to inform the societal context of clinical practice from a microlevel perspective. They demonstrate what nonsociological practitioners typically take for granted as they deal with microlevel phenomena. It is the task of an effective clinical sociology to situate them within the dynamic interplay of social structures at other levels, thereby removing them from their reified positions within contemporary society.

When looked at from the perspective of the small minority of the population actually afflicted with a mental disorder, the use of psychopharmacology would appear to be an important, if somewhat limited shift from the widespread use of electroconvulsive shock therapy and of physical restraints to a much more humane form of treatment for the mentally ill. The widespread societal use of tranquilizers, mood elevators, antianxiety, hyperactivity, and sleep-inducing medications, however, indicates a very real change in the way in which we view and deal with emotional and behavioral problems. Often, treatment involves little more than the prescription and monitoring of the proper psychoactive medication, which may consist of little more than a general awareness that the original behavioral or emotional problem has not recurred.

Similar to psychopharmacology is the use of behavior modification techniques, particularly with the mentally retarded and with children and adolescents in rehabilitative and correctional settings. This is also true, to a lesser extent, of learning environments and early child-rearing strategies employed by educated parents.

There has been a decided reinterpretation of the freedom of individuals to make choices about their personal identity, that is, sexual preference. This is not true of all segments of the larger society, but it has largely characterized the academic, legal, and political arenas for the individual who chooses to make his or her homosexuality known. Even with the outbreak of the AIDS epidemic, this change has maintained its position. It may be doubtful that this has changed the number of people with a homosexual preference, but it certainly has changed the self-identity of people with such a sexual preference, even from the time that the psychotherapeutic community considered it a diagnosable deviation.

By the late 1970s and early 1980s, the words *anorexia* and *bulimia* were regular parts of the language of the larger culture and had, for a few years, been part of the exclusive discourse of the psychotherapeutic community. These problems were quickly identified with the pressures of the culture on a young woman's appearance and with the dysfunctionality of certain family structures and dynamics.

Although we had long been aware of the problems of alcohol abuse, we "suddenly" became aware of the consequences of growing up in a family characterized by alcoholism and the family dysfunction that it causes. In short order, groups and techniques that offered help to the "Adult Child of an Alcoholic" (ACOA) sprung up all over the country. By the mid-1980s, these concepts and techniques were part of our cultural and individual discourse.

In the late 1970s, we began to see some alarming changes in the behavior of our preadolescent and older children. Previously untouched by the changes in our society, individuals in these age groups began to commit suicide in numbers that did not exist previously. Drug addiction and alcoholism also began to take on a younger face.

By the early to mid-1970s, the evidence became clear that there was a direct link between stress and a variety of mental health and physical problems, notably, chronic heart disease. People began to find myriad ways to insulate themselves from the specter of stress. They began jogging and engaging in other forms of aerobic exercise; they tried meditation, progressive relaxation, yoga, guided imagery, biofeedback, and many other stress-reducing strategies.

Our examples of change give little more than a glimpse of the context for clinical sociologists working at the microlevel of analysis. The important thing for the sociological practitioner at the microlevel to remember is that uniquely sociological insights about individual behavior and emotions relate to an understanding of the macro- and mesolevel structures within which they ultimately occur. It is too easy to get wrapped up in the nature of individual problems and to forget their sociological context. If one looks back on the few examples that have been listed, one will see that behavioral problems are generally treated as if they had existed forever and were unrelated to larger social issues and processes. Unless clinical sociologists make a point of those sociological dynamics, they will be indistinguishable from their psychological practitioner colleagues.

CONCLUSIONS

The formal discipline of sociology suffers from the one-sidedness of an intellectual enterprise without a genuine testing ground of practice. For far too long, sociologists have deluded themselves into believing that empirical research is the testing ground of the discipline. The genuine testing ground of empirical findings that are grounded in theory is the application of those findings to real problems in the real world. Every other discipline holds itself to this difficult but ultimately reasonable standard. It is a sleight of hand maneuver or simply intellectual cowardice to propose that the mere interplay of theory and research is an adequate test of the mettle of an intellectual enterprise. I submit that the rest of the academic world and a good bit of the nonacademic world has figured this illusion for what it is. It is high time for sociology, itself, to come to grips with its accountability to its ultimate clientele. One does not have to look far to recognize the omens that portend the dismal future of a sociology that does not quickly and thoroughly rethink its raison d'être.

We have learned that the dimensions of social change involve new physical technologies and their impact on social structures. We do not fully appreciate or adequately understand many of the new social technologies.

We have seen other practitioners take as ultimately real, clinical problems that are reflections of larger social changes. Responding to a problem without a global, dynamic perspective that is uniquely available in sociology not only obfuscates our understanding of it but results in a process of reification of the problem.

We have noted the way in which our interventions are, themselves, dimensions of social change. We must isolate interventions to minimize the possibility of unintended consequences. We have an ethical obligation to measure outcomes. We must determine what kinds of simulations we can develop to anticipate the effects of our interventions and to determine the degree to which we are bound to perform them and the situations in which it is acceptable to study interventions *in vivo*. We need to create standards that we can use as "templates" for determining the level of intervention that we should design. And we need to uncover the principles of the effects of microlevel changes on meso- and macrolevel structures (as well as all of the possible permutations of each level affecting the other levels).

All of these complex and challenging ethical and professional issues will face a clinical sociology that is serious about its role in the arena of interventions. In some cases, we have the advantage of following interventionist colleagues who have trod similar paths, and we can save ourselves a few unnecessary steps. In other cases, the nature of sociologically based interventions are so unique that we will have to go alone into the uncharted territory that lies ahead.

REFERENCES

 1. Mills, C. Wright (1959). *The sociological imagination.* New York: Oxford University Press.
 2. Szasz, Thomas (1970). *Ideology and insanity.* New York: Anchor Books.
 3. Demos, John & Virginia (1973). Adolescence in historical context. In Michael Gordon (Ed.), *The American family in social-historical perspective* (pp. 209–221). New York: St. Martin's Press.
 4. Aries, Phillippe (1962). *Centuries of childhood: A social history of family life.* New York: Knopf.
 5. Thomas, W. I. (1923). *The unadjusted girl.* Boston: Little, Brown.
 6. Haley, Jay (1976). *Problem-solving therapy.* San Francisco: Jossey-Bass.
 7. Minuchin, Salvador (1974). *Families and family therapy.* Cambridge: Harvard University Press.
 8. Ladner, Joyce (1973) (Ed.). *The death of white sociology.* New York: Random House.
 9. Bell, Daniel (1973). *The coming of postindustrial society.* New York: Basic Books.
10. Naisbitt, John, & Aburdene, Patricia (1985). *Re-inventing the corporation: Transforming your job and your company for the new information society.* New York: Warner Books.

PART III

CLINICAL SOCIOLOGY IN SPECIFIC SETTINGS

CHAPTER 9

Clinical Sociology with Individuals and Families

LANCE W. ROBERTS

INTRODUCTION

Ideas have consequences and, like all objects of our attention, we can be over- or undercommitted to ideas. Sometimes over- or underidentification carries serious consequences. From a clinical sociologist's viewpoint, many of our colleagues remain undercommitted to the proposition aptly stated on a button promoting the discipline: *SOCIOLOGY is a verb, not a noun.* In short, "sociology applies." Lenski's[1] judgment, although rendered in a different context, identifies the consequences of believing otherwise: "Without such a commitment it is difficult to justify public support of sociology." Starting from the belief that sociological ideas have practical implications, this chapter's goal is to stimulate thinking regarding how a sociological orientation can contribute to counseling individuals, couples, and families.

This chapter is not intended to be a definitive statement on the place of sociology in individual, marriage, and family therapy. Clinical interventions related to helping troubled persons or groups do not constitute a scientific practice. Instead clinical assessment and intervention are more appropriately conceptualized as an art that can be scientifically informed. Accordingly, my outline of the place of sociology in clinical practice is suggestive rather than definitive. The ideas presented are offered as a stimulus to the thinking and practice of clinical sociologists. As an additional caveat, it is important to note that this chapter emphasizes the broad application of some sociological ideas to the concerns of troubled individuals, couples, and families. Clearly, it is unreasonable to undertake here a discussion of how to manage presenting problems such as grieving, sexual dysfunction, alcoholism, or separation. The task is not to present specific directives but to

LANCE W. ROBERTS • Department of Sociology, University of Manitoba, Winnipeg, Manitoba, R3T 2N2 Canada.

illustrate the plausibility of using sociological concepts and principles to help persons in need of counsel.

Within this delimited framework, the chapter begins with a brief statement of the relevance of sociology to counseling. Next the case is made for an approach to counseling that is guided by sociological themes, rather than being programmatic in character. After establishing the relevance of a thematic approach, an illustration of one such guiding theme is presented, which portrays the tension between individual autonomy and social constraint. The chapter then outlines three stages of the counseling process (intake, assessment, and intervention) and illustrates some ways sociological concepts and principles can be used at each of these stages. The intention of these sections, again, is to highlight the relevance of a sociological orientation rather than articulate its possibilities. Having argued for and exemplified sociology's relevance to the counseling enterprise, the chapter concludes with some general remarks on the connection between sociology and this area of clinical practice.

THE RELEVANCE OF SOCIOLOGY TO COUNSELING

Roger Straus[2] noted that sociological training allows us to claim the right to intervene because so many of the problems that people face are rooted in their social circumstances. For reasons that are unclear, however, sociologists have not been widely interested in directing their resources toward counseling individuals, couples, and families. The field of practice continues to be dominated by social workers, psychologists, ministers, family physicians, and psychiatrists. It is my contention that sociologists can and should play a greater role in this area of clinical practice because their orientation and training give them special intellectual resources to undertake the challenges of clinical intervention. The important resources that sociologists have are theoretical and methodological in character, some of which deserve mention.

With respect to theoretical orientation, sociology is a discipline that concentrates on units that are extremely significant, but typically neglected, by other practitioners. With few exceptions, the perspectives of both concerned clients and consulting practitioners have a psychological bias. The focus of concern is on the *character* of people and stresses their intrapersonal deficiencies. Without denying the relevance of such individual variation, it has become increasingly apparent to the therapeutic community over the last quarter century, in part because of the limitations in psychotherapeutic interventions, that attention must be given to other relevant variables, especially those that are interpersonal in character. As two psychiatrists[3] noted in reviewing various treatment approaches, the emergence of an approach emphasizing microsocial structural issues "seems to be the right treatment at the right time." Interpersonal variables that define the structure of the relationships between troubled persons are the central focus of sociology. The growing recognition of the relevance of taking social structural considerations into therapeutic account (if not our discipline) provides an excellent opportunity for sociologists to enter the field of clinical practice with individuals and groups.

Methodologically, sociology also equips us for clinical practice. The fact that sociology stresses a "scientific orientation" (however much we might argue about the specific attributes of the term *science*) means that we orient ourselves to problems in a systematic manner and emphasize the importance of empirical evidence. Even though counseling is not a scientific practice, a scientific orientation and training is a benefit to clinicians. An interest in identifying particular problems, specifying objectives to be pursued, assessing alternative means, planning interventions, and observing outcomes stands in refreshing contrast to clinical practice that too often appears based on unfounded intuition and chaotic follow-up.

Besides the broad relevance of taking a systematic and informed approach to counseling, which a scientific outlook promotes, the specific methodologies that comprise sociological training are also relevant to clinical practice. For example, our training provides us with interviewing skills that make us appreciate the art of asking questions and sensitive to the meaning of responses. We also have access to the methodologies relevant to interpreting naturalistic acts of the type clinical counselors have to cope with, as well as observational skills regarding the same. In addition, we appreciate the importance of triangulation and are skeptical of accepting words as valid indicators of deeds.

The roster of theoretical and methodological considerations that sociology has to offer clinical practice can easily be extended. The point, however, is that although sociologists take these tools for granted, they are not the stock in trade of those outside our discipline. Witness, for example, the response to the point that "the causes or nature of an individual's problem may not be clear from a study of that person alone but can often be better understood when viewed in the context of a family social system."[4] For some clinicians such an appreciation is regarded as a "whole new way of conceptualizing human problems, of understanding behavior, the development of symptoms, and their resolution."[4] There is a tendency for sociologists to assume that because we take these considerations for granted they must be commonly held by other professionals. They are not. Clinical practitioners have only recently started coming to terms with the relevance of theoretical and methodological perspectives that sociologists employ. Consequently, this time affords an excellent opportunity to enter the area of clinical practice in a way that can make a meaningful contribution to clinical development. The remaining sections of this chapter will illustrate some ways theoretical and methodological considerations from sociology can be tied to clinical practice with individuals, couples, and families.

A THEMATIC APPROACH TO SOCIOLOGICAL COUNSELING

Sociology supplies us with a set of concepts and principles that encourage the observation and interpretation of experience from a particular perspective. Our discipline is a perspective not a practice, in that its principal contribution concerns how we *think* about social experiences as opposed to a set of *technologies* for intervention. Of course, the perspective we take toward our concerns has important implications for the practical interventions we recommend; hence the justification for clinical sociology.

It is my contention that the *discipline* of sociology provides the basis for a meaningful and effective approach to helping people in need. In other words, the "knowledge" our discipline contains can serve the counseling function. For present purposes, it is important to recognize, however, that "knowledge of" social experience is distinctive from "doing something about" this experience. In this sense, knowledge is *not* power. Several kinds of connections exist between "knowing" and "doing" (Nettler, 1972),[5] ranging from informed intervention through effective but uninformed doing to useless knowledge. Sociology, as a discipline-based study, has a built-in bias that emphasizes "knowledge" over "action." We are not "social engineers" as much as we are students of society.

These considerations, among others, lead me to believe that our discipline more appropriately equips us to take a thematic, rather than programmatic, approach to counseling. Programmatic approaches to counseling emphasize "doing" in the sense that they specify a series of steps that must be taken or rules of thumb that need to be followed during the course of counseling. The counseling recipes of behavioral psychologists are examples of a programmatic orientation. By contrast, a thematic approach is more suggestive than definitive. It recognizes the intricate complexities of social experience and appreciates that no nomothetic approach can capture actual, idiographic experience. This is one of the reasons there will likely never be a "science" of counseling. A thematic orientation approaches the uncertainties inherent in giving counsel by recognizing them as conditions of therapy, rather than managing uncertainties by trying to fit all presenting problems into a preestablished schema.

A thematic approach to counseling relies on the knowledge of the discipline to sensitize us to a number of general considerations that can be applied flexibly and creatively to a range of concerns. It is my view that sociological thinking is "disciplined" (i.e., restricted) in that it emphasizes the impact of culture and group life on human conduct and attempts systematically to identify the role of these influences in a scientific manner. Others may differ in what they consider to be the salient features of the discipline, but the generic point holds—because our approach is disciplined, our perspective and our counsel are limited.

The restricted perspective of clinical sociology implies a reluctance toward developing overly programmatic intervention strategies. Models of programmatic intervention are based on specific assumptions, theories, and evidence; in short, they are discipline bound. The actual circumstances of troubled persons, couples, and families are more complex and include more considerations than any discipline selects to emphasize. Consequently, an inevitable misalignment is bound to exist between any disciplined orientation and the circumstances the client faces. Because the client experiences the risks of following our counsel (e.g., disappointment, disillusionment, iatrogenic effects), it seems reasonable to adopt an approach that is flexible enough to accommodate the complexity of the client's experiences. A thematic approach has more degrees of freedom than a programmatic one and therefore recommends itself.

The advantage of the thematic over the programmatic approach to clinical counsel extends to the relationship of clients to counselors. Clients assume that counselors "know" what they are talking about, and indeed they often do. But to recognize that counselors have more knowledge than clients about clinical matters is quite different from believing that they have complete knowledge. Nonetheless, there is a tendency for clients to overestimate what clinicians know, especially with regard to translating knowledge into action. Many clients, in other words, believe the clinician "knows the answer" to their problems, where *knows the answer* is translated to mean "can give instructions that direct action to predictable, effective outcomes." No clinician can legitimately claim such expertise or power. However, there is a tendency for programmatic strategies to perpetuate such beliefs. By contrast, thematic approaches resist such unrealistic expectations and work to empower clients by engaging them in developing more adaptive strategies. A thematic approach cannot directly or indirectly provide the answers; it suggests approaches that clients can work from with their clinicians toward living more efficiently and effectively. The following section illustrates one therapeutic theme that is sociologically informed.

AUTONOMY AND CONSTRAINT: A GUIDING THEME

By the time people seek professional counsel they typically have a biased view of their problems. This is not surprising because they have been unsuccessful in struggling to resolve their concerns, are frustrated, and have often retreated into defensive coping strategies. They are troubled individuals trying to adapt as well as their resources permit. A common bias in their perspective, which acts as an impediment to successful resolution, is that they neglect some fundamental social facts of their circumstances.

One of the most helpful sociological themes that can guide clinical practice is that everyone is *both* an autonomous actor *and* a "victim of circumstance"; in other words, we are free *and* constrained. This fundamental tenet of sociology, that we are the products and the producers of our social circumstances, is one of the first things that people lose sight of when they are troubled. The common reaction is to over-emphasize one of these social facts or the other. An illustration of each case will suffice.

Recently I saw a 35-year-old woman who dysfunctionally overestimated the degrees of freedom she had in her relationship with her adulterous husband. After a series of blatant extramarital affairs, the husband continued to live with his wife but, on investigation, expressed no intention of restricting his sexual outlets. The wife's response was to continue to believe that, if she "tried hard enough," she could "make him change." Not surprisingly, her efforts repeatedly failed, and she became more and more despondent over time, filled with self-doubt and low esteem. The more she "tried," the worse her circumstances became, which she interpreted as a deficiency in her commitment to finding and implementing a solution to her husband's conduct. This woman's pain was compounded because she overestimated the difference she could make and underestimated the circumstantial constraints beyond her control.

By contrast, another dysfunctional coping mechanism displays itself in the reverse case; namely the person who overestimates the circumstantial constraints and underestimates his or her individual autonomy. A family with two teenagers arrived for counsel because they were "stuck in a cycle of destruction." The parents and teenagers had maneuvered themselves into distinct coalitions. For two sessions, each side attributed blame to the other and complained relentlessly about the "family situation." However, no one expressed any responsibility for the family's circumstance. When probed, the teenagers ritualistically repeated that "this mess is our parents' fault"; likewise, the parents' view was that "there's nothing we can do" to change the situation. This is an example of what Berger calls "bad faith"; that is, the actors are pretending "something is necessary when in fact it is voluntary."[6] With such an orientation, this family really is "stuck," because no possibility of change is admitted as being within their control.

Repeatedly these exaggerated themes of independence *or* dependence are expressed by persons in troubled circumstances. Routinely, people overidentify themselves as either "controllers" or "controlled." These orientations are unrealistic and, consequently, acting upon them usually generates more difficulties than they resolve. One helpful sociological theme that can guide our counsel to those in need is the reiteration of an *interactionist* perspective. Such an outlook reminds us that social life is created (and thus recognizes our autonomous ability to make a difference), while at the same time recognizing the limits of such constructions (thereby recognizing our dependence). As social psychologists tell us, our social experience is analogous to a "prisoner's dilemma" in that, although we can always make choices, our fate is to some extent always in the hands of others. Clinical sociologists can use this theme in their practice, not only by making clients aware of it, but by helping them come to terms with *how much* of *what types* of freedom they possess as well as the conditions of their experience that are beyond their control.

Recognizing and developing applicable sociological themes such as that of freedom and constraint is just one way to advance a sociologically based approach to counseling. Another approach involves the recognition that counseling is itself a relatively ordered social process and that, like all orderly processes, proceeds through a set of stages. The following section divides the counseling process into three such stages and indicates how sociology might be utilized at each stage.

COUNSELING STAGES AND SOCIOLOGICAL CONTRIBUTIONS

The therapeutic process is divided into roughly three phases. Different theoretical and methodological concerns are relevant at different stages. The process begins with the issue of intake and introduction, proceeds to assessment and evaluation, which is followed by intervention and follow-up. These stages are discussed in turn.

Intake and Introduction

Therapy always begins with an individual, couple, or family coming to a session to introduce themselves and their concerns. It is critical that the counselor manage this initial set of encounters properly if future sessions are to be productive.

The goals of the introductory session(s) are threefold. The first task of the therapist is to develop a meaningful social connection with the client(s). The second task is to acquire a clear understanding of what specific concerns bring the client(s) for counseling, as well as what solutions have been previously attempted. The final task of the introductory sessions is to negotiate a reasonable goal for the therapeutic process.

In the first instance, it is essential that the therapist make the clients feel as if their presenting concerns have been thoroughly aired and understood. It takes no great insight to appreciate that, if people are going to share their concerns and disclose themselves and their vulnerabilities, such exposures must take place in an atmosphere of trust. An experienced therapist will reinforce the importance of the initial encounters to establishing this type of social bond and recognizes that this sets the stage and tone for subsequent work. Clients who have unsuccessful counseling experiences typically report a lack of genuine empathy for their difficulties as high on their roster of complaints. If the therapist is going to make a difference to his or her clients, then it is essential that a meaningful relationship with them be established at the outset. Moreover, it is important to emphasize that the "meaningfulness" of the relationship is from the *client's* viewpoint, not the counselor's.

Therapists of all persuasions have had the experience of not being able to connect adequately with clients at the outset and have had this deficiency affect the course of later events. There is no simpler or more effective way to create a meaningful social bond with clients than to make them feel understood through empathetic role taking.

Empirical research confirms that the experience of being "meaningfully heard" by others is surprisingly infrequent. For most people, their personal or professional socialization has *not* provided them with effective listening skills. Relevant data on this account come from Carkhuff and Berenson[7] who used the ability to reproduce or reiterate a speaker's points as a benchmark of empathetic listening. If a listener merely restated the other's points before giving his or her own view, they were categorized as an effective listener and were scored 3 on a 5-point scale. A score of 3 indicated a level of understanding interchangeable with that expressed by the client. A rating scale of 1 identified therapist expressions that either "do not attend to" or "detract significantly from" the client's formulation. At the other extreme were scores of 5 in which the therapist responses "added significantly" to an accurate expression of the meaning and intention of the client's expression. In Carkhuff and Berenson's studies to assess levels of empathetic listening in various groups, the following modal scores were found: general public 1.5, teachers and nurses 1.7, guidance counselors 1.9, psychology graduate students 2.1, professional therapists in training 2.7. Because a score of 3 represented a response that was minimally facilitative, these findings suggest that being an effective "active listener" is not a skill that can be taken for granted, even among professionals. Consequently, it is imperative that clinical sociologists engaged in counseling practice develop their listening skills. Although the mechanics of developing such skills cannot be detailed here (see Martin[8] for an excellent guide), the critical ability is that clinicians continually work at expressing the presenting problem *from the client's viewpoint*. It will become clear in the assessment and evaluation section that it is not necessary (or highly likely) that the clinician will rely on the client's definition of the situation. However, it is critical for purposes of establishing the social bond that the clinician express an understanding of the client's viewpoint. By contrast, in the initial counseling stages, the *least productive* course of action a therapist can follow is to try and define the nature of the client's concerns in terms of the concepts and principles that guide the therapist's theoretical outlook.

Having established a bond with the clients, the therapist has already progressed toward the second goal of initial client encounters; that is, toward gaining a clear appreciation of the presenting problem. It is worth noting that, with surprising frequency, the process of empathetic listening is constructive to the clients because it encourages them to articulate and confront the specific nature of their concerns. Often a complicating source of clients' concerns is that they are unclear of what specifically is troubling them. By providing accurate precis of their self-reports, the clinician is providing a therapeutic mirror that assists clients to see their circumstances more clearly. The clinician's task here is to learn how the clients view their situation. This is critical because future interventions must be tied to and build upon the clients' present experiences as they define them.

Initial sessions with clients should be more than empathetic in tone; the therapist also needs to have clients define, as specifically as they are able, what changes are required in order to improve their circumstances. Placing this item on the agenda serves several important functions. First, it encourages clients to specify and order their concerns, something clients typically have not done before seeking counsel. Responses to the issue of required changes take many forms, the least common being a clear statement on which there is consensus. Illustrative responses include long, unordered complaint rosters with responsibility attributed to others, vague talk lacking stable empirical referents, and specific but contrasting concerns among members. A second utility of a discussion of needed changes is that it sets the groundwork for establishing goal-directed counseling. Such purposefulness helps avoid sidetracking and makes it at least possible that clients may achieve a degree of satisfaction. Without agreement on ends, any amount of change is potentially insufficient. Considering the issue of required changes also gives the clinician a sense of whether the therapeutic expectations are within his or her sphere of competence. Clearly the expertise of any therapist is restricted, and any professional ought to be conscious of these limitations. An early exploration of what may need to be accomplished provides the opportunity for clinicians to commit themselves or disengage (preferably through referral) from the encounter. Finally, the struggle that clients typically engage in to come to terms with the issue of expectations regarding change can be useful to the clinician as an example of the processes they use to confront problems.

The initial encounters should also explore what solutions the client has already tried. Clients usually come for counsel only after they have exhausted all of their own means of solving their problems. Seeking counsel is an activity of "last resort." To help solidify the social bond and begin planning later evaluations and interventions, it is worthwhile for the therapist to know what has already been unsuccessfully tried and what brings the clients for counsel at this time. There is usually some precipitating cause for people seeking counsel, and such information can be helpful in understanding the present situation of the clients.

Finally, during the initial session, a third useful goal is for the counselor and clients to establish a set of realistic expectations about the nature and extent of change that can be accomplished in a specified period. Usually clients arrive for counsel with the idea that the competence of the therapist includes some mysterious properties that will permit resolution of their concerns in a short time and with little effort. Although one can appreciate the hope underlying such expectations, this does not make the expectation any more realistic. The openness and trust established during the introductory sessions provides an opportunity for the counselor to send a simple, direct message to the client about his or her situation. This message should state that most people gradually work themselves into their present, unfortunate situation (i.e., the modal precipitating cause of misfortune is not dramatic or tragic) and that it will take the expenditure of considerable resources of time, effort, and sacrifice to change the architecture of their experience. Moreover, this change is advisably approached in small, solvable steps, even though the possibility of dramatic improvement remains a possible by-product.

Assessment and Evaluation

When the first phase of the therapeutic process has been successfully accomplished, the therapist will have gained considerable information about the clients and their presenting concerns. The next task is to conceptualize this extensive information load. Because the initial phase was empathetic in tone, what the therapist can expect to have gained is an intimate, privileged depiction of and acquaintance with the clients' outlook. The principal assessment and evaluation task is to take these insider reports and reconceptualize them so that they make theoretical sense. In this stage the clinician will analyze and interpret the reports with a degree of detachment characteristic of an outsider's viewpoint. Because the clinical sociologist's theoretical framework is one that, in some form, emphasizes the relationship between actors, the evaluation of the data from the initial interviews will typically be interpreted in structural terms. Before developing this point, it deserves noting that the introduction and assessment stages are not necessarily or usually sequential. It is common for assessment to take place while the clients are describing their circumstances.

The assessment stage is critical. It shapes the clinician's outlook on the case and, in turn, defines the possibilities for later interventions. In scientific terms, the evaluation establishes the "working hypotheses" that the clinician will later test by trying various intervention strategies. As critical as this stage is, it is also complicated, both theoretically and methodologically. Training in sociology can assist the clinician in managing some of the complexity in each of these domains at the assessment and evaluation stage. The following comments on each of these dimensions illustrates this utility.

Methodologically, a principal clinical problem regarding assessment is the heavy reliance on self-report data. One of the more reliable findings our discipline has documented is the generally modest correlations between persons' reports of their conduct and their actual behavior. This fact of social life, that people's reports tend to be biased in a way that is self-justifying, must remain a salient clinical consideration during assessment. Individuals construct and report different realities from the same shared experience, often even more dramatically than sociologists anticipate. The concordance correlations reported by Booth and Welch[9] illustrate this point.

These researchers individually interviewed spouses from 321 married couples about their marital experiences in the *previous month*. The self-reported findings serve as a reminder of the degree to which couples construct separate marriages. The correlation coefficient expressing couple agreement of the "frequency of fighting" was .46, on who generally "gets their way" in disputes .22, on how much time the couple spent together the *previous day* was .40, and the frequency of intercourse was .68. Note that these modest correlations are from fairly innocuous and empirically grounded issues. Clinicians' experience shows that, as the issues become more sensitive and subject to interpretation, the concordance of clients' self-reports of shared experience will drop from even these modest levels. In short, it seems reasonable to view couples as having "his" and "her" marriages, rather than a marriage.

What does a clinician do with this appreciation? Although self-reports probably provide us with an obscure picture of actual events, they can be taken as direct information of the respondents' interpretive and rationalization strategies. Appreciating this dimension of clients can be useful when developing meaningful intervention tactics that must be connected to the clients' frame of reference. Moreover, the generally low correlation between clients' self-reports and their conduct suggests that clinicians ought to try to triangulate self-report findings wherever it is feasible. Triangulation establishes the reliability of a finding by using two or more sources of information to document it authenticity. Two strategies along this line are illustrative.

For some kinds of issues, having clients keep a daily log recording the incidence of conduct that the therapist considers relevant can be an instructive counterbalance to the self-justifying rationalizations and selective perceptions reported in counseling sessions. I have used such logs successfully on a number of occasions with reference to the issue of time allocation. Early on, for example, I was impressed by how grossly individuals overestimate the time they actually devote to constructing intimate relationships. Consequently, I regularly ask clients to keep a log for a week or two of how much time they spend in the following categories: personal time, couple time, family time. For many clients it has been a consciousness-raising experience when their belief that they devote ample time to their marriage or family or private interests is confronted by the discipline of data.

Another illustration of reliability assessment occurs when clients are in clinical sessions. In this situation, besides the content of their verbal reports, clients are presenting the clinician with another sort of data, namely their interaction patterns. For example, when clients report how supportive they are, this can easily be compared to the actual supportive behavior they display during the counseling session. From a sociologist's viewpoint, the *structure* of relationships between participants is as or more important than the *content* of their reported concerns. An observation of a couple's or family's conduct can be used as a sample of their typical interaction patterns. In this way, whatever the clients say the nature of their relationships are, the accuracy of these assertions can be assessed by comparison to the actual structures observed in therapeutic session.

These illustrations only point out sociology's relevance to the methodology of assessment; they do not define its possibilities. In a similar fashion, sociology's theoretical relevance to this stage of the therapeutic process can be highlighted. To appreciate this contribution, an important starting point is the realization that the presenting problems as described by clients are expressed in insider's terms. The clinical sociologist's assessment and evaluation, however, are phrased in outsider's terms. There are a number of reasons for this conceptual misalignment between client and clinician's perspectives. First, most persons have a psychologically biased appreciation of their circumstances. For example, when asked to give their understanding of some concern, the typical response I hear is clients identifying the (usually deficient) "character traits" of themselves and/or significant others. Rarely is a response formulated by clients that emphasizes sociological considerations such as the system of relationships that has been developed to integrate the members and maintain order. Most people do not practice systemic thinking and, consequently, a clinical sociologist is likely to present issues in very different terms from those of the client.

In addition to this difference in theoretical orientation, there are other reasons why the sociologist's conceptualization will differ from his or her clients. For instance, because most people take their personal and social circumstances for granted, they tend to have unsophisticated appreciations of these domains. Consequently, when they are asked "why" they or their loved ones act as they do, they often do not know, either because they lack the relevant theoretical training or simply are not used to seriously considering such questions. Of course there is considerable client variation in this regard, but few clients approximate a capable sociologist's insights.

Finally, there is a point that follows from the earlier observation that people reconstruct and report realities. Given the propensity of actors to shape the presentation of experience it is probable that, even if clients did know why they acted in a particular manner, they would offer socially desirable reports. In this manner the causes of their conduct (assuming that they are known), which specify the actual reasons for conduct, will be mixed (to some unknown degree) with plausible rationales for action. This situation supports the idea that a clinical sociologist will make an evaluation of the client's situation quite different from that which a client is likely to report.

For at least these reasons, the sociological counselor's assessment of the presenting problem(s) will be different in form from but will use the content of the client's reports. The theoretical task is to come to terms with the information collected, in a "disciplined" way, by formulating a sociological reconstruction of the experience. The theoretical richness of our discipline provides a vast array of alternatives on this account, one of which is illustrated in the following.

As noted earlier, the therapeutic community has recently realized the relevance of social structural circumstances to the creation and maintenance of personal troubles, as well as its importance to suggested remedies. Sociology emphasizes the relevance of social facts of life and contributes to the kind of "systemic thinking" that is considered pertinent. To translate the notion of "system" into the social domain requires specifying the relevant "variables" and "relationships" because, by definition, any system is both a set of variables and relationships between variables.

From my perspective, the variables of interest to assessing a presenting concern in sociological terms are statuses and their associated roles, whereas the relationships between these variables refer to the values and attitudes that underlie the mutual expectations actors occupying statuses have for each other. Using this translation procedure, the assessment task is to clarify, in social structural terms, what is occurring. Conceptualizing "systemic thinking" in this way provides immediate access to a set of theoretical tools, distinctly sociological, that includes, for example, the notions of role and status set; career; role articulation, ambivalence, conflict, and strain; aligning actions; social capital; identity formation; sincerity and authenticity. The meaning and relevance of these fundamental concepts need not be reviewed here, but the central conceptual question for the clinician is worth underlining and echoes that found throughout sociological inquiry: Recognizing that actors are independent persons possessing distinctive personalities that require coordination, what social system can be constructed that optimizes personal autonomy and organizational integration?

A sociological education provides the conceptual apparatus and intellectual flexibility best suited for addressing this issue. There are, in addition, more specific techniques available that can assist in the task of coming to terms with the character of the social system and its influence on individual actors. One tool worth mentioning is graphically diagraming the nature of a client's system of social arrangements. This procedure provides a handy, short-hand encapsulation and assessment of the structural character of a client's circumstances. The general procedure is set forth by Minuchin[10] and can be modified for any sociological therapist's purposes. Along the same line, a structural portrait can be found in the sociometric process known as *sculpting*. Goldenberg and Goldenberg[4] describe this technique as an attempt to "translate systems theory into physical form by creating an arrangement of people placed in various physical positions in space that represent their relationships to each other at a particular moment in time. While it may be very difficult for an individual to verbalize his or her perceptions of how family members relate—how intimate or distant they are, how loving or indifferent—sculpting allows the person to reveal his or her private view of invisible but meaningful boundaries, alliances, subsystems, roles, and so on."

By whatever means, the sociological clinician is trying to develop an appreciation of what the social configuration of the actors is and how this structure limits the possibilities for change. I like to think of this effort as a "sociological work-up." With this sort of model, consideration can be given to how clients might release themselves from the constraints of their current social situation. It is worth underlining that this formulation of the client's situation is always done with data supplied by the client. The task is similar to the kind of grounded theory development common among qualitative researchers in our discipline. The goal in this phase is descriptive, not prescriptive, in character. For example, it is the nature of the statuses *father* and *daughter* and the mutual expectations that bind them *from the actor's viewpoint* that are the essential conceptualization material. It is not the nature of these statuses and relationships as defined by the culture or the counselor that is important in the assessment phase.

INTERVENTION AND FOLLOW-UP

Earlier we mentioned that "knowing" and "doing" are separate but related competencies. This separation suggests that an isomorphic correspondence between assessment and intervention will probably not exist. Our assessment models are nomothetic and cannot capture the complexity of individual, couple, or family concerns. Moreover, an analytical assessment, especially a sociological assessment, employs a conceptual frame of reference that is foreign to most clients. Consequently, even translating an assessment, let alone developing an intervention, is riddled with communication difficulties. This sort of reasoning leads me to believe that intervention is more "artistic" than "scientific" in character. There is no set of interventionist steps that reliably produces predictable results. Given this view, I will set forth a general theoretical model, based on sociological findings, that I find a helpful guide in constructing clinical interventions. This model will be followed by some illustrations that point out our discipline's relevance to this phase of clinical practice.

A General Approach

In the section on assessment and evaluation, the emphasis was on conceptualizing the presenting problems in *relational* terms. Social relations occur in structural contexts characterized by statuses clients occupy and the roles they enact that are connected with their respective statuses. Paralleling this emphasis of social relationships in the assessment process, the intervention stage is characterized in similar interpersonal terms.

An important point in thinking about intervention is to recognize that, in the final analysis, the client must be willing to change. This obvious point is too often lost in the therapeutic encounter, where time and again it is assumed (often by clients, less frequently by clinicians) that the therapist can (somehow) "make" the client change in a particular direction. Therapists can easily test the limits of their ability to control clients in this manner and will readily find their power is meager compared to displays of client resistance. Nonetheless, a therapist can exert considerable influence over a therapeutic encounter. Given these facts, the question becomes: To encourage clients to change in specified directions, what conceptualization of the situation most appropriately takes account of therapeutic influence? My experience suggests a useful answer to this question can be found in the socialization literature.

In order for clients to decide to change, they must experience some change in their self-concept. That is, for changes to be *relevant*, conduct (not just words) must change. If changes are to be *lasting*, they must be accepted by the person making the change. Such changes in orientation and conduct constitute changes in people's self-concepts (i.e., they think and behave somewhat differently). The socialization literature identifies two dimensions that are important in encouraging self-concept changes—power and affect (Boldt, Lindquist, & Percival[11]; Brim[12]; Coser[13]). From my experience, successful interventions establish an appropriate mix of these dimensions. Figure 1 displays a gradient of mixtures of the power and affect dimensions as they relate to structural tightness and looseness.

In Figure 1, the extreme characterizations of the therapeutic encounter are labeled as *structural tightness* and *structural looseness*. The structurally tight situation is one that contains high degrees of power and low amounts of affect, whereas the structurally loose circumstance has the reverse proportions of these variables. The structurally tight designation characterizes a demanding situation in which the expectations for change are imposed on the client (Boldt & Roberts[14]). By contrast, the structurally loose situation is characterized by normative suggestions rather than impositions and effusive affective support. Structurally loose expectations for change are proposed to (rather than imposed on) the client.

These extreme situations represent the kinds of circumstances that ought to be avoided by therapists. In the structurally tight circumstance, where the attempt is to demand changes from the client, the likely result is high client resistance and

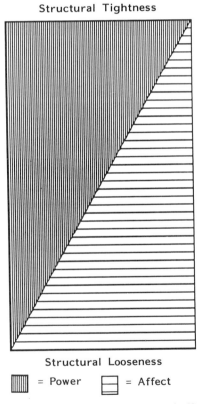

FIGURE 1. Continuum of power and affect.

little or no lasting change. This organizational arrangement is experienced by the client as a threat to his or her self-concept, which receives little affective support under these conditions. A common response by clients is to exit from such circumstances. Where clients continue in tightly structured situations, the most probable type of change will be short-term acquiescence or compliance. Change in structurally tight situations is governed principally by instrumental considerations. Clients in tight circumstances are "motivated by the desire to gain a reward or avoid punishment" (Aronson[15]). Where there is extreme conformity pressure to change in some direction, the typical response is to invest minimal resources in meeting the demands and allocate remaining energies to self-maintenance through avoidance and resistance.

Under the conditions of structural looseness, the opposite situation exists—affection is high, and demands are low. The result is that the existing self-concept(s) of the client(s) are highly reinforced, and the likelihood of change in a specified therapeutic direction is lowered. This, of course, does not deny the possibility of personal change or development under structurally loose circumstances. However, the learning process in this situation is likely to be of the "identification" sort (i.e., "social influence [is] brought about by an individual's desire to be like the influencer"[15]) with the unpredictable results that this process typically implies.

In order to encourage lasting change in a specified direction, Figure 1 suggests that some midpoint between structural tightness and looseness is optimal. In the middle range of this continuum, the therapist will be working to structure a learning situation that both demands specified changes while at the same time affectively supports the self-concept of the client. In doing so, the therapist will be adopting the role of a "warm demander" (Kleinfeld[16]). Clearly specified changes will be demanded of the client, but their overall self-concept will not be challenged. In doing so, the self-respect and dignity of the person initiating the change can be maintained at the same time that he or she is trying to move in a positive direction. It is this social circumstance that minimizes frustration while still carrying the expectation for change and development.

In summary, using the conceptual model presented in Figure 1, the lesson for intervention is that we do not ask too much (structural tightness) or too little (structural looseness) from our clients. By being aware of these extremes, we increase the chance of cultivating therapeutic situations where the lasting, meaningful changes associated with internalization can occur. As Aronson[15] reminds us, "the internalization of a value or belief is the most permanent, most deeply rooted response to social influence. The motivation to internalize a particular belief is the desire to be right." Moreover, the simplified model in Figure 1 also gives therapists an overall conceptual scheme to return to when their interventions are not yielding desired results.

This model can be elaborated to include all sorts of sociological concepts including, for example, the notions of sincerity and authenticity, socially constructed identities, attitudinal and behavioral conformity. However, the task at hand is illustrative rather than demonstrative. The point is that this kind of model, developed from the socialization literature, exemplifies the sort of nomothetic contribution our discipline can make to the art of intervention. We shall also illustrate some interventionist strategies that are sociological in character. Before doing this, however, another distinction from the sociological literature that can guide productive interventions deserves mention.

On Expressive and Instrumental Action

The process of devising appropriate interventions benefits from an appreciation of our discipline's distinction between expressive and instrumental action. Instrumental action concerns itself with efficiently achieving an identifiable objective; it involves purpose and calculation and is interested in considering alternative means for achieving a specified end (Nettler[17]). Expressive action, by contrast, is guided by considerations of affect and value and is interested in expressing moral sentiments. For therapeutic purposes, the relevance of this distinction is that people "often confuse what they *want to do* with what they *propose to achieve*" (Nettler[18]). In doing so, their actions move along the gradient from rational to irrational conduct. This confusion between conduct that expresses our values and that which helps us achieve our purposes occurs in everyday action. However, it is especially prevalent among those who seek professional counsel. This is not surprising because clients are troubled, are in pain, and are often frustrated and resentful. It is common for clients to keep their anger and pain inside, sensing that expressing themselves might only make matters worse. When counseling provides a legitimate opportunity to reveal these sentiments, expressive conduct is in large supply, whereas the prevalence of instrumental action recedes.

The point here is not to deny the importance of action guided by impulse or conscience, but such expression should not be identified as the means for helping people achieve desired changes in their lives. The deficiency many clients have is in moving beyond the expression of outrage or injustice toward developing and implementing a reasonable strategy for producing meaningful change. For this purpose, being able to distinguish instrumental from expressive conduct is fundamental. Because these separate types of conduct often constitute different agendas, many clients will be confronted with the dilemma between doing what, morally or emotionally, seems "right" and following an instrumentally "correct" line of conduct. Recognizing the distinction between instrumental and expressive conduct does not resolve the difficult choices that have to be faced when "rightness" and "correctness" clash, but at least it makes clients and counselors cognizant of what is occurring.

Besides helping conceptualize interventions with distinctions like that between instrumental and expressive conduct, sociology can also guide the generation of specific intervention ideas. The following section exemplifies this kind of contribution.

Specifying Facts and Likely Consequences

Given the variety of problems that a clinical sociologist is bound to encounter, no suggested intervention is going to apply across a broad spectrum of circumstances. However, when clients are thinking of developing strategies of instrumental action, a useful sociologically based intervention derives from our general knowledge of institutional and career patterns. Sociological and other social scientific research provides a more informed appreciation of how various social sectors operate. As a result, compared to those clients who are not acquainted with such understanding, we can specify the likely consequences for a client who considers selecting one course of action or another. Such an "information-giving" function is, under some circumstances, just what clients need in order to move on. This occurs especially when the anxiety associated with an uncertainty of the unknown is so great that it paralyzes actors, even those in "unhealthy situations."

The work of Ebaugh[19] on the process of role exit provides an excellent illustration of this function. As Robert Merton says in the foreword to this work, "From these pages, we learn that the recurrent social process of role-exit in diverse spheres of American social life varies within quite narrow bounds." Ebaugh demonstrates that persons leaving social statuses and their attendant roles go through a predictable set of stages. This piece of sociological knowledge can be used by clinicians to inform clients of "what they are in for" should they decide to follow a particular course of action.

In this same vein, besides being informative, the clinician can use sociological knowledge as a "corrective" to misinformed beliefs on which their clients may be premising their conduct. For example, a woman who came for counsel convinced that her "sex drive was abnormal" and that she was "frigid." It became evident that she was basing her pejorative self-evaluation on the fact that she "only felt like having sex every second day." Here a simple recitation of the distribution of intercourse frequency provided a corrective frame of reference. Likewise there is the case of the mother, ignorant of the stages of moral and cognitive development, who refused to discipline her 3-year-old son's unruly and destructive conduct because "he should know better." She had concluded that it was an inadequacy in her son's "conscience" that was giving rise to her parenting problems. In short, clinical experience confirms that many persons, "commonsense" ideas of both character formation and the operation of the social world are based on large tracts of either misinformation or ignorance. In these instances, a potent intervention can derive from the clinician's authoritative (not authoritarian) correction of the beliefs underlying dysfunctional situational definitions.

Reality Construction and Time Allocation

A fundamental sociological premise is that social facts, including social relationships, are the products of human effort. In my experience, a reliable feature of many who appear for marriage or family counseling is that they do not share this premise and, more often, believe the opposite. Their orientation is that social arrangements can be "taken for granted." There is a common tendency for such persons to assume that the bonds of marriage, friendship, and family, for instance, are just there for their use.

As these clients see their relationships to significant others deteriorate, an opportune time presents itself to dissuade clients of their taken-for-granted approach to social relationships. In these circumstances, I have found it instructive to have couples, for example, keep a systematic log of the time they devote in a week to "couple time," that is, sharing experiences that are relevant *not* to their needs and interests as separate persons, or as parents, or to any institutional affiliation, but just to the construction and renewal of their bond as husband and wife. Frequently couples who perform this exercise report that "only a few hours per month" are given to nurturing these bonds. This counting exercise is sociologically informed, simple, and effective for it points to how few resources are given to creating meaningful personal, couple, or family life.

Establishing Rituals

Another kind of intervention, extending from the notions of time allocation and reality construction, stems from the importance of ritual and ceremony to the creation and maintenance of meaningful personal and social experiences. Ritualistic performances are typically "social" in character; they emphasize the expression of relationships between statuses, rather than persons. For example, we display our deference to the university president, not the Fred or Jane who occupies this office. Participating in rituals and ceremonies is one way actors transform their individual acts into social connections. Through ritualistic means, actors are able to connect themselves with a larger social order that has a significance beyond their personal purposes. Initially, rituals are used for dedication to and consecration of social commitments. Later they are used to celebrate and commemorate our social connections.

My experience has shown that often troubled persons have very little experience connected to established rituals and, following sociological reasoning, there is a deficiency of purpose and meaning in significant sectors of their lives. It is no accident, for example, that questioning troubled married partners often reveals a negligent attendance to celebrating their anniversary or that families who come for counsel infrequently share meals together. Although many people dismiss such ritualistic activity as "meaningless ceremony," they are, in a sense, demoralizing themselves. Rituals help establish a social connection and continuity to our lives. Moreover, their practice signifies a willingness to serve a collective reality beyond that of individual interests. Redefining their importance and helping people institutionalize rituals in their social experience can be a significant intervention. Lieberman *et al.*[20] underline this point and suggest a set of procedures for developing and implementing meaningful rituals. Ceremonial practice takes time, however. When low time allocations to couple or family interests appear alongside negligent ritualistic activity (as they often do), a dual intervention can easily be constructed. As was noted earlier, marriage reconstruction requires that a couple work at it in and over time. Institutionalizing a simple ritual such as "going out to dinner together every Thursday" can serve as a meaningful first step toward devoting time and other resources to the reconstruction of a social bond.

Follow-Up: Clinical Interventions as Hypothesis Testing

Specifying likely consequences, time allocation, and establishing rituals illustrate some of a long roster of sociologically informed interventions that can be generated. In addition, family therapy handbooks and counseling manuals (e.g., Wolman & Stricker[21]) also contain strategies for encouraging change, many of which have sociological justification. Whatever interventions the clinical sociologist deems appropriate, it is important that these initiations not be practiced ritualistically.

Earlier we argued that a thematic approach to counseling was more appropriate than a programmatic one for sociological clinicians. One advantage of the thematic approach is the flexibility it permits. An important offshoot of this flexibility is that clinical interventions are treated as hypotheses. By contrast, programmatic orientations toward counseling, almost by definition, are underwritten by a sense of assuredness regarding assessment and intervention. The clinician's theoretical approach is, more or less, assumed to be correct, and the problem becomes one of either tailoring the system to the client's needs or, as often, trying to induce the client to conform to the requirements of the program. In this fashion, many programmatic counseling approaches become ritualistic. Under such circumstances, where the clinician is committed to a theoretical viewpoint or program of intervention, the investment of the clinician makes it difficult to falsify their ideas, and interventions become more tests of the client's ability to meet clinician demands than tests of the clinical approach.

Given the complexity of the social circumstances in which people live, the individuality and degrees of freedom people have, the theoretical, methodological, and personal limitations operating on the clinician, it is reasonable to think that counselors do not accurately know about the past, present, and future of clients' conditions with a great deal of certainty, especially where the test of "knowing" is the ability to intervene accurately in a way that produces predictable outcomes. Clinical sociologists need not be embarrassed by describing their practice in these terms; the same holds true for all of the social science disciplines (cf. Collins[22]). Of course some theoretical schemes and interventions are more efficient and effective than others. However, no existing scheme is so thoroughly developed that it can legitimately claim to "have all the answers."

Given these facts, the appropriate course of action is to treat clinical interventions as hypotheses to be tested. This attitude is not only appropriately modest, but it is also clinically functional. By conceptualizing our interventions as educated guesses, we are encouraged to attend carefully to the outcomes and treat "failures" (that is, unsuccessful interventions) positively. Our errors provide us with meaningful information that can be used in the *reformulation* of our assessments and future interventions. In this way, the sociological clinician can treat his or her work as "research," where we literally study or look again at clients as we create conceptualizations and subject our ideas to the discipline of data.

CONCLUSION

As emphasized throughout this chapter, the process of giving counsel to troubled others takes place in a complex network. There is a dense causal web of forces operating intra- and interpersonally in every case a counselor sees. In this sense, every case is idiosyncratic. When idiographic circumstances such as these are met with any discipline's nomothetic models, there is likely to be an imperfect alignment. Given these facts, my suggestion is that clinical sociologists interested in counseling troubled individuals, couples, or families work from the strengths of their discipline. These strengths include at least a scientific orientation that encourages a systematic approach to each of the counseling stages; an emphasis on the structural character of people's concerns, which encourages a view that social systems are means for coordinating individual interests for humanistic ends; and an approach to issues that is intellectually flexible. My goal has been to provide a sense of how sociological themes, theories, and techniques can be translated into therapeutic practice. Studying sociology, in one sense, constitutes a liberal education, and this liberated outlook holds considerable potential for helping troubled actors. As a discipline we are just beginning to turn our attention to translating our "knowing" into "doing" (e.g., See & Straus[23]; Swan[24]; Fein[25]). The history of our discipline has a humanistic undercurrent, and developing our discipline along the lines suggested in this chapter is one way of keeping this tradition current.

ACKNOWLEDGMENTS.   The author acknowledges the careful reading and contribution of E. Boldt, R. Clifton, A. Pressey, D. Rennie, and the editors to the development of this chapter.

REFERENCES

1. Lenski, G. (1988). Rethinking macrosociological theory. *American Sociological Review, 53*, 163–171.
2. Straus, R. A. (1982). Clinical sociology on the one-to-one level: A socio-behavioral approach to counselling. *Clinical Sociology Review, 1*, 59–74.
3. Glick, I. D., & Kessler, D. R. (1980). *Marital and family therapy*. New York: Grune & Stratton.
4. Goldenberg, I., & Goldenberg, H. (1985). *Family therapy: An overview*. Monterey, CA: Brooks/Cole.
5. Nettler, G. (1972). Knowing and doing. *The American Sociologist, 7*, 3–7.
6. Berger, P. L. (1963). *Invitation to sociology*. New York: Doubleday.
7. Carkhuff, R. R., & Berenson, B. G. (1977). *Beyond counseling and therapy*. New York: Holt, Rinehart & Winston.
8. Martin, D. (1983). *Counseling and Therapy Skills*. Monterey, CA: Brooks/Cole.
9. Booth, A., & Welch, S. (1978). Spousal consensus and its correlates. *Journal of Marriage and Family, 40*, 23–34.
10. Minuchin, S. (1974). *Families and family therapy*. Cambridge, MA: Harvard University Press. Minuchin, S. (1981). *Family therapy techniques*. Cambridge, MA: Harvard University Press.
11. Boldt, E. D., Lindquist, N. E., & Percival, A. (1976). The significance of significant others. *Canadian Review of Sociology and Anthropology, 13*, 345–351.
12. Brim, O. G. (1966). Socialization through the life cycle. In O. G. Brim & S. Wheeler (Eds.), *Socialization after childhood* (pp. 1–49). New York: Wiley.
13. Coser, R. L. (1979). *Training in ambiguity*. New York: The Free Press.
14. Boldt, E. D., & Roberts, L. W. (1979). Structural tightness and social conformity. *Journal of Cross-Cultural Psychology, 10*, 221–230.
15. Aronson, E. (1988). *The social animal*. New York: W. H. Freeman.
16. Kleinfeld, J. S. (1975). Effective teachers of Eskimo and Indian students. *School Review, 83*, 301–344.
17. Nettler, G. (1976). *Social concerns*. New York: McGraw-Hill.
18. Nettler, G. (1988). *Criminology lessons*. Cincinnati: Anderson.

19. Ebaugh, H. R. F. (1988). *Becoming an ex: The process of role exit*. Chicago: University of Chicago Press.
20. Lieberman, R. P., Wheeler, E. G., de Visser, L. A., Kuehnel, J; & Kuehnel, T. (1980). *Handbook of marital therapy*. New York: Plenum Press.
21. Wolman, B. B., & Stricker, G. (1983). *Handbook of family and marital therapy*. New York: Plenum Press.
22. Collins, R. (1989). Sociology: Proscience or antiscience. *American Sociological Review, 54*, 124–139.
23. See, P., & Straus, R. (1985). The sociology of the individual. In R. Straus (Ed.), *Using sociology* (pp. 61–80). Bayside, NY: General Hall, Inc.
24. Swan, L. A. (1988). Grounded encounter therapy: Its characteristics and process. *Clinical Sociology Review, 6*, 88–100.
25. Fein, M. L. (1988). Resocialization: A neglected paradigm. *Clinical Sociology Review, 6*, 76–87.

CHAPTER 10

Public Policies and Clinical Sociology

ALFRED McCLUNG LEE

BASIC QUESTIONS AND TASKS

When a clinical sociologist starts to serve as a change or intervention agent in a public policy on behalf of an individual or organizational client, what are probable first steps to be taken? Specifics differ widely from case to case, but certain general concerns are fairly common, and they lead to a search for workable answers to these questions.

In the client's consideration of the policy problem, how realistic and practical is the client's own role conception? And how realistic is the client's perception of that role conception's impression in various publics? In discussions of the policy, how accurate and informing are communications from and to constituents and others? How is the clinical sociologist likely to penetrate existing social barriers and distances that separate the client's view of the policy from those of relevant publics? How can the sociologist provide to the client credible empathetic perceptions of relevant people and situations concerned with the policy? Above all, how realistic and attainable are current policy goals likely to be through strategies in use or available for use?

These questions or introductory investigative steps do not often lead to categorical or absolute answers. In our complex society, one learns to be satisfied with practical approximations. Only thus can one reach a decision as to the viability of a client's leadership and program potentialities.

These steps to help visualize a client's relationship to a given public policy situation remind one of the often quoted statement by W. I. and Dorothy S. Thomas[1] that when people "define situations as real, they are real in their consequences" (p. 572). Among illustrations of this point, they mention the "often

---

ALFRED McCLUNG LEE • Brooklyn College, Brooklyn, New York 11210 and Drew University, Madison, New Jersey 07940.

conflicting definitions" of a child's problems given by the child, the child's parents, teachers, and other associates, and "such facts as can be verified about the situation by disinterested investigators." For any client, conflicting definitions of situations and conflicting value positions have significant consequences in policy definition. The practitioner gradually determines how to understand and how to deal with them.

When the late clinical sociologist Irving Goldaber was called upon to help cope with a conflict situation in a town or in a prison, his clients in the sense of being his employers were town or prison officials, but his search for a "definition of the situation" did not derive only from them. With his colleague Holly G. Porter[2] in the nonprofit Community Confrontation and Communication Associates (CCCA) of Grand Rapids, Michigan, he had recourse to a "laboratory confrontation program" in each case. They brought together group-selected leaders—usually 6 to 10 from each of the identifiable adversaries. They insisted that these people come together in "a closed door, issue-oriented, eyeball-to-eyeball group dialogue . . . conducted in a neutral setting over a three- to five-day period." Each group was asked to bring its agenda of problems and possible policy modifications. In the confrontation, Goldaber and Porter were able to guide the participants from "positions of polarized antagonism to collaboration through a process which encourages 'gut level' ventilation of hostilities." In this dramatic joint experience, "explanations are offered, communication skills are developed, trust is built up, and as feelings are altered, forces are joined to formulate common objectives and to prepare a scheme for implementation."

The first laboratory confrontation was just the start of the Goldaber–Porter effort, an exploratory experience. It was then followed in riot-torn places like Asbury Park, New Jersey, by a variety of efforts that involved many local organizations, the police, businesspeople, teenagers, churches, and other laboratory confrontations. But the first confrontation always helped substantially to define the situation more clearly.

Every public policy problem is different, but the Goldaber–Holly procedure suggests an orientation toward the "definition of the situation" that can be adapted with profit to a great many contentions. As Roger A. Straus[3] notes, the social problems of clients "cry out for sociological intervention" (p. 57). This means, he adds, "reconstructing the operational definition of the situation with reference to the multiple, interacting layers of social context framing any particular case." That redefinition may be achieved through the presentation in many ways of many types of credible factual materials, but it usually also requires therapeutic interpersonal or group procedures—as in laboratory confrontations—to make change understandable, acceptable, and then useful to policymaking and implementation.

Think of the complexities of a local drug problem. A clinical sociologist is called in usually to certify that the most adequate ways to cope is to organize a more thorough and systematic educational program for the young and for appropriate adult groups. But what about existing collusive deals among drug peddlers, police, and politicians? What about drugs being pushed in some local schools, hotels, eating establishments, houses of prostitution, manufacturing plants, business offices, political offices, jails, and prisons? What sorts of protective deals are being made with certain judges? What are the channels through which drugs so easily reach this area? Who controls and benefits from those channels? How essential is drug pushing as a way of life among the unemployed and unemployable? If the clinical sociologist examines only the prevalence of addiction and the virtues of an educational approach, a procedure all too much in line with current public policy, the perspective is much too limited to be of any great service to the community even though that is what the client wants to pay for.

To go beyond the kind of job the client would like to have done requires courage. Just how far the professional can go to make the more adequate overall picture influence the client's policies and program of public policy intervention depends upon the practitioner's reputation and diplomatic therapeutic methods. The latter are the "packaging" that has much to do with establishing credibility even though the wisdom of a counselor provides the actual basis for a continuing and constructive relationship. As Irving Louis Horowitz[4] notes, "What is at stake as a result of this newly acquired influence [in policy formation by clinical social scientists] is not the feasibility of social science, but the credibility of social scientists" (pp. 262–263). The achievement of credibility and of a reputation for competence and responsibility depends upon both the profession's standards and the individual's accomplishments.

Let us look in more detail at aspects of the clinical sociologist's typical tasks in relation to public policy concerns. These include (1) getting acquainted with the client's personnel, equipment, and operations, (2) visualizing the relation of the client's functions to the changing social setting, (3) diagnosing aspects looked upon by the client and others as problematic, (4) studying current and potential policy goals, (5) developing strategies, (6) intervening diplomatically in operational and public relations policies through instructional and other therapeutic procedures, (7) continuing program adaptations in the light of opportunities, and (8) adjusting programs to meet ethical concerns and issues.

Getting Acquainted

This point may or may not be obvious. It is easy to try to place a client in a preconceived category that may be inaccurate. The more accurately the practitioner can perceive clients—individuals, and organizations—the more useful the sociological contribution can be. In an organization, this includes examining the necessary relationships with management and with existing research, marketing, public relations, and personnel recruitment offices. Getting acquainted requires time, effort, and cooperation. Like a lawyer or a physician, a clinical sociologist needs to have as intimate and practical knowledge of the client and the client's complaint and social setting as possible. Time spent in participant and empathetic observation can save time and effort later.

In dealing with a public policy problem, there is the possibility that the client may also be employing specialists in marketing, opinion polling, public relations, or politics. Marketing firms are concerned not only with sales procedures and advertising but also with research to reveal possible markets and to discover consumer reactions. Their findings may be useful, but their preoccupations are usually narrowly with the bottom line of current profits rather than with public policy matters. Opinion polling outfits can also provide useful data, but clinical sociologists can well become dissatisfied with the superficiality and even inaccuracy of many poll results. As Craig Reinarman[5] notes, "The broad structural conflicts between state and market, workers and management, the little guys and the big guys, do not register clearly in the polls and at the polls" (p. vii). For example, a *New York Times*/CBS poll in October 1985 said 85% had an opinion on: "Will President Ronald Reagan's Star Wars plan work?" To this, 58% said "yes" and 28% "no." But a *Wall Street Journal* poll the same month tabulated only 48% who thought themselves knowledgeable enough to have an opinion on the question! Such variations are due to differences not only in audience sampling procedures but also in "the comprehension of the questions asked—their meaning to respondents as well as their meaning to interviewers."[6] Similarly, the growing percentage of possible voters who stay away from presidential elections presents no simple picture. Voting statistics cannot at all clearly indicate what people are actually thinking. Who and what do they imagine they were voting for? Why? What kept nonvoters away from the polls? What do they think would have encouraged them to vote? Clinical sociologists need to try to answer such questions.

Public relations and political specialists focus upon their definitions of their tasks and may resent what they regard as encroachment by a clinical sociologist. It is thus well to be aware of their presence, attitudes, and methods of operation in this getting-acquainted step. When appropriate, they can become colleagues rather than competitors in a decision-making process about goals and strategies.

Visualizing the Social Situation

To comprehend existing sex education, affirmative action, hospitalization, mental illness, homelessness, child and spouse brutalization, or health care policies and procedures requires both micro- and macroprobings of propaganda- and myth-ridden situations. As is suggested, public opinion polls can make a contribution to this search process when they are carefully supervised and critically interpreted. Reinarman,[7] as a microinvestigator of individual relations with public policies, reports on "the oddities and anomalies, concealed inconsistencies, and vagaries of valence I found in my subjects' accounts of their beliefs, as well as the multiple possibilities for disarticulation and misinterpretation that occur when these are severed from their context" (p. 222). He shows how the "political technology" of the polls, surveys, ballots, voting tallies, and media reports "take away from us the voice with which we speak in political life" and use it as its controllers see fit—not as we would like.

Thus, to the extent possible, clinical sociological perceptions of social situations should be based upon intimate and dependable social data. The practitioner should find or develop "the rare poll," as Leo Bogart[8] observes, that "allows us to see opinion as multifaceted, multilayered, and intricate" (p. 20).

It is not necessary in this treatment to go into details about the various sampling and interviewing methods that have been developed and tested. They include the use of nonrepresentative, panel, "political scout," quota, and probability samples and of open-ended, forced-choice, thermometer-rating, semantic-differential, and other types of questions and interview procedures.[9] A drawback to the more perceptive, in-depth, and observational surveys is their expensiveness, but such probing of even a small and reasonably representative sample can yield significant results that can give useful depth to a broader survey.

As a kind of shortcut, exploratory method, the "political scout" technique has considerable merit once it is made operative. This method calls for the selection of a network of what might accurately be called "neighborhood gossips" to act as reporters of the opinions and understandings of people in representative parts of an area or even the country. The gossips include bartenders, grocers, clergypeople, local politicians, persons active in civic, neighborhood, and other organizations, including trade unions and businesses. This is the sort of sampling device politicians and journalists have more or less systematically used for generations. It has its limitations but also its virtues. It is quick, and it gives some notion of popular understanding rather than just of expressed opinion. It then needs to be checked with more systematic survey data.

Elizabeth G. Herzog,[10] experienced with U.S. Bureau of the Budget survey problems, rejected the assumption that "the ideal is impracticable [in social surveying], and that there is no alternative to pursuing accepted methods of strict quantification, resigning ourselves to their blindspots until practice makes them perfect" (p. 31). Such amplifications and adaptations of survey methods as I have suggested become more and more useful alternatives.

Significant aspects of situation comprehension that the foregoing does not mention are the historical and the closely related legal and judicial. In working with Kenneth Clark, Thurgood Marshall, and others in race relations, I saw vivid evidences of these influences on policy formation. Cases and appeals had to be developed with evidence that eventually succeeded in getting the U.S. Supreme Court in 1954.to set aside the "separate but equal" prosegregationist doctrine for public schools and to order integrationist procedures. In addition to the work of legal consultants, this meant that the clinical social scientists involved had to do careful social historical analyses that could then be related to other types of social research under way—classroom, ecological, bussing, and other studies. In addition to printed accounts in newspapers, periodicals, government reports, and books (all to be considered critically and in historical context), sometimes recourse to oral sources, to accounts by long-term participants in the social situation, may be invaluable.

Diagnosing Problems

The preceding aspects of the clinical sociologist's tasks for a client with public policy concerns can involve what amount to beginnings of diagnostic procedures; by this step the practitioner has presumably been retained and can get this task fully underway. The practitioner uses available evidence and experience to make a preliminary analysis of a person's, organization's, or movement's policy aspirations and possible strategies. The practitioner can thus be equipped to provide aid to the client in situation definition, stimulation, and guidance, but decision making about what is problematic is best cast into a group discussion framework. The client needs to see and understand the problem.

In effect, a clinical sociologist at this stage needs to be both a diagnostician and a group therapist with an ability to arrange instructive and challenging group discussions. As Mary C. Sengstock[11] emphasizes, it is necessary to involve "individuals/group members in the planning process, to maximize the likelihood that they will have an investment in the outcomes" (p. 132), and thus want to help implement them. Howard Rebach[12] points out: "The small group has been 'rediscovered' as a technique in social planning and administration, community organization and development, and organizational development in large formal organizations" (p. 201).

Such diagnostic groups may be drawn from an organization, from the client's community, or from available specialists or interest representatives. They focus on policy needs, possible experiments or variations in policy and program and/or research plans for longer term efforts to mold public policies and behavior. The effectiveness of the Porter-Goldaber "laboratory confrontation" method was mentioned before.

The practitioner has the responsibility of exposing such decision-making groups to relevant surveys, research reports, and informed viewpoints. As Doris Y. Wilkinson[13] indicates, in a discussion of modifying national health policies, "If policy makers are to design coherent planning strategies, they must understand the organization of economic activity, intrinsic and environmentally induced health care needs of the population, and the different patterns of medical service utilization by class, age and sex" (p. 142). This sounds highly complicated, but it is the sort of interdisciplinary data that needs to be fed into client committees to clarify the nature of the problems faced.

Some of this discussion may raise the question of how broadly one should define the area in which a clinical sociologist should be able tenably to claim expertise. At what points would a client think it necessary to bring in other social scientific specialists? Thomas J. Rice,[14] of the consulting firm Interaction Associates, insists: "The reality of consulting is that you draw on whatever knowledge you have to solve the problem at hand" (p. 8), and you attempt to convince the client that, although you have been helpful, the client has defined the problem and diagnosed it. He takes the position that "interdisciplinary boundaries" are a "luxury we cannot afford to indulge" in clinical sociology.

Defining Goals

Is the client trying to represent or even lead an evolving policymaking movement locally, regionally, nationally, or internationally? How tenable does the effort appear to be? How accurately is the movement perceived and described? Are there short-term as well as long-term goals that can and should be sought? What are related, contrasting, and competing movements?

Is the individual or organizational client undergoing a crisis because of incompetence, lack of funds, lack of visibility, changed social conditions, competition, or organized opposition? Some such situation is a common reason for seeking outside expert help. It may be accompanied by an inaccurate definition of possible goals and strategies.

Too often strategies are bound by habitual perceptions and practices and by the vested interests of "insiders" in procedures. Many voluntary, governmental, and commercial organizations suffer from failure to search for, discover, and accept techniques for renewal, to experiment with novel procedures, structures, and personalities, and to reach out toward different publics and organizational alliances. Such adaptations are too often seen as endangering the security of current administrators or technicians. As Jan M. Fritz[15] says, "Clinical sociologists are change-agents who use a sociological perspective as the basis for intervention" (p. 577). She illustrates this by the ways "they try to foster changes in students' attitudes and/or behavior as a direct result of classroom experiences." So practitioners "in the field" must similarly influence their clients through appropriate applications of group therapies.

Confusion between long-term and short-term goals must be understood and avoided or placed in perspective. The establishment of a birth control clinic or of a sex education program in a school are useful steps or short-term objects in a planned parenthood program, but each such step needs to be viewed as a step; the overall program requires continued planning and stimulation.

The goals of an organization (society, corporation, or whatever) and of its leaders, functionaries, and constituents must be considered in relationship. Opportunities for expression and recognition for individuals build morale and also give a personalized aura to a program. The Gray Panthers have gained greatly from the leadership and dramatization of goals by Maggie Kuhn and her picturesque image and manner. Black civil rights efforts gain greatly from identification with the images of such persons as Martin Luther King, Jr. and Jesse Jackson. Similarly our presidential campaigns owe more to the projected images of the principal candidates than to specific promises and party support.

In addition to outstanding personality images, public policy movements get tied to stereotyped issues, spectacular events, and promises of constituent gains. Think of the many stereotyped definitions and redefinitions and even rewritings of the federal Constitution's first amendment clause about the separation of church and state. Religious, civil liberties, and educational bodies and political parties have asserted: It is a "wall of separation." It does or does not permit private or public prayer in public schools.[16] "Right to life" antiabortionists and Planned Parenthood "freedom of choice" activists similarly struggle with constitutional interpretations to try to achieve their goals. Carefully formulated issue stereotypes are most helpful in any public policy struggle.

An example of a spectacular event's influence on policy struggles is provided by the F.B.I. and Naval Investigation Service report on Operation Ill Wind of "rampant bribery" in the Pentagon's military contracting. It "may rank as one of the biggest federal white-collar crime cases ever prosecuted" (pp. 16–18).[17] Those immediately concerned—industrialists, politicians, religious leaders, and social actionists—found the report to be a reason to reexamine and perhaps revise their strategies and goals.

The long-term struggles for more egalitarian treatment of ethnic and racial minorities provide many illustrations of goal and strategy complications. A significant continuation of this campaign was led by N.A.A.C.P. attorney Thurgood Marshall and by social psychologist Kenneth B. Clark. This resulted in 1954 and

1955 in the landmark U.S. Supreme Court *Brown* decisions.[18] Many then thought "that was that." Public schools would have to be desegregated as those decisions were implemented. Many took the position that they could rest for a while from the struggle. Such was not the case. The implementation of those decisions required a continuous series of efforts to offset attempts to set their implications aside. The *Brown* decisions and other developments were followed by resurgences of racist agitations, of sophisticated rationalizations for denying employment, housing, and educational benefits to blacks and other minorities.[19]

Even though the *Brown* decisions were tremendously useful to modifiers of public policies and practices, they were victories in a long, continuing, and much broader struggle. Those involved in fighting for or against equal rights realize that they need to have both long-term and adaptable short-term goals and strategies that can contribute to the overall struggle in many types of public policy of related sorts. The nineteenth amendment to the Constitution giving voting rights to women was just a way station, as it were. Women's organizations have had to continue to fight for legislation and judicial decisions on property rights, divorce, abortion rights, employment opportunities, and the like, and above all for their practical implementation in society.[20]

Significant public policies are embedded in our evolving societal, local, class, ethnic, and vocational cultures. They are reflected, in their various interpretations, in the goals and strategies selected for ongoing struggles. The resulting complications that need to be sorted out and attacked are well illustrated by organizational reactions to the spread of the AIDS infection. In addition to campaigns to fund diagnostic, treatment, basic research, and preventive educational procedures, the whole policymaking scene becomes elaborated by homophobia, racism, anti-birth-control, and evangelical and other mystical explanations and pressurings. As is almost always the case on significant policy problems, attention cannot solely be focused on short- and long-term goals for constructive policymaking and funding. Strategies to cope with opposing thrusts must be prepared for dramatization.

Developing Strategies

On the basis of what is learned from pursuing these four tasks, clinical sociologists next need to turn to analyzing and advising clients on strategic possibilities with their potential objectives, alternatives, risks and benefits, and consequences. How can precedents, allies, opponents, and neutrals be used? What talent, media, and costs are involved? What are other sources of commitment, support, and participation? What sort of a schedule is practical for events, reports, other statements, and their possible repetition in the same or modified form?

At this stage, clinical sociologists need to become stimulators of scenario formations as well as to serve as therapeutic interveners in what L. Alex Swan[21] calls "grounded encounter" relationships with clients. This involves (1) drafting policy statements, (2) possibly suggesting redefined roles, networks, and organizational structures, images, and community relations, (3) planning dramatizing procedures and events, (4) planning the use of available personalities, and (5) developing financial support and schedules. Each of these can best evolve, as Swan says, from "social interaction [with the clients] in which disclosure and discovery lead to an understanding of the social context out of which the problems emerged" (p. 7). Let me illustrate each of these briefly.

Drafting policy statements not only helps to crystallize goal definitions but also provides useful guidance for spokespeople and for communications media purposes. Such statements need to be as clearly stated as possible. Policy proposals should also be given carefully worded labels and, if practical, characterized by a slogan. The American Civil Liberties Union, to illustrate, consistently represents itself as upholding citizens' rights under the federal Constitution, such rights as freedom of speech, assembly, and the press. The clarity and consistency of its position has protected it from many attacks. An example of a useful label is "the greenhouse effect," the concern of all the organizations trying to keep the planet from heating up.

Redefining roles and structures can be the most touchy aspect of strategy negotiations. Client representatives perform certain roles. Their notion of those roles and of how to perform in them may well be a significant part of the client's problem. Inept public statements by a spokesperson may be damaging to the client. Participation in social networks that do not help the client or even give the client a "bad image" must be avoided. An organizational image that identifies a client with some particular source of funds may well keep other sources from providing needed support. The multiplicity of organizations concerned with public policies prompts cooperative efforts among those with similar goals, but such associating must be done only after a careful examination of the public images and potential public images of each.

Planning and dramatizing procedures and events calls for an ability to dramatize program purposes. It is an old story that the mass media look upon large demonstrations and confrontations as more newsworthy than mere statements of an organization's objectives. Those concerned about deforestation hold ceremonial tree plantings. Those seeking to promote planned parenthood procedures give away sample condoms in public spots. Americans United for the Separation of Church and State and Americans for Religious Liberty promote their concerns in religious freedom by participating in constitutionally significant court trials.

Planning the use of available personalities capitalizes upon the symbolic value of attractive individuals. I have mentioned the usefulness of Maggie Kuhn to the Gray Panthers and of Martin Luther King, Jr., and Jesse Jackson to the civil rights movement. Media portrayals of such as Ronald Reagan and George Bush make them far better known than their political policies. Good stage presences can accomplish much for an organization even if they are not as yet well known. In view of this, clients do well to select carefully spokespersons who can represent their contentions. This procedure carries with it the danger of the one selected becoming too enthralled with personal publicity and placing personal gains above the organization's public policy aspirations, but that risk can be borne in mind and controlled.

Developing financial support and schedules necessarily tie together. To keep a program alive, money raising is usually an ancillary goal of many programs. Some do this by associating their programs with holidays or seasons of the year. The Salvation Army is ubiquitous at Christmas time. College and university efforts become more prominent in football seasons and at graduation time. Programs to modify legislation must be keyed to election campaigns and other governmental agendas.

Sometimes there are shortcuts that help to simplify the development of a useful strategy. For example, let us assume that the client is a local public school with a library that contains such popular books as Maurice Sendak's *Where the Wild Things Are* or Harper Lee's *To Kill a Mockingbird*. Some parents in Las Cruces, NM, organized to have the first book removed "for promoting secular humanism and the occult." Some parents in Morrisvale, WVA, formed a crusade against the second book on the grounds that it contains "dirty, filthy language." The school people began to organize resistance to this attempted censorship. They gained support, but the struggle might have been difficult if they had not discovered unexpected aid. The federal secretary of education, William J. Bennett, a Reagan conservative, had issued a list in which both books appeared as desirable stimulants to young people's curiosity and intellectual growth.[22] That made the censor's task too difficult. School officials realize, however, that continuing parent consultation and involvement are needed to prevent recurrences of such events.

Intervening Diplomatically

With tentative strategy plans agreed upon, implementation calls for clinical sociologists to provide their key role as intervener in or reformer of the existing action program. To help clients deal effectively with a public policy problem, the clinicians may be able to do the necessary diplomatic instructing and negotiating themselves. Many times, however, they may have to employ others to assist in developing and staging suitable events, planning and carrying out publicity arrangements, and guiding legal procedures and political forays. To the extent employed, outside professionals should be aids rather than principals in order to avoid a competitive or confusingly contradictory situation. Their work assignments need to be developed cooperatively, and their reports should be integrated into the overall effort.

Spectacular events sometimes occasion the retention of a clinical sociologist. In any event, struggles over a public policy by business, political, or professional leaders are often part of a client's initial problem. Immediate recourse to obtaining favorable media attention, evidence of cooperation from other organizations, and endorsements by notable individuals are among public relations devices that can help the client to get beyond an emergency emotional first stage as rapidly as possible. Such an event as George Bush's attack on Michael Dukakis for being a "card-carrying member" of the American Civil Liberties Union was poorly handled by Dukakis supporters. They permitted themselves to be embarrassed by it rather than to glory in the pro-federal Constitution character of the label. The ACLU on the other hand benefitted from the attack. It exploited the event by providing its constituents with "card-carrying-member" labels to stick to their automobiles. It also made descriptions of its pro-federal-Constitution character available to the media and members.

Interventions of the sort discussed take place on personal, intergroup or intraorganizational, inter-organizational, and societal levels. They may also be in the form of direct, indirect, or cooperative procedures. Although these levels and forms can be typified separately, they are frequently mixed together in practice.

The *personal level of intervention* with the client's leader may be crucial. It may mean helping the person clarify notions of interracial or interethnic or intergender relations. Sometimes the leader's personal background and current family life may be handicaps. The practitioner's awareness of such personal problems can determine whether or not some form of individual counseling or group therapy, instruction or recreation might improve the administrator's or spokesperson's functioning. Whether to use direct, indirect, or cooperative procedures in helping people on the personal level depends upon one's day-to-day contacts with them.

Sometimes the most important use of personal intervention is among selected people who are, for some reason, trouble spots in the organization. I have often seen how the arranging of some degree of personal recognition and perhaps public identification can involve such persons constructively in a program. To the extent possible and practical, morale and drive can be improved and even made dynamic by avoiding appearances of depersonalization, of unthinking routinization. More comprehensively, as Roger A. Straus[23] asserts, this involves attention to "role structure, taking into account such factors as authority relationships, consensus regarding roles and their boundaries, degree of involvement in roles, role strain or conflict, [and] informal versus formal realities" (p. 57).

Intergroup level interventions within an organization or movement often focus, as Straus adds, on "the degree to which the operational definition of the group facilitates or hinders attainment of its collective purposes." These interventions can be all the more direct to the extent that the earlier stages of work with the client have been conducted on confrontational "gut level" bases.

Many race relations, civil rights, planned parenthood, and other social policy organizations run into problems of minor but disrupting internal ideological differences. Group-level interventions can do much to smooth over such differences in the interest of overall concerns. Unwise personnel selections and lack of opportunities for participant discussions and other aids to the development of morale have consigned many organizations to what amounts to organizational graveyards, killed through lack of such therapeutic intervention on a constructive and continuing basis.

A recent development in the movement to assure women of their right to reproductive choice illustrates a useful way to intervene in the relations among cooperating or potentially cooperating groups. Many religious denominations and welfare institutions favor women's right to an abortion, but they differ on the nature of the need and on the maximum timing during pregnancy of such a recourse. The differences are often seized upon and exaggerated by "prolife" antiabortionists in order to support their efforts. Americans for Religious Liberty in 1988 brought together a conference of many organizational representatives to develop a manual for the movement that would emphasize their similar views. The resulting manual, published in 1989, is *Abortion Rights and Fetal "Personhood."*[24] It contains religious, scientific, and legal articles, written in clear English by recognized experts, that indicate a "united front" on the definition of basic issues. It also reports that opinion polls indicate that nationally a majority of the members of each religious segment favors abortion rights. It sets forth the formal supporting statements by denominations and theologians, including evangelicals and Roman Catholics. This provides substantial ammunition for this movement to use in upcoming legislative and judicial battles.

Interorganizational level interventions require adequate personnel, diagnostic, ideological, and strategic preparations. The more one can learn about the opposition the more effective this level of intervention can be. For example, if one can obtain a person identified with the opposition to take the client's position, it is much more effective than statements from the home camp. In the case mentioned about the abortion struggle, the scholarly Roman Catholic theologian Marjorie Reiley Maguire was enlisted to write a chapter that gave priority to female "personal autonomy" over "fetal personhood."[25] She documented her proabortion stand with Roman Catholic statements.

The struggles of the NAACP Legal Defense and Educational Fund (LDF) are so varied that they illustrate many aspects of interorganizational intervention. For example, LDF had Louis Harris conduct a national poll (reported in 1989) for diagnostic purposes. That survey "found that blacks and whites are 'worlds apart' in their perception of race relations, with a majority of whites believing that blacks are treated equally in America and a majority of blacks disagreeing." On the hopeful side, "53 percent of all those surveyed both black and white—said 'more' should be done to promote greater equality for blacks and other racial minorities."[26] This and other aspects of the survey support the NAACP's ideology and the LDF's program of lobbying and litigation for equal rights. Aided by the growing number of Afro-American figures of prominence, such as Jesse Jackson and Bill Cosby, Barbara Jordon and Lena Horne, the NAACP's educational program supports the LDF's activities.

On the *societal level of intervention*, dramatic speeches and other events predominate. They provide access to the media and to private-interest mythmaking. They require careful analyses of both the client's and the oppositions' propagandas.[27] Interventions are best achieved through arranging cooperative moves with other similarly motivated or focused bodies. Efforts on this level do much to achieve public policy modifications.

The Reagan–Bush phalanx of private organizations and public agencies demonstrate how a substantial network of socially manipulative instruments is brought together and implemented. It has included religious bodies, business groups, labor institutes, militarists, and New Right propagandists. Its most influential members have been the Center for Strategic and International Studies at Georgetown University, the Heritage Foundation, and the Council for Inter-American Security, all conservative think tanks. Active as lobbyists have been the Conservative Caucus, Free Congress Foundation, National Defense Council for Inter-American Security, the New Christian Right, the Moral Majority, and the Christian Anti-Communist Crusade among others. The National Endowment for Democracy, Freedom House, and the Center for International Private Enterprise work to "export democracy," as defined by the current administration's supporters. The federal government itself has a complex of national and international propaganda agencies, centered in the

White House. The United States Information Agency has 204 posts in 127 countries and operates the "Voice of America" and the Cuba-oriented "Radio Marti." The influence of all these agencies on the mass communications media, social leaders, and education has often been discussed. Clinical sociologists often need to know the workings of this vast network in handling public policy problems for a client.

Continuing Program Adaptations

The goal of a public policy modification program should not be the implementation of a single policy statement as such. It should be the development of an ongoing process of policy adaptation to changing opportunities and social conditions. Individual policy statements are useful as temporary or long-term goals. One constantly needs to realize, however, that they are imbedded in social struggles in a changing social environment. Their current form can soon become dated at least in rhetoric if not in intent. Thomas Jefferson[28] pointed to this principle of attention to social change when he asked, "What country can preserve its liberties, if its rulers are not warned from time to time, that this people preserve the spirit of resistance?" (pp. 19–20). And he adds: "A little rebellion, now and then, is a good thing, and as necessary in the political world as storms in the physical."

Consider the changing nature and settings of policies that attempt to deal with our rising tide of homelessness, with entrepreneurial abuses of the Medicare, Medicaid, and general health situation, with the exportation of manufacturing enterprises, with the neocolonialist exploitation of "Third World" areas, with the pollution of earth, water, and air, with the nuclear and nuclear waste threats locally and nationally, and with the Greenhouse warming of the earth and potential rising of the oceans. Think of policy statements that have been put forward, fought for, and adopted with regard to the status of women politically and economically and how these have become dated and changed. Ponder the efforts to militarize our society further and to demilitarize it. And then there is the spread of the AIDS virus, dangers perceived in genetic experimentation with animals, diseases, and even humans, and the presence of chemical warfare weapons. All these and other stimulants to continuing and changing policy struggles have both micro- and macroaspects of concern for clinical sociologists whether they are counseling individuals, corporations, governmental agencies, or voluntary bodies. A client concerned with any one of those struggles has day-to-day current problems and policy objectives. These then have to be seen as clearly as possible in relation to longer term developments and opportunities in order to be ready to adapt. Some speak of it all as being a "very challenging game." Maybe that is a stimulating way of thinking about program adaptations, but they are often too complicated and important to be reduced to such a simplification.

Ethical Concerns and Issues

The value situation in sociological research and application is an intricate, difficult, and haunting one. I have tried to explore it extensively in my books,

Sociology for Whom?[27] and *Sociology for People.*[29] It has also concerned many other sociologists, for example, Pitirim A. Sorokin[30] and Robert S. Lynd.[31] As I see it, those who wish to function and be regarded as creative and ethical social scientists make their findings or services available only to clients whose activities they regard as being socially constructive in a democratic society. By this, I do not mean that social scientists agree on what is creative or constructive or ethical. They may disagree on the nature of specific aspects of what a democratic society are or should be. But their dedication to such objectives and concerns gives them much to hold in common, a basis for mutual respect.

As T. V. Smith[32] concludes, "Ethics is the organization or criticism of conduct in terms of notions like good, right or welfare." The criteria for these notions derive from our religious and political traditions. These criteria have much in common and are widely held in our society.

As an academic, I have always found it enlightening to participate in discussion groups of nonacademics: labor union organizers, investigative media reporters, advertising and public relations specialists, politicians, and miscellaneous professionals. I have also listened to discussions of ethical issues by groups of clergy from various denominations. These groups have been of different colors and ethnic backgrounds. Like academics, these people soon make it clear that they are employed and to a degree bound by the practical problems of existing institutions. They have to do the kinds of thinking, acting, and writing that their employers accept and will reward. At the same time, many of them have had intimate experiences with the unemployed, abused, abusing, imprisoned, psychotic, exploiting, lying, thieving, degenerate, and whatever. In their discussions at such meetings, they tend to talk more about people that they know rather than about stereotypes. They also suggest the labels and thought formulas with which they or their colleagues can simplify their lives by pushing the problematic into pigeonholes. But at the same time, they often have twinges of conscience that make them criticize currently accepted public policies and the ways in which they or their colleagues "have to" compromise and even violate such policies. Some become whistle blowers and risk conflict with their superiors in order to do what they regard to be ethical.

Another perspective that I have had on professional ethics has been provided by my study of the development of ethical codes by journalists, advertising specialists, and public relations counselors and by my participation in ethical decisions in the American Sociological Association. These experiences give me a clear impression that organizational codes of ethics are intended primarily as public relations devices, especially to the advantage of those engaged in the commercialization of a profession. Fortunately such codes also provide a reason for not accepting professionally unethical assignments from a client. A great many sociologists are, in my estimation, highly ethical as a part of their dedication to their discipline. They do not need the pressure of a society or a code to keep them from violating scientific and humane principles. Those who have had the field experience that makes them know people and their needs on many levels of society try to serve society more broadly.

Some intelligent public relations specialists that I know provide me with another perspective on sociological ethics. Their view of the utility of clinical sociology, interestingly enough, often applies an ethical measure to those they employ. They characterize available sociologists either as accurate and ethical operatives or as propagandists. They may hire both types. The former do investigations and offer strategies and therapies useful for their own guidance and for the counseling of their clients. The reports and interpretations of these clinical sociologists may be upsetting and difficult for them to use. They look upon sociological propagandists, on the other hand, as merely part of their manipulative staff. They are known to do what they are told to do.

What I regard as a by-product of the ethical clash between the mandates of employers and the folk wisdom and dedication of professionals has given us, in the field of mass communications, a valuable information source for clinical sociologists concerned with public policies. I am referring to the media of communication that are called "alternative." Many of their articles or sources of information are derived from employees of the "mass" media. Some of these reporters eventually free themselves and find greater opportunities to investigate and to publish books as free-lancers or to work full-time for alternative newspapers, magazines, or radio or TV stations. Their critical treatments of "the respectable" may not be acceptable in many cases, but it provides possible bases for more objective perspectives on many public policies. It is the sort of thing that made Lincoln Steffens, Upton Sinclair, George Seldes, and I. F. Stone famous and influential in the discussion of many public policies.

My illustrations are meant to suggest that the experience necessary for the training of competent clinical sociologists develops in them an attachment to ethical values of a constructive sort. Even when their financial "bottom line" tempts them to become careless with humane values, they often prefer to plead against short-term experiments of a selfish nature that ignore longer term social consequences. Without such built-in enlightenment in many types of practitioners, our capitalistic democracy would be far less viable and durable.

What I am saying is that clinical sociologists perform their social roles most acceptably and adequately when they have learned the value of intellectual autonomy, have been immersed in enough participatory experience and sociological knowledge to understand necessary humane concerns, and advise their clients accurately rather than merely expediently. The more such clinical sociologists we have, the more the usefulness and employment of their contributions will expand. It will also assure that they will make continually more effective modifications of public policies.*

REFERENCES

1. Thomas, W. I., & Dorothy S. (1928). *The child in America*. New York: Alfred A. Knopf, 3rd ed., 1983.
2. Porter, Holly G. (n.d.). *Laboratory confrontation*, mimeo., pp. 23–24, and Goldaber, Irving, and Porter (n.d.) *Notes on "laboratory confrontation."* Grand Rapids: Community Confrontation & Communication Associates.

* My thanks for critical suggestions to Howard Martin Rebach, John S. Bruhn, Deborah Backes, and especially Elizabeth Briant Lee.

3. Straus, R. A. (1984). Changing the definition of the situation. *Clinical Sociology Review, 2*, 51–63.
4. Horowitz, I. L. (1968). *Professional sociology.* Chicago: Aldine.
5. Reinarman, Craig (1987). *American states of mind.* New Haven: Yale University Press.
6. Fienberg, S. E., & Tanur, Judith M. (1989). Combining cognitive and statistical approaches to survey design. *Science, 243*, 1017–22.
7. Reinarman, *op. cit.*, p. 222.
8. Bogart, Leo (1972). *Silent politics, polls, and the awareness of public opinion.* New York: Wiley-Interscience.
9. Abramson, P. R. (1983). San Francisco: W. H. Freeman & Co. Cannell, C. F., & Kahn, R. L. (1968). Interviewing. In Gardner Lindzey & Elliot Aronson (Eds.), *The handbook of social psychology* (Vol. 2, Chapter 15). Reading, MA: Addison-Wesley.
10. Herzog, Elizabeth G. (1947). Pending perfection: A qualitative complement to quantitative methods. *International Journal of Opinion and Attitude Research, 1*(3) (September), 31–48.
11. Sengstock, Mary C. (1987). Sociological strategies for developing community resources. *Clinical Sociology Review, 3*, 132–44.
12. Rebach, Howard (1987). Review of P. H. Glaser & N. S. Mayadas, *Group workers at work.* Totowa, NJ: Rowman & Littlefield. In *Clinical Sociology Review, 5*, 201–203.
13. Wilkinson, Doris Y. (1987). Transforming national health policy: The significance of the stratification system. *American Sociologist, 18*, 140–145.
14. Rice, T. J. (1986). Life on the applied/clinical side. *ASA Footnotes, 14*(8) (November).
15. Fritz, Jan M. (1979). Practicing clinical sociology. *American Behavioral Scientist, 22*, 577–588.
16. Swomley, J. M. (1987). *Religious liberty and the secular state.* Buffalo, NY: Prometheus Books.
17. Magnuson, Ed (1988). The Pentagon up for sale. *Time,* 131, 26 (June 27), pp. 16–18.
18. Clark, K. B. (1965). *Dark ghetto: Dilemma of social power.* New York: Harper & Row.
19. Pinkney, Alphonso (1984). *The myth of black progress.* New York: Cambridge University Press. Wilhelm, S. M. (1983). *Blacks in white America.* Cambridge, MA: Schenkman Publ. Co.
20. Richardson, Laurel (1988). *The dynamics of sex and gender.* New York: Harper & Row. Weitzman, Lenore. (1985). *The divorce revolution.* New York: Free Press. Foner, P. S. (1980). *Women and the American labor movement.* New York: Free Press.
21. Swan, L. G. (1988). Grounded encounter theory: Its characteristics and process. *Clinical Sociology Review, 6*, 76–87.
22. *St. Louis Post-Dispatch,* Sept. 8, 1988; New York *Times,* Sept. 1, 1988.
23. Straus, *op. cit.*, p. 57.
24. Doerr, Edd, & Prescott, J. W. (Eds.). (1989). *Abortion rights and fetal "personhood."* Long Beach, CA: Centerline Press.
25. Maguire, Marjorie R. (1989). Symbiosis, biology, and personalization. In *ibid.,* Chapter 2.
26. Johnson, Julie (1989). Blacks and whites are found "worlds apart." *New York Times,* January 12.
27. See Lee, A. McC. (1986). *Sociology for whom?* (Rev. ed.). Syracuse: Syracuse University Press.
28. Jefferson, Thomas (1787). *Thomas Jefferson on democracy.* Ed. by S. K. Padover. New York: New American Library, 1946.
29. Lee, A. McC. (1988). *Sociology for people: Toward a caring profession.* Syracuse: Syracuse University Press.
30. Cowell, F. R. (1970). *Values in human society: The contributions of Pitirim A. Sorokin to sociology.* Boston: F. Porter Sargent.
31. Lynd, R. S. (1939). *Knowledge for what?* Princeton: Princeton University Press.
32. Smith. T. V. (1937). Ethics. *Encyclopaedia of the social sciences, 5*, 602–607.

CHAPTER 11

The Clinical Sociologist in Medical Settings

YVONNE M. VISSING AND DAVID J. KALLEN

INTRODUCTION

As medicine has come to recognize the importance of psychological and sociological variables in the role of health and disease, the demand for clinical sociologists in medical settings has increased. In this chapter, the history of medical sociology will be reviewed, the special roles of clinical sociologists in medical settings will be discussed, and the usefulness of sociological theory in delivering health care services will be noted. Fertile areas of development for clinical sociologists, including medical ethics, chronic disease, and the establishment of personal and social wellness, will be outlined. In order for clinical sociologists to deliver services, they must gain professional acceptance, so some discussion of credibility for clinical sociologists in medical settings is included. This chapter should provide the reader with an understanding of the special needs of patients and providers in the health care professions. More important, it will demonstrate how the unique skills of clinical sociologists can be used in medical settings and show that clinicians working within a medical framework may find the opportunities to help bring about monumental social change.

HISTORY OF MEDICAL SOCIOLOGY

The use of sociological theory and methods in health settings was first discussed in the 1930s by Wirth,[1] in the context of the usefulness of sociologists in

YVONNE M. VISSING • Family Research Laboratory, University of New Hampshire, Durham, New Hampshire 03824, and Department of Pediatrics, Boston City Hospital, Boston, Massachusetts 02118. DAVID J. KALLEN • Department of Pediatrics and Human Development, Michigan State University, East Lansing, Michigan 48824.

child guidance clinics.[2] The utility of sociologists as part of medical school instructional and care giving faculty was suggested by the dean of the Yale School of Medicine in a series of papers in the early 1930s.[3,4] Neither of these efforts bore fruit, and clinical sociology in medical and other settings languished until around 1972 when Dunham[5,2] again suggested the utility of the sociological perspective. Both Wirth and Dunham were concerned with the usefulness of a sociological understanding of individual, primarily deviant, behavior.

Traditional medical sociology, which forms a base for much clinical sociology in health care settings today, developed initially as part of U.S. sociology.[6] As late as 1980, Wolinsky[7] reported that the majority of research and publication in medical sociology came from the United States. The autobiographical accounts of careers in medical sociology, edited by Elling and Sokolowska,[8] also reflects this American push.

Concern over the relationship between social factors and disease resulted in the development of "social medicine" in the United States during the 1920s and 1930s. This concern was bolstered in the 1940s and 1950s by an increase in epidemiological studies. The first medical sociologist was appointed to the faculty of the Department of Psychiatry and Preventive Medicine at the University of Ontario in 1949; in the 1950s, medical sociologist Robert Straus, set up a department of behavioral science as an integral part of the new medical school at the University of Kentucky. The movement of sociologists into positions in medical schools led to the use of sociological theory in teaching in medical schools, but little was written about clinical sociology in medical settings until the early 1980s, with the reemergence of clinical sociology as a major subdiscipline within sociology.

For the most part, American medical sociology has not been *clinical* in its focus. It made an early distinction between the sociology *of* medicine as "the use of medicine as an arena to study important social processes, such as stratification, professional socialization and politics, with no particular concern with arriving at insights useful to practitioners"[9] and sociology *in* medicine, which focused on "*research* that was structured more to serve medical care needs than to promote new basic knowledge."[9] (emphasis added) More recently, it has been recognized that this distinction is not useful; theory adds to practice, and practice adds to theory.

Even today, a recent review of the field of medical sociology, prepared under the aegis of the Medical Sociology Section of the American Sociological Association[10] continues the tradition of research and analysis and contains no discussion of sociologists using their knowledge to bring about change desired by a client. Nonetheless, the work of traditional medical sociologists forms much of the knowledge base for clinical sociologists working in medical settings, just as the understandings developed by these clinicians are contributing to the knowledge base.

USE OF THEORY IN CLINICAL MEDICAL SOCIOLOGY

Although clinical sociologists may be able to use a variety of psychological and sociological theories in their practice, it is likely that their sociological roots direct their selection of theoretical perspective. The perspective will influence whether the client's problem is seen as due to forces in the macro-social structure, such as economics, discrimination, or organizational conflict or, if a more microperspective is used, whether the interaction between the client and significant others is the issue; problems in the definition of social cues, problems due to the reference group the client has selected; problems due to past experiences that have resulted in script development that constructs a certain kind of "reality" to which the individual responds. To what extent does conflict, be it macro or micro in nature, affect the reason that the clinical sociologist is contacted?

It is important for clinical sociologists to keep their theoretical positions in mind while providing clinical service in medical settings. Understanding the impact of all the different social units with which the client comes in contact—the individual, the family, the physician, the other health care providers, the organization of the hospital/care facility, important other social units (i.e., job, school)—is a major challenge. Yet this complex, interwoven set of relationships must be carefully considered when working with a client. The needs of the patient may be different from the needs of the family or the needs of the physician or the needs of the hospital, and these needs can be in direct opposition to one another. The clinical sociologist must be clear whose side he/she is on.[11]

The link between theory, research, and practical applications is critical. In order for the sociologist to become a change agent, sound theory and research must have been developed. The clinician is in the unusual and helpful position of being able to identify when the theory does not hold true, as well as when it is useful as the basis for intervention. The clinical sociologist may also determine what kinds of research should be generated in order to solve problems. The clinician may be able to recommend social change and new social policies based on the disparity between available knowledge and the information that needs to be acquired.

SPECIAL ROLES OF CLINICAL SOCIOLOGISTS IN MEDICAL SETTINGS

There are many roles that a clinical sociologist can assume, just as there are many roles for medical sociologists. The merging of medical and clinical sociology produces a unique set of skills for the sociologist. This section will provide information on a few of the specialized roles that clinical sociologists can play in medical settings. Emphasis will be placed on the role of clinical sociologist as counselor in dealing with patients and their families, but mention will also be made of the clinical sociologist as program developer and as a "teaching attending" in a hospital.

Counselor in Medical Settings

The clinical sociologist can provide a variety of counseling services in health care settings and can introduce a biopsychosocial perspective into the traditional understanding of both physical and mental illness.[12] Some of these counseling services include (1) helping the individual change undesired behaviors, such as failing to adhere to a diet, that will result in inability to lose weight, (2) helping the patient deal with the consequences of physical or mental disability/disease, (3) helping the patient's family cope with the consequences of mental or physical disability/disease, and (4) helping the patient modify role perceptions that influence the development of behavioral or health problems.

Clinical sociologists have important skills to contribute, including in-depth interviewing and the use of grounded theory methodology, which are essential for understanding human behavior. Research interviews have been found to become therapeutic interviews for some subjects,[13] and the line between interview data collection and therapy may become fine indeed. The sociological study of emotion is useful in counseling because it facilitates an understanding of how patients experience emotion, how they objectify it, and the strategies they use to handle emotions. Sociologists may also be able to unravel communication and language misinterpretations between the physician and the patient because of their understanding of culture.[12] Physician–patient discrepancies in verbal and nonverbal communication may also be important arenas for counselor involvement. Understanding how linguistic frames and schemata provide structures of expectation, which control the interaction between physicians and patients, can be used to improve the interaction patterns between physicians and patients.[14]

Clinical sociologists may provide therapy to help the patient resolve situations that cause tension within himself or herself or in interaction with the wider social world. Changes in their views of themselves, in their relations with others, and in patterns of behavior may all be of assistance to patients. As Cuthbertson[12] points out, at times it will be necessary for drug therapy, psychological therapy, and possible other forms of treatments to occur simultaneously to enable the patient to work on these changes. This collaboration suggests an important role for the clinical sociologist, a role that is interdependent with the roles of other specialists.

It is important to remember that the clinical sociologist involved in counseling is a *sociologist*. Therefore, the counseling that takes place deals more with interpersonal relationships or with the relationship that the person has with the social world than it does with the internal working of the psyche. Swan's[15] approach to sociotherapy involves *grounding*, allowing "the problems, their explanations, and the strategies and techniques for treatment to emerge. . . . [from] a process of interaction in which disclosure and discovery lead to an understanding of the social context out of which the problems emerged." This process has similarities with the research process suggested by Glaser and Straus.[16] In health care settings, this approach is particularly useful in those instances where family difficulties impact on the health care process; for example when difficulties between husband and wife make it difficult for them to adhere to a treatment regimen for their child, or when tensions in their relationship exacerbate health conditions, such as high blood pressure.

Many health care issues in which counseling is helpful are related to definitions of the situation,[17] to role relationships, or to ways in which the individual constructs social reality. For example, in counseling an overweight woman who wants to lose weight but is having difficulty doing so, Straus[18] points out that social definitions of the situation both support behaviors that make it difficult for the client to lose weight and add to her self-definition of an overweight person. Unsuccessful attempts to lose weight result in definitions of self as failure.

Intervention can take several forms. The client may be helped to understand that definitions of appropriate weight are arbitrary and dependent on the standards of the social group.[19] Counseling will help the client to understand how much of the behaviors that contribute to the obesity are grounded in social behaviors and social expectations, supported by norms and behaviors of a variety of groups to which she belongs. They are lifestyle issues, rather than social or psychological defects in the person. Change can be brought about by helping the client redefine the situation; Straus points out that one way to be changed is to act changed. Acting as though one has changed may depend on social support from significant others, and the counselor may need to work with family members to get them to accept and support the changed behaviors of the client. These changes, in turn, lead to changes in the relationships within the family group.*

Important educational functions are performed by the clinical sociologist in health settings. In the case of chronic disease[23] or of sexual dysfunctions,[24] the counselor can help specify sets of social expectations and can help the client discover the social origins of his or her own expectations. Sometimes, simply providing data on the social distribution of problems or events may help the client place his/her own behavior in a broader social context. For example, many men have episodes of erectile difficulty; providing this information may help a client recognize the fact that the difficulty is not unusual and hence relieve anxiety about it.

Educational and social constructionist perspectives are also helpful in crisis intervention. As Byers[25] points out, a crisis is a social interpretation of events that may have other interpretations. When situations or events are interpreted as a crisis, the client will take action; the same events may be interpreted as normal, and no action will result. Health care issues may be defined as a crisis when an individual is diagnosed as having a life-threatening disease or when medical care is necessary and the client does not have the necessary funds. When a physician and a patient interpret the same event differently, a crisis may be created by the failure of the patient to take the action expected by the physician. Clarifying roles and expectations and redefining the situation as one in which appropriate action may be taken will often remove its crisis aspects and result in appropriate action.

A good deal of sociological intervention in health care situations involves changing the definition of the situation, with a consequent redefining of appropriate, expected, and normal roles. Fein[26] indicates that giving up certain unhealthy behaviors may require resocialization. Resocialization involves the process of reexperiencing failed roles learned earlier, letting those failed roles go, and substituting new and more satisfactory roles. The process involves both cognitive and emotional experiences. It is particularly useful in the treatment of alcoholism. Alcoholic behavior is supported by present social relationships and by roles and sense of self learned in earlier relationships.

Counseling in health care settings is a growing and important activity for clinical sociologists. As the health care professions show increasing concern with

---

* Kargman's[20] approach to marriage counseling assumes a similar position. See also Church,[21] and Voelkl and Colburn.[22]

chronic illness and chronic disease and deal increasingly with the aging population, the need to help patients negotiate social realities, construct new lives for themselves, and renegotiate social roles is bound to increase.

Program Developer

Clinical sociologists can be used by hospital and care giving facilities to develop special programs or units to serve the needs of patients and their families. The clinical sociologist can develop programs or units to meet the health care needs of the patients while addressing important social and psychological characteristics of those to be served.

As an example, Kallen[27] helped organize an adolescent inpatient unit in a community hospital. Adolescents were admitted to the unit because of an acute physical problem. The unit was designed to promote the healing process and encourage adolescent social growth. Activities were developed to provide role continuity between the required sick role in the hospital and normal roles that adolescents played outside the hospital. Patients were encouraged to play as many of their outside roles as possible, given the requirements of their medical condition. This required renegotiation of some of the traditional caretaker roles, as some encouraged self-care activities of the patients conflicted with the traditional caretaker role of the nurses. Clinical sociologists encouraged the incorporation of an activities room, designed as a "safe haven" where adolescents could play and communicate with each other with the assurance that no medical procedures would take place in the room. Much use was made of small-group process to help adolescents reduce the sense of isolation that illness and hospitalization brought to them and to help create a normative structure to promote continued development.

Attendance on Teaching Rounds

Clinical sociologists can make a significant contribution by working with physicians on the wards in determining diagnosis, treatment, and care of patients. Despite the reforms of the Flexner Report,[28] much teaching in medicine still retains an apprenticeshiplike character, which is readily apparent in hospital teaching rounds. A description of teaching rounds will be followed by a discussion of how clinical sociologists can contribute to them.

Teaching rounds generally take the following form: A group of students, including third or fourth year medical students; first, second, and third year residents; and fellows and a senior physician meet in the hospital to review the treatment of patients who are under the residents' care. Someone presents the salient facts about a patient, including a complete medical history. For a patient who has been in the hospital for one or more days, minimal changes in treatment plan may be called for. Teaching is accomplished when participants question the more junior participants about the patient's condition and treatment. Because rounds serve both a socializing and an instructional purpose, the team members will frequently draw upon their own experience with similar cases to make points.

The focus of rounds normally is on the traditional medical aspects of patient care. Anspach[29] has noted that the language commonly used makes for depersonalization of the patient, focusing on the disease entity, with an emphasis on impersonal workings of interventions rather than on the actions of health care providers. The pediatric residency program in the College of Human Medicine at Michigan State University combatted this impersonalization by having a clinical sociologist make teaching rounds with the attending physician. (Rounds were also made by anthropologists and psychologists.) The mere presence of the sociologist (and other behavioral scientists) focused attention on the human problems of the patients.

Clinical sociologists should realize that teaching rounds require skills that are quite different from those required by direct patient care or traditional classroom teaching. The subject matter of the teaching frequently is not known until rounds are under way but stems from something noticed on rounds or during the discussion of a patient. For example, a patient being presented on one day might come from what appeared to be a normal family, facilitating a discussion of the nature of the typical family, whereas on another day, the discussion might focus on a child hospitalized for failure to thrive. Teaching could center on the nature of mother–child interaction and the frequent indication, in cases of failure to thrive, of a disarrangement of optimal mother–child interaction,[30] or, when appropriate, on the problems of adolescent parenthood. The inability to obtain a special diet for a child could result in a discussion of how bureaucracies operate, the coexistence of formal and informal social structures in the hospital, and how the informal structure can be utilized to help the patient when the formal structure creates major roadblocks. Teaching rounds provide an ideal opportunity for the clinical sociologist to merge macro- and microknowledge to result in more humane treatment of a patient.

THE CREDIBILITY CRISIS FOR CLINICAL SOCIOLOGISTS

Although we have established the fact that a clinical sociologist working in medical settings can provide service to both the physicians and patients, the acceptance of the clinical sociologist as part of the medical team may not be easy. An important reason for this lack of acceptance has to do with a perceived credibility crisis for clinical sociologists.

Clinical sociologists who practice in medical settings must understand that medical sociology suffers, according to Gold,[31] from a "crisis in identity"; traditional medical sociologists are perceived to be playing a subordinate, handmaiden role to physicians. To the extent that the medical sociologist adopts existing medical value assumptions, this support for the medical model may minimize the theoretical and political integrity of medical sociology. Although cooperation between the various disciplines is necessary in any research effort, this does not give one discipline license to dominate another.[7]

Part of this credibility problem seems to stem from a lack of consensus over the definition of health and illness. Twaddle and Hessler[32] put it succinctly—"We all know what health and illness are. Or do we?" Physicians may have different conceptual and operational definitions of what constitutes health and illness than may clinical sociologists. According to Wolinsky, there are social, psychological, and medical dimensions to the definition of health and illness. This three-dimensional approach views strict allopathic diagnosis as but one component in the ultimate decision as to whether one is sick or well. The social and psychological components, which clinical sociologists can help physicians understand, are also of major importance in defining a person's condition as healthy or ill.

Some sociologists have lost credibility with physicians by assuming a practice of "doctor bashing." Doctor bashing represents a critical stance toward the practice of medicine that frequently fails to recognize the reality of medical practice, finds fault with the health care system, and lays the blame on medical practitioners. The if-they-would-only-listen-to-me syndrome is reflected, for example, in many of the articles on medical education appearing in a recent issue of *The Journal of Health and Social Behavior*.[33] After analyzing structural impediments to the training of humane physicians, the authors suggest that if the medical schools would only listen to the sociologists and change their curriculum (which, in turn, would require a restructuring of the entire medical school), the problems would be solved. These approaches fail to take into account the complex influence of accrediting bodies on training programs and the material acquisition necessary for such physician qualification tests as the national boards. Furthermore, these suggestions fail to include a commitment on the part of the critics to help design and implement the necessary structural and curricular changes for such a massive revision of medical training.

In order for the practicing sociologist to establish credibility in the health care system, she or he must demonstrate the ability to do things that are useful for the system. Although theoretical criticism is useful in the abstract, the sociologist whose clinical actions make the life of the health care practitioner easier is the sociologist who will be listened to. Credibility, in medicine, is established primarily through clinical work, that is, through the willingness to put one's ability and skills on the line in the service of caring for patients. This may be through direct patient care or through the indirect care implied in the instruction of medical students and house staff on the hospital ward or in outpatient settings. The instruction must be of a consultative nature, translating the knowledge of the clinical sociologist into terms and activities that the resident can apply to a specific patient, rather than an abstract lecture on a theoretical topic.[34]

AREAS OF EXPANSION FOR CLINICAL MEDICAL SOCIOLOGISTS

Because the use of clinical sociologists in medical settings is recent, sociologists are still in the process of determining areas of medical practice that may especially benefit from their involvement. A discussion of three of these fruitful areas—medical ethics, chronic disease, and wellness—will deal with ways in which increased involvement from clinical sociologists could facilitate health care and health care decisions.

Medical Ethics and Clinical Sociology

Although sociologists have had an interest in biomedical ethics, this interest has been more concerned with the ethics of research than with the ethics of patient care decisions.[35,36] There has been concern with the distribution of scarce resources or with the ethics of deciding who will receive organs for transplantation.[37,38]

As Fox[39] and Grey[35] both point out, major ethical concerns arise from the high level of technology presently available to keep the body alive, the ability to preserve life through transplantation of bodily parts that are in scarce supply, the privatization of health care, and problems of access to health care in a society in which major issues of income differential exist. Sociologists tend to approach these issues from a structural point of view; ethics are frequently seen in terms of *social justice*. On the other hand, medical ethics, as viewed by physicians, tend to focus more on *individual patient rights*, or on the interdependence of individuals (i.e., patient and family).

Sociologists, by training, tend to be relativistic in their assessment of moral issues. Durkheim[40] pointed out that social facts are dependent on the norms of the society, and what is normative is relative to a particular society at a given point in its history. In this view, there are no absolutes except those that a given society declares to be absolute. At the same time, sociologists as citizens have values and beliefs that guide their behavior. Their relativistic understanding is apt to enable them to accept varied patterns as valid for a given society or subgroup within society, rather than to hold all to a universal standard.

Much of the debate in medical ethics has been over whether or not there are universal rights. Some of the questions that are raised follow: Does a patient with a fatal disease have a universal right to be told of the prognosis, or should the physician decide whether or not to tell the patient on the basis of the physician's assessment of the benefit to the patient of knowing or not knowing the prognosis?[41] Does a patient who is apparently being kept alive by respirator have the right to have that respirator turned off?[42] Whose interests are served by which decision? Who has a right to intercede for the patient or for the family? What interest does the state have in the outcome?

Sociologists have not been greatly involved in these decisions, which are frequently stressful for those who must make them. There is a major difference between supporting social justice by calling for a health care policy that provides equal access to health care and participating in clinical decisions, such as deciding whether to turn off a respirator or to deny access to a needed organ transplant to a known individual.

There are several ways in which clinical sociologists can become involved in issues of medical ethics. They include the following:

1. Many medical schools and hospitals have ethics conferences in which ethical dilemmas are reviewed. Frequently, these are oriented around a specific case that provides an example of the issue. Participating in such a conference will afford the clinical sociologist an opportunity to learn more about the area of medical ethics and to represent the sociological viewpoint in the discussion.

2. Increasingly, hospitals are forming ethics committees to review instances in which ethically difficult decisions must be made. For example, a decision might

have to be made regarding whether to perform open heart surgery on a severely brain-damaged infant who shows no signs of sentient thinking but responds to pain and will take nourishment. The ethics committee frequently consists of medical personnel and middle-class representatives of the community. The sociologist could explain why parents of modest means, who find the economic burden of high technological care for a child whose quality of life will, at best, be negligible, may choose not to have heroic measures used on their deformed infant. Alternatively, the sociologist may be able to explain why a woman whose life career is motherhood and child rearing wants extreme measures taken to preserve the life of an infant whose care would be viewed as an intolerable burden by most observers.

3. Due to increasingly scarce resources, hospitals may be faced with making decisions about using technology that will enable a patient to live or die. Sociologists are aware that a conflict between the good of an individual and the good of society as a whole often exists. Societies frequently ask their members to sacrifice themselves so that the society can survive (i.e., in wartime). Issues of health care are more subtle but may reflect the tension that exists between the good of an individual and the good of society. The clinical sociologist may be able to use this knowledge to address dilemmas in health care delivery, for example, deciding whether to prolong the life of an aged individual with Alzheimer's disease. The family and the patient have a vested interest in the decision, but society must also decide how much of its resources will be allocated to the care of such patients. The issue is further complicated by the fact that whatever the decision, it will have systematic effects on the moral order. Another example of a moral dilemma in health care delivery is related to organ donation; some poor people have expressed willingness to sell their organs to wealthy people who need them.[43] The question arises whether a person who has something he or she is willing to sell to someone who will pay what he wants for it has a right to do this if the item of value is a body part or whether the selling of body parts should be outlawed, because it perpetuates the ultimate form of capitalism—the rich buying parts of other human beings (who are poor) to preserve their own existence.

4. As organ transplantation has become a more routine medical procedure, decisions about who should receive and donate organs must be made. Often, decisions are made on the basis of "objective criteria," including age of the respondent, general physical condition, and distance from the transplantation center, which are intended to prevent bias and favoritism from entering into the decision about who will get the next available organ. However, some of the criteria used may be so correlated with values about social worth as to introduce a major bias into the selection process without awareness of the system. For example, if employability following transplantation is a criteria, uneducated blacks who statistically have little chance of employment, even when healthy, will have significantly lower chances of receiving organs than will college-educated white men. The clinical sociologist may be aware of these institutionalized biases in the selection criteria or can examine data on who is served by a given program to determine the existence of systematic bias in the selection procedures.

5. Brody[44] has indicated that empirical studies in medical ethics are increasingly important and require methodological rigor that sociologists are trained to provide. For example, Erde[41] asked patients in a family practice setting whether

they would want to be told if they developed Alzheimer's disease. Brody and Tomlinson[45] indicate that they find major methodological problems with the study. Certainly, clinical sociologists can work with ethicists in the design and analysis of such studies and bring their methodological skills to bear on these important issues.

Whether the client is an individual, a family or other small group, an institution, or a whole society, responsibility for client welfare may emphasize the ethical problems and dilemmas involved. Just as the clinical sociologist must abstract from sociological theory to formulate specific interventions to assist the client, so must the clinician abstract from generalized ethical principles to apply them to the specific needs of a specific client.

CLINICAL SOCIOLOGISTS AND SERVICE IN CHRONIC ILLNESS

As the population ages, as childhood diseases are controlled or wiped out, and as scientific medicine advances, the major focus of medicine of the future will be the care of those with chronic illnesses. A chronic disease represents an ongoing medical condition for which there is no cure, a condition with which the patient must learn to live. Whether or not it is incapacitating depends partly on the nature of the physiological problems and partly on the social arrangements of the patient's life. Strauss and Corbin[46] assert that new modes of thinking are required to effectively treat the increased numbers of chronically ill patients. This, in turn, will require a restructuring of the present health care system.

Because modern medicine cannot eradicate chronic disease, it is necessary to determine the kind of health care delivery that is required. Primary care is regarded by Werbach[47] as first-line medicine, where primary care physicians are contacted in the diagnosis and treatment of a disease. If they cannot successfully do so, they refer to specialists, who provide care known as "second-line medicine." As specialists have been unable to conquer chronic disease, patients have felt personally and financially frustrated; no amount of money has been able to cure the disease, and the costs associated with trying to do so have been staggering.[48,49] Patients may long for alternatives to what physicians typically provide, alternatives that they hope will ease the burden of the disease. Werbach has coined the term *third-line medicine* to refer to what he thinks will be the next approach to health care delivery, an approach that includes the use of both orthodox and alternative treatments. The health care system of tomorrow, according to Werbach, will need to provide more socioemotional support, show greater understanding of the psychological and social variables that are contributing to the illness, and demonstrate a willingness on the part of the care providers to view the patient as a consultant in the healing process.

Adequate care of the patient with a chronic illness requires a team approach, in which team members with a variety of skills work together to help the patient reach his or her maximum capacity. The team needs to consider such issues as the impact of the ill member on the family and of the family on its ill member, economic costs of care, and the need for socially scarce resources. There are several ways in which clinical sociologists can become part of this effort. First, they may be able to help the team function as a team. Through a knowledge of small-group process, and of organizational behavior, and through a knowledge of the relationships among roles, the sociologist can provide feedback to the team about its functioning and thus help it work more effectively.

As outlined in the section on counseling, many intrafamily relationships are affected by the chronic illness. Modern approaches to the treatment of chronic disease emphasize the role which the family plays as part of the health care team. Families, however, need help in reducing role confusion or implementing role change, which may be a necessary consequence of having a family member with a chronic disease. The clinical sociologist is able to assist the family with this role renegotiation. Similarly, a social worker or a psychologist may need to help the patient or other family members with intrapsychic issues raised by the chronic condition. These demands on the family will increase with time, and the family increasingly will be considered a crucial part of the health care delivery system.[50,51]

Members of the medical profession frequently view their patients as the focus of their efforts and lose sight of the impact of treatment suggestions on other members of the family. Viewing the family as a social system enables the sociologist to see the effect a given course of action will have on other members of the family. Although a knowledge of these effects may not change the recommendations for treatment, the acknowledgment of their existence will enable the team to make a more reasoned judgment about what they wish to do.

Physicians frequently do not recognize the complex nature of the patient's social, psychological, and economic worlds. Behaviors, which are seen as counterproductive by the health care team, may be seen by the patient as perfectly appropriate, given his or her ethnic group or a social class. People behave in ways that make sense to them; the challenge to the sociologist, as to other members of the health care team, is to discover in what way behaviors, which are seen as problematic, make sense to the patient.

Pilisuk and Parks[52] assert that human interrelationships provide the direct link to health maintenance. The transient nature of many relationships, moving to obtain jobs, fragile family ties, and other isolating processes may not yield the kind of support that is most desirable for the maintenance of good health. The authors believe that people will attempt to compensate for the loss of social networks through counseling, intentional communities, and mutual self-help groups. The clinical medical sociologist can help people who are sick to establish support networks, or "healing webs," so that wellness can be established. This approach views the need for social support to be so vital to the health of a person that clinical intervention is needed in a variety of social contexts where caring relationships are formed, tested, and sometimes destroyed—places like the school, the workplace, and the community at large.

FACILITATING WELLNESS: CLINICAL SOCIOLOGY'S ULTIMATE CHALLENGE

Medical sociologists deal with health as well as illness and see them as two extremes of the same continuum. Antonovsky[53] believes that a health care approach based on the dynamics of well-being is essential if health care professionals are to respond constructively to the world's health problems. Although many people talk about the usefulness of a wellness approach, Antonovsky illustrates how one's sense of coherence of self and situation is directly related to neurophysiological, endocrinological, and immunological pathways to health outcomes. The mind and body relationship is becoming increasingly substantiated.[54,55] Helping clients to achieve self-understanding and to find ways to handle situations that make them uncomfortable are important health care activities for clinical sociologists.

The medical profession is beginning to regard health and disease on the same continuum and to recognize that health and illness are not just physical states but also psychological and social. Personal mental health and illness was the focus of medicine in the 1960s, but today there is an emphasis on social health and illness. Pollution, war, family violence, poverty, famine are all forms of social illness. Intervention at the societal level—a social action approach—is necessary to adequately approach solutions to these issues. Physicians founded the organization, Physicians for Social Responsibility (PSR), to promote world peace. As former PSR president Helen Caldicott[56] questioned, "What good is it to immunize children so they will not get pertussis; what good is it to make sure there is family harmony so they can grow up to be happy and healthy, with the knowledge that in a nuclear war, they will all be dead?" The current emphasis is on creating a social world that is healthy, so that the children and all the members of the planet can also be healthy. If the social world around us is not healthy, then all of the medical care that is given will not create personal or social health. It is in this arena that the skills of the clinical sociologist may have the greatest impact.

REFERENCES

1. Wirth, L. (1982). Clinical sociology. *American Journal of Sociology, 37*, 49–66. Reprinted in *Clinical Sociology, 1*, 7–22.
2. Glass, J., & Fritz, J. (1982). Clinical sociology, origins and development. *Clinical Sociology Review, 1*, 3–6.
3. Fritz, J. (1990). Dean Winternitz, clinical sociology and the Rosenwald Fund. *Clinical Sociology Review, 7.*
4. Gordon, J. B. (1990). Notes on the history of clinical sociology at Yale. *Clinical Sociology Review, 7.*
5. Dunham, H. W. (1982). Clinical sociology, its nature and function. *Clinical Sociology Review, 1*, 23–33.
6. Pflanz, M. (1974). A critique of Anglo-American medical sociology. *International Journal of Health Service, 4*, 565–574.
7. Wolinsky, F. (1980). The sociology of health. Boston: Little, Brown.
8. Elling & Sokolowsha (1978). *Medical sociologists at work.* New Brunswick, NJ: Transaction Books.
9. Mechanic, D., & Aiken, L. J. (1986). Social science, medicine and health policy. In L. J. Aiken & D. Mechanic (Eds.), *Applications of social science to clinical medicine and health policy.* New Brunswick, NJ: Rutgers University Press.
10. Aiken, L. J., & Mechanics, D. (Eds.). (1986). *Applications of social science to clinical medicine and health policy.* New Brunswick, NJ: Rutgers University Press.
11. Becker, H. (1967). Whose side are we on? *Social Problems, 14*, 239–247.
12. Cuthbertson, B. (1990). The therapeutic community in a psychiatric facility: Does clinical sociology have a place? *Clinical Sociology Review, 7.*
13. Warren, C. A. B. (1985). Clinical and research interviewing in sociology. *Clinical Sociology Review, 3*, 72–84.

14. Tannen & Wallet (1987). Interactive frames and knowledge schemas in interaction: Examples from a medical examination/interview. *Social Psychology Quarterly, 50*(2), 205–216.

15. Swan, L. A. (1988). Grounded encounter therapy: Its characteristics and process. *Clinical Sociology Review, 6*, 76–87.

16. Glaser, B., & Straus, A. (1967). *The discovery of grounded theory strategies for qualitative research*. Chicago: Aldine.

17. Thomas. W. I. (1931). *The unadjusted girl*. Boston: Little, Brown.

18. Straus, R. (1982). Clinical sociology on the one-to-one level: A social behavioral approach to counseling. *Clinical Sociology Review, 1*, 59–74.

19. Kallen, D. J., & Sussman, M. B. (Eds.). (1984). *Obesity and the family*. New York: The Hayworth Press.

20. Kargman, M. W. (1957, 1986). The clinical use of social system theory in marriage counseling. *Marriage and Family Living, XIX*, 263–269, reprinted in *Clinical Sociology Review, 4*, 19–29.

21. Church, N. (1985). Sociotherapy with marital couples: Incorporating dramaturgical and social constructionist elements of marital interaction. *Clinical Sociology Review, 3*, 116–128.

22. Voelkl, G. M., & Colburn, K. (1984). The clinical sociologist as family therapist: Utilizing the strategic communication approach. *Clinical Sociology Review, 2*, 64–77.

23. Ventimiglia, J. (1986). Helping couples with neurological disabilities: A job description for clinical sociologists. *Clinical Sociology Review, 4*, 123–139.

24. Lavender, A. D. (1985). Social influences on sexual dysfunctions: The clinical sociologist as sex educator. *Clinical Sociology Review, 3*, 129–142.

25. Byers, B. D. (1987). Uses of clinical sociology in crisis intervention practice. *Clinical Sociology Review, 5*, 102–118.

26. Fein, M. (1986). Resocialization: A neglected paradigm. *Clinical Sociology Review, 6*, 88–100.

27. Kallen, D. J. (1984). Clinical sociology and adolescent medicine, the design of a program. *Clinical Sociology Review, 2*, 78–93.

28. Flexner, A. (1910). Medical education in the United States and Canada. New York: Carnegie Foundation for the Advancement of Teaching.

29. Anspach, R. R. (1988). Notes on the sociology of medical discourse: The language of case presentation. *Journal of Health and Social Behavior, 29*, 357–375.

30. Kallen, D. J. (1987). Failure to thrive and the problem eater. In A. Rudolph (Ed.), *Pediatrics*. Norwalk, CT & Los Altos, CA: Appleton and Lange.

31. Gold, M. (1977). A crisis of identity: The case of medical sociology. *Journal of Health and Social Behavior, 18*, 160–168.

32. Twaddle, A., & Hessler, R. (1977). *A sociology of health*. St. Louis: Mosby.

33. Colombotos, J. (Ed.). (1988). Thematic issue: Continuities in the sociology of medical education. *Journal of Health and Social Behavior, 29*, 4.

34. Kallen, D. J., & Pack, C. A. (1985). Medical sociology, the clinical perspective. In R. A. Straus (Ed.), *Using sociology*. Bayside, NY: General Hall Publishers.

35. Grey, B., & Osterweis, M. (1986). Ethical issues in a social context. In D. Mechanic & L. H. Aiden (Eds.), *Applications of social science to clinical medicine and health policy*. New Brunswick, NJ: Rutgers University Press.

36. Barber, B. (1973). *Research on human subjects*. New York: Russell Sage.

37. Fox, R. (1959). *Experiment perilous*. Glencoe IL: The Free Press.

38. Fox, R. (1979). *Essays in medical sociology*. New York: John Wiley and Sons.

39. Fox, R. (1986). Medicine, sciences and technology. In D. Mechanic & L. H. Aiken (Eds.), *Applications of social science to clinical medicine and health policy* (pp.). New Brunswick, NJ: Rutgers University Press.

40. Durkheim, E. (1938). *Rules of sociological method*. Translated by S. A. Solovay & J. H. Mueller. Edited by G. E. G. Catlin. Glencoe IL: The Free Press.

41. Erde, E. L., Nadal, E. C., & Scholl, T. O. (1988). On truth telling and the diagnosis of Alzheimer's disease. *The Journal of Family Practice, 26*(4), 401–404.

42. Armstrong, P. W., & Colen, B. D. (1989). The courts and the PVS patient. *New Jersey Medicine, 86*(1), 27–30.

43. Kinsley, M. (1989). Take my kidney, please. *Time, 13*(88).

44. Brody, H. (1983). Empirical studies of ethics in family medicine. *Journal of Family Practice*, 1061–1063.
45. Brody, H., & Tomlinson, T. (1988). Commentary. *The Journal of Family Practice, 26*(4), 404–406.
46. Strauss, A., & Corbin, J. (1989). *Shaping a new health care system.* San Francisco: Jossey-Bass.
47. Werbach, M. (1986). *Third line medicine: Modern treatment for persistent symptoms.* New York: Arkana.
48. Knowles, J. (1977). *Doing better and feeling worse.* New York: Norton.
49. Navarro, V. (1986). *Crisis, health and medicine: A social critique.* New York: Tavistock.
50. Levin, L. (1976). *Self care: Lay initiatives in health.* New York: Prodist.
51. Calnan, M. (1987). *Health and illness: The lay perspective.* New York: Tavistock.
52. Pilisuk, M., & Parks, S. H. (1986). *The healing web: Social networks and human survival.* Hanover: University of New England Press.
53. Antonovsky, A. (1987). *Unraveling the mystery of health.* San Francisco: Jossey-Bass.
54. Simonton, O. C., Simonton, S. M., & Creighton, J. (1978). *Getting well again.* Los Angeles: Tarcher.
55. Siegel, B. S. (1986). *Love, medicine, and miracles.* New York: Harper & Row.
56. Physicians for Social Responsibility (1981). "The Last Epidemic." A film produced by Thiermann. Distributed by Educational Film and Video Project.

CHAPTER 12

Health Promotion and Clinical Sociology

John G. Bruhn

THE CONCEPT OF HEALTH PROMOTION

The causes of disease always have been categorized as biological phenomena. However, disease has another dimension—it is mediated and modified by social activity and the cultural environment. During the nineteenth century, medicine developed as a social science, principles of public health and social medicine were clarified, and three basic themes were identified: The health of people is a matter of direct social concern; social and economic conditions have an important effect on health and disease and must be subject to scientific investigation, and steps must be taken to promote health and combat disease; every member of the community is entitled to health protection, just as every person is entitled to the protection of liberty and property.

In the mid-nineteenth century, American health reformers, recognizing the link between health and behavior, expressed an interest in personal hygiene and public health. They encouraged daily baths, moderation in diet and sexual behavior, exercise, athletics, and the outdoor life. Health-reform-minded figures, such as Sylvester Graham, William Alcott, Horace Mann, Ellen White, William James, and Anne Riley Hale, brought a missionary zeal to what amounted to a religious crusade and eventually reached an expanding audience. Today, as the twentieth century wanes, the link between health and a healthy lifestyle has been accepted by a large segment of American society. The contemporary view of health educators emphasizes recommended choices among styles of life rather than rigid imperatives tied to science, scientism, or righteousness.[1-3]

The broader view of health, as related to lifestyle, helped reshape the definition of health. "Traditionally, health has been defined by what it is *not*. Just as peace

---

JOHN G. BRUHN • The University of Texas Medical Branch, Galveston, Texas 77550-2782.

has been defined as the absence of war, and sanity as the absence of insanity, health has been defined as the absence of illness."[4] The absence of illness may have been an adequate definition of health when "illness" referred to infectious disease. However, in America, the leading cause of premature disability and death is no longer infectious disease but is frequently associated with how we live. Our conceptualization of health must take into account the increasing numbers of individuals who are ill and impaired due to chronic conditions whose etiologies are tied to lifestyles. The prevention of chronic illness and disability has become an increasingly important aspect of health and must be linked to the promotion of positive health strategies. Telling people what *not* to do to avoid becoming sick is not enough. We also must determine, in a positive way, what can be done to remain or to become healthy.[4]

The characterization of health as a positive state brings us closer to the etymological derivatives of the word *health*, which literally means *wholeness*. This conceptualization is embodied in the World Health Organization definition of health as "a state of complete physical, mental, and social well-being," not merely the absence of disease or infirmity. The challenge for health enhancement is greater than the prevention of disease; it must involve positive strategies that go beyond prevention and are oriented toward optimal health and well-being.

Maslow's theory of self-actualization is relevant to the concept of health promotion. He proposed that healthy people have sufficiently gratified their basic needs and so are motivated primarily by trends to self-actualization. Self-actualization is a relative state achieved by few people; for most people, it is a hope, a yearning, a drive—"something" wished for but not yet achieved—showing itself clinically as a drive toward health, integration, and growth.[5] Health promotion could be considered part of the process of self-actualization. Like self-actualization, health promotion is concerned with individual potential, and both are, therefore, matters of individual meaning and definition.

Bruhn[6] has proposed a model of health that views "wellness," or health promotion, as a positive lifelong process. The process involves an individual's active work to improve his/her total health and well-being. Wellness will be an ideal for most, and a reality for a few. Wellness does not become a complete entity all at once; rather it is a cumulative process that can be influenced by environmental, physical, behavioral, psychological, social, and genetic factors. An individual continually seeks to attain, and, once achieved, retain wellness.

Garfield[7] has studied "peak performers" in organizations, that is, people who are willing to evolve and grow, to learn from work, as well as to complete it. The difference between peak performers and ordinary performers is that the former consciously, persistently, and intelligently refine and develop the characteristics they value most. Peak performers are in a process of self-actualization. If they include their health in this process, they are attempting to achieve a state of wholeness, wellness, or total well-being.

Health promotion is implicit in the concepts of "wholeness," self-actualization, peak performance, and wellness. Health promotion means that individuals can take the initiative to enhance their state of health and, through sustained action, improve their physical and mental health. It is assumed that many illnesses can be prevented, or at least delayed, in onset, by promoting one's health. The promise underlying health promotion is that an individual can improve the quality of his/her life; hence, the cliche, "You can add life to years, not only years to life."

Relevance of Health Promotion to Clinical Sociology

Perhaps the greatest current modality for advancing health in the United States is through influencing behavior. Those concerned with public health are gradually coming to grips with personal behavior as a health factor and are seeking ways to influence it favorably. Comprehensive health promotion includes three modalities: preventive medical measures, environmental measures, and influences on behaviors that are favorable to health. The goal for all three is not only the avoidance of specific diseases but also the achievement of "physical, mental, and social well-being.[8]

Health promotion has not been a commonly accepted goal in the United States. As Fuchs said, "Within limits set by genetic factors, climate, and other natural forces, every nation chooses its own death rate by its evaluation of health compared with other goals."[9] We make choices about what is important to us as a nation and as individuals and families, how we will spend our time and allocate our resources, and health has not been at the top of our list of values. We feel little or no personal obligation to help prevent our illnesses. Instead we expect sophisticated medical technology to be capable of resolving most illnesses. Health is seen as a responsibility of the health care system and not of the individual.

Because the behaviors associated with health that we learn are deeply rooted in culture, we need to understand differences and similarities between people's health practices vis-à-vis their cultures. Health promotion cannot be expected to be an important goal in all cultures. Without cultural meaning, no intervention to alter current health behavior or promote health could be expected to be accepted. Therefore, the clinical sociologist is uniquely qualified to study, understand, and effectively intervene in matters related to sociocultural phenomena.

According to Webster, to *intervene* means to become a third party, to come between points of time or events. This is an unusual role for the sociologist who is most often an observer of people and who carefully avoids value judgments and active participation to change social situations. The role of the clinical sociologist, on the other hand, is usually one of active involvement to change situations.[10] Health promotion is an area of concern that involves action—individuals and groups must actively work to enhance or optimize health. Health promotion requires changing social situations, as well as behavior. An example might be employees deciding to enforce a smoke-free work environment and making necessary adjustments to accommodate fellow employees who smoke. The role of the interventionist, perhaps, captures most situations in which clinical sociologists would find themselves. Types of intervention range from those involving an individual (e.g., smoking cessation), a family (e.g., family therapy), a small group (e.g., drug abuse counseling), an organization (e.g., developing a health promotion program), a community (e.g., team member in AIDS education program), or countries (e.g., implementing a family planning program).

Typically, interventions in the field of health are designed for individuals after they become patients or after a problem presents itself. Health promotion suggests the need for intervention to prevent problems. This requires a perspective beyond the individual level. Clark[11] suggests many possible roles related to health promotion for clinical sociologists in his description of a healthy organization. He states that a healthy organization must afford the individual, small groups, intergroups, and the total organization chances to fulfill their tendencies and capacities for equilibrium and growth. The organization must also exhibit reactive (maintenance) behavior as well as proactive (growth) behavior.

In the Marshall Company, a healthy organization studied by a group of Harvard investigators, there were norms that helped individuals grow and learn. Individuals were rewarded by learning new tasks, but they were not pushed into new behavior unless the organization's proaction required it, as it did in acquiring faster machinery. Moreover, a person could choose not to learn any new tasks at all, so long as he did not prevent others from satisfying their proactive needs. Individual behavior, which did not support proaction, was reacted against by other members of the group. The companywide codes supported requesting and giving help after an individual had tried on his own. This fostered reciprocity and proactive behavior between groups. Social reciprocity was institutionalized in such a way as to meet reactive and proactive needs at all levels of the company. In knowing what "health norms" are for organizations, clinical sociologists can serve as consultants and contribute to the design and evaluation of interventions to remedy stunted creativity of individuals, the alienation of group members, or intergroup conflict that may have contributed to the disequilibrium of a total organization.

Many studies in the social and behavioral sciences and medicine have shown social support to be one factor among many that contributes to disease resistance. Social support appears to offer a stability that protects people in times of transition and stress. Given the complexity of social support and the newness of research in this area, it is too early to specify the mechanisms by which social support enhances health. We also need to learn more about which type of support works best in what situation.[12] Nonetheless, interventions have been designed to take advantage of our preliminary knowledge of the relationship between social connectedness and health. Strengthening the social support of widows has been shown to improve their health significantly following bereavement. Human companionship has been shown to effect the course of labor and childbirth. Interventions to strengthen social support have also improved compliance with medical regimens and decreased subsequent mortality. There is evidence that social support is effective in reducing stress in medical experiences. Preliminary findings indicate that increased social interaction can prompt measurable psychoendocrine changes that are consistent with favorable health outcomes. Syme and his colleagues are working on recommendations that might help prevent hypertension among San Francisco bus drivers by involving the drivers in making more realistic route schedules. Also being considered is improving the quality of social support for the drivers by moving the rest stops from remote, isolated parts of the city to areas where they can talk to their peers. Investigation into how social support influences health is a new frontier. Although the traditional focus of medical interventions has been the sick individual, interest and evidence, which support health as a reflection of social support, are now growing.[13] Interventions to strengthen social support are appealing to the clinical sociologist because they have the potential to promote health and enhance resistance to disease.

LEARNING HEALTH PROMOTING BEHAVIORS

Health is the result of individual choices that, in turn, are related to the social institutions from which we learn our values. The family is one of the key institutions where we learn about health behavior. Margaret Mead has said:

> So much of our behavior and methods of child rearing reiterate the old Puritan dichotomy between "good" and "good for you". . . one concerned with pleasure and the other with duty, neither with goals. The individual learns to eat spinach, brush teeth, go to bed early, and take a bath by being rewarded, if he fails to do so, he is punished. But he learns something deeper, he learns that all of these activities are unpleasant, otherwise, he would not have to be rewarded for doing them.[14]

As Mead pointed out, the child learns that one could not possibly enjoy or perform most of these behaviors of one's own free will. She also emphasized the importance of understanding the concept of culture, values, beliefs, and judgments about what is desirable and how people should behave in promoting health.

Health behavior and health values are usually learned in childhood, first in the context of the family, by observing and modeling the health behavior of parents, and later in school, by engaging in behavior that is highly valued by peers. Pratt[15] proposed a family type, the "energized family," in which family members are more likely to engage in a broad variety of health behaviors. The dimensions of family structure that were found to have the strongest relationship to good health were a low level of aversive control and obstructive conflict, a high level of autonomy, support, and encouragement, and interaction among members. She concluded that the level of health is greater in families that tend to support their members' personal needs and interests, assist the members' efforts to cope and function, and tolerate and encourage members' moves toward self-actualization and personal development. Pratt noted that a large majority of the middle-class parents in her study sample explained to their children (aged 9 to 13) about health care procedures, such as the proper way to use a toothbrush, the proper kinds of foods to eat, the effects of smoking on health, when and how much to exercise, effect of sleep on health, importance of bowel regularity, and how to maintain cleanliness. How reproduction takes place was the one topic neglected by two-thirds of the parents.

Pratt's work demonstrates how family structure can affect the learning and practice of health behaviors by family members. Family structure is also important in getting family members to change their health behavior. Baranowski and his colleagues[16] carried out an intervention in which family members were encouraged to support each other's attempts to reduce fat in their diet and increase aerobic exercise. These researchers regarded social support as a form of family communication that could play an important part in promoting positive health behavior among well families. Twenty-four families from three major ethnic groups who had at least one child in the fifth or sixth grade were randomly assigned to experimental and control groups. Experimental group families met for group discussions about what is good diet and exercise, set behavioral change goals, and kept track of their eating and exercise behaviors. Control group families received educational brochures and monitored their diet and exercise behavior but did not attend weekly discussion groups. The findings suggested that the promotion of social support for change among family members can encourage more changes in diet, than in exercise. Social support was promoted by group discussion of opportunities for support and by contracting exchanges of support within families. Baranowski notes, however, that parents resisted the idea that their children could support the parent's dietary or exercise change. Indeed, parents often attempted to suppress or divert the conversation when such support was discussed. This may be related to Pratt's finding that family structure shapes young children's health habits more than those of the adults because the adult's practices have been moulded by sources other than the family over a period of time. It would follow, therefore, that the health behavior of children and adults are more likely to be changeable when a family has the characteristics of an "energized family."

The difficulties in getting individuals to change unhealthy behaviors brings to the forefront the fact that, even in the context of the family, health behavior is often learned segmentally, accidentally, and with threatened negative consequences, that is, "your teeth will fall out if you don't brush them." We do not teach children about health in such a way that they develop a concept of it, feel a personal responsibility about keeping their health, or that they should be concerned about the social and economic consequences of losing their physical and/or mental capacities. Ideally, education about health promotion should engage families and schools in a reinforcing partnership.

Bruhn and his colleagues[17,18] designed a curriculum to teach positive health behaviors to 4-year-old children enrolled in a day care program with an educational emphasis. Because the preschool population was relatively stable, it provided an opportunity to teach children over a period of time, reinforcing knowledge and skills and involving parents in these efforts. The Preschool Health Education Curriculum was based on social learning theory, which proposes that human behavior is determined by continuous interaction among cognitive, behavioral, and environmental factors. The curriculum was structured around selected age-appropriate behaviors that children can learn in assuming greater responsibility for their health. The behaviors were dissected conceptually to identify what the children needed to learn to be able to perform the selected behaviors. The learning activities were designed to provide modeling, practice, and reinforcement to promote children's self-confidence in performing the selected behaviors (self-efficacy); their feeling that it was important to do the behaviors (value expectancies); and their belief that they can have some control over their health (locus of control). The curriculum was developed, taught, and evaluated in an early childhood learning center and field-tested and evaluated in 13 day care centers.

Children who received the curriculum showed statistically significant increases from pre- to posttesting in their health and safety behavior intentions and in their health and safety preference scores. No differences were found with respect to locus of control. The lack of change in locus of control may suggest that either the curriculum was not effective in reinforcing internal locus of control, or the effects may have been canceled by more powerful influences in the child's environment. This study needs to be replicated in other school settings with special attention given to the carryover between home and school with respect to what is learned about health behavior in both settings.

Gochman[19] has suggested that family factors may *not* be primary determinants of children's health concepts despite deeply held assumptions to the contrary. It is also unlikely that the school alone is a primary determinant in learning health concepts. We have experiential evidence about the strong influence of mass media and peer pressure on both children's and adults' health behavior. However, we have little information about how all of these influences interact and reinforce each other at different times in life.[20]

PARADIGMS OF INTERVENTION

The ideology of prevention in our health care system is tied to the notion of early intervention among populations who are at high risk for certain diseases. Therefore, the first step is to find people who have identifiable problems they wish to prevent. The ideology of health promotion is not something that is the responsibility only of our health care system nor the sole purview of the medical doctor or dentist. The assumption is that one's health status can be enhanced whether or not a person has an identified problem. Health promotion is a step beyond prevention. Harris and Guten[21] asked randomly selected adults, "What do you do to protect your health?" They found that virtually everyone performed some health-protective activities, but the most commonly performed activities did not involve the use of the health care system. These findings affirm that individuals are producers of health rather than simply consumers of health care.

Kaplan[22] identified several problems underlying many of the interventions used to promote lifestyle changes and to maintain and enhance health. First is the assumption that specific behaviors create risks for serious illnesses. Second is the assumption that behavior and disease are positively correlated and that a modification in risk-related behavior will reduce the incidence of disease. Third is the assumption that behavioral changes are lasting. Fourth is the assumption that the most reasonable approach is to express benefits from health programs in terms of the extra years of life they produce. Health promotion as discussed in this chapter, based on the concepts of wellness, wholeness, and self-actualization, avoids these problems. First, health promotion involves more than a specific behavior—it involves sets of behaviors, some of which may not be directly related to health; it involves a proactive attitude and values that may be more personal than altruistic. Health promotion does not involve isolated or separate activities that are engaged in at designated times. Indeed, health promotion is a continuous part of a daily philosophy, which permeates all of an individual's actions and thoughts. Second, it is erroneous to think that an individual who is health promoting will be illness free. There are illnesses whose etiologies develop despite individual protective behavior, such as accidents and stress, which are not totally within an individual's control. Third, health promotion makes no presumption about how easy or difficult health behavior is to change. Health promotion is an ongoing set of activities, which are interrelated and tied to "where an individual is in his life and development at particular points in time." Fourth, the objective of health promotion is not only to add years to life but to add quality to life. Fifth, although motivation to enhance one's health is important in both prevention and promotion, in promotion, the motivation pervades one's thoughts and actions and is self-sustaining. Indeed, the qualitative benefits of health promotion activities give impetus to an already existing high level of motivation. Motivation to continuously enhance one's health is intimately tied to one's self-esteem and feelings of power; health is something one prizes, works to keep, and uses one's decision-making powers to improve or enhance. This differs from prevention activities, which require motivation and/or varying degrees of support from others to change a specific behavior or make changes for a short period of time. Therefore, health promotion activities are not easily subject to cost-benefit analysis. Certainly, one would assume that individuals, families, or workplaces that engage in health promotion should experience less use of health services and qualitative increases in factors such as morale, productiveness, and enjoyment of life and work. However, staying healthy requires some financial cost. It is assumed that the cost of illness is greater than the cost of staying healthy. Although there is some preliminary evidence that the latter is true in the workplace, the real cost of health promotion is still elusive.

Lifestyle Change

There are three general paradigms for intervention in health promotion (see Figure 1). The first is intervention to move an individual from an illness-producing to a health promoting lifestyle. In order to intervene among at-risk individuals, one needs to have some formulation about the etiology of the lifestyle. Lifestyle intervention, if there is to be any expectation of success, must include consideration of psychological, social, cultural, and environmental factors, current and retrospective as well as consideration for an individual's expectations, hopes, and aspirations. Too often, interveners are seduced by an individual's motivation. Changes are difficult to effect even among the most highly motivated. For example, the death of a parent or spouse from a heart attack or stroke might heighten an individual's interest in changing unhealthy habits, yet, motivation, alone, is not likely to sustain a major or lasting change in lifestyle. One of the greatest pitfalls in getting at-risk persons to change their behavior is the belief that they just need to be convinced about the need to change and that once motivated, with some reinforcement, the effort will be effective. This paradigm becomes even more difficult to carry out if applied to larger social units such as organizations, communities, or countries. Indeed, the controversial efforts by the U.S. surgeon general to modify behavior on a national scale regarding smoking, sex, nutrition, and seat belts, and the mixed results of these efforts illustrate the complexity of health promotion. The outcome of health promotion efforts cannot be assessed only by the number of persons who changed their behavior in the hoped-for direction. Change is a process and,

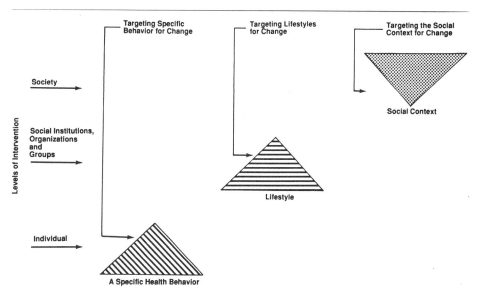

FIGURE 1.   Three levels of intervention and targets to promote healthy behavior.

therefore, the point at which success or failure is judged is arbitrary. Furthermore, precipitants to change may be additive and seldom attributable to a single intervention. Therefore, this is the most difficult of the three paradigms offered to implement and evaluate.

The critical elements to effect lifestyle change require an ecological perspective. This perspective is not popular because it requires much data gathering and analysis before an intervention is planned. Only when there is an understanding of what is involved in the change can an appropriate intervention be designed. Usually a potpourri of available intervention techniques are offered, singly or in combination, to a client in hopes that, along with sufficient motivation, he/she will change. Failure is too often attributed to the individual's level of motivation rather than to the appropriateness of the methods of intervention.

Targeting Behavior for Change

The second type of paradigm of intervention is to target specific health behaviors for change. This is the most common type of clinical intervention, usually directed toward individuals or families. Although this approach may be effective if the goal is to change only one behavior, it is unrealistic if the goal is to move an individual from an illness-producing to a health promoting lifestyle. Numerous intervention studies have focused on weight control, a healthful diet, smoking cessation, coping with stress, alcohol, and drug abuse, and so forth; most of these studies have selected one or two health behaviors as the target for change. The results of these studies are mixed, mainly because, in targeted studies, we have sought to modify a harmful behavior or two in isolation from the social life of people in which those behaviors, such as in smoking and drinking alcohol, might be strongly reinforced. Moreover, health behaviors, good and bad, are all interrelated and part of the normal life of people. Langlie[23] examined 11 different preventive health behaviors. She found that such behaviors fell into two sets: indirect preventive health behaviors, such as seat belt use, nutrition habits, and medical checkups and immunizations; and direct preventive health behaviors, such as driving behavior, personal hygiene, and nonsmoking. She reports that people who engage in one set of preventive health behaviors are not necessarily likely to engage in the other. Furthermore, there are somewhat different predictors for each type of behavior. A strong sense of control over one's health status, perceptions that preventive actions are worthwhile, and membership in a higher socioeconomic group tend to predict indirect preventive health behavior. Conversely, women and older people are more likely to exhibit direct preventive health behavior. Similarly, Harris and Guten[21] found that an average respondent in their study practiced between 5 and 19 specific behaviors aimed at health promotion. They identified 5 types of health promoting activities: health practices, safety practices, preventive health care, environmental hazard avoidance, and substance avoidance. These authors, like Langlie, found that health protective behavior is not unidimensional. People who sought preventive examinations or who practiced certain nutritional habits were generally not much more likely to engage in other preventive practices than were individuals who did not practice preventive examinations or nutrition.

These studies provide important information for the design of intervention programs. They tell us that health promotion behavior is complex and multifaceted, that it is difficult to effect the change of only one health behavior. It is also unrealistic to expect that people will exhibit consistent behavior with respect to health promotion. In addition, a change in one health behavior is certain to influence other health behaviors, for example, negatively, some people who give up smoking eat more, or positively, some people who engage in physical exercise do not drink alcohol or smoke tobacco.

Certainly, there are examples of relative success in altering single healthy behaviors, such as the national campaign to discourage cigarette smoking. On the other hand, national efforts to discourage the abuse of alcohol and other drugs have not been successful. Even if people are convinced of the need to adopt appropriate health habits, it is often difficult for individuals to remain in control of their own health behavior. Attention must be paid to the settings in which people live, work, and travel, and to what is "acceptable" behavior in some settings, for example, drug and alcohol use for leisure, relaxation, and escape.

Changing the Social Context

Although health promotion eventually must reach the individual level, it should begin at a societal or community level. Educational efforts must include interventions at the political, economic, and social institutional levels if change is to involve large numbers of people, if change is to be lasting, and if health behavior is to be reinforced and valued. McKeown[24] pointed out the role of nutrition, changing personal habits, and sanitation in achieving the marked improvements in health status over the past century. He believes that improved medical care and technology are the major reasons for this improvement. LaLonde[25] suggested that providing access to health care and improving the quality of care were not the most effective ways to improve the health of the population. He proposed that approaches should be geared to four areas: human biology, physical and social environments, lifestyle, and health organization.

Health promotion for the elderly is an example of the third paradigm, changing the social context. Until recently, the elderly were not included in wellness or health promotion activities. Somers, Kleinman, and Clark[26] note that the little attention given to health promotion for the elderly reflects the attitude that 65 is "too late." Health promotion policies have also focused on the young and the individual. Only recently have the public and private sectors taken responsibility for initiating change in social institutions and the political and economic system to promote a healthier environment that would be supportive of healthy lifestyles. In 1985, the Department of Health and Human Services launched a 2-year public information and education campaign for the elderly to encourage participation in specially organized fitness programs designed for older adults.[27] A national program of health promotion for the elderly, however, has not been developed. Promoting healthy behaviors among the elderly, in the absence of positive reinforcement from social institutions, especially if there are no economic incentives or rewards, is likely to be a short-lived movement involving only small groups of the elderly.

THE PARADIGMS ILLUSTRATED

Targeting Behavior for Change

Smoking cessation has been a common target for intervention in health promotion programs. Various strategies have been used to help people stop smoking including behavioral modification, cessation clinics, drug therapy, individual counseling, group therapy, hypnosis, and the use of tobacco substitutes. Because the criteria of success among programs vary, it is difficult to assess the effectiveness of these different interventions. Although study after study suggests that it is possible to persuade smokers to stop for varying lengths of time, these same studies note that most former smokers will not continue to abstain from smoking. Thus it would appear only logical to deal with the problem of smoking before people become addicted. This would necessitate the increased targeting of smoking prevention programs to nonsmokers, beginning with children. An ideal program would follow the example set by Finland[28] where a 25-year effort, with the objective of making those born in 1975 a nonsmoking generation, has begun. The program began with expectant parents in 1974 and is presently concentrating on withdrawal clinics and other measures to develop a nonsmoking environment for those children born in 1975. Educational efforts for adults and children, increased governmental control on advertising and marketing of tobacco products, and an all-out effort to create a nonsmoking generation in a nonsmoking environment is being supported by both governmental efforts and the general public.

Targeting Lifestyle for Change

Acquired immunodeficiency syndrome (AIDS) is caused and spread by a set of behaviors that are part of a lifestyle. Depressed immune function has been shown to be associated with poor health habits including the large consumption of tobacco, alcohol, and drugs, poor nutrition, inadequate sleep, and exercise and stress. Depressed immune function sets up the opportunity, when blood and semen are exchanged, for infection by the AIDS virus. The surgeon general has launched an intensive public campaign aimed at informing all persons of the ways to reduce the likelihood of infection by this virus. In addition, intensive educational efforts are being undertaken by numerous groups and organizations through conferences, films, videotapes, pamphlets, and the mass media to get individuals to change behaviors that might put them at risk for AIDS. Counseling programs associated with HIV-screening clinics alert individuals who are HIV positive about the need to change their personal habits. It should be pointed out that the targets for change are the risk behaviors and attitudes associated with those behaviors, not sexual preference. Changing one's sexual preference would not, in itself, alter one's risk for acquiring AIDS. Educational efforts have been successful in changing personal habits among homosexuals, one of the groups at risk. Efforts have been least successful among another high-risk group, IV drug abusers. Indeed, the appeal to IV drug abusers is to not share contaminated needles, rather than to give up drugs.

Interventions dealing with behaviors that are closely related to a person's lifestyle must target the behaviors for change, not the lifestyle, lest the intervention alienate the individual or group of concern from participation. For example, in the case of reducing risk behavior among coronary-prone persons, it is not likely those with Type A personalities will change their personalities. Indeed, the warning to "not work so hard" is one way of rejecting what that person may value most; such persons may be willing to modify personal habits to reduce their risk for disease, but only if their lifestyle is not attacked.

Targeting the Social Context for Change

Minkler and Pasick[29] point out that the focus of current health promotion on individual responsibility for health is not accompanied by how the environment affects one's ability to respond to one's personal health needs. For example, the elderly are told about the importance of walking, but how can they walk safely in high-crime, inner-city neighborhoods? They are told about the importance of consuming a balanced nutritious diet but not how they can afford such a diet on a small, fixed income. Such approaches to health promotion remove the individual from the context of his/her environment.

There are several examples of projects for elders that have incorporated the larger social context. The Growing Younger Program implemented in Boise, Idaho, proposed not only to improve the health of citizens over age 60 but also to improve the social quality of life by fostering friendships among people and encouraging more smiles, hugs, and laughter in their daily routine. The final objective was to broaden community attitudes toward aging. Highly significant positive changes were found in four of five behavioral change indexes measured. Participants reported exercising more, eating better foods, increasing stress management and social activities, and improving their management of health care problems. The only area in which significant improvements were not noted was that of drinking and smoking, which were extremely low behaviors reported at the start of the program. Graduates of the program are becoming involved in the community in a variety of activities. Growing Younger Programs are now found in 12 states, and the program is being replicated in clinics, hospitals, senior centers, rehabilitation centers, and public health agencies.[30]

Another project for elders, which was designed to alter the social context, is reported by Wechsler and Minkler.[31] The Tenderloin area of San Francisco had a long history of crime and high rates of suicide, alcoholism, drug addiction, and prostitution. The area was also one of the largest "gray ghettos" in the United States with 8,000 elderly men and women, many living in single-room hotels. In 1979, a university-sponsored project, based on social support theory, proposed to increase the level of social support, sense of personal control, and health status of the elderly in the area. Informed assessments indicate that the sense of control, sense of community, and mental health of the residents have improved. As a result of empowering and supporting the elderly, barriers that previously reduced individual choices were lifted. By working with the police, local stores, and the media, the residents have been effective in implementing change.

Other examples of changing the social context to effect changes in health behavior came from community interventions to reduce the risk of coronary heart disease. The Five City Project of the Stanford Heart Disease Prevention Program proposed to transform the knowledge and skills of individuals to reduce the mortality and morbidity of coronary heart disease. A second goal was to carry out the educational program in a way that created a self-sustaining health promotion structure that continued after the project ended.[32] The authors point out that in health promotion programs with multiple objectives not everything can be done all at once for everyone. Therefore, the selection and sequencing of actions is very important. They used the concept of social marketing to help break up the community into manageable pieces. The application of social marketing to community health promotion rests on the promoter's ability to control or arrange the elements of product, promotion, price, and place. Their general plan for community organization was derived from the social planning or locality development strategies of Rothman[33] in which "exogenous organization leads to exogenous education." An example of exogenous organizing leading to exogenous development is the joint establishment of smoking classes in the communities by the County Health Department and Stanford. Stanford provided the educational training and development expertise. The major function of community organization following the early phases of development was to provide the environment for the educational products to be used effectively. The results of this 9-year project will be forthcoming in a few years.

ROLES FOR CLINICAL SOCIOLOGISTS

Bruhn[10] has viewed the clinical sociologist as a health broker. Brokering is an applied and active role. Indeed, the clinical sociologist's role in health promotion activities and projects is that of a change agent. The goal is to plan intervention activities that will enhance healthy behaviors and promote well-being or self-actualization. Sashkin, Morris, and Horst[34] note three ways in which a change agent can behave. One is as a consultant, essentially in a role that tries to help find new solutions by using rational problem solving. The second role is as a trainer. Here the aim is to help a client develop new skills that will lead to an ability to function more effectively. The third role is that of a researcher. One of the aims of this role is to develop a systematic evaluation. Another aim is to add to the general knowledge of the social sciences. Following the ideas of Sashkin and his colleagues, a change agent or broker can perform all three of these roles and, therefore, is in the best position to help to bring about change at many levels. In another sense, the change agent can be seen as the link between the client's culture, values, needs, and so forth, and the change agent's professional knowledge. Thus, the change agent can plan change that will be meaningful to the client. Figure 2 illustrates this process.

One of the biggest differences between the role of the sociologist and the clinical sociologist is that of values; the former carefully guards against bias, maintaining a "value-free" position, whereas the latter's biases must be addressed as a factor in the process of intervention to bring about change. Indeed, results in intervention studies are all bound to be influenced (positively and negatively) by the interaction between the intervener (the person seen as a helper) and the client. This is especially true in longitudinal studies where the client is seen by the same researcher or clinician repeatedly over time. Although concern about bias is not unique to sociologists, one would expect their level of awareness about bias to be high and that they would be cautious about bias in interpreting and generalizing results.

STRATEGIES FOR HEALTH PROMOTION

Blum[35] discusses two broad approaches to risk reduction: microapproaches in which individuals make behavioral changes and macroapproaches in which groups, communities, or societies make behavioral changes to reduce health risks. There is a third approach, a mixture of micro- and macroapproaches wherein behavioral changes are planned to become mutually reinforcing. The micro- or individual approach is the most popular because it is easiest to design, implement, and evaluate, whereas the macroapproach is the most difficult to design, implement, and evaluate. Indeed, if one takes the view that one's social environment is a continual influencing factor in a person's life, it is difficult to separate out which level factors, that is, personal or societal, have been most influential in bringing about the expected change. The assessment of diet modification in individuals, groups, and society as a whole illustrates this problem.[36] Cultural and psychological factors, especially television advertising, are powerful influences on food preferences.

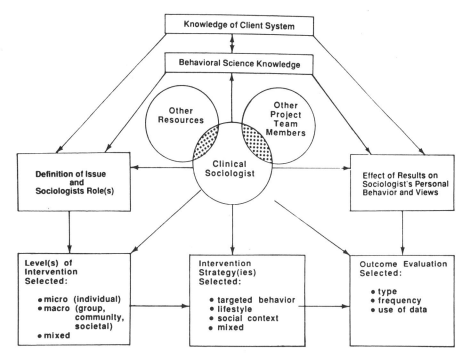

FIGURE 2. Possible roles of the clinical sociologist in the process of conducting health promotion activities (redrawn from Sashkin, Morris, & Horst, 1973).

Methods used to track changes in dietary habits are highly dependent upon our ability to measure food intake accurately. Current methods are self-report, 24-hour dietary recall, naturalistic observations in public settings, food intake of people in controlled environments, and measurement of serum albumin concentrations. Attempts to modify the dietary habits of the American public have begun only recently. Because of the complexity of factors involved in shaping dietary habits and the crudeness of available methods for assessing dietary habits, results of nutrition education programs are mixed. Results from the Stanford Three Community Study, however, indicate that media interventions are as effective over the long term in modifying dietary behavior as traditional and more expensive face-to-face programs.

Childhood is the ideal time to establish health promoting dietary habits. This belief has led several educators to establish nutrition education in school curricula. This approach can involve teachers and parents as models, provide a semi-controlled environment for instruction and reinforcement, and provide an opportunity to follow children's dietary habits over a period of time. The question of whether enhanced knowledge improves dietary behavior should be answered as several current longitudinal studies of dietary behavior among children report their findings.

Numerous strategies that have been used to bring about change at the microlevel include behavior modification, hypnosis, group confrontation and support, counseling, aversive conditioning, information, and so forth. The most common strategies to change behavior at the macrolevel include television, video, films, group pressure, mutual help organizations, literature, controlled environments, punishment, and so forth. Efforts to effect change at the microlevel are labor intensive, and efforts at the macrolevel are very expensive. One strategy, which combines both micro- and macrolevels, is the idea of networking: the involvement and training of natural groups and natural helpers.[37-38] A number of descriptive studies suggest ways of enlisting natural caregivers, including working with neighbors who provide neighborhood day care services for children; identifying central figures who provide needed services within their neighborhood to the elderly; working with a natural network of managers of boarding homes for discharged mental patients in an urban poverty area; developing an outreach program to the newly bereaved; and developing mental health services in a rural area.

Networking and the use of natural groups have not been used extensively as a strategy in health promotion efforts. Because social support has been shown to be such a potent factor in the maintenance of health status, networking and its implicit supportive features could be valuable in promoting health among the well. Although this has occurred informally in the formation of, for example, exercise groups, these are not natural enduring networks, and their members are highly selective with respect to age, sex, and other characteristics. There is a need for model programs, which utilize natural groups and natural helpers, in promoting health.

OVERCOMING BARRIERS TO HEALTH PROMOTION

Buck[39] has discussed some of the factors that must be changed if health is to be improved. She discusses four factors that she feels impede health promotion: inertia, the fragmented structure of the political and bureaucratic apparatus, short-sighted vested interests, and a philosophy that misery is part of the human condition. Certainly, these factors are present in varying degrees and affect the solution of many national problems, including health. It is difficult, as Buck says, to change these factors because they are so deeply embedded in our social structure. Yet, if health promotion is ever to become more than an ideal, we need to create ways to work around these barriers.

An additional barrier to health promotion becoming a realistic national goal is the expectation that health promotion will result in financial savings to society. As Higgins[40] has pointed out, it is inappropriate to judge health promotion solely on the basis of financial savings. Successful health promotion results in health gains valued by those who benefit. Hence, they are primarily health programs rather than cost-containment measures. As such, they should be viewed as offering benefits at some additional costs. Because of this, Rogers, Eaton, and Bruhn[41] suggest that cost-effective analysis of health promotion programs are preferable to cost-benefit analysis.

The best strategy for overcoming barriers to health promotion is a long-term educational intervention targeted at our preschools and schools. Students who excel in sports are rewarded and glamorized by their peers, parents, and the community as a whole, but no parallel attention is given to maintaining good health behavior. We need to begin by at least age 4 to teach about health as an individual responsibility, the rewards of which are a higher quality of life. Information about health and behavioral skills related to health promotion can be adapted to various age levels. Learning about health should be experiential, reinforced, and modeled. Teachers should be models of healthy behavior; for example, schools should have and enforce no-smoking policies and apply them to teachers as well as students. Teaching about health in schools should be oriented around the benefits of health promotion and not solely around specific social problems such as drug and alcohol use. Unhealthy behavior does not occur in isolation; it is part of a complex of behaviors related to health. Therefore, there is a need to promote the health of the school-aged child through cooperative ventures that link and integrate the family, the school, and community agencies and services. The nation's public schools have the potential to act as powerful and effective agents in building a national coalition to effect positive attitudinal and behavioral changes regarding health promotion among future generations. Clinical sociology has a unique opportunity to participate in this movement.

A POTENTIAL HEALTH PROMOTION PARADIGM

A recent government report notes that because positive health behavior requires the adoption of discrete and definable behaviors, the general "wellness" message alone is adequate. A paradigm for intervention on a national scale is proposed in detail.[42] The model has three dimensions: age, subpopulation, and risk factor. Further subpopulations exist, and dimensions such as sex and socioeconomic status will have to be included to capture the dimensions necessary to plan many of the interventions. One segment of each dimension would represent all of the components for that dimension, that is, all subpopulations for the subpopulation dimension, all risk factors for the risk factor dimension. The union of the three summary segments could include all ages, subpopulations, and risk factors. The message from this cell would be a "general awareness message" that the target risk factors are important to all people, that all people improve their quality of life by reducing risk-factor levels, and that striving to reduce levels of personal risk is socially fashionable (Figure 3). This level of intervention would "set the agenda."

The next level of generality would result in three types of messages: all risk factors addressed to all ages of a single subpopulation, for example, all Hispanics; a single risk factor for all ages and subpopulations, for example, dietary needs; and all risk factors for a single age group but multiple subpopulations, for example, adolescents. These would be more specific messages and would be tailored to the needs and perceptions of the groups represented by the cells.

The third level would consist of messages about a specific risk factor tailored to a specific age and specific subpopulation. The message at this level would be very

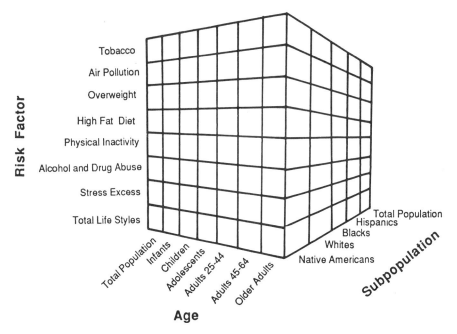

FIGURE 3. Conceptual model for developing a health promotion program from U.S. population (modified and redrawn from U.S. Department of Health and Human Services, *Integration of Risk Factor Interventions*, November 1986, p. 39).

specific and tailored to the needs and perceptions of the subpopulation, for example, dietary needs directed at Hispanic teenagers.

The suggested strategy would be to start with a general awareness campaign for "wellness" that would feature people of all racial, ethnic, age, sex, and socioeconomic groups. A media campaign, which might resemble those of soft drink manufacturers, would give the message that the quality of life can be improved by taking a few steps, and it is socially desirable to take those steps.

Health promotion as a way of life in the United States is a realistic goal. It will, however, take at least one, if not two, generations to change our attitudes and behavior. These efforts must begin at the earliest possible time among our youth, involve the family and community, and be reinforced continually as we progress throughout the life cycle. The school is the logical initiator of these efforts, but health curricula alone will not ensure long-term healthy habits. Individuals personally must learn to value their health, take responsibility for it, and continually work not only to keep it but to enhance it. Clinical sociologists have an important role in helping to plan, implement, and evaluate health promotion programs in a variety of levels. They can help set realistic goals for health promotion relevant to the level of intervention. Health promotion is new territory for clinical sociologists. The need for involvement in health promotion is a great challenge because of the complexity in establishing a new attitudinal and behavioral base in our country from which to view health. Clinical sociologists can play a critical role in helping us value health as an end in itself.

REFERENCES

1. Sokolow, J. A. (1983). *Eros and modernization: Sylvester Graham, health reform, and the origins of Victorian sexuality in America.* Cranbury, NJ: Associated University Press.
2. Whorton, J. C. (1982). *Crusaders for fitness: The history of American health reformers.* Princeton, NJ: Princeton University Press.
3. Burnham, J. C. (1984). Change in the popularization of health in the United States. *Bulletin of the History of Medicine, 58,* 193–197.
4. Ng, L. K. Y., Davis, D. L., Manderscheid, R. W., & Elkes, J. (1981). Toward a conceptual formulation of health and well-being. In L. K. Y. Ng, & D. L. Davis (Eds.), *Strategies for public health: promoting health and preventing disease* (p. 44). New York: D. Van Nostrand Reinhold.
5. Maslow, A. (1968). *Toward a psychology of being* (2nd ed.). Princeton, NJ: D. Van Nostrand.
6. Bruhn, J. G., Cordova, F. D., Williams, J. A., & Fuentes, R. G. (1977). The wellness process. *Journal of Community Health, 2,* 209–221.
7. Garfield, C. (1986). *Peak performers.* New York: Avon Books.
8. Breslow, L. (1983). The potential of health promotion. In D. Mechanic (Ed.), *Handbook of health, health care, and the health professions* (pp. 50–66). New York: Free Press.
9. Fuchs, V. R. (1984). *Who shall live? Health, economics, and social choice.* New York: Basic Books.
10. Bruhn, J. G. (1987). The clinical sociologist as a health broker. *Clinical Sociology Review, 5,* 168–179.
11. Clark, J. V. (1969). A healthy organization. In W. G. Bennis, K. D. Beene, & R. Chin (Eds.) *The planning of change* (2nd ed.; pp. 282–297). New York: Holt, Rinehart & Winston.
12. Ornstein, R., & Sobel, D. (1987). *The healing brain.* New York: Simon & Schuster.
13. House, J. S., Landis, K. R., & Umberson, D. (1988). Social relationships and health. *Science, 241,* 540–545.
14. Mead, M. (1947). Positive motivations in health education. In New York Academy of Medicine, *Motivation in health education: Health education conference of the New York Academy of Medicine.* New York: Columbia University Press.
15. Pratt, L. (1976). *Family structure and effective health behavior. The energized family.* Boston: Houghton Mifflin.
16. Baranowski, T., Nader, P. R., Dunn, K., & Vanderpool, N. A. (1982). Family self-help: Promoting changes in health behavior. *Journal of Communication, 32,* 161–172.
17. Bruhn, J. G., & Parcel, G. S. (1982). Preschool Health Education Program (PHEP): An analysis of baseline data. *Health Education Quarterly, 9,* 116–129.
18. Parcel, G. S., Bruhn, J. G., & Murray, J. L. (1984). Preschool Health Education Program (PHEP): Analysis of educational and behavioral outcome. *Health Education Quarterly, 10,* 149–172.
19. Gochman, D. S. (1985). Family determinants of children's concepts of health and illness. In D. C. Turk & R. D. Kerns (Eds.), *Health, illness, and families* (pp. 23–50). New York: John Wiley.
20. Green, L. W. (1984). Modifying and developing health behavior. *Annual Review of Public Health, 5,* 215–236.
21. Harris, D. M., & Guten, S. (1979). Health-protective behavior: An exploratory study. *Journal of Health and Social Behavior, 20,* 17–29.
22. Kaplan, R. M. (1984). The connection between clinical health promotion and health status. *American Psychologist, 39,* 755–765.
23. Langlie, J. K. (1977). Social network, health beliefs, and preventive health behavior. *Journal of Health and Social Behavior, 18,* 244–260.
24. McKeown, T. (1976). *The role of medicine: Dream, mirage or nemesis?* London: Nuffield Provincial Hospitals Trust.
25. LaLonde, M. (1974). *A new perspective on the health of Canadians: A working document.* Ottawa: Ministry of National Health and Welfare.

26. Somers, A. R., Kleinman, L., & Clark, L. (1982). Preventive health services for the elderly: The Rutgers Medical School Project. *Inquiry, 19*, 190–221.
27. Estes, C. L., Fox, S., & Mahoney, C. W. (1986). Health care and social policy: Health promotion and the elderly. In K. Dychtwald (Ed.), *Wellness and health promotion for the elderly* (pp. 55–60). Rockville, MD: Aspen.
28. Puska, P., Vartiainen, E., Pallonen, V., Salomen, J. T., Poyhia, P., Koskela, K., & McAlister, A. (1982). The North Karelia Youth Project: Evaluation of two years of intervention on health behavior and cardiovascular risk factors among 13 to 15 year old children. *Preventive Medicine, 11*, 550–570.
29. Minkler, M., & Pasick, R. J. (1986). Health promotion and the elderly: A critical perspective on the past and future. In K. Dychtwald (Ed.), *Wellness and health promotion for the elderly* (pp. 39–54). Rockville, MD: Aspen.
30. Kemper, D. (1986). The Healthwise Program: Growing Younger. In K. Dychtwald (Ed.), *Wellness and health promotion for the elderly* (pp. 263–273). Rockville, MD: Aspen.
31. Wechsler, R., & Minkler, M. (1986). A community-oriented approach to health promotion: The Tenderloin Senior Outreach Project. In K. Dychtwald (Ed.), *Wellness and Health Promotion for the Elderly* (pp. 19–36). New York: Macmillan.
32. Farquhar, J. W., Fortmann, S. P., Maccoby, N., Wood, P. D., Haskell, W. L., Taylor, C. B., Flora, J. A., Solomon, J. D. S., Rogers, T., Adler, E., Breitrose, P., & Weiner, L. (1984). The Stanford Five City Project: An overview. In J. D. Matarazzo, S. M. Weiss, J. A. Herd, N. E. Miller, & S. M. Weiss (Eds.), *Behavioral health: A handbook of health enhancement and disease prevention* (pp. 1154–1165). New York: John Wiley.
33. Rothman, J. (1968). *Three models of community organization practice.* National Conference on Social Welfare, Social Work Practice. New York: Columbia University Press.
34. Sashkin, M., Morris, W. C., & Horst, L. (1973). A comparison of social and organizational change models: Information flow and data use process. *Psychological Review, 80*, 510–526.
35. Blum, H. L. (1982). Social perspective on risk reduction. In M. M. Faber & A. M. Reinhardt (Eds.), *Promoting health through risk reduction* (pp. 19–36). New York: Macmillan.
36. Wadden, T. A., & Brownell, K. D. (1984). The development and modification of dietary practices in individuals, groups, and large populations. In J. D. Matarazzo, S. M. Weiss, J. A. Herd, N. E. Miller & S. M. Weiss (Eds.), *Behavioral health: A handbook of health enhancement and disease prevention* (pp. 608–631). New York: John Wiley.
37. Vallance, T. R., & D'Augelli, A. R. (1982). The professional as developer of national helping systems: Conceptual, organizational, and pragmatic considerations. In D. E. Beigel & A. J. Naparstek (Eds.), *Community support systems and mental health: Practices, policy, and research* (pp. 224–237). New York: Springer.
38. Israel, B. A. (1985). Social networks and social support: Implications for national helper and community level interventions. *Health Education Quarterly, 12*, 65–80.
39. Buck, C. (1986). Beyond Lalonde: Creating health. *Journal of Public Health Policy, 7*, 444–457.
40. Higgins, K. W. (1988). The economics of health promotion: *Health Values, 12*, 39–45.
41. Rogers, P. J., Eaton, E. K., & Bruhn, J. G. (1981). Is health promotion cost effective? *Preventive Medicine, 10*, 324–339.
42. U.S. Department of Health and Human Services, Public Health Service, Office of Disease Prevention and Health Promotion. *Integration of risk factor interventions.* November 1986.

CHAPTER 13

Clinical Sociology in the Mental Health Setting

TAMARA FERGUSON, JACK FERGUSON,
AND ELLIOT D. LUBY

Mental patients are no longer secluded in mental institutions for long periods of time but are released to the larger society after only a short period of hospitalization. This is a dramatic change and has many consequences, not the least of which is the type of treatment they receive in the institution and afterwards. All of this has been accelerated by cost containment, limitations of health insurance, and starting in the 1950s—the prescribing of psychotropic drugs. Hospitalization has become increasingly costly. The virtues of deinstitutionalization and an increase of civil rights cannot be ignored. There are new challenges for therapists, patients' families, and communities when patients are being rapidly discharged from the sheltered environment of the hospital into a highly technical society where there is little room to survive without skills and the ability to get on with others. Clinical sociologists, who are trained to evaluate the structure and functional integration of components of life, can evaluate the consequences of different types of interventions for individuals, small groups, and institutions. In this chapter we shall clarify the contribution they can make in a hospital setting and in the community.

The average length of stay of mental patients can now be counted in days, instead of weeks and months. In this short period of time, medication can alleviate the patients' more florid symptoms, and they may learn to discuss their feelings and some of the traumatic events that led to their hospitalization. There is little time, and frequently little planning, for the patients and families to learn to interact more successfully with each other and differentiate between their needs and the demands made by significant others and the community.

TAMARA FERGUSON, JACK FERGUSON, and ELLIOT D. LUBY • Harper Hospital, Detroit, Michigan 48201.

When discharged, patients usually still have many problems. Some do not have a place to live, other do not have jobs to return to, knowledge for retraining, or families and friends to support them. Most are ambivalent about their personal value and their ability to succeed. Their doubts are sustained by the stigma attached to having been hospitalized and the side effects of medication. The sick role may appear the only one in which they can excel.[1]

Continuity of care is a big problem because there has been a proliferation of different types of therapies. There are now more than 250 techniques,[2] and therapy is conducted by psychiatrists, psychologists, social workers, and counselors with different levels of training and theoretical orientation. Patients who have been advised by therapists with different theoretical orientations and who are no longer in therapy may be at a loss to know to whom to turn when undergoing new stresses. They believe that their future is hopeless: They overmedicate themselves or suddenly give up all medications—and find themselves hospitalized once more.

Families have their own predicament. The importance of family therapy is increasingly recognized. In 1973 there was only one journal in this field. Now there are about two dozen therapy journals published in English and other languages. New books on this subject are constantly appearing, and there are now 300 training programs in family therapy.[3] But although research has documented the efficacy of family therapy, it has provided little explanation about how families operate and change.[4] Left without a structure to deal with their problems, families tend to shop around for new therapeutic insights. The trials of families seeking a miracle cure, vitamin pills, a place where patients could work, or institutions where patients could be sheltered after their parents' death are vividly described in *Families in Pain*.[5] The lack of a biopsychosocial role theory that can be operationalized has made it more difficult to devise a common language and a conceptual framework that can be understood by all concerned.

There has been an increasing demand for an eclectic approach to therapy and a theory that would explain how this could be achieved.[6] In a seminal article, Engel[7] discussed the importance of investigating the patients' physiological, psychological, and social needs. Later, Schwartz and Wiggins suggest that "we must devise concepts that apply generically to all systems as such—whether biological, psychological, or social—while we also construct more specific concepts that set forth the differences among them"[8] (p. 1213).

We are attempting to address this problem here, and we shall present a biopsychosocial role theory of mental health that we have developed and tested before discussing the role of clinical sociologists because the theory gives us a structure to look at social problems at different levels of generality.

A BIOPSYCHOSOCIAL THEORY OF MENTAL HEALTH

Two surveys led to the development of the theory. At first we tried to operationalize Erikson's theory of the psychosocial development of children to test a proposition on the repetitive pattern of maternal deprivation. Erikson[9] proposed that a person had to go through a series of psychosocial crises to achieve a sense of identity, of knowing who he is, and what he wants to do. The main finding of our first study was that children trusted others and acquired autonomy only *if their self-expectations and their expectations of others were realized*.[10]

The study that led to a new theory—the theory of alternatives—was a survey on the adjustment of a hundred young widows.[11,12] We found that the widows' problems were biopsychosocial. They experienced severe emotional and physiological responses to their loss and at the same time had to solve a wide range of financial, social, and ethical problems. This study led to the replacement of Erikson's concept of psychosocial crises by the concept of basic needs, or life vectors, derived from Malinowski's cultural imperatives.[13] Life vectors were defined as the basic biopsychosocial needs that are institutionally defined and sanctioned by the individual. These needs run through the life of a person and are interdependent.

Sense of Attainment

We propose that to function in a society you have to achieve a sense of attainment: the knowledge that you are achieving your self-expectations and that your expectations of others are being met in all of your life vectors.

By self-expectations, we mean what you want to do for yourself and for others, your rights, and your obligations. And by expectations of others, your expectations of their rights and obligations.

Complement of Life Vectors

Our interaction with others is not confined to one life vector. When you grow up, the demands that society makes on you increase in size and scope, and you start interacting with an increasing number of people. Life vectors are latent in a person, and the period in which they become manifest depends on maturation and the culture in which you live (Table 1).

Survival is a prime concern for the infant and the aged so that health, nutrition, shelter, and motor development are all crucial to their welfare. Learning to communicate through speech and acquiring an education becomes activated during childhood. In adolescence, social life, love and sex, the choice of an occupation, and finance become increasingly important. A commitment to art, a respect for law and order, an interest in politics, religion, and ethics may start in youth or become significant later on in life. The life vectors are not stages of development but are concurrent dimensions that can occur simultaneously or sequentially. Life vectors can be conceptualized at different levels of generality. Under law and order we can

Table 1. Complement of Life Vectors

Health	Speech	Occupation	Law and order
Nutrition	Education	Finance	Politics
Shelter (housing)	Social life	Parenthood	Religion
Motor development (exercise)	Love and sex	Art	Ethics

classify how a child is punished by his or her parents and whether this child adheres to the laws of society.

Interaction between Two Persons and Role Theory

The basic precepts of role theory are that in each of your statuses, or roles, you have rights and obligations that are defined by you and society.[14] Role enactment occurs when you achieve your expectations and role complementarity when you and the other person agree on your mutual rights and obligations. The theory of alternatives is basically a role theory for it explains that you *fulfill* your basic needs by functioning in different roles and interacting with others. But the human tragedy is that only performances are visible, and you can only infer expectations from performances.

Figure 1 represents the interaction between two persons, you (Ego), and the other person (Alter). The circle in the middle of the diagram shows that only performances are visible. The long arrow from Alter to Ego shows that when Alter acts, he or she meets his or her obligations to you and recognizes your rights, and the long arrow from Ego to Alter shows that when you act you recognize Alter's rights.

When you and Alter have the same expectations, when there is role comple-

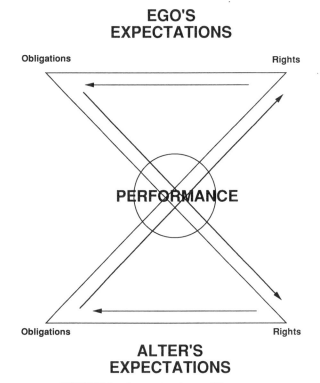

FIGURE 1. Interaction in one life vector.

mentarity, there is no problem. When this is not the case, you can experience anger if you believe that your rights have been overlooked by Alter, or you can experience guilt if you believe that you did not live up to Alter's rights. You can also experience anger and guilt for you blame yourself and Alter. But instead of letting your feelings dictate your behavior, you can assess the situation more objectively.

Assessing a Stressful Situation and Selecting Alternatives

For example, if you are in hospital and your therapist is late, you realize that the ward nurse is the person who probably knows why your therapist is late. She may tell you that the therapist has an emergency and will arrive in 20 minutes and ask you to wait. She may not have told you before because she was busy. So you settle down, read a paper, and when the therapist arrives, you proceed with the interview. You have been aware of your therapist's professional obligations and because of this have modified your expectations and performances.

Patterns of Reaction and Defense Mechanisms

But early traumatic experiences can make it more difficult for you to assess a situation objectively. Freud proposes that we use defense mechanisms to avoid conflicting ideas and feelings. He changed his definition of defense mechanisms several times,[15] however, and Anna Freud did little to clarify this problem.[16]

Vaillant[17] suggests that a distinction should be made between mature and immature defense mechanisms, between concepts such as sublimation and projection. He classifies "acting out" as an immature defense mechanism. But his definition does not differentiate between different types of acting out.

We make a distinction between expectations and performances. Horney[18] states that a person can move against, toward, or away from people. You move against people if when you were a child you were aware of the hostility around you and were blamed if anything went wrong. You move toward people if you were brought up to feel helpless and preferred to be dependent and lean on others than to be left to your own devices. A third possibility is that you withdraw from the situation because you felt as a child that no one understood you. We have derived the following four patterns of reaction from Horney's comments:

Patterns of Reaction Habitual, observable, and unproductive performances when facing a stressful situation	
Brutalization	You physically or verbally force a performance on another
Self-brutalization	You force a pseudoperformance upon yourself: eat or drink too much, stop eating, or take drugs
Victimization	You submit to the performance of another although it is contrary to your expectations
Insulation	You withdraw from the situation

We have added a fourth pattern of reaction—self-brutalization. You feel angry and guilty because as a child you were never sure who was to blame and so you punish yourself and others. But your action is a pseudoperformance because it does not solve your problems. Patterns of reaction allow us to differentiate between different types of responses to a stressful situation. For example, instead of trying to find out why your therapist is not coming, you allow his behavior to reactivate previous traumatic experiences that you have repressed. Your therapist's behavior reminds you of your father who never kept his promises and did not attend your high-school graduation. Your repressed anger at your father's behavior prevents you from assessing your present situation objectively. Instead of finding out why your therapist is late, you react by insulting her when she arrives; getting drunk, eating too much, or stop eating; agreeing to see her even if she is chronically late; or refusing to see her when she arrives.

Defense Mechanisms
Rigid and destructive cognitive methods when facing a stressful situation

---

1. Avoidance of reality

Denial	You refuse to recognize certain expectations or performances
Rationalization	You force your expectations to fit your performance
Regression	You focus on a set of expectations held at an earlier stage of development

2. Cannot differentiate between self-expectations and expectations of others

Projection	You attribute a derogatory expectation to another person that you hold of yourself
Displacement	You transfer an expectation about a person to another or to an object
Identification	You adopt the expectations of another

We have grouped defense mechanisms under two headings: denial of reality and inability to differentiate between self-expectations and the expectations of others because you have first to acknowledge a problem and differentiate between self-needs and those of others before you can negotiate expectations and performances.

When we explain the theory to the patient we keep the list of defense mechanisms short, but a more comprehensive list has been published elsewhere.[19] Figure 2 shows that a stressor[20–23] creates unmet expectations. You can either assess the situation objectively and regain your equilibrium by modifying expectations and performances and negotiating them with others or respond with patterns of reaction and compound your problem because you may worry that you are not more effective.

METHODOLOGY

Our interview schedules were designed to (1) provide the patient with a structure to identify his problems and realize their functional interdependence and

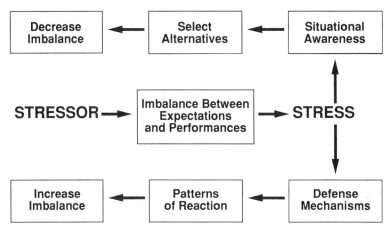

FIGURE 2. Response to imbalance in one life vector.

(2) test the main propositions of our theory. Our main propositions were tested on a sample of 80 schizophrenic, depressed, alcoholic, anorexic, and bulimic inpatients, and their parents; a follow-up group of 18 patients; and a control group of 347 first-year university students.

The patients who were still in high school and their relatives were interviewed only once, but the other patients were interviewed twice. Each interview lasted about an hour. The first interview was designed to establish the patients' functioning at a similar point in time: the last year in high school. Questions were asked to find out the respondents' expectations and performances and relations with significant others in each life vector and the family mode of response to stress. We also inquired about the parents' demographic background, level of aspirations, discipline methods, and plans for the respondents' future.

All the interviews were structured in the same manner. We grouped the life vectors under the following seven themes to make the respondent more aware of the interdependence of life vectors.

Interdependence of Life Vectors	
Doing the work you like	Taking care of your body
Education	Nutrition
Occupation	Exercise
Speech	Health
Options in saving and spending	Be part of this world
Finance	Art
Housing	Politics
To love and be loved	Law and order
Social life	At peace with yourself
Love and sex	Ethics
Your children and their future	Religion
Parenthood	

When we approached the patients, we explained that we would like to discuss their achievements and not just their problems. We mentioned that our interviews were based on a theory of alternatives that we would explain to them when the interviews were completed. We specified that we had grouped areas of behavior under these seven themes so that they could realize the interdependence of their problems. Most hospitalized patients were mulling over either a few very specific problems or believed that they had failed in all areas of behaviors. When they realized that their outlook in life might have been biased, they regained some hope and became more willing to express their concerns.

We explained to the respondents the rationale for grouping life vectors in this fashion:

Education, occupation, and speech are grouped together under "Doing the Work You Like" because the job you can get depends on your educational level and your ability to express yourself.

"Options in Saving and Spending" covers both finance and housing. Your house may be your biggest financial asset, and you cannot move if you do not have money. Going back to school implies that you are going to delay financially your rewards.

"To love and be loved" covers both social life and love and sex for your boyfriend (girlfriend) or husband (wife) should be your friend.

"Your Children and Their Future" emphasizes that the goal of parenthood is to train your children to become self-sufficient and independent.

"Taking Care of Your Health" groups together health, nutrition, and exercise because all three life vectors are important to feel good.

Under "Be Part of this World" are listed art, politics, law and order because you are part of the world.

"At Peace With Yourself" includes religion and ethics, for if your behavior conflicts with your values, you are not at peace.

For each of the life vectors we chose one obvious indicator guided by the critical incident technique.[24] Attitude questions were coded on a 4-point scale ranging from very unimportant to very important. A patient was scored as having an imbalance in a life vector if a critical expectation was not met (Appendix A). A total score was obtained by adding up the number of life vectors in which there was an imbalance.

At the end of each interview, the patient was asked to rank each life vector on a 4-point scale from very important to very unimportant and check in which life vector he believed he had a serious problem. A positive answer was coded as 1 and the number of life vectors in which he had a serious problem added up. He was also asked to list his conflicts and priorities.

The second interview had the same structure as the first but focused on what had happened to the patient before his hospitalization. For certain pivotal life vectors, such as health, education, occupation, housing and sex, we asked him to give us a history of the main events that happened between high school and his present hospitalization.

Most studies on conflict resolution have measured different styles of coping. Our main concern was to find out whether the patients resolved their interpersonal problems by talking about them, used patterns of reaction, or both. Our measures were based on the patients' answers to four questions: How had he behaved when he had a problem at work; a sexual problem with a loved one; or a difference of opinion with his father and mother? Had he talked it over (alternatives) or got angry and had a quarrel (brutalization); given in and became depressed (victimization); drank or ate too much, stopped eating, took drugs (self-brutalization); or withdrew (insulation). An index was formed from the sum of these patterned responses.

The parents' interviews were constructed in the same manner, and three questions were asked to find their patterns of reaction: How had they reacted when they had a problem at work; a sexual problem with each other; or a difference of opinion with the patient.

The patient's level of stress was measured by his score on the SCL-90[25]—a psychological test composed of 90 items rated on a 5-point scale from 0 to 4. It was administered to the patient before he was interviewed for the first time, and it took about 10 minutes to complete.

RESULTS AND INTERVENTION

The following propositions were tested:

1. The greater the number of life vectors in which the patient had an imbalance according to our criteria, the higher his level of stress as measured by the SCL-90 total score.
2. The greater the number of life vectors in which the patient indicated he had a serious problem, the higher his level of stress as measured by the SCL-90 total score.

These two propositions were found to be statistically significant for all of the different diagnostic groups. Pearson r varied from $p<.01$ to $p<.02$. It was also true for the control group of university students, but the level of measurements was in a different domain.

The results of the interviews allowed us to discuss with patients and significant others, first separately and then together, a summing up of their interviews.

In order to discuss the results with the patient, we listed the life vectors they had checked as very important, the life vectors in which according to our criteria they had an imbalance between expectations and performances; the life vectors in which they considered they had a serious problem; their conflicts and priorities; their responses to stress according to the questions we asked and to three projective questions; and their total SCL-90 score (for a complete listing see Appendix B).

For example, Betty Smith was a 34-year-old divorcee, single, no children. She was a college graduate, employed, 5 feet, 8 inches, 145 pounds, a bulimic who also had a drinking problem.

Her father, an alcoholic, was very critical of her behavior. Betty became a bulimic in college: she felt *relatively* deprived[26] because she was tall and heavy compared to her reference group, the other girls, and a friend told her that vomiting was a good way to lose weight. She became addicted to this way of slimming. Her husband left her because she drank too much.

According to the interview with Betty's parents, John and Jane, John was deprived when he was a child. His parents were very poor. His father was a silent man with a grade-school education. His mother, a bitter woman, was very critical of John's behavior and was only pleased if he was at the top of his class. John became a schoolteacher to please his mother, but he was dissatisfied with his job because he earned little money. He started to drink. His very important life vectors were education, occupation, and finance—the same as Betty.

Betty's mother, Jane, dropped out of college when she married. Her parents were authoritarian like her husband. She never worked because her husband did not want her to work. Her very important life vectors when interviewed were health, nutrition, and housing. No one in the family thought that love and sex was a very important life vector.

After explaining the theory and our coding to Betty, the therapist went over the summing-up. Betty was then asked how she would solve her crucial problems and get on with her priorities. She said that before she came to the hospital she would have listed that her priorities were her work and "Mom and Dad." Now it was "being Betty, learning who I am." The information that was given to her about her parents' background made her realize that her father was so critical of her because he had been severely criticized by his own parents and that she had learned from her mother to repress her feelings and to obey. When she was asked how she would solve her first priority, she replied that her main problem was speech. She said that her father had told her not to trust anybody and that she "superimposed a father figure on all authority figures." Instead of telling her boss that her workload was too heavy, she complained to others and ran away from people.

An explanation of the Oedipus complex made Betty realize that her main role had been to be Daddy's little girl. Betty and her mother competed for John's love, and this triad[27] had prevented Betty from trying to make a success of her own love affairs. The last weekend before she was discharged, she went home to her apartment. She had a date with a boy friend. When she came back to the hospital after her outing, she said that for the first time she was able to date, have a good dinner, and did not vomit when she came home.

THE CLINICAL SOCIOLOGIST AS A MEMBER
OF THE CLINICAL TEAM

Hospitals are very hierarchical organizations. In a general hospital, the chief of the department, a psychiatrist, makes many of the major decisions about patient care: diagnosis, medical history, treatment plan, length of stay, and discharge plans. Each physician is legally responsible for his patient's welfare, and when dealing with very sick patients this is a heavy burden. The input of his staff members, who meet with him at weekly clinical rounds, is very real for most modern therapy uses a team approach. A comprehensive evaluation of the patients' problems increases the efficacy of the treatment unit.

The main duties of the staff members are well defined: psychologists give psychological tests; nurses supervise the patient's physical needs; social workers interview families and find out where patients can live when discharged; occupational therapists encourage the use of patients' practical skills. The behavior of the clinical sociologist is under scrutiny when he joins the team because his role is not clearly defined. Parsons points out that the health profession is a science and an art because the combination of uncertainty and strong emotional interests produces strain.[1,28] Working as a member of a team that has clearly defined responsibilities decreases the anxieties of the staff.

Interaction between clinical sociologists, patients, and parents is closely watched by the staff, and clinical sociologists have to be careful that their interview schedules do not provoke undue anxiety in their respondents but help them to mobilize their strengths. There is also a need to evaluate the operation of the unit and of different forms of therapies. Hospitals are competing for contracts with third parties, and all treatment units have to demonstrate that their approach encourages remission of symptoms. Clinical sociologists who can demonstrate that their evaluation of the patients' problems can lead to new therapeutic approaches and are willing to explain their methodology to members of the staff can make a contribution that will be recognized.

Clinical sociologists can also evaluate whether the recommendations made by marketing experts to cut costs are in the hospital's best interests in the long run. Patients and families may look forward to services that do not appear essential but that prevent patients from feeling incarcerated, such as weekly dinners in the dining room that patients and parents can share, as well as group outings. The patients' morale on the ward is often based on a well-run unit that makes them feel that their own welfare is considered.

Another important function of clinical sociologists would be to evaluate the efficiency of partial hospitalization. In an article in *Psychiatric News*, a journal of the American Psychiatric Association, the underutilization of partial hospitalization is stressed.[29] Despite three decades of existence, there is still no definition whether an organization "will be called 'a partial hospital', 'a day care center', an 'outpatient clinic,' or something else." But partial hospitalization frequently costs only half the usual day rate of a mental hospital. It can be a bridge between the sheltered atmosphere of the general hospital and the demands of the business world. Its function and relation to the department of psychiatry in a general hospital needs to be evaluated.

A frequent complaint made by patients is that they have problems functioning on the job. They complain about their workload, conditions of work, and interaction with an authoritarian boss. There is a trend to employ professionals to explain to management and unions the patients' problems. Concepts such as status crystallization[30,31] can help the clinical sociologist to recognize whether patients are under strain because they have too much education for their job and are bored, or they are under strain because their jobs have been upgraded and their training is obsolete. Another problem is that patients often displace on their boss the authority problems that they had with their parents and do not differentiate between the norms and values of their primary group and the needs of the organization. The counter-transference of the boss on his worker is another problem. Misunderstanding can be blown up out of proportion and needs intervention. And this type of intervention may prevent the patient from losing his job and becoming a chronic patient, increase the efficiency of the company who employs him, and improve the reputation of the hospital in the community.

Continuing medical education meetings are part of the training of the staff and are attended by hospital staff, residents, medical, and other students. At these meetings, clinical sociologists can be asked to present their findings and explain sociologically their intervention with patients. Collaboration with psychiatrists on research projects, presenting papers at professional meetings, also validate their role.

THE CLINICAL SOCIOLOGIST IN THE COMMUNITY

Clinical sociologists providing private therapy to mental patients may have a difficult time. They are licensed to practice in only a few states, and they do not have the backing of the medical profession. Many patients are physically as well as emotionally sick, and the availability of a physician who can recognize the organicity of the patients' symptoms is important. The clinical sociologist may also find it difficult to get malpractice insurance.

Clinical sociologists who are working in community mental health centers as part of a team have a contribution to make because they are trained to recognize the specific problems that patients of different social classes face and the needs of the communities where they work. Workers in community centers usually have a very heavy load of patients to supervise. Support groups with group leaders, who could be clinical sociologists, may be able to help patients to deal with daily problems—this has yet to be determined by clinical trials.

Continuity of care and the delivery of social services at the state and federal levels requires very careful planning. The clinical sociologist who has worked in state hospitals and community centers should be able to make recommendations based on experience.

TRAINING OF THE CLINICAL SOCIOLOGIST

The training of clinical sociologists have to be standardized and their usefulness demonstrated before the profession can push for national certification. A strong background in sociological theory and quantitative and qualitative methods of research is essential for this knowledge trains them to evaluate the social functioning of patients, small groups, and organizations—and thus set them apart from other professionals.

Our own theoretical framework has been influenced by the theories of Thomas, James, Cooley, and Mead. The importance that we attach to the respondent learning to assess a situation objectively and differentiate between his expectations and those of others stems from Thomas's definition of the situation[32] and the theories of James, Cooley, and Mead.

When discussing the I and the Me, James observed that we are concerned about how other people see us.[33] Cooley stressed that other people are for us a "looking-glass self" for we interpret how other people see us, and this judgment colors our evaluation of ourself.[34] We found that the anorexic who had the delusion that she was fat often had a mother or a "significant other" who teased her in adolescence about "her big butt" or her "heavy thighs." She internalized their opinion of her and even when emaciated thought that she was fat.

Mead realized that to function in society you have to know the rules of the game. The baseball player can only play if he visualizes the moves of the other players.[35] Schizophrenics who are brought up in families where the rules of the game are contradictory have not acquired this knowledge. They cannot take "the role of the other" and interact constructively with others.

Courses in occupations, organizations, symbolic interaction, the family, and race relations are indispensable. Concepts such as power, stigma, conflict, dyad and triad, vested interests, status consistency,[31] *relative* deprivation, and opportunity structure[36] are familiar to clinical sociologists and part of their training. A sociological perspective helps them to resocialize the respondents: to give them a broader perspective to evaluate their own socialization, their norms and values, and the consequences of their interaction with others—and so learn to function more efficiently in a society.[37] Most modern approaches to the treatment of mental illness are eclectic, and, for that reason, clinical sociologists should learn psychoanalytic, cognitive, interpersonal, personality theories, and behavior modification, and some basic psychopharmacology should be studied. An internship in a mental institution should also be part of their training.

The theory of alternatives provides a structure for the clinical sociologist to investigate in which life vector and at what level of generality the respondent has a problem. By reconceptualizing defense mechanisms as expectations and defining patterns of reaction as performances, the respondent's problem can be analyzed as an individual, a member of a small group, various organizations, and a citizen of his country, using the basic concepts of role theory—expectations and performances. Intervention can be done with respondents, their families, and the groups to which they belong using the same structure and language.

Appendix A. Coding of Imbalances between Expectations and Performances for Each Life Vector According to Set Criteria

Life Vector	Imbalance occurs if
Education	Did not get the grade he wanted (high school), or did not achieve his educational goals (adult)
Occupation	Had a job and did not like it, or did not have a job and would have liked one
Speech	Found it difficult to talk to people he had just met
Finance	Had financial problems
Housing	Would have preferred living somewhere else
Social life	Did not have a close friend and would have liked one
Love and sex	Was dating and did not like his date, or was not dating and would have liked to date (high school)
	Was not satisfied with is sexual life (adult)
Parenthood	Had serious problems with one of his children
Nutrition	Believed his weight should have been higher or lower
Exercise	Believed he should have exercised more or less
Health	Dissatisfied with his health
Politics	Believed he should have been more informed about current events (high school), or did not vote and felt he should vote (adult)
Law	Had legal problems and worried about them
Art	Should have been more or less involved in arts
Religion	Believed he should have gone to church or to a synagogue more frequently

Appendix B.   Summing-up of a Case History

BETTY SMITH
34-year-old, divorced, no chidlren, college graduate, employed,
white, Protestant, 5 feet 8 inches, 145 pounds

Very important life vectors
4
Occupation
Education
Speech
Finance

Imbalances between expectations and performances
(Our own criteria)
5
Nutrition
Religion
Health
Art
Love and sex

Serious problems
5
Social life, "Don't have any. Imperative to my recovery to get one."
Love and sex, "I need to be loved other than being father's little girl."
Health, "I am killing myself throwing up, binging, drinking."
Nutrition, "Same."
Ethics, "What I am doing is 100 percent degree different from what I think is the moral thing to do."

Conflict
1
"Feel out of my hands."

Priorities
4
"Being Betty, learning who I am,"
"Not being a reflection of anybody else."
"Asking help, taking it."
"Be free of this obsessive behavior."

Responses to stress
5 self-brutalizations
3 victimizations

Projective Questions
1 brutalization
4 self-brutalizations
1 victimization
1 alternative

Total SCL-90 Score: 88

REFERENCES

1. Parsons, T. (1951). Social structure and dynamic process: The case of modern medical practice. In *The social system* (pp. 428–479). Glencoe, IL: Free Press.
2. Herink, R. (Ed.). (1980). *The psychotherapy handbook. The A to Z guide to more than 250 therapies in use today*. New York: New American Library.
3. Bloch, D. A., & Weiss, H. M. (1981). Training facilities in marital and family therapy. *Family Therapy, 20*, 133–146.
4. Gurman, A. S., Kniskern, D. P., & Pinsoff, W. M. (1956). Research on the process and outcome of marital and family therapy. In S. L. Garfield & A. E. Bergin (Eds.), *Handbook of psychotherapy and behavior change* (pp. 565–624). New York: Wiley.
5. Vine, P. (1982). *Families in pain*. New York: Pantheon.
6. Garfield, S. L., & Bergin, A. E. (1986). Introduction and historical overview. In S. L. Garfield & A. E. Bergin (Eds.), *Handbook of psychotherapy and behavior change* (3rd ed.; pp. 3–22). New York: Wiley.
7. Engel, G. L. (1977). The need for a new medical model: A challenge for biomedicine. *Science, 196*, 129–136.
8. Schwartz, M. A., & Wiggins, O. P. (1986). Systems and the structuring of meaning: Contributions to a biopsychosocial medicine. *American Journal of Psychiatry, 143*, 1213–1221.
9. Erikson, E. H., (1956). The problem of ego identity. *Journal of the American PsychoAnalytic Association, 4*, 56–121.
10. Ferguson, T. (1962). *An exploratory study of the repetitive pattern of maternal deprivation*. Unpublished master's essay. New York: Columbia University.
11. Ferguson, T., Kutscher, A. H., & Kutscher, L. G. (1981). *The young widow: Conflict and guidelines*. New York: Arno.
12. Ferguson, T., & Ferguson, J. (1981). Alternatives after loss. In E. Chigier (Ed.), *Grief and bereavement in contemporary society* (Vol 2.). London: Freund Publishing House.
13. Malinowski, B. (1960). Basic needs and cultural responses. In *A scientific theory of culture, and other essays* (pp. 191–119). New York: Galaxy.
14. Sarbin, T. R., & Allen, V. L. (1968). Role theory. In G. Lindsey & E. Aronson (Eds.), *The handbook of social psychology* (2nd. ed., Vol. 1; pp. 488–567). Cambridge, MA: Addison-Wesley.
15. Vaillant, G. E. (1986). Introduction: A brief history of empirical assessment of defense mechanisms. In G. E. Vaillant (Ed.), *Empirical studies of ego mechanisms of defense* (pp. viii–xx). Washington, DC: American Psychiatric Press.
16. Freud, A. (1966). *The ego and the mechanisms of defense* (Rev. ed.). New York: International Universities Press.
17. Vaillant, G. E. (1986). Appendix III. Vaillant's glossary of defenses. In G. E. Vaillant (Ed.), *Empirical studies of ego mechanisms of defense* (pp. 111–120). Washington, DC: American Psychiatric Press.
18. Horney, K. (1945). *Our inner conflicts*. In *The collected works of Karen Horney*, Vol. 1. New York: Norton.
19. Ferguson, T., Schorer, C. T., Tourney, G., & Ferguson, J. (1981). Bereavement, stress, and rescaling therapy. In O. S. Margolis, H. S. Raether, A. H. Kutscher *et al.* (Eds.), *Acute grief* (pp. 158–166). New York: Columbia University Press.
20. Cannon, W. B. (1953). *Bodily changes in pain, hunger, fear and rage* (2nd ed.). Boston: Branford.
21. Selye, H. S. (1956). *The stress of life*. New York: McGraw-Hill.
22. Selye, H. S. (1974). *Stress without distress*. Toronto: McClelland and Stewart.
23. Pearlin, L. I., Lieberman, M. A., Menaghan, E. G., & Mullan, J. T. (1981). The stress process. *Journal of Health and Social Behavior, 22*, 337–356.
24. Flanagan, J. F. (1954). The critical incident technique. *Psychological Bulletin, 51*, 327–355.
25. Derogatis, L. R., Lipman, R. S., Covi L. (1976) Self-report inventory. In *ECDEU Assessment manual for psychopharmacology*, revised 1976; pp. 311–331. Rockville, MD: U.S. Department of Health, Education and Welfare.
26. Merton, R. K. (1968). Contributions to the theory of reference group behavior. In *Social theory and social structure* (Enlarged ed.; pp. 279–334). New York: Free Press.

27. Simmel, G. (1950). The isolated individual and the dyad. The triad. In *The sociology of Georg Simmel*, trans. K. H. Wolff (pp. 118–169). Glencoe, IL: Free Press.
28. Goode, W. J. (1960). A theory of role strain. *American Sociological Review, 25*, 483–496.
29. B. S. H. (1989). Partial hospitalization underutilized. *Psychiatric News, 24*, 1,19.
30. Lenski, E. G. (1954). Status crystallization: a non-vertical dimension of social status. *American Sociological Review, 19*, 403–413.
31. Jackson, E. F. (1962). Status consistency and symptoms of stress. *American Sociological Review, 27*, 469–480.
32. Thomas, W. I., & Thomas D. S. (1923). *The unadjusted girl; With cases and standpoint for behavior analysis*. Boston: Little, Brown.
33. James, W. J. (1961). The self. In G. Allport (Ed.), *William James psychology, the briefer course* (pp. 42–83). New York: Harper Torchbook.
34. Cooley, H. C. (1902). *Human nature and the social order*. New York: Scribner's.
35. Mead, G. H. (1934). In C. W. Morris (Ed.), *Mind, self, and society*. Chicago: The University of Chicago Press.
36. Cloward, R. A., & Ohlin, L. E. (1960). *Delinquency and opportunity*. New York: Free Press.
37. Fein, M. L. (1988). Resocialization: A neglected paradign. *Clinical Sociology, 6*, 88–100.

CHAPTER 14

Clinical Sociology in the Criminal Justice System

CLIFFORD M. BLACK, RICHARD ENOS, JOHN E. HOLMAN, AND JAMES F. QUINN

THE CONTEXT OF THE JUSTICE SYSTEM

Sociologists, particularly clinical sociologists, are implementing new models throughout the justice system as well as redesigning existing programs. They work in law enforcement, the judicial system, and corrections to develop and improve programs for use by all of the individuals and agencies affected by the criminal justice processes.

The American criminal justice system is undergoing many significant changes. Changes in judicial decisions (e.g., defining minimal standards for correctional facilities and programs) have resulted in overcrowding in correctional systems, leaving these systems in turmoil. These changes have had repercussions throughout the system, affecting law enforcement and the judiciary as well as corrections. There are not enough facilities to accommodate the changes, and it has become too costly to add more. This has lead to the return of many offenders to the community more quickly than is appropriate.

Sociology is making a significant contribution to the resolution of these problems. This chapter illustrates current work, plus the potential for further contributions by clinical sociologists in the criminal justice system. It explores the role of sociology and of clinical sociologists in earlier criminal justice programs and provides a brief introduction to the use of selected sociological theories in some programs and practices.

CLIFFORD M. BLACK, RICHARD ENOS, JOHN E. HOLMAN and JAMES F. QUINN • School of Community Service, University of North Texas, Denton, Texas 76203.

NEW DIRECTIONS AND MODELS IN THE JUSTICE SYSTEM

Clinical sociologists practicing within the criminal justice system are unique in two respects. They have appropriate training in sociological theory and methods, and they are committed to intervention. Each program discussed in this chapter reflects the four characteristics of clinical sociology: (1) a commitment to intervention,[1] (2) a commitment to interdisciplinary strategies and cooperation, (3) a concern with human and societal needs, and (4) a focus on holism. It should be recognized that clinical sociology is not primarily microsociological in perspective or practice but is able to work at all levels and relate the consequences of activity at one level to outcomes at another.[2]

This presentation of the programs and professional roles of clinical sociologists considers the variety of roles and actors found in the law enforcement, judicial, and correctional subsystems. Whenever appropriate, the programs will be identified by level of practice (i.e., micro, meso, or macro), and the interaction of levels in a specific program will be noted.

Clinical Sociologists in Law Enforcement Programs

Although many possibilities exist for clinical sociologists in law enforcement, few sociologists have chosen to direct their efforts in this direction. William M. Hall is one of the few clinical sociologists who is a law enforcement officer. He analyzed his role in a recent discussion of crime, deviance, and the sociological imagination.[3] Another of the few clinical sociologists who have been involved in law enforcement programs is Clifford M. Black. In 1986, Black was invited by the Governor of Texas's *Task Force On Crime Prevention* to provide clinical sociological training on human relations and interpersonal relationships. This involved training for police-to-police interaction, police-to-public interaction, and public-to-police interaction.

Persons trained in clinical sociology have taken occupational roles as county sheriffs, police administrators, police officers, secret service, and FBI agents. They also work as instructors in universities, community colleges, and police academy law enforcement programs, and as private counselors and consultants working with police and police families.

Clinical Sociologists in the Judicial System

Thornton and Voigt[4] assert that "testifying in court [is] the most frequent consulting activity of criminologists" (p. 115). They provide an informative discussion of the sociologist's role as expert witness in their discussion on the roles and ethics of the practicing sociologist (p. 113). The label of *criminologist* is used in the United States to refer to academicians and practitioners, usually trained in sociology with specialization in juvenile delinquency, deviance, or criminology (p. 129). Although the role of expert witness appears a logical one for clinical sociologists, Thornton and Voigt report that "research on this subject . . . suggests that most academic criminologists have never served in this capacity, especially on a regular basis" (p. 115).

Another example of a role for the clinical sociologist in the judicial system is the alternative sentencing consultant and planner. One of the former directors of the Southwest Regional Office of the National Center on Institutions and Alternatives, in Dallas, is a clinical sociologist. This organization works with defense attorneys to develop alternatives to incarceration that are acceptable to the victim, judges, and prosecutors. As these alternative sentencing programs grow and become widespread, they develop the potential to change court processes and correctional practices.

Clinical Sociology in the Corrections System

Considerable opportunity for the professional clinical sociologist exists in corrections. On the microlevel, several sociologists provide counseling for behavior change with actual or potential offenders. One example was provided by Powers who described her work with a chronic slasher.[5] Another example is that of a sociologist who conducted human relations training for prisoners and corrections officers, with emphasis on the needs of female prisoners. Other clinical sociologists have conducted training programs for prisoners as well as training and research with guards. The program for inmates at the Federal Correctional Facility in Fort Worth provides one example of this role.[6]

Sociologists working on a microlevel in law enforcement agencies and correctional institutions require sociological training, awareness of meso- and macrolevel issues, and the ability to integrate theory, research, and practice from each level while working with individuals and small groups. The examples provided are directly concerned with individual behavior change. However, the acceptance of a role for clinical sociologists within the correctional institution has great potential for bringing about mesolevel changes in correctional practices.

As one example of a mesolevel intervention, in 1986, clinical sociologists in Texas introduced electronic monitoring and house arrest in Dallas and in Denton. The sociologists worked closely with the probation departments, the courts, and the sheriff's department to implement and sustain these programs. Another program, created in Texas in 1984, is operated by a team of clinical sociologists. The Denton County Jail Computerized Life-Coping Skills Program complements traditional case management and fulfills the state-mandated jail counseling requirements. Clinical sociologists work with individual case managers to provide inmates with personalized training in areas in which many offenders have inadequate socialization, contributing to unemployment, excessive debt, family instability, general difficulties in social interaction, and, perhaps, to criminal behavior and recidivism. This computerized training includes simulations of specific problem resolution techniques.

Clinical sociologists are also active in drug treatment programs. In one state, a clinical sociologist is the director of drug and alcohol research. In another state, a clinical sociologist is a DWI probation supervisor in a large metropolitan district. Another new and rapidly developing area open to clinical sociologists is the private initiative prison, which offers considerable opportunities for consulting and practice at several levels. At least one team of clinical sociologists has worked in this capacity in Texas.

Although many of these programs intervene at the individual level, they have implications for broader change in correctional and judicial systems. Programs like these also have ethical implications and are not without their critics. However, considering the conditions within most state prisons and the potential of such programs for positive change, rejection of these programs raises far more powerful ethical questions. The challenge for sociologists is to apply theory and research in creative ways to develop and refine effective programs. Because of their sensitivity to the many levels at which social interactions occur, clinical sociologists are particularly well suited to practice within the criminal justice system.

THE ROLE OF SOCIOLOGY IN THE HISTORY OF CRIMINAL JUSTICE

Although much early work in the criminal justice system was done by sociologists and allied practitioners, the potential of the discipline has not yet been fully realized. The public and criminal justice personnel perceive sociology to have made significant contributions to the justice system. Personnel in the various components of criminal justice frequently receive some portion of their training in sociology, but little actual use has been made of sociological theory and practice.

The dominant models in the criminal justice system have been psychological, reflecting a strong tendency by the public and criminal justice personnel to perceive crime as an idiosyncratic and individual, rather than a social, problem. This has been reinforced by the strong political role of the American Psychological Association in regulating the programs and treatments that can be offered to individuals. The lobbying efforts of psychologists have helped to limit the market and practice areas of licensed psychologists. The fact that social workers frequently adopt similar models of, and approaches to, criminal justice practice strengthens this approach. Even though many of the problems thought to underlie crime are social in nature and even though problems of criminals can be traced to socialization, the programs that have received the most support and funding are individual counseling psychology models. Models that focus on social systems and the socialization process, although identified as significant, have yet to be fully implemented.

Sociology, and clinical sociology, have only begun to exert influence on the criminal justice system. A number of writers have emphasized the need for, and roles of, clinical sociologists.[7,8,9] These authors note that American sociology has, from its beginnings, included clinical and practice elements. They express concern for social problems and note that, until the early 1980s, criminology has been "one of the few explicitly applied subfields within sociology." In this section we will detail the historical development of clinical sociology in each of the three major components of the criminal justice system.

Law Enforcement

Bordua and Reiss[9] attribute the absence of sociological involvement in police organizations to three factors. First, police departments were "inaccessible to social science investigation." Second, sociology was identified with what Bordua and Reiss label *good government* forces whose role was to "expose" the police. Finally, they argued that sociologists felt "uncomfortable" with coercion, which is evidently the mode of operation associated with police work (p. 275).

Another reason for the limited application of sociology lies in the historical relationship between sociology and other intervention disciplines, which tended to focus on the problematic behavior of the individual criminal. Only later did sociology and clinical sociology direct its attention toward its potential roles in the criminal justice system.

Social workers initiated programs and intervention with police organizations. The police social worker sought to aid police with certain types of offenders, such as women and children. In some cases, intervention was extended to the families of offenders. However, police social workers had difficulty developing a positive image in police organizations, due, perhaps, to the fact that such roles were originally filled by women. They were also perceived as being of greater benefit to the offender than to the law enforcement officer.

Psychology developed a more positive image with the role of police psychologist. The greater prestige results from the higher status given to psychology. It also results from the perceived purpose of the role as one of assisting police officers, rather than aiding offenders. Though there is less role confusion and ambiguity for everyone involved, some resistance has been encountered. The model suggests that something is wrong with the officer who needs to work with the police psychologist.

We conclude from our experience that there is considerable need for a police sociologist. For example, one of the authors had considerable success working with the problems and issues that arise in families of law enforcement officers. Much of the stigma attached to psychological problems does not adhere to social problems. Although attention has been given to psychology in the training of police officers, insufficient attention has been given to the fact that much of the work performed by police officers involves social interaction and is conducted in a social environment. Thus many of the problems encountered by police are problems of interaction.

Education, including degree programs, has been the most obvious contribution of sociology. Many officers received undergraduate training in sociology and are now returning to graduate schools for advanced degrees. Two trends are observable: police departments are increasing the use of sociological expertise, either by (1) employing clinical sociologists or (2) providing police officers with training as sociologists or criminologists.[9]

Judicial

Zeisel[10] explored the application of sociology in law almost a quarter of a century ago. His work offers a framework for including the role of clinical sociologists in the judicial system. Zeisel limited the role of sociologists in the judicial system to research that would identify more effective judicial practices. Various research methods were used to examine the efficiency of pretrial conferences, differential sentencing by judges, the significance of the judge's instructions to the jury as related to jury decisions, the behavior of juries, and the merits of capital punishment.

A related role for clinical sociology is the analysis of juror behavior and has led to the use of demographic information by attorneys to assist in making informed decisions with regard to jury selection. Attorneys attempt to choose jurors who will be most likely to give their case a favorable hearing. This presents ethical and moral dilemmas for many individuals. However, equally difficult moral decisions must be considered if all the helpful information is not used in a system that has been structured so that both the defendant and the state have maximal opportunity to gain sympathy for their arguments.

In addition to research and evaluation, clinical sociologists have recently begun to assume the roles of expert witnesses and advisors in judicial settings. Within the courtroom, the expert witness role has long been assumed by psychologists rather than sociologists. For many years, psychologists have been called upon to interpret the criminal for the courts, especially in regard to establishing intent (i.e., mens rea). This seems a strange phenomenon when so many of the variables related to criminal behavior are social in nature.

Corrections

Clinical sociological practice in corrections began with the "child guidance" clinics of the 1920's.[11] Dorothy S. and W. I. Thomas were active in these clinics. "The . . . sociologists's contribution was not merely obtaining diagnostic insight into the juvenile's motives, attitudes, situational analysis, group and cultural participation, but also in controlling and reconstructing the juvenile's behavior."[12,13] Black and Enos[14] detail this control and reconstruction of the juvenile's behavior with their discussion of "beneficent framing" of the situation. Saul Alinsky,[15] another pioneer in clinical sociology, was involved in corrections and completed much work on the influence of social factors on crime.

In the early 1980's, Chandler[16] reported that postconviction work held promise for sociologists as practitioners (i.e., parole and probation officers) and in the development and administration of programs. In a more negative vein, Chandler stated that aside from selected reports that they provide their agencies, "their duties seem unrelated to sociology" (p. 202). Such a conclusion may have more to do with Chandler's understanding of clinical sociology than with the role of the clinical sociologist in criminal justice. Chandler described the unrelated duties as "counsel[ing] clients, do[ing] presentence investigations, write[ing] bureaucratic reports, and attend[ing] committee meetings about the agency's coordination, financial, and training problems" (p. 202). These activities represent clinical sociology in practice because they require a detailed understanding of the interrelationships between the micro-, meso-, and macrolevels of social phenomena.

Although Kahn[17] expressed some reservations with respect to the utility of sociology in the juvenile justice arena, his overall treatment of the role of the clinical sociologist in these roles is basically positive. He asserts that the intellectual bases used by many executives, officials, and social workers are fundamentally sociological and have brought about major changes in delinquency treatment programs. They have also played a significant role in the shift of emphasis toward prevention.

Chandler[18] ends his discussion with some positive predictions. He asserts that career opportunities in the postconviction portions of criminal justice are likely to continue to expand for some time. In his analysis, this is the only area in which "some job descriptions require sociology, where specialized academic preparation is available (criminology and criminal justice studies), and where those in authority have or are familiar with sociological skills" (p. 204).

THEORIES FOR CLINICAL SOCIOLOGICAL PRACTICE IN CRIMINAL JUSTICE

Much of the work of clinical sociologists is eclectic in that it includes theories and techniques from other disciplines. No discipline has a theory base sufficient to explain and predict human behavior with a high degree of reliability. The work of the criminal justice system is often based on sociological theories that have, in many cases, preceded, paralleled, and/or contributed to clinical practice and intervention. However, such theories have often been popularized by, and subsequently identified with, other disciplines. Black and Enos[19] are a particularly fruitful source for exploring this phenomenon in more detail.

This section outlines three important theories for sociological practice. Suggestions are made, and examples provided, to demonstrate the usage of each theory by clinical sociologists in the criminal justice system at micro-, meso-, or macrolevels of practice.

The interventions draw on the experiences of all who are involved in them, including clinical sociologists. Using a sociological perspective, the interventions involve clients in an active process of discovery and insight, including creative problem solving and experimentation in everyday life. Experiential learning can lead to insights that can come from such activities as one-to-one discussion, role playing, observation, imitation, and the "trying on" of the roles, structures, and behaviors of other persons, groups, and societies.

Intervention based upon cognitive learning is also important in clinical sociological practice. Instruction about social structures, institutions, groups, roles, and processes is an important intervention tool in itself. The affective dimension of the individual is often accessible through the cognitive. Interventions should be oriented toward opportunities to demonstrate human worth that support and reinforce the client's sense of self-respect. Various opportunities should be used to promote self-evaluation and the exchange of ideas on how clients and clinical workers view each others' presentations of self and perceptions of the social world around them.

Clinical practice, at any level, requires knowledge and understanding of the intervention needs and possible outcomes at each of the overlapping levels of social reality. The microlevel intervention, which most closely parallels therapeutic and counseling interventions, tends to focus on the individual and small group. Interventions at the mesolevel are closely identified with inservice education and training strategies. The macrolevel is dominated by policy concerns, which are usually implemented at the mesolevel.

One level of analysis and practice is provided for each theoretical perspective.

A macrolevel example is provided for conflict theory. An example at the mesolevel is provided for phenomenological theory. Finally, an illustration of micropractice and analysis is provided for social construction of reality theory. The interaction of these levels is of unique concern to the sociologist, and no theory is inextricably bound to any level of reality.

Conflict Theory

Conflict theory asserts that conflict and social change are the most significant processes in determining the nature and structure of human social interaction. Conflict is a constant but dynamic social process within every group and society, and change is often a product of the conflict resolution process in individuals as well as groups of all sizes.

The notion of conflict includes much more than violent manifestations such as war, genocide, and interpersonal violence. Sociologists studying competition among ethnic, racial, class, or other groups have conceived of competition as a form of "rule-governed" conflict. The evolution of labor and management conflicts into designated procedures for the negotiation of differences illustrates this point. Destructive conflicts often evolve into restricted competition. All societies are dynamic and experience degrees of social change. Neither resistance to social change nor participation in, or accommodation to, social change guarantees the survival or existence of a group or society. However, all societies must have mechanisms for managing conflict and competition. The more successful they are at responding to conflicts, the greater the probability of their survival. Responses to conflict can take various forms and have a variety of implications for social structures.

Conflict results from the competition for scarce resources such as power, prestige, status, privilege, and wealth. The significant issue for conflict theorists is that the individuals or groups that have power control the distribution of scarce resources. Therefore, they can define social processes and structures for their own purposes. Understanding the interaction of individuals within groups requires a clear comprehension of the power structure and an understanding of how power is used and maintained.

Macro

The macrolevel of analysis and practice can be used to demonstrate the clinical utility of conflict theory. Clinical sociological intervention in the criminal justice system commonly manifests itself in policy interventions. Hall[20] treats this as one of the methods for clinical sociological intervention in the criminal justice professions. He cites it as one method by which sociology can aid in the development of strategies to change crime patterns. He contends that sociologists are well equipped to develop theories and programs to modify criminal behavior. However, he cautions that the linkage of causal theories to ameliorative policies is often tenuous and indirect. He attributes this to the fact that "social policy can be implemented only within the moral boundaries of society" (p. 126).

For example, it can be asserted that organized labor has an essential role in the development of criminal justice programs and that there is an historic rationale for labor's involvement in such issues. Further, it can be shown that organized labor has helped to shape many aspects of contemporary correctional programs.

A contemporary manifestation of this can be seen in the example of The United Labor Comprehensive Criminal Justice Program—Fort Worth, Texas. This was an effort by organized labor in this region to respond to issues of crime and justice. The center provided services in four areas: (1) youth recreation and employment, (2) ex-offender employment, (3) prevention of crime against the elderly, and (4) victim/witness support services. Several attempts were made to develop this model of political intervention into a meso- and macroeffort. These included efforts to gain the support of several national labor organizations, to fund the efforts through labor foundations, and to link the Department of Justice and the Department of Labor in the development of the program. This intervention depends upon political action, public education, and community organizational efforts to encourage appropriate groups to take political action in order to change the current criminal justice systems and policies.

The preceding example suggests that clinical sociological interventions in the justice system are heavily predicated on conflict theory. Other historical examples, such as the use of police organizations to protect business and industry from workers and European immigrants, provide insights into current roles and relationships among various powerless groups in this country. The historic responses of the criminal justice system to strikes can be defined as a context in which the miscarriages of justice for disenfranchised groups can be framed. Sociological explanations of the history of legislation regarding child welfare and child labor can easily demonstrate legalized victimization in this society. Such discussions serve to sensitize organized labor to the need for involvement in the political process. This strategy is designed to provide a model for analyzing middle class and upper-class attempts to "properly" socialize the working-class child. Evidence for this perspective is cited from the history of "child savers" and the rise of juvenile institutions.

The unwitting role of organized labor in shaping criminal justice policy can be credited with encouraging labor groups to develop strategies for responding to crime and delinquency. Labor's response to prison employment, prison industry, work release programs, and community restitution centers is counterproductive to the current goals of labor organizations as well as to intelligent correctional practices and informed agency management.

Phenomenological Theory

The phenomenological perspective asserts that human behavior and social interaction can only be understood from the point of view of the actors. It assumes that both the generation and perception of behavior are ultimately based on an inner personal dimension, accessible only through the actor's point of view.

This perspective provides a method of introspection for the "controlled examination of awareness itself." Personal experience is analyzed so as to specify that which is "most directly experienced as social reality"[21] by the individual. This results in an assessment of the individual's perception of the structure and process of society. In this assessment, the individual identifies the determinants of human behavior, social interaction, and the structure and processes of society that direct that behavior and interaction. Such a process is felt to lead to insight and voluntary change on the part of the client.

Black and Enos[22] outline four areas in phenomenological theory that provide support for the use of this perspective in clinical work. One of these is communication. The clinical sociological practice approaches in criminal justice, outlined or suggested in this section, will focus only on this one aspect of human behavior, human social interaction, social structures, and social processes.

Meso

In demonstrating and explicating phenomenological theory, an example of analysis and practice by clinical sociologists at the meso-level can be used. One necessary clinical sociological practice, which is often aided by the use of phenomenological theory, is that of the clinical sociologist's role as an expert witness. For Cohen[23], this method assists the practitioner in knowing "persons and groups on their [own] terms" (p. 33). That is, "He thinks through what he would perceive, mean, feel, and act if he lived in that body, mind, social group, and with that person's and group's background and life experiences" (p. 33). Once data are obtained, they are placed in the most appropriate context for use by the judicial process.

Actors within the courtroom share in certain acts but view them from different perspectives. Such variations in perceptions dramatically effect the actions of the individuals. It is imperative for clinical sociologists, as expert witnesses, to anticipate the interpretations that are likely to be attached to their assessments by other actors. Several activities required of the expert witness in the courtroom illustrate the significance of this theory and the methodology for analyzing the meaning of witness behavior.

The interpretation of scientific studies that relate to litigation underscores the significance of phenomenological theory. The expert witness must respond to the differences in the interpretation of his statements as a scientist and as a witness. Although social scientists rarely speak in definitive terms, they must often learn to communicate in an unequivocal manner in order to successfully impact the judicial process.

Other situations also demonstrate the use of phenomenology in analyzing meaning and communication in the courtroom. The "rules of evidence" are one such area: In order to communicate the desired meaning, the expert witness must understand and follow the rules of evidence within a given jurisdiction while presenting his/her testimony. He/she should remain aware of the fact that an expert witness can "clarify and expand statements." The fact that expert testimony can take the form of an opinion is also crucial to this role.[24]

As expert witnesses, clinical sociologists must communicate their expertise to the members of the jury and the judge. They must also be aware of the structure and process by which such communication is accomplished. It is necessary that they understand the meaning of their actions to the jury.

Social Construction of Reality Theory

Social construction of reality theory assumes that all reality is socially constructed; there is no reality that is not socially interpreted. Thus socialization plays a significant role in the perception, interpretation, and communication of reality. The reality confronted by individuals is filtered through socially learned assumptions about the nature of the world and human social life. Thus the same reality can be interpreted quite differently by different subcultures and individuals. Such social constructions have great influence on human behaviors.

This perspective focuses upon the process by which certain perceptions come to be interpreted as reality. It focuses upon understanding how all other theoretical schools construct reality and on how the insights provided by these schools influence social processes and structures. This theory offers the benefit of being both critical and eclectic.

The social construction of reality viewpoint provides a theoretical foundation for a clinical sociological practice that enables clients and clinicians to examine multiple versions of reality. This permits an analysis of the impact a particular version of reality has in determining the behaviors of individuals and groups and helps transcend official reality. From this vantage point, it is possible to analyze the role an official version of reality has in determining the behaviors of individuals and groups.

Interventions grounded in the social construction of reality approach assume that comprehension of the process by which social realities are constructed equips individuals and groups to interact within the confines of these realities. Such insight enables them to effectively resolve the issues critical to their survival. The purpose of this model of intervention is to help individuals and groups become aware of the process of reality construction and its transmission through socialization.[25]

Micro

We have selected analysis and practice by clinical sociologists at the microlevel as the level that best illustrates the implementation of the social construction of reality theory. We use the Computerized Life-Coping Skills Program at the Denton (Texas) County Jail as our example. This program was designed and is operated by faculty, graduate students, and staff of the Institute for Criminal Justice Studies and the Department of Sociology and Social Work at the University of North Texas.

This program was generated from the theoretical perspective of the social construction of reality. Three concepts that are useful in operationalizing socialization are imitation, reinforcement, and incorporation. Imitation refers to the reproduction of ideals, values, and behaviors by individuals and groups that have been observed in reference groups. Reinforcement refers to individual and group responses to the ideas, values, and behaviors of others. Incorporation denotes the acceptance and self-regulation by individuals and groups of specific ideals, values, and behaviors. The basic premise of the life-coping skills program is that selected individuals have not been adequately socialized with respect to certain required social tasks.

Using computer-assisted instruction, participants receive individualized training in several areas in which many offenders have inadequate socialization. This deficiency contributes to a variety of problems that are thought to underlie criminal behavior and recidivism. This computer-delivered training includes simulation training in resolving specific personal problems related to employment, finances, family relations, and social interaction. Individual case managers are available to assist the offender in this skill development process.

TRANSLATING THEORY INTO PRACTICE
IN CLINICAL SOCIOLOGY

There are nine steps involved in the translation of theory into practice, each of which is built upon the previous step. The process is both additive and linear. However, the dynamic interaction between clients in the criminal justice system and the clinical sociologists intervening in that system is, most often, uneven.

The first step is the identification of the problem(s) to be solved. Clients for the clinical sociologist in the criminal justice system may come from or be involved with any one of the three major components of the criminal justice system: law enforcement, judicial, and correctional. Clients may present problems or situations for intervention at any one of the three levels of focus: micro, meso, or macro.

A second step involves gathering data to place the problem within an historical and contemporary context: the assessment of the client's history by the clinician. An assessment of the current state of affairs is also a prerequisite to action. This analysis reveals past interventions and outcomes while specifying the areas of need for current interventions.

The third stage is the choice of appropriate theoretical perspectives by the clinician. The selected perspective is used to generate general models and specific strategies for intervention. Such theories must be consistent with the four characteristics of clinical sociology. They should (1) lend themselves to intervention, (2) represent an interdisciplinary approach, (3) be humane, and (4) treat the client holistically. Sociological theories present alternative ways of understanding social interaction, social structures, and social processes. Appropriate theories provide an intellectual base for understanding human phenomena.

A fourth stage involves the operationalizing of significant concepts generated by sociological theories to identify behaviors. The process of operationalizing refers to the process of identifying the actual manifestation of social phenomenon in everyday life.

In the fifth step, theory(ies) and concept(s) are used to construct a model for intervention that encompasses the goals, strategies, and evaluation of the intervention. The medical model of intervention has tended to view the client as a patient, the problem or illness as a phenomenon beyond the control of the patient, the patient as someone to be acted upon, and the clinician as the main actor who possesses the tools to remedy the problem. Holistic and preventive medicine alter this model drastically, making the patient (client) an active partner in the process of recovery (change).

Once a model for intervention has been developed, goals, strategies, and methods consistent with the theory, concepts, and model are developed. A social construction of reality model, for example, conceptualizes the real world as one in which all reality is socially constructed. This model focuses on the shaping of individual behaviors, throughout history, by social constructions and social interactions, and, currently, by institutions, roles, values, and norms.

The sixth stage is the development of goals for the intervention. These emerge from actions that can be demonstrated to be realistic and consistent with the model. One goal of the social construction of reality model might be to encourage the offender to conform to the beliefs, values, and norms of the society or community. A second goal might be to assist the individual in perceiving and understanding how reality is constructed. A third goal might be to enable an individual to make necessary adaptations, whenever necessary, in order to survive.

In the seventh stage, objectives and strategies are developed for accomplishing these goals. Indicators must be developed that serve to translate the clinical process into measurable increments of change. The accomplishment of several specific objectives serves as an indication that a specific goal has been achieved.

In Stage 8, specific methods and techniques by which the objectives and goals can be accomplished, are developed. If individuals need to be taught the process by which reality is socially constructed, methods and techniques, which successfully accomplish the learning task, must be selected. Methods or techniques of discussion, dialogue, or debate might be appropriate. Experiments or problem-solving techniques might also be used to accomplish this goal.

In the ninth stage, the intervention process must be evaluated. This is similar to validating or refining a theory once a hypothesis has been submitted to scientific testing. Such testing assists in determining the utility of the theory. The evaluation of an intervention helps to determine whether the techniques and objectives had an acceptable degree of success in accomplishing the goals that had been outlined for the intervention. Various program evaluation and/or single-subject research designs can be utilized to accomplish this task.

REFERENCES

1. Black, C. M., & Enos, R. (1980). Sociological precedents and contributions to the understanding and facilitation of individual behavioral change: The case for counseling sociology. *Journal of Sociology and Social Welfare, 7,* 648–664.
2. Black, C. M., & Enos, R. (1981). Using phenomenology in clinical social work: A poetic pilgrimage. *Clinical Social Work Journal, 9,* 34–43.
3. Hall, W. M. (1985). Crime, deviance, and the sociological imagination. In R. A. Strauss (Ed.), *Using sociology* (pp. 118–135). Bayside, NY: General Hall.
4. Thorton, W. E., Jr., & Voigt, L. (1988). Roles and ethics of the practicing criminologist. *Clinical Sociology Review, 6,* 113–133.
5. Powers, S. (1979). Clinical sociological treatment of a chronic slasher. *Case Analysis, 1,* 169–179.
6. Black, C. M. (1984). Clinical sociology and the criminal justice professions. *Free Inquiry in Creative Sociology, 12,* 117–118.
7. Clark, E. J., & Fritz, J. M. (Eds.). (1984). *Clinical sociology courses: Syllabi, exercises and annotated bibliography.* Washington, DC: Clinical Sociology Association/American Sociological Association.

8. Chandler, D. B. (1983). Law and criminal justice. In H. E. Freeman *et al.* (Eds.), *Applied sociology* (pp. 200–214). San Francisco: Jossey-Bass.

9. Bordua, D. J., & Reiss, A. J., Jr. (1967). Law enforcement. In P. F. Lazarsfeld (Ed.), *The uses of sociology* (pp. 275–303). New York: Basic Books.

10. Zeisel, H. (1967). The law. In P. F. Lazarsfeld *et al.* (Eds.), *The uses of sociology* (pp. 81–99). New York: Basic Books.

11. Hall, *op. cit.*

12. Wirth, L. (1931). Clinical sociology. *American Journal of Sociology, 37,* 49–66.

13. Hall, *op. cit.*

14. Black, C. M., & Enos, R. (1982). Cultural relativity as a counseling paradigm in clinical sociology: A theory and case studies. *Humanity and Society, 6,* 58–73.

15. Alinsky, S. D. (1934). A sociological technique in clinical criminology. In *Proceedings of the Sixty-Fourth Congress of Correction* (p. 204). Houston, TX: American Correctional Association.

16. Chandler, *op. cit.*

17. Kahn, A. J. (1967). From delinquency treatment to community development. In P. F. Lazarsfeld *et al.* (Eds.), *The uses of sociology* (pp. 477–505). New York: Basic Books.

18. Chandler, *op. cit.*

19. Black and Enos, *op. cit.*

20. Hall, *op. cit.*

21. Martindale, D. (1960). *The nature and types of sociological theory.* Boston: Houghton Mifflin.

22. Black and Enos, *op. cit.*

23. Cohen, H. (1981). *Connections.* Ames: The Iowa State University Press.

24. Thorton and Voigt, *op. cit.*

25. Enos, R., & Black, C. M. (1983). A social construction of reality model for clinical social work practice. *The Journal of Applied Social Sciences, 7,* 81–97.

CHAPTER 15

Clinical Sociology and Mediation

John S. Miller

INTRODUCTION

Dispute resolution means efforts directed toward resolving disputes between people, groups, organizations, agencies, or nations. Typically, alternative dispute resolution (ADR) is conflict resolution through mediation, arbitration, and negotiation. ADR, in other words, is an alternative to traditional court adjudication. Instead of taking disputes to court or taking things in one's own hands, disputing parties work with a mediator or arbiter to resolve their dispute.

In this chapter, an overview of mediation is presented as a means of introducing the clinical sociologist to its potential for clinical practice. A case study is presented of a court mediation program in which clinical sociologists practice mediation. Finally, mediation opportunities for clinical sociologists are profiled. The author believes mediation can be a growth industry for clinical sociologists.

MEDIATION

Mediation typically occurs when two disputing parties agree to sit down with a disinterested third party to work out a resolution to their dispute. The mediator, in contrast to a judge or arbitrator, has no power to impose an outcome on disputing parties. Rather, the mediator's function is that of go-between, assisting the disputing parties to reach their own agreement.

Although mediation is often thought of in the context of labor disputes, or disputes among nations, it is utilized in many other areas as well. Disputes between family members are frequently mediated, as are disputes between persons having other continuing relationships, such as landlords and tenants, or neighbors. Media-

JOHN S. MILLER • College of Arts, Humanities, and Social Sciences, University of Arkansas at Little Rock, Little Rock, Arkansas 72204.

tion has also been used to resolve environmental and community disputes. Finally, mediation has been employed as an adjunct to the court structure, primarily in interpersonal disputes, small claims cases, and minor criminal and juvenile cases. The private sector, especially the insurance industry and corporations involved in environmental disputes, is becoming increasingly interested in mediation as an alternative to litigation.

The advantages of mediation over adjudication for certain disputes are numerous. Mediation is usually faster, less expensive, and better suited to tailoring outcomes to the needs of the parties. The involvement of disputants in fashioning their own resolution, rather than having one imposed on them, is said to lead to greater satisfaction with the outcome and to higher levels of compliance than with judicial decrees. Finally, the process of working out their own resolution, albeit with the assistance of a third party, is said to improve the parties' capacity to resolve future disputes without the need for external intervention.

MEDIATION OPPORTUNITIES: A CASE EXAMPLE

A number of societal and discipline related trends have converged to offer the clinical sociologist a wide range of opportunities in the area of mediation. A brief look at one example, the local justice system, makes this point clear. The effectiveness and efficiency of the local justice system has been and continues to be a focus of social research and public attention. Burdened by crowded dockets and demands for speedier justice and improved service, the justice system is examining and adopting alternatives to traditional adjudication, such as court-ordered arbitration, mediation programs, and private sector initiatives for handling disputes.[1,2]

Due to economic uncertainties, changing student interests, and increased public demands for accountability, the academic and political environment in which colleges, universities, and departments operate has become increasingly competitive. Resources have become scarce. Recently, undergraduate education, especially in the liberal arts and humanities, has come under increasing scrutiny. The diversity of today's college students and the highly competitive employment outlook has led to calls by college administrators, politicians, and pundits for universities to graduate students with assessable improvements, as measured by academic outcomes such as knowledge, intellectual capacities, and skills. Sociology has not been immune from these demands for accountability. In light of the turbulent environment faced by departments of sociology, it is not surprising that many see the clinical skills of the discipline as a means of dealing with the growing list of internal and environmental contingencies.[3]

An example of a clinical program that emerged in response to trends inside and outside the university is the University of Arkansas at Little Rock–Pulaski County Mediation Program (LRMP). This program developed as an innovative alternative to the traditional courtroom resolution of disputes in municipal–small claims, juvenile, and criminal court. The program brings together, in a cooperative venture, the needs, facilities, support, and strengths of the Pulaski County judicial system and the human and administrative resources of the University of Arkansas at Little Rock (UALR). In this joint venture, the needs of the judicial system are matched with the resources and needs of the contemporary urban university.[4,5] Based in the College of Arts, Humanities, and Social Sciences, the program is instructive to departments of sociology and/or individual clinical sociologists who wish to apply their sociological skills and/or introduce a clinical component into the curriculum.

Like judicial systems throughout the United States, the Pulaski County courts are understaffed and inadequately funded to meet the growing citizen demand for litigation and the rising crime rate. The LRMP aids in alleviating these persistent judicial problems and enriches the department's and individual faculty's outreach and community service mission in several ways. The project facilitates access to the justice system by providing a free alternative to traditional litigation. Faculty assist citizens in reaching mutually acceptable and lasting solutions to their disputes. Dispute resolution is provided in a cost-effective, efficient, and personal manner. The project provides a positive first experience with the justice system for many local residents.

Using college faculty as mediators and students as interns, the LRMP provides a means for faculty and students to apply their clinical skills. Faculty report that participation has enriched their teaching and research in clinical practice. The project furnishes an excellent paid clinical internship for three to four senior-level students each year, and faculty participation has led to increasing positive publicity for the program and the utility of clinical practice, both outside and inside the university.

Since April 1981, UALR's College of Arts, Humanities, and Social Sciences has provided mediation services to the Pulaski County judicial system. Funding for this unique program has come from local and national foundations and the county judge, the chief administrative and elective officer of county government. The funding compensates faculty mediators $30.00 a case, supports two student interns at minimum wage, and underwrites training workshops for participants.

The primary assumption of the program is that the liberal arts, such as sociology, teach skills useful for the resolution of disputes. Clinical sociologists who have a concern for people and a desire to increase understanding among people, can be a natural ally and/or an alternative to the courts where litigation often occurs because of failed communication.

Clinical sociologists have skills that are useful in the resolution of disputes when applied within the structure of mediation. Clinical sociologists with an understanding of small-group dynamics, especially the "triad" and symbolic inter- action or the ability to "take the role of the other," can be effective mediators. Attention to the symbolic interaction occurring and the dynamics of the "triad" within the mediation or arbitration setting can be combined with skills used daily in the classroom or in other small-group settings such as counseling sessions. These skills include listening, probing, moderating, summarizing, speaking, explaining, evaluating, and balancing. Clinical sociologists will find a familiarity with the social meaning of roles and statuses such as age, sex, race, and ethnicity and an under- standing of the social stratification system an aid in "taking the role" of the plaintiff and defendant and in assisting each to understand the other's position.

PROJECT STRUCTURE

Administration

The program director acts as project coordinator in the various courts and oversees the administration of the LRMP. This role can be played by a senior program participant. It is the program director's responsibility to assure the integration of the mediation program into the courts, to supervise the training of the interns and mediators, and to assist in evaluating the program.

A paid student intern coordinates cases appropriate for mediation. Upper-level undergraduates and graduate students apply for the intern positions as they become available. Each intern applicant is interviewed by the program director and the court administrator. Interns are expected to work 20 hours a week at the court-house acting as intake officers and arranging mediation sessions. While on the job, the intern, like any other court employee, reports directly to the court administrator.

Appropriate cases for the LRMP are those that fall within the small claims statute and those referred to the project by the various courts. These would include small claims disputes, such as landlord–tenant disputes, disagreements between individuals and businesses and between two individuals, and nonviolent juvenile and criminal cases. In a typical case, a plaintiff comes to the courthouse and files a formal complaint. The intern discusses the case with the plaintiff and explains the mediation program. If the plaintiff elects to use the mediation program, the intern contacts the defendant and the mediator and arranges for a mediation session at a mutually agreeable time. All cases are mediated in the municipal courtroom in the county courthouse. Interns observe most mediation sessions to learn from and to informally evaluate the work of the mediators.

Training

The success of the program is, in part, based on the training that each mediator receives. A mediation handbook has been prepared for each mediator.[6] The handbook, written by a participant in the program, discusses the purpose and philosophy of the program, the role of the mediator and the mediation procedure, and suggests mediation strategies.

Short papers, descriptive case examples, and materials focusing on techniques prepared by experienced mediators[6] are also effective in orienting new mediators and in keeping experienced mediators current in the field. Training is conducted in a yearly 1 ½-day workshop. Workshop topics include a description of the mediation program, the role of the mediator, small-group techniques, negotiation skills, and the justice system. Consultants with expertise in mediation and negotiation are used to highlight general mediation strategies and skills. Interns and interested justice system officials and staff as well as new mediators attend the training sessions.

Evaluation

The program director evaluates the success of the various components of the project on a day-to-day basis. It is the director's responsibility to make changes necessary in the workings of the courts, interns, and mediators. Each mediator is asked for an evaluation of the program at the close of the budget year.

An advisory panel made up of court personnel and program faculty meets periodically for a thorough evaluation of the program. The director frequently contacts court personnel as a means of monitoring the program. Plaintiff and defendant also complete evaluation forms, which are returned to the program director for analysis. Success is measured by the level of satisfaction expressed by the clients, staff, and mediators of the program and by the percentage of cases resolved.

Program Impact

Quanitatively and qualitatively, Pulaski County's mediator program has had a significant impact on citizens using the county's justice system. Since its inception, nearly 80% of 2,000 cases processed have been resolved. An enumeration of the evaluation forms completed by plaintiff and defendant after each mediation session points to the objectivity, sensitivity, and effectiveness of the mediators. Eighty percent of those using the mediation services said they believed the mediator was impartial and balanced in his/her approach. Eighty-five percent believed the mediator encouraged them to reach a settlement, and 90% said they would recommend the mediation program to others. Overall, 75% said they were satisfied with the program.

The program has had an impact on participating faculty and student interns. Mediators report that involvement in the program has resulted in an increase in their perceptiveness and understanding of the everyday problems of local governments and citizens. Faculty report that work with the mediation program has enriched their clinical research and teaching. Professors have incorporated aspects of alternative dispute resolution into their teaching, both substantively and methodologically.

The joint county–university mediation project has been responsive to a number of contingencies faced by the university. The program currently provides participating faculty with an avenue for community service. Since its inception, a dozen student interns have participated in the program. The project has resulted in a growing amount of positive publicity for the program, and the university, both on and off campus. Students, faculty, administrators, and the general public are increasingly aware of the positive aspects of the program.

A "Typical" Mediation

How does mediation work? Although each case is different, the mediation process follows a fairly routine course. A "typical" case in small claims court can be described as follows. The mediator reports directly to the small claims office and receives a file containing the plaintiff's complaint and mediator's form. Mediation actually takes place at a table in the courtroom, or in an adjacent office.

Cases in small claims court vary widely but have a common theme. The plaintiff is asking for a monetary (under $300) award for some documented grievance. The money, however, is only part of what the plaintiff wants. The plaintiff also wants to tell someone about being treated badly by the defendant. If the mediator keeps in mind this desire for sympathy on the part of both parties, it can be an important tool during mediation.

Before the session begins, the mediator becomes familiar with the complaint. The complaint is read, and the mediator thinks about what other information is required to fully understand the problem.

Beginning the Mediation

The mediation sessions begin with the introductions including an explanation of the purpose of mediation and clarifying to all involved that mediation is voluntary. For example, the mediator might say,

> "Let me introduce myself. My name is ———. I am NOT a lawyer, and I am NOT a judge. This is NOT a court. My purpose is to try to help you resolve your dispute without going to court. There are several advantages to both of you in resolving this problem today. First, there are no court costs; mediation costs you nothing. Second, in a court, someone wins and someone loses. We have the option of compromise. Any solution that is agreeable to everyone concerned is acceptable. Lastly, we are not bound by the same rules that apply in court. Judges are limited in what they can hear as evidence; we can look at anything that is reasonable.
>
> I want to emphasize that we are not obligated to come to an agreement today. This is extremely important. If we do NOT find an agreeable solution, your case will go to court without delay or penalty. You will have lost nothing by coming here today. If we DO find an agreeable solution, we will all sign it, and then the judge will sign it. At that point it becomes the order of the court. Remember, though, that we do not have an obligation to settle this today.

Opening Statements

Mediation itself begins with a statement from the plaintiff. The mediator asks him/her to explain the problem and tell what he/she is asking from the defendant. The mediator tries to get the plaintiff to be as specific as possible. Discussion might begin with broad diagnostic questions such as "What is your view or interpretation of the disagreement?" Most mediators take notes on all statements for later reference. At this point, the plaintiff usually wants to appear reasonable in front of a third party and will often ask for less than the amount specific on the complaint form. The mediator should realize that this is sometimes the first opportunity that the defendant has had to hear the formal complaint against him/her, so it is important to get this statement.

The plaintiff might bring along repair bills, copies of a lease or contract, or some other form of support for his/her claim. The mediator usually will examine these and let the defendant look at them. In mediation, there is no hard and fast rule about what the mediator should look at. Anything reasonable and relevant to the complaint will do.

Most mediators tend **not** to look at things related to past problems (for example, **other** clothes that the cleaner ruined, which are not mentioned in the complaint). If the dispute is over bodywork on a car and there is disagreement regarding the damage, the mediator has the option of going and **looking** at the car.

After the plaintiff is finished, the mediator asks the defendant what he/she would like to say about the problem. The mediator encourages the defendant to be specific and to respond to every point raised by the plaintiff. The mediator does not allow the plaintiff to interrupt. Here, the mediator will try to discover specifically what (if anything) the defendant is willing to do to resolve the problem. The defendant also wants to appear reasonable and will often offer to do more after telling his/her side than he/she has in the past.

Bringing the Two Together

After both sides have had a chance to speak, the mediator looks at his/her notes and tries to find some points of agreement. At this stage, the mediator's job is to remove the adversarial positions that the individuals have taken and emphasize agreement between the two in order to begin communication. A landlord and tenant, for example, may agree that the screen was broken but disagree about how much repairs should cost or about who broke it. The mediator reviews these points of agreement, no matter how trifling.

The mediator then encourages both parties to comment on points of agreement, in order to give them a chance to say **something** that they can agree about. This is where the clinical sociological skills of "taking the role of the other" and the definition of the situation as to age, sex, race, income, prestige, and so forth come into play. The mediator must be able to "see" the problem from the point of view of both plaintiff and defendant. Sensitivity to real or perceived power differentials based on sex, race, or age must also be exercised. Occasionally (but not often enough), they will begin to work things out at this point by themselves. If this happens at any time during the session, the mediator should encourage it.

If the parties do not start talking at this point, the mediator may begin to review some of the points on which they disagree. This is done one point at a time, beginning with those points that seem least important to the dispute or on which the parties seem to be closest to agreement.

Next, points of disagreement are reviewed, and the nature of the disagreement clarified: Is it the amount of money that is disputed; the cause of the damage; the amount of the damage? If necessary, the mediator may want to phone an expert concerning a technical point.

The Root of the Problem

Frequently, the mediator will find one central point of disagreement and others that are relatively unimportant. The mediator must use the skills of questioning, summarizing, probing, and moderating to reach agreement on exactly what the issue is. Questions of clarification as to "Who did what, when, and why" are crucial in making sure everyone is talking about the same things. Asking the parties to summarize their position or their view of the situation is useful at this point. The mediator can close this phase of the process by summarizing the two points of view—their agreement or disagreement—in his/her own words such as "What I hear you saying is . . ." Should the central problem be a misunderstanding of some sort, if the mediator can point out the misunderstanding without assigning blame to either party, things will proceed quickly. For example, a complaint was brought by a young woman who had bought a car from a dealer who advertised "no money down." She had negotiated to buy a new car and was given an estimate of the monthly payment.

When she picked up the car, she was surprised to find that she had to pay sales tax on the spot. She had made it clear to the salesman that she had no money with which to make a down payment, and she understood that she would need no money when the car was delivered. As the plaintiff and defendant talked, it became clear that the central problem was a basic misunderstanding—she thought that "no money down" meant "no money needed to pick up the car," and the salesman assumed that everyone knew that "no money down" simply meant that there was no down payment but that sales tax had to be paid on delivery.

When the mediator suggested to the parties that their basic problem was a simple misunderstanding about the meaning of the phase *no money down*, they were perfectly willing to work out a solution. When they could agree that neither was trying to cheat the other—thus dissolving their adversarial positions—they were able to come to an agreement quickly.

Keeping the Peace

Sometimes, when parties begin to discuss their points of disagreement, they become angry. Mediators try to prevent this, if possible, because anger serves to solidify antagonistic positions. It is important that both parties express their feelings, but hostility is counterproductive. If the parties get angry, the mediator can direct the conversation to himself/herself. The parties will rarely shout at the mediator. When they calm down, they can talk to each other again.

It is possible that the parties will begin negotiating at this point. If they do, the mediator should step back and let them. There is sometimes a feeling that the mediator must be in **control** of the situation. In reality, the mediator's job is more like that of a guide; the only time that the mediator should have to actively assert control is when things are going badly.

Piecing Together Solutions

After the sources of disagreement are clear, the mediator can have both parties suggest possible solutions. During this phase of mediation, the parties are asked to suggest solutions, and negotiation often ensues. Here, the sociological skills previously enumerated come into play. Creativity may be called for at this point in the process. Specifically, questions of action and or decision can be raised by the mediator. For example, "What is the most important issue?" or "Which issue or issues should he address?" If that fails, the mediator can take the initiative and suggest, "From what you have told me . . . appears to be the key issue(s). Am I correct?" If none of the solutions offered are accepted by the other party, the mediator can solicit new ones. If none are offered or if those offered are strongly rejected, the mediator may offer suggestions. The mediator should be creative.

Generally, once the parties see new ways to solve their problem, they will actively participate in negotiating solutions. If they do not, and all else fails, mediators are encouraged to remember Solomon: Cut the baby in half. "Mrs. ——, you are asking for $100, and Mr. —— is offering $50. Would you accept $75?"

Concluding the Agreement: Three Options

If, despite the mediator's best efforts and repeated tries, it becomes clear that no solution will be reached, the case can go to court. If a solution is reached, a form is compiled stating the specific nature of the solution, the amount of money (if any) to be paid, and the date of payment. If the solution involves the performance of services, they are specified, and a deadline established for performance. Both parties sign the form and return it with the file to the intern.

There is a third option. The mediator can continue the case. This will not happen often, but it should not be disregarded as an option. Continuance means that the mediator will meet at another time (or place) to resolve the problem. It may be, for example, that more data are needed before a resolution can be reached.

NEW DIRECTIONS

The successes of the project have not led to complacency. To the contrary, these successes have proven the viability of the original idea and encouraged the experimentation and expansion of the project. In the future, the group of trained and experienced mediators created by this project will participate in several new areas. At the request of the Pulaski county judge, mediation is available to disputing governmental agencies. In addition, work has begun with the Pulaski County prosecuting attorney's office to establish a postconviction mediation program and a preformal complaint mediation/diversion program. Finally, at the judge's request and with the support of the lawyers involved, divorce mediation cases are now being accepted.

OUTREACH OPPORTUNITIES FOR CLINICAL SOCIOLOGISTS

Clinical sociologists have skills that are useful in the resolution of disputes when applied within the structure of mediation. The justice system has a need for these skills, and most departments are looking for ways to interface in a mutually satisfactory manner with key elements in their environment. This chapter has described one successful program of county–college cooperation. Additional opportunities abound for the sociologist working through a department, college, university or as an independent practitioner.[7] Several are outlined next.

1. *Mediation in the local court system.* Most court systems are overloaded and searching for ways to divert cases. Small claims court is a natural place to start. The stakes are usually low, and the parties want an inexpensive and quick resolution. Juvenile court is another component of the justice system where mediation of

disputes between juveniles, adults, and schools, or business may be open to alternative dispute resolution (ADR). In a number of jurisdictions, experienced mediators are accepting cases of a nonviolent nature in criminal court. Divorce mediation, either as part of the court system or as part of a private practice, is becoming increasingly popular.

2. *Mediation for the Better Business Bureau.* Each community of any size has a Better Business Bureau (BBB). The BBB is interested in resolving disputes between its member businesses and customers. Clinical sociologists with mediation skills should find the local BBB cooperative in working with local businesses.

3. *Mediation within the public school system.* Local public school systems are often interested in training provided by and/or using outside mediators in resolving complaints between students and the school, between students, and between the student/family and the school.

4. *Mediation within the university.* A number of universities are adopting, considering, or experimenting with mediation as part of or as an alternative to their normal grievance procedure. Clinical sociologists could play a role as consultants and/or mediators.

5. *Mediation within the private corporation or public agency.* Like universities, corporations and governmental agencies are taking closer looks at their personnel policies related to grievances. Clinical sociologists can act as consultants and/or contract with the public or private agency to perform mediation.

6. *Mediation with a local law firm.* Some law firms are now offering a mediation option. For many cases, a legal background is not needed to resolve a dispute. Clinical sociologists can work on retainers for law firms taking referrals.

7. *Mediation in family counseling.* Mediation can be an important skill used by clinical sociologists as part of their private family practice.

8. *Mediation consulting.* Clinical sociologists with mediation skills will find a growing number of opportunities to consult with other individuals and organizations about implementing mediation procedures within an organization.

9. *Mediation workshops.* For those establishing mediation programs and for those with ongoing programs, training workshops in "how to perform" mediation offer the clinical sociologist an opportunity to train others in mediation methods.

10. *Mediation as a specialty in clinical sociology.* Clinical sociologists may find their university or college fertile ground for a mediation emphasis within sociology, criminal justice, or social work. The Department of Sociology at George Mason University has established the Center for Conflict Resolution with graduate degrees in conflict management, and John Jay College of Criminal Justice offers a certificate in dispute resolution.

11. *Mediation research.* As more individuals become involved in mediation and more programs using mediation are established, the need for systematic research on mediation becomes increasingly critical. Clinical sociologists acting as applied or basic researchers and/or evaluators will find opportunities and financial support for their work.

12. *Mediation of environmental and public policy disputes.* Clinical sociologists will find increasing opportunities to assist governmental, public, and private interests in resolving public policy disputes in areas such as the environment.

MEDIATION: A GROWTH INDUSTRY

The foregoing list can easily be lengthened. The opportunities for clinical practice in mediation certainly abound. Disputes will always be with us, and our institutions are crying out for more efficient and effective way to deal with disputes.

In their best-selling book, *Getting to Yes: Negotiating Agreement without Giving In,* Roger Fisher and William Ury, of the Harvard Law School, conclude that "conflict is a growth industry."[8] Certainly, the demand from the justice system is growing. Universities and departments also need to involve faculty in the community and students in internships. Clinical sociologists, however, face two major impediments to becoming part of the mediation movement: apathy and exclusion. Other professionals, such as psychologists, social workers, lawyers, and psychiatrists are entering the field. If practicing sociologists do not act quickly, the field may be controlled by others.[9]

This leads to the second point—exclusion. In some states, laws mandating mediation in some situations already are being considered. These laws set out who is to perform mediation and what credentials they are to have. Clinical sociologists must monitor these developments to ensure they have the opportunity to apply their sociological knowledge.

REFERENCES

1. McEwen, C., & Maiman, R. J. (1984). Mediation in small claims court: Achieving compliance through consent. *Law and Society Review, 18,* 11.
2. Greason, J. (1980). Humanists as mediators: An experiment in the courts of Maine. *American Bar Association Journal, 66,* 576–584.
3. Miller, J. S. (1985a). Applying the liberal arts. *Issues in Higher Education, 17,* 307–315.
4. Miller, J. S., & Ledbetter, C. (1986). Liberal arts faculty as mediators: The Pulaski County program. *Arkansas Political Science Journal, 7* 74–79.
5. Miller, J. S. (1985b). Sociologists as mediators: Clinical sociology in action. *Clinical Sociology Review, 3,* 158–164.
6. McNally, K. A. (1982). *Mediation: Little Rock's alternative to the courts.* Little Rock: University of Arkansas at Little Rock.
7. Herrman, M. (1986). Sociology and alternative dispute resolution. *Clinical Sociology Newsletter, 8,* 5–6.
8. Fisher, R. & Ury, W. (1981). *Getting to yes.* New York: Houghton Mifflin.
9. Volpe, M. (1986). Sociology and dispute resolution. *Clinical Sociology Newsletter, 8,* 4–5.

CHAPTER 16

A Clinical Perspective on Organizational Development

DAVID W. BRITT

INTRODUCTION AND OVERVIEW

There are almost as many definitions of organizational development as there are people writing about the field.[1-4] In spite of that, there is considerable overlap among these definitions on the focus of organizational development. The definitions emphasize enhancing the adaptive capacity of organizations in the face of environmental changes, technological changes, and internal problems. The definitions bring out the paradox of organizational development: To create an organizational capacity to adapt requires creating the capacity to tear down (or at least challenge) basic assumptions about the organization and control of work and creating the ability to build more viable social forms.

Interventions in clinical sociology are case-based, problem-oriented, focus on causes, and seek to build organizational capacity to cope with demands and opportunities. This involves examining environments in which organizations are embedded, their technologies, structures, processes, and people, their histories, and their prospective futures. It also requires digging under the observable reality to examine deeper processes that drive surface observations. In this chapter, organizational development will be discussed as a series of dilemmas created for the clinician having to confront these issues.

DAVID W. BRITT • Department of Sociology, Wayne State University, Detroit, Michigan 48202.

TYING DEFINITIONS TO MAJOR THEMES
IN CLINICAL SOCIOLOGY

Case-Based Intervention

Case-based intervention is strongly rooted in clinical sociology. It is not merely the study of a case but the formulation of a program of adjustment and treatment.[5-10] Applied to intervention in organizations, two parallel dilemmas must be confronted by the clinical sociologist: (1) how much should the client adjust to the context, and (2) how much and when to involve the clients in the problem definition, assessment, implementation, and evaluation of interventions.

Adjustment/Context

The first of these dilemmas involves the adaptation of the organization to the internal and external forces in which it is embedded: Should the client be assisted in adjusting to the constraints of environments, constituents, and technologies? Or, should environments, constituents, and technologies become part of the change process with the client assuming a more proactive role in shaping external and internal forces than constrain behavior?

Several authors have offered an action research model for proactive reassessment of contexts for departments using an outside consultant to facilitate the process.[11-14] The key elements of the approach are:

1. Develop a study team of all relevant managers, specialists, and union representatives. Ensure that leadership is exercised by line managers rather than staff specialists.
2. Develop methods for assessing current effectiveness according to external standards of performance. Use hard data and the opinions of clients of the organization.
3. Develop methods for assessing projected effectiveness according to external and internal standards for performance. Use hard data and the opinions of present and potential clients of the organization.
4. Have the team and the external consultant reassess the distribution of authority, responsibility, and resources in light of what needs to be done to ensure future effectiveness.
5. Develop concrete activities and objectives necessary to achieve future effectiveness.
6. Develop a support system for those involved in the project and for the project itself.
7. Ground the purposes of the organization in a value system that emphasizes the interests of its emerging and existing clients.
8. Rationalize the distribution of rewards to reflect the values inherent in moving toward desired future conditions.

There are direct and indirect changes developed from interventions that follow steps such as these. As a direct consequence, problems will have a good chance of being resolved. As an indirect consequence, the process by which problems come to light, are studied, and resolved is shaped and future problems have a greater chance of being resolved. The result is greater adaptive capacity of the organization.

Clinical sociologists have noted that the clinician should not stop with helping clients solve a problem but must examine and act with respect to the larger context of the problem.[6,9] The development of proactive assessment of environmental demands is within this tradition. It also suggests the underlying theme of this review: The clinician should try to leave the organization in a better position to solve its own problems. Examining the larger context is a step in that direction.

A useful way of thinking of the desired goal of such a relationship between a client and a clinical sociologist is captured by Whyte's concept of "social inventions for solving human problems."[15] Such *inventions* may be new patterns of authority or sets of procedures for coordinating behavior, new roles, and so on. *Interventions* are problem solutions brought into the organization from the outside, whereas *inventions* are arrived at by organization members themselves. With social inventions, problems get solved, but clients arrive at the solution themselves that reinforces the process of internal problem solving and contributes to the adaptive capacity of the organization.

Proactive, imaginative thinking and action about alternatives must precede inventions. Lippitt developed the distinction between *proactive* and *reactive* responses to address the challenge of reducing the size and scope of an organization to a more manageable scale. But the logic can be generalized to include problem solving stimulated by a greater variety of external and/or internal changes (see Table 1).[16]

Table 1. **Proactive versus Reactive Organizational Coping**[a]

Proactive coping	Reactive coping
Imaging potential positive results	Focusing on pain (problems)
Assuming alternatives can be found	Helpless, hopeless responses
Rethinking priorities of operational goals	Assuming all elements of current operational goals are equally legitimate
Involving everyone in the generation of ideas	"Closet decisions" at the top
Environmental scanning for relevent inventions	Internal focus and discussion only
Exploring collaborative exchange and sharing of resources	Jealously guarding turfdom
Exploring alternative sources of support	Blaming regular sources of support for problems
Preserving problem-solving resourcefulness in reducing personnel	Cutting personnel in proportion to their vulnerability
Exploring new markets	Cutting back on innovation resources
Expanding human resource options	Contracting human resource options
Technological changes used to enhance personnel capacity	Technological changes solely to restrict personnel capacity or eliminate personnel
Rethinking relevance of existing coordination and control mechanisms	Reifying existing coordination and control mechanisms

[a]Adapted from Lippitt[16] and Britt.[17]

Proactive coping builds departmental and organizational adaptive capacity. Reactive coping may have short-term benefits but may leave the adaptive capacity of the organization at the same or even a diminished level[17] as environmental demands continue to change.

Most of the strategies in Table 1 are derived from Lippitt's suggestions for shaping proactive coping responses.[16] What Lippitt,[16] Kanter and Buck,[11] and Schein[18] all called interventions lead to the development of inventions by organization members. The first time through the process, the clinical sociologist may provide more guidance and suggestion for activities. As problems get "solved" and organization members get feedback on their success in proactive coping with problems, the clinical sociologist's role can begin to recede. As a general rule, clinicians should stay involved with the process at least until formal appraisal and reward systems have been allowed to function to support the process and/or a new cohort of members has been socialized into the process. Withdrawal before this point risks having an apparently successful intervention destroyed by an inhospitable climate.

Client Involvement

Client involvement is not a dilemma about *whether* clients should be involved but how to involve them. Three patterns often characterize clients' reaction to outside consultants. These patterns are marked by variation in the amount of control the client tries to exercise over the process. Schein described the first pattern as analogous to a patient playing the sick role, helplessly going to a physician and getting a prescription that can be easily followed.[18] A related pattern is analogous to an engineer fixing a piece of broken machinery, as if organizing work is amenable to simple rational analysis and quick but permanent repair. In both cases, the challenge is to engage clients in the process rather than letting the external consultant do everything and make recommendations. At the other extreme, clients may want too much control over the process. In this case, the clinical sociologist risks being co-opted (with the consequence of justifying existing arrangements and power distributions). The amount of control clients want over the change process is affected by their capacity for studying problems and implementing changes and by their commitment to the change process. Clients may want to control the process when they feel they are competent or when they are threatened by changes that might ensue and are not committed to the change process.

There is a resolution to the client involvement dilemma in high-threat/high-control situations. Clients tend to think of themselves as competent if they have the technical skill or credentials required to produce certain goods or services or if they have a good record of solving problems themselves. Schein[18] called for the former technical competence and the latter process competence. *Technical competence* reflects knowledge needed to produce the products and services that are central to the organization's or department's mission. *Process competence* reflects an ability to mobilize technical and human resources so that the stages from problem identification to solution implementation may be carried out. Process competence exists when there are high levels of communication, trust and feedback, and low levels of destructive competition within and between groups.

In many high-threat, high-control situations, the perception of competence based on technical skill is more likely than a perception of process competence. Organizations with widely distributed process skill have less need for external help in solving problems. Technical competence in a department or organization, however, is no guarantee of its being able to cope, proactively, with internal and external problems. Different technical skills in different units that need to coordinate their actions make problem solving difficult.

Proactive problem solving is also difficult when technical skill and process skill are unevenly shared by different factions that need to coordinate their activity. I was involved in an intervention to try to resolve a 5-year, protracted conflict between two factions in a safety and health department of a printing plant. One faction had limited education and training (as well as authority) but enjoyed great respect and influence in the plant, built up over a long period of helping workers operate their machines safely and informally resolving safety problems that came up. They had, in Schein's words, process competence, but had only their experience with somewhat outmoded technologies and a few training courses as claims to technical competence. The other faction had advanced educational credentials and technical training (as well as authority) but had not been able to establish any rapport with the departments they were supposed to help with safety issues. They had good technical skill but only modest process skill.

The client involvement dilemma in this case was further complicated by the fact that both factions were concerned about maintaining control over resolution of the conflict. The duration of this conflict and the rigidity of each groups' position made it advisable to use several techniques for ensuring client involvement:

1. The consultation team was balanced by race and sex because these issues confounded the apparent underlying problem.
2. The endorsement of the plant manager and division head was symbolically reinforced by having the division head present at the initial confrontation meeting and express his and the plant manager's support for the intervention.
3. The neutrality of the team was symbolically reinforced by not having anyone in authority chair the confrontation meeting and by having an opening statement by the team. The opening statement indicated that the team had been asked to investigate whether they would join in the effort to resolve the problem. It was emphasized that the team would not come in unless (1) the team was convinced that all were sincerely concerned in jointly working on a solution, (2) all concerned were convinced of the appropriateness of the involvement of the team, and (3) proposed resolutions had to be ratified by the entire group.
4. The previous experience of the consulting team in handling similar problems in other organizations and successfully completing a similar project a few years before in the organization was emphasized.

Both factions were persuaded that the consulting team was not biased toward one faction or the other, that the team's concern was genuine, and that the team was committed to joint assessment and problem resolution. The more members of a client system are hostile or distrustful of one another, the more effort is necessary to establish an entry posture conducive to joint involvement. The most intense threat is found between opposing factions with uneven authority, but all problems are at least mildly threatening.

Situations involving clients who feel helpless require a somewhat different strategy. With apparently helpless clients, the central tasks are getting clients to risk involvement and ensuring that their efforts are rewarded. The following more specific recommendations are offered:

1. In early negotiations, discuss the difference between solving a particular problem and building problem-solving capacity.
2. Have the language of the contract reflect the intention of joint client/ consultant involvement in the problem-solving process and the objective of increasing problem-solving ability. Follow this up with a letter reinforcing these points to those involved in the process and those underwriting the effort.
3. Do sufficient focus group and/or single interviews to get a sense of the range of problems and their dynamics. Then use an initial organizing meeting to develop some problems to work on. The initial problems should be relatively easy to resolve and resolvable in a relatively short time. Feedback from internal and external sources on early successes should be used to catalyze further joint problem resolution.

Bear in mind that there are underlying reasons for apparent helplessness. Frequently, individuals are either officially or unofficially discouraged from engaging in proactive efforts. Unless these factors are changed as well, building more proactive internal coping mechanisms will have only a short-lived impact on the capacity of the organization to adapt.

A difficult situation occurs when the client views problems as mechanical breakdowns and wants the clinical sociologist to fix the problem as if it were some sort of machine breakdown. Schein[18] called this the engineering model. Clients may feel too busy to get involved, may desire to maintain distance from the problems and desire to maintain some veto power over the problem resolution or may feel that the division and integration of work is machinelike. When initial meetings suggest one of these structures, the following are recommended:

1. During negotiations, emphasize (1) the importance of joint involvement of client and clinician and tangible evidence of upper echelon support, (2) the fragile, non-machine-like nature of all strategies for organizing work, and (3) the unwillingness of the consultant team to get involved in situations where a genuine commitment to change is absent.
2. Have explicit language in the contract regarding stages of review by each party so that both clients and clinician may reconsider objectives and intent after assessment and early problem resolution cycles.
3. Choose as initial problems those which most directly expose the risk of assuming that the organization of work is machine-like and may be taken for granted once set in place.

4. Spend more time after initial problem resolution sitting in on strategic and routine upper level meetings, trying to balance the clinical sociologist's obligation to puncture assumptions which are inconsistent with the change effort with the client's right to terminate the contract if they believe diminishing returns are being achieved.

Problem Oriented

A focus on problems appears to be at the heart of the clinical sociological perspective.[5,6,19,20] There are seven major dilemmas that must be confronted by clinical sociologists working with organizations: (1) the relationship between presenting and actual problems, (2) the differences among technical-system, structural (coordination and control), and process problems, (3) the confounding of coping responses and problems, (4) moving forward without becoming trapped in the past when dealing with litanies of problems, (5) differences in the scale of problems, (6) differences in problem depth, and (7) deescalation biases.

Presenting versus Actual Problems

The validity of distinguishing between presenting and actual problems has been discussed by several sociologists.[20,21] There is a client bias toward presenting superficial symptoms rather than fundamental problems. There is also a bias toward defining problems based on assumptions shared by the dominant coalition in an organization. The relationship between presenting and actual problems is sometimes difficult to discover. For example, turnover is frequently cited by organizations as a presenting problem. Turnover may be associated with more fundamental problems that differ from one area of a plant or office to another. Some jobs are more stressful and less rewarding than other jobs. These more fundamental problems may have a common thread. They may be exacerbated by fluctuations in the extent to which the organizational system is overloaded. And, for each of these "problems," there may be varying definitions by the people involved in different areas and different levels in the hierarchy.

What then, is the problem? It is imperative to build into the client/consultant contract an understanding that the presented problem is a starting point and that the clinical sociologist and client, working together, have the license to follow different paths in redefining the problem(s). The initial and continuing task of assessment becomes more manageable once the actual problem gets defined.

Assessment may take a variety of forms[2,22] with the choice depending on the time available for the project, the complexity and rate of change of the situation, the apparent scale of the problems, and the skills of the clinical sociologist. The more quickly assessments are needed, the smaller the budget, or the more complex and changeable the work situation, the more assessments should be some combination of focus groups, intensive interviews, observation, and secondary data analysis. The broader the scale of the problems, the more useful standardized instruments (such as Dyer's[23] "Team Building Checklist") and routinely gathered hard data become.[24]

There are several approaches to assessing the extent of process problems. Researchers have developed scales to measure the climate within which organizational processes take place.[18,23,25,26] Some of these are reliable and valid but suffer from being expensive to administer and somewhat cumbersome. Other approaches attempt to use secondary data, routinely gathered by organizations, or develop short forms that permit quick assessment of process problems. For example, Britt[17] constructed a reliable scale of organizational strain (a proxy for process problems) based on changes in just four perceived characteristics (conflict, tension, morale, and quits) that had an alpha coefficient of .75.

Under no circumstances should a clinical sociologist rely on one source of data for problem definition. Jick[27] made a strong case for triangulating data-gathering methods in organizations. In my experience, new sources of data are frequently presented to consultants and organization members working with them as they try to find out what is wrong. Once, I was summarily presented with a carton of memos and notes that bore directly on the extent to which communication had become formalized and unproductive between two individuals.

Engaging organization members in the assessment process has direct and indirect benefits. A direct benefit is that the data developed are likely to be more varied and reveal what is happening in the unit under investigation and among its constituencies. It will, therefore, be less parochial and more useful. Indirectly, organization members will acquire assessment skills and be willing to use them to answer questions. The assessment phase of a project, then, becomes a clinical tool to begin shaping a proactive approach to gathering and analyzing data on the unit and its environment.

Differences among Problem Types

It is possible to distinguish among different kinds of problems within organizations. There are technical problems, control and coordination (structural) problems, and process problems. The dilemma these problems create for the clinical sociologist is that "problems" rarely fall into only one domain. And when they interact, the different kinds of problems tend to exacerbate one another. For example, in a salvage operation of a chicken processing line, a switch was made from knives to scissors because the scissors made better cuts and reduced accidents. Unfortunately, the scissors caused aches and pains in the forearms of the salvagers. This may seem like a purely technical problem, but it was not. Forearm pain was not experienced by everyone. Relationships among salvage workers deteriorated as some were forced to work harder to make up for the problems others were having. This escalated process problems. The situation got still worse when a promise was made by the supervisor to purchase lighter scissors but then never followed up. Workers become alienated from one another and from their supervisor. The dilemma was how to assist people to define and act on the problem to make constructive change possible. Process is a major intersection through which all other problems eventually pass. But process problems are too abstract for many people to grapple with when their everyday worlds are concrete. The clinician may appreciate Schein's insight that communication breakdowns, mistrust, destructive conflict, and competition may reflect poor social relationships, dishonest communication, and lack of shared purpose.[18]

Neither supervisors nor salvagers would be likely to grasp and/or appreciate the subtlety of process concepts. What they can readily grasp is a distinction between *how* changes are brought about and the changes themselves. The salvage operation can jointly experiment with different scissors until a mutually satisfactory and cost-effective solution can be found. The scissors eventually selected (the change) and the scissor selection process (how the change was developed and implemented) both contributed to problem resolution. But the scissor selection process had a greater effect on adaptability. For the clinical sociologist, such an approach boils down to using more concrete representations of problems to attack process problems that are more difficult to grasp. The indirect benefits were again pronounced. Working through this concrete problem increased the chances that proactive problem solving will be used the next time a similar problem arises.

More generally, structural interventions that, at an early stage, do not involve members who are going to be affected by the changes may be perceived as arbitrary. These structural interventions will certainly lead to a period of disruption because of changes in jobs, relationships, feedback patterns, and so forth. Consequently, it is usually recommended[2] that there be a bias toward process change at an earlier point. Selective involvement of others who have needed skills and want to be involved, mapping changes, anticipating impact, and general proactive conduct is consistent with earlier recommendations on client involvement.

The Confounding of Problems and Coping Mechanisms

Sociologists have been familiar with the interaction between the behavior of groups in organizations and the control mechanisms that organizations use, at least since Merton's early statement.[28] Social actors use whatever discretion they have to make their work less stressful, not necessarily better. Organizations add or change rules or technologies to regulate the conduct of groups or individuals. Tighter regulation, however, often polarizes relations between managers and workers. Lowered commitment by workers and an increase in the frequency and intensity of the behavior that the rules were intended to regulate can occur. So can other manifestations that are equally appalling to those making the changes. The assumptions, policies, and behavioral outcomes become self-fulfilling and mutually reinforcing.

The dilemma created for clinical sociologists is the intractability of such feedback cycles and the difficulty of defining the problem in straightforward terms. Is the problem the behavior and difficulties of the group? Or is it the controls that try to regulate the behavior but that often lead to worsening the situation? To define the problem too narrowly is tantamount to legitimizing one position at the expense of the other. This reduces the likelihood of a mutually satisfactory resolution to which both sides become committed. To define the problem for those involved as a complex feedback loop runs the risk of obfuscating the issues and alienating both sides.

Solution of this dilemma may be possible using several strategies. A useful place to start is with Walton's[29] work on interpersonal peacemaking and Laue's[30,31] continuing work on conflict resolution. In these approaches, problem definitions, assumptions, and resolution strategies emerge from mutual confrontation of the issues. The following general guidelines may be helpful:

1. In individual or focus group interviews with managers and staff, try to document:
    a. How the changed rules and/or technologies have been interpreted by staff in terms of levels of trust and support by management.
    b. How the behavior and problems of the staff are interpreted by management in terms of how committed the staff is to unit goals and how much managers may trust staff to carry out their jobs.
2. Before engaging in a confrontation between the two groups, develop top management support, your own credibility, and test the willingness of both parties to jointly resolve the problem.
3. Engage in the confrontation meeting(s) following the guidelines laid out by Laue or Walton.
4. Seal the resultant understandings of both sides by having them implement a revised control structure and procedure for evaluating its effectiveness, and sharing that information with people who are directly involved as well as managers.

The indirect effects on the quality of the relationship between the parties are as important as the short-term resolution of conflict. The augmented capacity to deal with problems emerges with successful resolutions. In the short term, a successful resolution is marked by agreement that the revised control structure is legitimate, provides support for those doing their jobs, increases the level of trust between managers and staff, and increases the capacity of both individuals and the unit to perform effectively.

Being Trapped in the Past

A problem orientation risks being frozen in an irrelevant past and mired in a situation that appears hopeless because of the magnitude of problems uncovered by assessment. The clinical sociologist faces the dilemma of developing a problem focus with organizational clients without suffering the negative side effects of lowered morale, scapegoating, searching for quick fixes, and the sense that in fixing one problem, two more develop. All of these are characteristic of reactive coping.

Two concrete things must happen for organizations to "adapt to new conditions, to solve problems, [and] to learn from experiences,[7,11] to proactively create new social inventions.[15] Problems must become opportunities,[19] and actions must be anchored in "images of potentiality."[16] Small straightforward, technical system problems are useful as opportunities for change. Small-scale technical problems limit costs and the number of people involved and make participation easier. Technical problems are neither so self-evident that discussion appears contrived nor so complicated that discussion appears futile. Considering what scissors to use to replace the knives presents such opportunities. The joint process of finding the right scissors can have powerful indirect effects both on the capacity of the department involved to surface and work through future problems and on the quality of members' relationships.

Anchoring changes and problem discussions in positive images of the future improves group reactions. Group members will get less depressed as the number and magnitude of problems mounts. Group members should mobilize fewer defenses against responsibility for action as these problems appear to become insurmountable. And group members will focus less on escape and avoidance as confronting problems becomes more painful.[16]

The challenge of dealing with problems without getting trapped by them is heightened when there are already difficult problems or when there have been changes that generate problems. In the latter case, the organization is already in a more proactive posture. Consequently, imagining positive futures and treating problems should be easier because of the proactive posture and the less severe problems.

Lippitt suggested tactics for working out of the dilemma of getting trapped in the past. They involve actions that focus attention on successes of the recent past (lists of "prouds" and "sorries" and imagined trips back a few years and then forward a few years). The short-term effects of this approach are positive, just as positive and negative events have contrasting effects on individuals.[32,33] However, there is a risk in concentrating on what has been done well. Odiorne coined the phrase *activity trapping* to refer to the tendency of individuals to engage in things they are comfortable doing rather than things that need to be done. Positive events should be seen as a platform for developing ideas for improvement through literature searches, developing task forces, and visiting sites where new ideas and social interventions are being tried.

Problem Scale

Some problems are larger scale than others. They affect more people and create a number of smaller problems. The dilemma posed for the clinical sociologist stems from choosing to work on larger or smaller problems first. The dilemma is made worse with pressure to accept definitions of the situation that are smaller scale and more nearly individualized. These require less change in the status quo. For example, the clinical sociologist might be asked to deliver a series of stress management seminars oriented toward individuals when the problems are clearly structural. If the intent is to cool out pockets of discontent, then the clinical sociologist is at risk of being co-opted by managerial definitions.

One resolution of this dilemma, suggested by Gutknecht, is bargaining "for open, humanistic, system-wide changes: decentralized power, just reward systems, democratic decision making development of the whole employee at all organization levels."[34] This is nice in theory, but clinicians often have limited bargaining power, and organizations must be ready for system wide changes. Unfortunately, a more realistic alternative is also more vague: Use the exploratory interview to test the commitment of the client to the possibility of larger scale change, to development of an internal capacity for surfacing and solving problems, and, generally, to increase the adaptive capacity of the organization.[18] Where commitment seems authentic, starting with smaller problems may facilitate surfacing and working through larger problems. Organization members may develop the sense that adaptation is possible and their skills for action planning may be refined.

My recent foray into a chicken processing plant turned up several modest technical problems on the order of the scissor/knife problem. These smaller problems were driven by a larger problem: increases in the volume of chickens processed (akin to a speedup). An exploratory meeting convinced me that there was more than rhetorical commitment to moving beyond "the turnover problem." My assessment (conducted through a series of focus groups and an analysis of trends in organizational strain measures) suggested that early process-oriented interventions aimed at technical problems had a greater chance of facilitating movement on the larger issues presented by the speedup problem rather than retarding such movement.

Unless clients develop the sense that broader change is possible and that they have the skills, starting with large-scale change can be very risky. Large-scale change should be attempted when the skills are present or the situation is critical and failing to address larger problems would lead to a worse crisis.[12,15,35]

Problem Depth

A fundamental reality of clinical work is that problems may be hidden under the surface. The dilemmas are to understand how deep the problems are and what strategies to use to work on them.

Critical theory[36] reminds us that lack of overt dissatisfaction may not reflect satisfaction with the operation of a system. Individuals may be afraid to express resentment. They may be unaware of how oppressive a situation is. Or they may express their resentment in ways that remain undetected by usual organizational indices. The dissatisfaction may occur in other, nonorganizational contexts, like child abuse, or in ways that are not thought of as discontent (illness, for example). The wider the assessment, the greater the chance of catching problems that are not easy for either the clinical sociologist or organization members to see and talk about.

Even when dissatisfaction surfaces, there may be only a vague sense of the problems. This leaves their dynamics and how to deal with them also vague. For example, there may be short-term individual and organizational ways of coping with stress and anxiety that only make the anxiety of organization members worse in the long run.[37] This often makes problems difficult to see given their different manifestations. However, if there is a department with some people abusing alcohol or drugs, others with patterns of tardiness and absenteeism, and still others in which interpersonal conflict is taken for granted, there are probably some common threads that bind these problems together.

Another, related view of "depth" comes from Harrison,[38] who classified interventions by the extent to which the self-concepts of participating individuals were at risk of being negatively affected. Beer[2] also argued that problems form a rough hierarchy based on how challenging they are:

Least Personally Challenging

> Task issues: techniques, goals, procedures, etc.
> Process issues: role expectations, delegation, etc.
> Personal and interpersonal issues: leadership styles, interpersonal styles, etc.
> Competence issues: knowledge, experience, credibility, etc.

Most Personally Challenging

Task issues are closer to the surface and less threatening. Competence issues are more ego involving and more difficult to discuss. Also, the self may become invested in procedures, patterns of delegation, or leadership styles that serve a protective function. Thus any of these issues may threaten some individuals. The challenge to the clinical sociologist is deciding how deep to go, how vulnerable to threat the various individuals are, and therefore, how to proceed. In addition, latent conflicts between gender and racial groups often are confounded with differences in position. These overlapping and mutually reinforcing patterns may erode trust and create deep-seated conflicts resistant to the most skillful short-term interventions.

All of these factors, anxieties that may be only partially job related, insecurities about the self, and latent conflicts of one kind or another make it difficult to understand the problems of an organization. And the clinical sociologist must be constantly aware of the dilemmas such factors create for intervention. The dilemmas can be framed as follows: Can the unspoken threatening problems be surfaced and confronted? Are there environmental and technological changes taking place that increase the chances of continuing conflict if the subsurface issues are not addressed?

Strategies for resolving depth dilemmas should consider the following ideas:

1. Develop with clients an understanding of the emerging technological and environmental forces that make demands on the unit.
2. Examine with clients how emergence of these demands coincide with conflicts among gender, racial, and ethnic groups.
3. Develop a consensus on where the environment and the technologies are going. Use this shared information as leverage to discuss, in sequence:
   a. *Task issues.* What goals and objectives flow from the collective sense of where things are going? How should work be coordinated?
   b. *Process issues.* How can the relationships be changed to make coordination easier?
   c. *Personal and interpersonal issues.* What leadership style would be best suited to these role changes?
   d. *Competence issues.* How can we best make use of existing skill and competence. What do we need to learn?

These issues must be addressed. However, it may take several months before sufficient progress has been made on surface issues to permit attacking more difficult problems. As a rule of thumb, interventions that provide short-term positive feedback offer an excellent platform for taking groups and departments forward on the more difficult issues. Where the problems are not so deep seated, structured process interventions (role negotiation, conflict management, etc.) may be tried sooner if the external situation suggests a worsening crisis unless these problems are addressed. If the external situation is less pressing and if several surface issues exist, working through some of these to build experience in successfully attacking problems is a better alternative.

Deescalation Bias

External consultants come into organizations to help solve problems, reduce risks, and deescalate conflicts. But if the major goal is increasing the capacity of the organization to adapt to changing conditions, it may sometimes be useful to stimulate frustration and conflict. For example, Ford[39] argued that, to ensure the airing of alternative views, stimulating conflict and tension may be a valuable tool to see that problems are surfaced and confronted. Van de Vliert[40] extended this idea to include several escalative interventions. Change in the distribution of rewards or deliberate stimulation of parochial interests were examples given.

For most situations, however, the dilemma for the clinical sociologist is not whether to stimulate conflict or tension. The dilemma is how to make sure that the conflict that does develop is constructive, leads to problem surfacing, data gathering, arguing about options, and other proactive activities. The conflict should not overwhelm or lead to distrust, insecurity, and a lowered sense of competence.

Cause Focused

Assessments lead to model development that leads to intervention choices. The progression is not always a linear one. A sense of what is going on, however, leads to the dilemma of how to attack the problem. Some clinical sociologists focus on the directness of the intervention effort. Straus[9] distinguished between direct and indirect interventions. If a family member has a drug problem, for example, a direct intervention would treat the behavior and attitudes of the drug-abusing person. An indirect intervention might have the family members alter what they are doing about it, rather than direct treatment of the drug problem.

To clarify the direct/indirect distinction for organizations, consider Straus's example adapted to an organizational context. A male worker has a drug problem that interferes with his productivity. Direct intervention would treat the drug problem perhaps through an employee assistance program. An indirect intervention would move back in the causal chain to attack elements of organization structure and process that may, at least in part, cause the drug abuse. For example, intradepartmental roles could be a source of stress and need to be negotiated more equitably. Or it could be that interpersonal relationships within a department need to be strengthened, to borrow Straus's phrase.

An even more indirect intervention would move even further back in the causal chain. Such an intervention might inquire about the environmental, technological, and organizational conditions that make roles stressful or leave role conflicts and ambiguities unresolved. For example, procedures may not exist for reevaluating what people in a department do, the nature of their interdependence, and how changing environments and technologies shape their action and interaction. Instituting such procedures could lead to ongoing clarification and adjustment of roles, reduced role stress, and reduction or prevention of indexes of strain, such as drug abuse.

A direct intervention, then, is one in which a problem is attacked head on. Interventions are more indirect as we move to the organizational conditions that cause the problem. Interventions become even more indirect when we consider the fundamental conditions that affect the immediate causes of the problem.

The further back in the causal chain the intervention takes place, the more prevention oriented it is. Prevention can be classified as tertiary, secondary, and primary.[41-44] Tertiary prevention treats problems after they have already become widespread and severe. Secondary prevention tries to attack problems before they escalate. Primary preventions try to stop the onset of problems. Primary prevention, then, is less concerned with directly treating the problem and more concerned with attacking the causes of the problem to prevent its occurrence. Following the example I constructed from Straus, primary prevention might include intervening with workers at risk of drug abuse to build their competence to cope with stress (individual level), strengthening the work group to bond the individual to more prosocial behavior (group level), renegotiating task roles among group members to reduce role ambiguity and conflict (group level), or facilitating a proactive posture with respect to the technical and environmental changes that may generate role ambiguity and conflict (organization level). These are methods of primary prevention that do more than simply intervene with workers who already abuse drugs.

In the example, prevention activities tried to institutionalize conditions that increased individuals' capacity to deal with stress, develop work group attachments, and define roles. More generally, drug abuse and similar individual and group activities provide an opportunity to work with clients to establish more proactive, adaptive activities and mechanisms to reinforce these activities.

Organization development is accomplished through establishment of a proactive stance. If successful, managers and workers identify and solve social problems as routinely and with as much confidence as they identify and solve financial problems.[2] The following guidelines are offered for resolving the cause versus problem dilemma:

1. The more serious and widespread the problems, the more attention must be paid to reducing the incidence and prevalence of the problems.
2. The less serious and widespread the problems, the more attention can be shifted to prevention-oriented efforts.
3. Attacking the proximate causes of problems is the most effective way of intervening in the short term.
4. Attacking only proximate causes of problems risks organizational regression to old ways as soon as the consultant leaves. The more prevention oriented the efforts can be, the less the risk of regression.

The Intervention Cycle Dilemma

It is incumbent on the clinical sociologist to be concerned with what Argyris,[1] Lippitt,[16] and others have termed *entropy prevention*. That is, the prevention of changes from running down because of loss of meaning, routinization, complacency, and a premature sense that problems have been fixed. Most interventions have life cycles composed of several phases ranging from starting up to declining to stopping. Each phase has sets of activities appropriate to the problems being addressed. There are different challenges facing the clinical sociologist during each phase (see Table 2).

In the initial phase, there is concern with building credibility and rapport, developing working teams, and establishing consensus about what is to be worked on. The intervention could be placed at risk if this phase takes longer than it should. The project can be derailed by groups hostile to it. Inadequate commitment of resources and the poor skills or organization members associated with the intervention can also cause an intervention to deteriorate. Consequently, the clinician should be particularly concerned with meeting these challenges so the project can move forward as smoothly as possible.

A critical challenge comes after the first set of problems has been worked on. Solving a finite set of problems can lead to an organization's becoming less con-

Table 2.   Phases in an Intervention's Life[a]

Phase	Activities	Challenges
Start-up	Rapport and credibility generation Working team development Training	Hostile groups Inadequate funding Low process or technical skills
Assessment	Problem identification and analysis Working model development Training	Weak analysis skills Weak process skills Disagreement over nature of problems
Approval of initial recommendations	Presenting recommendation Training	Resistance by management and/or labor groups Weak presentation skills
Implementation	Relevant groups act on suggestions	Prohibitive costs Resistance by groups that must implement Premature conclusion that problems are over
Lateral and preventive expansion	Expanding focus to other problems Expanding focus to more prevention-oriented resolutions Building proactive activities Creating a demand for proactive activities	Resistance from management and/or labor groups Inadequate funding Inadequate commitment by organization Weak technical and process skills Lack of demand for proactive activities

[a]Adapted in part from Mohrman and Lawler.[51]

cerned about adaptation as it becomes more successful in the short term. Resolution of simple problems is different from adopting a proactive strategy for surfacing, confronting, and working through problems.

A CONCLUDING NOTE ON ENVIRONMENTAL AND TECHNOLOGICAL CHANGE

To this point, several dilemmas for clinical sociologists working in organizations have been reviewed. These dilemmas arise from the case-based, problem-oriented, cause-focused nature of organizational work. The perspective emphasizes proactive coping in organizations to increase their capacity to anticipate and adapt to changes and make them saner places to work. It is fitting, at the close of this chapter, to draw attention to working assumptions that may be useful to clinical sociologists in their efforts to expand the proactivity of organizations.

Environmental and technological changes press organizations, and the people in them, to respond. Anticipating, planning, and retraining for such changes on a continuing basis has several advantages. Organization members should experience less trauma. The capacity and willingness of organization members to cope with these changes will be greater. Heightened capacity to adapt should be reflected in several organizational outcomes.[46–48]

1. Groups should be more resistant to shortfalls in productivity and increases in organizational strain.
2. The resilience of groups in bouncing back from problems should be greater.
3. The adaptive capacity of groups should be retained at higher levels for longer periods after working through problems.

A major challenge for clinical sociologists is helping organizations to create a demand for proactive and flexible planning, reinforced through the organization's coordination and control mechanisms.[49,50] Sensitivity to the dilemmas faced in clinical practice with organizations should improve the capacity of clinical sociologists to work effectively with their clients.

REFERENCES

1. Argyris, C. (1971). *Management and organizational development: The path from XA to YB.* New York: McGraw-Hill.
2. Beer, M. (1980). *Organization change and development: A systems view.* Glenview, IL: Scott, Foresman, & Co.
3. French, W. L., & Bell, C. H. (1984). *Organization development: behavioral science interventions for organization improvement* (3rd ed.). Englewood Cliffs, NJ: Prentice-Hall.
4. Huse, E. H., & Cummings, T. G. (1985). New York: West Publishing Co.
5. Freedman, J. A. (1982). Clinical sociology: What it is and what it isn't—a perspective. *Clinical Sociology Review, 1,* 34–49.
6. Lee, A. M. (1979). The sources of clinical sociology. *American Behavioral Scientist, 22,* 487–512.
7. Lippitt, G. (1982). *Organization renewal.* Englewood Cliffs, NJ: Prentice-Hall.

8. Straus, R. (1982). Clinical sociology on the one-to-one level: A social-behavioral approach to counseling. *Clinical Sociology Review, 1,* 59–74.
9. Straus, R., (1984). Changing the definition of the situation: Towards a theory of sociological intervention. *Clinical Sociology Review, 2,* 51–63.
10. Wirth, L. (1931/1972) Sociology and clinical procedure. *The American Journal of Sociology, 31,* 49–66; reprinted in *Clinical Sociology Review, 1,* 7–22.
11. Kanter, R. M., & Buck, J. (1982). From strategy to structure: Reorganization at Honeywell. *Organizational Dynamics,* Summer, 5–27.
12. Lippitt, G. L., Langseth, P., & Mossop, J. (1985). *Implementing organizational change.* San Francisco: Jossey-Bass.
13. Beckhard, R., & Harris, R. T. (1987). *Organizational transitions.* Reading, MA: Addison-Wesley.
14. Weisbord, M. R. (1987). *Productive workplaces.* San Francisco: Jossey-Bass.
15. Whyte, W. H. (1987). Social interventions for solving human problems. *Clinical Sociology Review, 5,* 45–64.
16. Lippitt, R. (1985). *Six problem solving contexts for intervention decision making. Clinical Sociology Review, 3,* 39–49.
17. Britt, D. W. (1989). *Constructing Adaptability: Proactive and reactive coping changes in response to an environmental jolt and increased organizational strain.* Wayne State University, unpublished manuscript.
18. Schein, E. H. (1987). *Process consultation: Its role in organization development.* Reading, MA: Addison-Wesley.
19. Deegan, M. J. (1986). The clinical sociology of Jesse Taft. *Clinical Sociology Review, 4,* 30–45.
20. Gouldner, A. (1965). Explorations in applied social science. In A. Gouldner & S. M. Miller (Eds.), *Applied sociology* (pp. 5–22). New York: The Free Press.
21. Denzin, N. K. (1970). Who leads: Sociology or society? *The American Sociologist, 5,* 125–127.
22. Weisbord, M. R. (1978). *Organizational diagnosis: A workbook of theory and practice.* Reading, MA: Addison-Wesley.
23. Dyer, W. G. (1987). *Team building: Issues and alternatives* (2nd ed.). Reading, MA: Addison-Wesley.
24. Macy, B. A., & Mirvis, P. H. (1983). Assessing rates and costs of individual behaviors. In S. E. Seashore, E. E. Lawler, P. H. Mirvis, & C. Cammann. *Assessing organizational change* (pp. 139–176). New York: John Wiley.
25. Moos, R. (1981). *Manual: Work environment scale.* Palo Alto, CA.: Consulting Psychologists Press.
26. Cammann, C., Fichman, M., Jenkins, G. D., Jr., & Klesh, J. R. (1983). In S. E. Seashore, E. E. Lawler, P. H. Mirvis, & C. Cammann. *Assessing organizational change* (pp. 71–138). New York: John Wiley.
27. Jick, T. (1979). Mixing qualitative and quantitative methods: Triangulation in action. *Administrative Science Quarterly, 24,* 602–611.
28. Merton, R. (1949). Bureaucratic structure and personality. In R. K. Merton, *Social theory and social structure* (pp. 151–160).
29. Walton, R. (1987). *Managing conflict: Interpersonal dialogue and third-party roles* (2nd Ed.). Reading, MA: Addison-Wesley.
30. Laue, J. (1981). Conflict intervention. In M. E. Olsen & M. Micklin. *Handbook of applied sociology* (pp. 67–90). New York: Praeger.
31. Laue, J. H., & Cormick, G. W. (1978). The ethics of intervention in community disputes. In G. Bermant, H. C. Kelman, & D. P. Warwick (Eds.). *The ethics of social intervention* (pp. 205–232). Washington, DC: Hemisphere.
32. Delongis, A., Coyne, J. C., Dakof, G., Folkman, S., & Lazarus, R. S. (1982). Relationship of daily hassles, uplifts and major life events to health status. *Health Psychology, 1,* 119–36.
33. Allen, L., & Britt, D. W. (1987). Appraisal of stressful life events, future expectations, and self-limiting symptoms. *Journal of Community Psychology, 15,* 132–140.
34. Gutnecht, D. B. (1984). Organization development: An assessment with implications for clinical sociology. *Clinical Sociology Review, 2,* 94–108.
35. Tichy, N. M. (1983). *Managing strategic change: Technical, political and cultural dynamics.* New York: John Wiley.
36. Johnson, D. P. (1986). Using sociology to analyze human and organizational problems: A humanistic perspective to link theory and practice. *Clinical Sociology Review, 4,* 57–70.

37. Menzies, I. E. P. (1970). *The functioning of social systems as a defense against anxiety*. London: Tavistock Institute of Human Relations.

38. Harrison, R. (1970). Choosing the depth of organizational intervention. *Journal of Applied Behavioral Science, 6*, 181–202.

39. Ford, J. D. (1986). The management of organizational crises. *Business Horizons, 24*, 10–16.

40. Van de Vliert, E. (1985). Escalative interventions in small-group conflicts. *Journal of Applied Behavioral Science, 21*, 19–36.

41. Albee, G. W., & Joffe, J. M. (Eds.). (1978). *Primary prevention of psychopathology* (Volume 1): *The issues*. Hanover, NH: University Press of New England.

42. Felner, R. D., Farber, S. S., & Primavera, J. (1983). Transitions and stressful life events: A model for primary prevention. In R. D. Felner, L. A. Jason, J. N. Moritsugu, & S. S. Farber. *Preventive psychology* (pp. 199–215). New York: Pergamon.

43. Goldman, H. H., & Goldston, S. E. (1985). *Preventing stress-related psychiatric disorders*. Washington, DC: U.S. Government Printing Office (DHHS Publication No. [ADM] 85-1366).

44. Klein, D. C., & Goldston, S. E. (1980). *Primary prevention: An idea whose time has come*. Washington, DC: U.S. Government Printing Office (DHHS Publication No. [Adm] 80-447).

45. Quick, J. C., & Quick, J. D. (1984). *Organizational stress and preventive management*. New York: McGraw-Hill.

46. Britt, D. W. (1988). The changing shape of adaptability in response to environmental jolts. *Clinical Sociology Review, 6*, 59–75.

47. Myer, A. D. (1982). Adapting to environmental jolts. *Administrative Science Quarterly, 27*, 515–537.

48. Golembiewski, R. T. (1985). Lessons from a fact-paced public project: Perspectives on doing better the next time around. *Public Administration Review, 43*, 547–556.

49. Walton, R. (1985). From control to commitment in the workplace. *Harvard Business Review, 85*, 77–84.

50. Walton, R., & Hackman, R. (1986). Groups under contrasting management strategies. In P. S. Goodman *et al. Designing effective work groups* (pp. 168–201). San Francisco: Jossey-Bass.

51. Mohrman, S., & Lawler, E. (1985). Quality circles after the Fad. *Harvard Business Review, 85*, 64–71.

CHAPTER 17

Clinical Sociology in the Workplace

ARTHUR B. SHOSTAK

INTRODUCTION

It is hard to imagine a sector of life as clearly in need of the services of clinical sociology as the world of work. Having spent nearly 30 years in both academic and consulting roles focused on workplace challenges, I forecast a remarkable rise in job openings for work-savvy clinical sociologists eager to assist corporations, labor unions, vocational centers, relevant government agencies, and the like. Should this upbeat forecast be misguided, however, the near future is likely to suffer from a downhill slide in productivity starkly at odds with our national well-being!

Why clinical sociology? Though clinical sociology has been previously defined in this *Handbook*, I think it best to precede a discussion of its utility in workplace reforms with some definitional thoughts.

Sociology often sounds like a dizzying cacophony of out-of-tune voices, a hard-to-follow score from the pen of a composer with a tin ear. Ceaseless controversy sets structure-functionalists against class theorists, positivists against subjectivists, macrotheorists against microresearchers. In addition, the entire subject confronts scores of commonsense beliefs settled centuries ago by tradition, coercion, or habit, but no less in error. Clinical sociology lends welcome clarity with its intriguing contention that "groups and group members who have sociological ailments need and deserve the care of sociological therapists."[1] Clinical sociology, in short, is "the application of a variety of critically applied practices which attempt sociological diagnosis and treatment of groups and group members in communities" (p. 5).[2]

In practice, this perspective adds many different "tools" to my kitbag:

ARTHUR B. SHOSTAK • Drexel University, Department of Psychology and Sociology, Philadelphia, Pennsylvania 19014.

- It focuses attention on the *social arrangements* between constituent groups of a company, plant, office, or union and their consequences for the people involved.
- It sensitized me to *conflicts* between the interests, the stated and unstated goals of different people and groups.
- It heightens awareness of the *pathology of normalcy*; the notion that what other people do and say, whereas average and normal in our culture, is not the only standard for choosing personal behavior.[3]
- It predisposes me to see things in *political terms* and to do an analysis of relative power positions and self-interest agendas.
- It encourages an *interdisciplinary orientation*, an appreciation for many and varied inputs from diverse social sciences.
- It helps me uncover points of intervention for planned change and keeps up my confidence in such prospects.

Above all, clinical sociology helps me obviate both blame and single-cause reasoning in my workplace consulting. Instead, I struggle to take the role or perspective of other persons or groups to help treat destructive processes involved in workplace structures and human interactions.

WORKPLACE CHALLENGES

Although there are many topics to choose from, I opt to illustrate the applicability of clinical sociology to five vexing issues now draining profit, productivity, and well-being from the American workplace: Each is an issue I know from direct personal experience, and it should be clear from the outset that my search for resolutions goes on unabated.

Substance Abuse

Nowadays, alcoholism and drug use lead most lists of workplace difficulties. Employers complain that employees are often too "hung over" or "spaced out" to complete adequate or accident-free assignments. Employees, in turn, resent the loss of privacy associated with mandatory drug testing, and many complain of a double standard that winks at a three martini lunch for top executives but punishes a three beer lunch for hard-hatted workers.

Plainly, then, the workplace is a promising venue for efforts to reduce substance abuse. To be sure, structural arrangements, such as mandatory shift work or mandatory obeisance to insufferable customers, prompt compensatory resort to alcohol, cocaine, crack, and other addictive chemical substances. Patterns of the workplace, such as giving booze as a holiday gift or overdoing it at "T.G.I.F." gatherings, enable employees to excuse self-destructive practices. As well, the culture of many work settings, especially those predicated on macho endorsement of "six-pack" or cocaine use, masks many health costs entailed. Even with all of this, the possible loss of a job in the aftermath of a crackdown appears one of the most powerful incentives to rehabilitation presently available.

From my limited experience as a consultant (primarily to trade unions), I believe clinical sociologists can help in five particular ways:

- We can expose half-truths, falsehoods, and gaps in knowledge about chemical dependency, the better to help labor and management share a common, valid base of knowledge.
- We can devise, administer, and analyze surveys to accurately measure substance abuse in a client's workplace, the better to substitute reliable data for vague, self-serving impressions.
- We can sensitize the parties to the significance of the culture and social class of the work force.
- We can also sensitize the parties to the related significance of the culture of the workplace.

Above all, we can help the parties understand the intractability of many chronic abusers and thereby prepare them for the complex challenge of rehabilitation efforts.

Clinical sociologists will find the substance abuse arena exceedingly trying. A counterproductive mix of prejudice, nostrums, and recidivism makes success elusive. Not surprisingly, the main actors have quite different needs:

- Local union officials want alcoholics and drug users given every possible chance to recover, though not if it means inordinate health plan costs for coworkers or a bitterly divided work force (substance abusers versus all others).
- Supervisory personnel want substance abusers fired, especially if their presence causes problems in safety or productivity.
- Managerial personnel want to avoid firings that lead to costly arbitrations, even as they want to reduce, sharply, the "detox" costs of chemically dependent employees.

To add to the problem, the frequency of backsliding by employees who have completed 28-day rehab programs saps the morale of everyone.

If a clinical sociologist should feel drawn to assist in this matter, five types of preparation are advisable:

- The very large body of current literature, cross-indexed in a highly refined way, should be read to provide a basic education.
- Guided tours through competitive treatment centers in the area will lend earthy reality to library material.
- Prearranged visits to AA, Al-anon, NA, and other such chapters will help to humanize the subject.
- Frank discussions with relevant "helpers" (physicians, therapists, nurses, treatment center staffers, academicians, etc.) should lend depth.

In addition, searching discussions with substance abusers in every stage (initial identification, denial, treatment, posttreatment, recidivism, recovery) remains indispensable, even if fraught with difficulty. Making contacts, earning trust, "translating," and retaining rapport will take the utmost in a sociologist's skills.

This much seems clear: Given the wide availability of destructive self-medications (alcohol, cocaine, "designer" drugs, heroin, marijuana), and the availability of testing paraphernalia to deter substance abuse, both labor and management will welcome the services of clinical sociologists in focused workplace interventions for many years to come.

Sexual Harassment

Sexual harassment in the workplace came out of hiding recently, thanks to the refusal of long-suffering victims to continue to accommodate the situation. Here again, the special sensitivities and tools of the clinical sociologist make a strong case for increasing professional involvement.

Although the law, at every level, lends its special brand of clarity to this offense, sexual harassment at work encompasses any and every act, word, or intent, deliberate or in its consequence, which seriously undermines an employee's ability to perform and is rooted in the gender or sexual preference of that employee. Plainly, we deal here with multifaceted, emotion-laden, explosive matters.

Clinical sociologists can help reduce the workplace toll in several ways:

- Male offenders often appreciate fresh insights into male socialization and role content. Such insights give them a new perspective on their misdeeds.
- Female offenders, in turn, may appreciate insights into socialization and corporate culture that can illuminate their own harassment misdeeds.
- Males, in general, profit from "consciousness raising" that sensitized them to the entire subject. Many do not interpret as harassment, scores of acts, words, and intentions perceived as such by potential victims.
- Females, in general, profit from training in assertiveness, the better to deter, ward off, dilute, rebuff, or retaliate.

Drawing on decades of sociological study of the "battle of the sexes," clinical sociologists can detoxify tense confrontations, clarify ambiguities, correct miscommunications, recast corporate culture, and, in many related ways, make a valuable contribution.

Three guidelines may help assure the sociologist's contribution comes close to its potential. For openers, he or she should follow such relevant topical sources as *Changing Men, Ms., Signs, Working Woman,* and the like. Attendance at many of the workshops now available in assertiveness training is also advisable. And third, searching conversations with concerned working women are indispensable, for the subject's complexities boggle the mind.

Although almost all the attention on gender issues has been directed at the modern business organization, the American labor organization has its fair share of this challenge and should not be overlooked as a needy recipient of reform attention. Costly use of the "glass ceiling" (sexist restrictions on the advancement opportunities for females) and of the "mommy track" (sexist confinement of child-rearing female employees to dead-end jobs), haunt labor as they do business, and all such cancerous forms of discrimination appear prime candidates for remedial attention.

A clinical sociologist drawn to this topic is well advised to locate and study organizations where caring, healthy, and productive relations exist among males and females, and among heterosexuals and homosexuals. Commonly known to an area's "grapevine" and to area specialists in human resource management, these exemplary firms (and their local union counterparts) can be "mined" for valuable reform ideas. Studied over several years, they can illuminate the three-part process (unfreeze, alter, refreeze) at the heart of a thoroughgoing large-scale upgrading of a workplace culture.

Quality Circles

Many employees want to help shape the workworld they inhabit, and in response, a large (though unknown) number of employers in the 1980s created small reform-proposing discussion groups at work. Ever since, however, they have gotten more than they bargained for! Uneven in purpose, tone, and significance, the nation's quality circles may help usher in a new era of cooperative employer–employee relations, or their possible fall from grace may initiate a new era of antagonistic workplace relations. Clinical sociology could help tip the scales in favor of a "win–win" scenario, provided that no effort is spared in preparing for this challenge.

A thoroughgoing background should be secured in the official and unofficial history of quality circles. As far back as World War I for example, the British created Whitney Councils in thousands of war plants to head off costly union–management disputes and iron out disagreements that threatened to weaken critical production. In the late 1920s, in this country, many nonunion employers adopted an anti-AFL blueprint called the American Plan, and under its aegis thousands of quality circles were created from coast to coast. Large numbers were rapidly transformed into company unions and were used as a shield to fend off AFL (and later CIO) organizing campaigns (critics characterized company unions as barely capable of getting shower stalls added to employee locker rooms, seldom able to get plumbing installed, and never able to get the water turned on).

Clinical sociologists reviewing this record will quickly pick up on the stigma of past exploitation, manipulation, deceptiveness, and chicanery associated by many contemporary workers with the concept of quality circles. Work with quality circles also requires a thorough background in the constraints posed by an existing collective-bargaining agreement. Under the legally binding terms of such a contract, all talk of "wages, hours, and working conditions" belongs exclusively to union–management dialogue. No changes can be made until they first have been the subject of formal contract renegotiations (and many contracts have clauses that bar negotiations during the years covered by the agreement). Given the natural propensity of quality circles to "trespass" (venture into discussion of "working conditions," controversies, and specific reforms), many local union officers are wary of this tool and expect a clinical sociologist consultant to appreciate the grounds for their misgivings.

Finally, there is the knotty matter of client sponsorship, one germane to every item discussed in this chapter and especially well raised by quality circle problems. None of the research with which I am familiar identifies a single local union as the initiator of a worksite quality circle. This social invention appears everywhere to be the product of managerial sponsorship. Accordingly, as the circles drift into fore-seeable problems (including supervisory resistance to reform ideas, executive vetoes of "large tag" reforms, personality squabbles, union political turmoil, and the sheer intractability of certain long-standing worksite challenges), we can expect management sponsors to seek assistance from applied social scientists. If possible, an outside consultant should request joint approval of his or her involvement and joint review by union and company representatives. Cost sharing by worker–management groups enhances the commitment of each to making the most of the consultants' services.

One important question permeates this entire matter, "Productivity for what?" An invaluable service can be provided by clinical sociologists who tactfully help the parties consider the deep basic structure of ongoing quality circles: Who and what are they ultimately serving? At their best, they can empower every participant (worker, union leaders, supervisor, and executive), and help align varying workplace visions in a newly rewarding way. At their worst, they can revert to the duplications and alienating ways of yesteryear's American Plan, thereby significantly setting back the cause of labor–management partnership.

Stress at Work

As the foregoing makes clear, the modern American workplace has more than its fair share of dysfunctional stress (otherwise known as distress). The ferocity of overseas competition, the rapidity of technological change, the rapacity of financial raiders, the uncertainties of corporate decision makers, and turmoil in policy- and law making help ensure an indefinite continuation of workplace distress.

Clinical sociologists should find this a major source of employment in the 1990s, provided they quickly and dramatically demonstrate their mastery of three major insights:

1. The client's definition of the problem is part of the problem. This axiom urges consultants to undertake their own analysis of the actual sources of distress at work and rely far more on their insights than on self-serving notions of the client (such as assigning all blame to the other side).
2. Quick relief is indispensable but generally also inadequate. This axiom recommends rapid use of field-proven relief measures, but it also insists that the job is not done until contributing sources are uncovered, analyzed, and remedied.
3. New sources of distress are inevitable, and their relief generally requires fresh remedies. This axiom cautions against expecting to achieve a work culture that is permanently free of distress, and it highlights the need to help the client learn how to invent novel responses to sources of distress.

These three insights, if discreetly conveyed to the labor and management parties directly involved with a distress challenge, should effectively establish a clinical sociologist's bona fides.

Definitions of distress abound, though most agree that we are talking about an unpleasant psychological and physical reaction that manifests itself in costly symptoms of emotional and physiological disability. Distress generally stirs fear in employees, undermines self-esteem, and leads many to worry about loss of control over vital aspects of their lives, at and away from work.

Clinical sociologists drawn into stress-relief work can profit from the use of a handsome array of tools:

- Gainsharing plans, first used 50 years ago, are more popular now than ever. Their current success (whether in the form of Scanlon, Rucker, or other such varieties) draws on their ability to share both the responsibility and the financial rewards for making a worksite more productive. Capable of securing dramatic, across-the-board gains, these bonus plans can use the "translator" and trust-building acumen of a clinical sociologist.
- Health care cost-containment plans are the newest stress-relief measures, so painful to everyone is the seemingly uncontrolled rise in health care costs. Joint labor–management efforts, beginning with second opinion programs and prehospitalization counseling, have been expanded to include early detection of disease (hypertension screening, periodic physical exams, etc.), control of biological risk (hypertension treatment, cardiac rehabilitation, etc.), detection of high risk behavior (health risk profiles through screening instruments, etc.), and the development of a healthy workplace culture (day care, on-site, job sharing, flex-time, noise control, smoking restrictions, etc.). Clinical sociologists can help by promoting compassion, tact, and creativity to insure the continued centrality of humanistic values.
- Comparable worth adjustments are possibly the most stressful of all current reforms, though they have potential for raising some of the basic questions at the root of innumerable workplace distressors. Designed to uncover and correct sexist wage inequities, these adjustments spur a rigorous reevaluation of pay rates in dissimilar jobs. This sort of research commonly vindicates the claims of female employees who allege gender prejudice in (earlier) rate settings. Given the obvious emotionality of the matter, a role for mediation by a clinical sociologist is obvious.
- Wellness pay continues to gain adherents as it proves a solid "bottom line" asset for cost-conscious managers. Predicated on the behavior-modifying use of a cash reward for desirable behavior, this reform provides cash bonuses to employees who make an extra effort not to miss work because of illness. As well, it discourages unnecessary trips to an MD ("the fender bender of the health business") and tries to shift workplace culture from reliance on sickness-recovery efforts to that of illness-prevention efforts. Plainly reliant on craft in communication and persuasion, this far-too-rare option would clearly profit from the help of a clinical sociologist.
- Supervisory redirection, although less "hard-edged" than the reform options listed, is no less significant. Clinical sociologists can school supervisors in consensus-building skills and lessen their reliance on hierarchical posturing. They can promote evaluation schemes that reward supervisors who achieve low levels of worker grievances, low absenteeism, and so on. They

can design, implement, and assess education programs to equip supervisors and employees alike with new interpersonal skills.

Above all, clinical sociologists can convey to everyone at work the vulnerability of negative stress to high-quality reforms: If a stress-reduction campaign is realistic in its goals, amply reinforced by critical resources, and patient and tactful in its execution, the likelihood of success remains quite high.

Outplacement

My own nominee for the "sleeper" issue of them all is outplacement, a sophisticated service to help former employees design a job-search strategy that can result in a totally new career. Outplacement goes so far beyond its antecedents in reemployment efforts as to make a compelling case for the presence of a vital new participant—the clinical sociologist.

Outplacement is a social invention that dates back only to the recession of 1981–1983, and its very youthfulness helps assure its continuous change in the months and years immediately ahead. It is novel in three particular ways: It does not entail rushing after every possible job lead, does not seek the shortest gap between a previous job and a new post, and it includes manual workers as well as the executives with whom it originally began (and, of course, everybody in between).

Outplacement is a patient, deep-reaching process that sensitively raises fundamental questions about an individual's obscure or veiled vocational goals. Very much in the spirit of clinical sociology, this process asks a participant to reflect anew on his or her vision of a truly desirable job. Earlier methods often assumed we wanted more of the same (though with better pay, easier work, and finer work conditions). Outplacement makes no such assumption. Instead, it encourages a free-wheeling consideration of widely diverse job options. Clients are given a battery of tests designed to uncover vocational aptitudes and interests, counseled in creative techniques for self-analysis, and their questions about a possible radical switch in career and life direction are given respectful treatment.

If outplacement is to live up to its potential and "liberate" people threatened with loss of a job to dare to attempt a new way of life, a number of sociological challenges must be met: An employee, for example, will want relevant insights into the culture of a proposed job, into the quality of relevant labor–management relations, and into the job's twenty-first century prospects. He or she will want a profile of prospective workmates and an inspiring account of reasons why others have left the job disillusioned. Above all, someone contemplating entry into a new work culture will want success tales of predecessors, along with lessons grounded in their example, as processed and shared by a clinical sociologist.

Assuming I am correct about the suitability of clinical sociologists to help meet ongoing workplace changes, I cannot emphasize enough three preconditions for making a desirable difference.

Anyone brave enough to venture into workplace consulting should be exceedingly worldly; however becoming innocence or naivete may be in certain (rare) settings, it is dangerous to all in workplace matters. Whether unionized or not, most workplaces are a hothouse of jealousies, rivalries, rackets, swindles, plots, and counterplots. Intrigues abound, and office politics honor no Marquis of Queensbury rules; alliances remain tentative, at best, and illusionary, at worst. Unless a clinical sociologist is psychologically armoured for "jungle warfare," he or she is best advised to seek a less treacherous setting.

Anyone brave enough to venture into workplace consulting should be agile enough to rebound from highly likely corporate "shocks" of a cataclysmic variety. Never before in business history have so many firms been so vulnerable to unwelcome changes in ownership engineered by so devious and greedy a stripe of financial bucanneer. "Job gutters" are rampant in executive suites across the land, and a paralyzing fear of unfriendly takeover attempts keeps otherwise able managers from "doing the right thing," such as keeping up support for a trial workplace reform implemented by a clinical sociologist. Bitterly resisted (or resented) takeovers often put a traumatic end to inherited reform projects and leave many reformers "shell-shocked" in aftermath.

Finally, there is the matter of homework, a strategic issue oddly neglected in handbook essays of this type. More specifically, anyone brave enough to join the rest of us in workplace reform efforts must understand beforehand that every day's issue of the *New York Times* and the *Wall Street Journal*, along with every issue of *Business Week, Dunn's, Forbes, Fortune, Harvard Business Review*, the *ILR Review*, the *Labor Law Journal, Personnel, Personnel Journal*, and many such others warrant careful scrutiny. There is no latitude for coasting in this high-stakes, fast-changing atmosphere. There is only room for consistently high-level study, analysis, and application.

Keeping up with current is not enough; a related necessity is organizational membership and attendance at annual meetings, monthly chapter gatherings, and the like. A clinical sociologist who is serious about workplace reform should be a card-carrying member of the Industrial Relations Research Association, the Labor Studies section of the Society for the Study of Social Problems, the Sociological Practice Section of the American Sociological Association, and various groups of personnel relations and/or organizational development specialists. This, of course, only makes sense if the literature of these groups is carefully read and their various meetings given responsible attention.

SUMMARY

With nearly 30 years of personal involvement to support my contention, I have tried to encourage clinical sociologists to join me in what I believe is one of the brightest of all areas for our employ. Modern workplaces host more change, planned and otherwise, than anyone can recall having bargained for. Every aspect, from A through Z, is in flux, with "future shock" more conspicuous here than in many better publicized areas of life. A combination of computer impacts, technological innovation, productivity pressures, worker shortages, and union innovation, to cite just a few, makes it clear that change will wrack the workplace for decades to come.

The situation plainly calls for the services of clinicians with a sociological orientation, clinicians earnest about immersing themselves in the complex and contradictory world of work. Such men and women must be prepared to work harder than ever before. They will confront tougher cross-pressures and conflicting agendas than they may have previously known, but they may achieve greater personal satisfaction than many earlier thought possible. The stakes are as large as the work lives of millions, and work remains the central defining experience of most adults. Conspicuously absent, to date, from the work reform efforts and overshadowed by the availability of industrial psychologists, personnel consultants, and the like, clinical sociologists are overdue as key agents of (overdue) workplace reforms.

APPENDIX: CLINICAL SOCIOLOGIST AND UNION WORK

Going back to 1954 when I began my pursuit of a BS degree in industrial and labor relations and continuing on through my 1958–1961 Ph.D. graduate program in industrial sociology, I have always sought effective ways of helping organized labor. This is a cause my father briefly served during the Depression when he was an organizer of fellow bread-truck drivers. His brother also contributed as a lifelong activist in the New York City teachers union. And even now one of my brothers is an activist in the AAUP/AFT local of college professors at the University of Pittsburgh.

Since becoming a clinical sociologist in 1961, I have found five ways of lending a (sociological) hand: (1) As a teacher I enjoy trading insights into possible reforms of work with unionists who take my courses at the AFL–CIO's George Meany Center for Labor Studies (Silver Spring, MD); (2) as a public speaker I enjoy popularizing insights from sociology for union-sponsored conferences, workshops, and the like; (3) as a researcher I do my best to provide unions with clear and timely answers to pressing sociological questions about childcare centers, drug rehab designs, and so on; (4) as a writer I try to find a reading audience among rank-and-filers, union leaders, and staffers for reform-advocating mono-graphs like *Robust Unionism*, *Blue-Collar Stress*, and *Blue-Collar Life*, along with volumes I coauthor with unionists, such as *The Air Controllers' Controversy*, and my current writing project, *The Air Controllers' Comeback*.

In my fifth role, that of clinician and survey researcher, I generally combine the other four and thereby enjoy myself all the more. For example, in 1980 when PATCO, the union of air traffic controllers, asked me to help clarify what underlay the unprecedented discontent of their 14,000 members, I devised five surveys for use at 3-month intervals. After collecting the data, I explained my computer-based findings to key PATCO activists. When it came time for the union to capitulate or strike, I reported my findings indicating that 78% of the respondents had said they would "hit the bricks" (that is, strike), a survey response off by only 3% from the actual turnout. (During the ill-fated strike, I reviewed my survey findings as a speaker at various PATCO rallies and began the scores of interviews that resulted 3 years later in my coauthored book on this subject.)

Now, when I am frequently asked by students like yourselves why I think this particular social movement is worth all the help sociologists can give it, I dwell on two sets of personal convictions, the first focused on the workplace; the second, outside of it.

Where the workplace is concerned, I believe we will probably always have unions, as we will always have employers distracted from sensitive personnel relations by greed, competi-tion, or callousness. I also believe shop stewards and the grievance process are indispensable buffers between a lone worker and an impersonal managerial powerhouse. And I believe locals are obliged to adequately service members by the threat of a costly decertification challenge or a raid from a rival labor organization.

Outside of the workplace, I believe labor makes a critical contribution by "bird dogging" every relevant governmental agency (e.g., OSHA [Occupational Safety and Health Administration], the Department of Labor, etc.). I also believe labor helps with its efforts to raise workplace standards in developing nations. And I believe labor's sustained political effort on behalf of the have-nots and the lower middle class (today's "working class") helps provide an indispensable element—an elevating conscience and vision—in our social and economic order.

None of which is to deny the great distance labor still has to go to set its own house in order. Like many of you, my heart aches when I read or watch media coverage of labor's various shortcomings. Far too few women and minorities hold powerful office and far too many discouraged bureaucrats keep unions from trying innovations that might revive both sagging morale and membership. Organized crime has too much influence (as it does in the business world), and decades of antagonistic relations undermine efforts at forging new labor–management cooperation on behalf of urgently needed productivity gains.

Working as I do, however, on the inside, and working as I have over a 25-year period, I am more encouraged than ever by the commitment to reform by shopfloor activists and labor leaders alike.

When PATCO, for example, was destroyed in 1981 by the firing of 70% of the air controller workforce, many commentators thought this sounded the death knell of the modern labor movement. You and I were told that PATCO replacements would never unionize, as they were the "new" breed of workers—antiunion, self-centered, career-protecting "yuppies." We were told that management would never make the same mistakes twice; that is, it would never repeat the poor personnel practices that had given PATCO such a loyal following prior to the 1981 strike. Above all, labor organizers could not mount a classy, modern, and appealing enough organizing campaign to ever win a majority vote of the post-1981 controllers.

Given the first law of sociology, "things are seldom what they seem to be," the outcome in June 1987 should have come as little surprise. With an extraordinarily high turnout of 84% the new union of air traffic controllers—one I now hope to serve, as in the past, as a clinical sociologist—received a greater than 2:1 margin of victory (70% to 30%). What antagonists had heralded as a death knell in 1981 appears, just a few years later, to be a symbol of recovery and renewal, a symbol of labor's new possibilities in a postindustrial America and another exciting invitation to sociologists to lend a hand.*

REFERENCES

1. Glassner, Barry, & Freedman, Jonathan A. (1979). *Clinical sociology.* New York: Longman, p. v.
2. *Ibid.*, p. 5.
3. See, in this connection, Erich Fromm (1965). *The sane society.* New York: Fawcett, 1965; Harry Cohen (1985). Sociology and you: Good living. In Roger A. Straus (Ed.), *Using sociology: An introduction from the clinical perspective* (pp. 44–60). Bayside, NY: General Hall, Inc.

---

*An earlier version of this appendix essay appeared in Beth B. Hess *et al.*, *Sociology.* New York: Macmillan, 1988, pp. 328–329.

CHAPTER 18

Clinical Educational Sociology

Interventions for School Staff

BRUCE SAUNDERS

INTRODUCTION

In my clinical practice, I often work with teachers and other school personnel who are angry, depressed, overwhelmed, feel guilty, and think of themselves as role failures. They are not idealistic tyros, but experienced educators who know a great deal about the mechanics of educating young people. The locus of their problems lies outside themselves, in the structure and organization of schools. Public schools are often chaotic, misorganized institutions and the people who work in them may respond by becoming sick, confused, dispirited, and unhappy. What appear to be individual problems are normal responses to working in an environment that is distorted by deep, virtually unresolvable structural problems.

At the individual level, intervention is twofold. Initially, the clinical sociologist helps school-based clients gain insight into how their schools are organized and function. Troubled staff need to understand how their work environment affects their feelings and behavior. The second step of the intervention is to help school personnel become actors in their own right. The clinician works with them to develop the power, the will, and the skills they need to make changes in their schools so that they can do their work well and gain satisfaction from it.

This chapter will describe clinical interventions for the "occupational hazards" of teaching and working in public schools in America. It will begin with an analysis of what is wrong with the public schools (structurally and as organizations), and then discuss the effects of these problems on the school-based clients a clinical educational sociologist sees in practice. In this chapter, I will sort out some of the problems besetting public schools, show how structural problems in and beyond the

BRUCE SAUNDERS • College of Education, University of Washington, Seattle, Washington 98195, and Clinical Sociology Associates, Seattle, Washington, 98115.

school affect school staff, and describe interventions that are workable and effective at the individual and staff levels. I will discuss only microlevel interventions with the school staff who seek clinical help; interventions at the school, district, state, or policy/analytical levels will not be discussed.

WHAT IS WRONG WITH SCHOOLS?

The roiling national debate on the quality and results of American education centers on problems such as drugs, school safety, falling test scores, equity issues, accountability, and making programs work for all children. Important as these problems are, they are only a part of what is wrong with public schools. Unless other, less obvious problems are addressed, there is little hope for bringing solutions to the issues that rouse the nation. The argument of this chapter is that there is little wrong with schools *per se*: They are good at doing what they have always done, educating children. However, the nation's expectations for schools have risen beyond what schools as institutions are able to accomplish. Reformers, who do not understand the limits of what schools can do, attack and feed on schools like frenzied sharks. The press and media pour out stories about what is wrong with schools. Proposals for reform stir up explosions of criticism and counterproposals in a self-sustaining, expanding chain reaction. Unfortunately, attempts to make schools better often harm schools and harm the people who work and pass through them.

How are schools and people who work in them harmed? Let us begin by defining what we refer to as a school. Years ago, one would point to a building, an experienced staff, a curriculum, and a student body that progressed through the grades in a stable cohort. Observers of today's urban elementary schools, who witness rapid changes in leadership, escalating turnovers of staff and students, and radical changes in programs each year, might wonder about the meaning of *school*. Only the building seems permanent. Modern schools have become temporary institutions. Staff and students are replaceable and programs come and go like sitcoms in the fall television lineup.

Redesigning education is a national pastime. This frantic compulsion to change education is not accidental or mischievous. It is the result of good impulses to help children and schools that have gone wrong. The public school system has become America's great experimental social laboratory, the place where every social researcher goes to try out his or her agenda.[1] Schools (districts and buildings) struggle to fend off attempts of well-meaning academics, unions, foundations, national commissions and boards, courts, legislatures, parents, businesses, and community groups to revise, reorganize, redirect, or dictate how schools function and what they teach.

America's school system is reeling from too much attention. No institution functions well if it is constantly dissected, reorganized, or given new functions. No institution thrives if it is bent and twisted to make it perform functions that it is structurally incapable of accomplishing. What is wrong with schools? They are beset with iatrogenic disease. A fragile institution is plagued with a core of physicians determined to mend what was never broken. In our attempts to make schools do what they cannot, we are destroying the system, piece by piece. The definition of what is wrong with schools and what needs to be done to fix them is up for grabs. The nation is awash in analyses and prescriptions for fixing schools. There are too many ailments, too many physicians, too many cures, and too little regard for what schools are and how they function.

Everyone, it seems, has a different use for schools. Every social problem that cannot be solved elsewhere is dumped on teachers' desks. Kids and teachers can become the targets of ameliorative social policy. Each social problem can be conceptualized as a consequence of failed socialization, and schools are society's official socializing agents. The problem with the "education solution" for social problems[2] is it does not work. Schools are not especially good at solving problems with which other institutions cannot deal. Acting on the unexamined belief that schools can straighten out social problems merely shoves these problems behind classroom doors, damaging the schools.

Power to control schools and their purposes has become diffuse, divided, and removed from the classroom. Parents, district leaders, politicians, members of the larger community, state and federal officials, jurists, and lawyers have muscled their way into schools. Elected school boards, which have formal legal responsibility for public schools, were established to shield schools from outside pressures. However, school boards have ceased to be shock absorbers; instead, they transmit (and in some cases multiply) pressures from the community to the schools. Our system of public schooling becomes increasingly politicized. No group has the power to mandate its particular vision of public schooling, but many groups have a *de facto* veto over school policies. The resulting pluralistic elitism[3] creates stasis and stalemate, or worse, reactive, *ad hoc*, crisis-oriented policy.

Organizations and institutions that cannot satisfactorily resolve contradictory requirements are "frustrated" and function in contradictory ways. School leaders respond to frustration, not by trying to reconcile or rationalize conflicting demands or by rejecting unwise, inconsistent demands on the schools by a divided public, but by changing program elements and moving students and personnel around the district. These changes are superficial displacement activities that draw attention away from the underlying problem: The institution is forced to do too much incommensurate work.

When we look at America's better private schools, we see an entirely different picture. Parents and outsiders (though involved) are kept at a distance. Governance is collegial. Resistance to change is great, and existing policies are sensibly guarded. Workloads are monitored, and time is carefully rationed. Policies are not changed without good reasons. Much thought is given to possible consequences of proposed policies before any change takes place. The genius of America's private schools is that they find a good way to do something and stick with it. They are not volatile or frustrated institutions. They resist attempts of misguided outsiders to control what they do. Public schools, on the other hand, attract every strange sentimental fancy and vagrant issue in society. Administratively, they are almost helpless in the face of determined attacks from without, so they are pushed into a series of increasingly radical cultural revolutions.

WHAT TEACHERS FACE

Public schools are tough on teachers. Most teachers try to be good professionals and do their work well. Teachers feel defensive, under assault, apologetic, and guilty for not doing everything they are "supposed to do." Their workload is high, and it keeps growing because school staffing lags behind swelling manpower needs. In a climate of scarce resources, teachers, principals, and districts make do, putting together patchwork programs that do little more than meet technical requirements.

What Teachers Feel

Teachers feel they get little help from students, parents, the public, the press, the state, the federal government, or their districts. They mistrust their unions and professional associations and sometimes feel exploited by them. Teachers have little confidence in the wisdom of the central office (but they do tend to like and trust their principals). School staff feel trapped in a limbo between bureaucratic and professional statuses and role orientations.[4] No one has decided whether teachers are professionals ministering to student/clients or semiskilled workers who need constant supervision and regulation. In the classroom, and in relations with students, teachers have the autonomy of professionals. In status, salary, and conditions of employment, teachers are bureaucratized employees, subject to the whims of their bosses.

Economic incentives that might make public school careers more tolerable for teachers are inadequate. For most teachers, the opportunity structure of teaching is flat. The status of teaching as an occupation barely holds its own, whereas, in the long run, teachers' salaries, relative to others in real dollars, fall.

Working in Reservoirs of Pain

Schools are hard places for sensitive people to work. Schools are vast reservoirs of pain, negative affect, and anxiety. Children are emotionally volatile, and schools throb with barely contained sentiments and feelings. Each day, every student's claim to his or her status set is tested. Identities and sources of accorded esteem are precarious, and role failure is a constant threat. The status system of the school churns as kids crawl up and are knocked back in the performance arenas of the school. Role support, positions, and esteem are awarded competitively by staff and peers on the basis of performance and manifested traits.

Kids are squeezed into a world that is too small for them, and they kick about it. The social system in which students compete for desirable roles and statuses has fewer role and status opportunities than the outside world. Because schooling is mandatory, all possible types of persons have to be squeezed into the social system of the school. The microcommunities in the larger world that separate different social types and reduce conflict are compressed in schools. Very different people have to struggle with the problem of fitting their lives together and maintaining their identities in a walled community that allows only a limited number of models for persons to fit.

Because schools reproduce the existing society with its existing differences,[5] children are differentiated along most of the dimensions that differentiate persons in the parent society: age, ethnicity, social class, gender, ability, attractiveness. In the outside society, groups and persons with different traits are differently situated in the social system, maintain social distance, and have little formal interaction. In schools, as in other inmate cultures, social distance is difficult to establish and defend. To maintain order, schools impose a strict system of rewards and punishments on students. Except for the persuasive arts and charismatic leadership, staff have few means of compelling students to do what they are told. The system of rewards and punishments is inadequate to get more than token compliance from many students, particularly those in upper grades. The kids wear away at each other and at the school that confines them, and staff are taxed, bruised, and emotionally strained.

Workloads

The work of teachers, if not controlled, expands without limits. Delivering the formal curriculum is only part of teachers' jobs. A formal curriculum is bounded (in theory), and teachers can deliver it in the allotted time. But teachers are also expected to deliver an unofficial, or hidden, curriculum[6] that is open ended. Children must be taught to be good citizens, patient, responsive to authority, tolerant of others' differences, gregarious, good team players, ambitious (but not selfishly so), to defer gratification and limit impulsiveness, to be self-confident and capable. And do not forget the social agendas that are part of both curriculums: the wars against drugs, racism, sexism, premarital sexual experimentation, unplanned pregnancy, and communism that must be fought while students are being taught the basics.

Blamed for Learning Failures

It is a prevalent educational myth that there are no student failures, only school failures. This myth illustrates how the moral climate of schools has changed. In the nineteenth century, children were held accountable for their behavior, and learning failures were individual failures. In the twentieth century, the locus of blame for student failure shifted from kids to their parents, the community, and the larger society. Today, the responsibility for learning and behavior failures is attributed directly to the schools and, by implication, to the staff. Teachers would love to have every child succeed, but they do not know how to do it. Neither does anyone else. This is not surprising. Thirty years of research into educational and status attainment processes has shown that easily manipulated school variables contribute very little to the variance around learning outcomes. Educational "success" appears to load strongly on variables that schools intrinsically cannot control as Coleman[7] and Jencks,[8] among others, have shown. These findings are controversial and do not prevent us from blaming different schooling outcomes on teachers. The findings do explain why schools have so much trouble finding something that "works."

Loss of Authority

Teachers are expected to control the behavior of students and compel them to learn. Power and authority are necessary to compel children to obey and learn, and teachers are being stripped of these. Teachers once had the law, community sentiment, moral authority, and a monopoly of legitimate power on their side. Now, the nature of the school's authority over students has changed.[9] Old bases for authority are being replaced with a ramified and complex legal code that gives teachers less power over students and, by legitimating and increasing student rights, creates thorny problems of its own. Teachers do not know which system of authority to use (and often find none of them works). Authority is crucial because teachers are dirty workers,[10] who perform in isolation before audiences of captives who are at best ambivalent, and more often apprehensive or unappreciative about what is done for them. Teachers face a chronic shortage of role support, and every interaction with students risks role failure. Teachers cannot find much role support in their communities either. The crisis of authority and legitimacy that plagues teachers in schools extends to the community level as well.

Cut off from Intellectual Capital

Teachers are less actors than objects in educational research and debates on education policy. Teachers' associations and unions are powerful lobbies, but teachers feel their associations do not speak for them. They feel invisible and unheard. In research, "the teacher" is studied as an object, but the teacher, speaking in her or his own voice, is mostly missing in public forums and in the research literature. The intellectual capital that informs school debates is provided by the research community, policy analysts, and staffs of prestigious boards and commissions. The knowledge teachers have about their own occupation is denigrated to the point that teachers, themselves, do not think it is valuable.

Consequences of Professionalization

Decades of efforts to professionalize teaching have produced an unanticipated result. Expectations governing the role relationships of teachers and students are becoming quasi-professional, but with unforeseen consequences. In the professional/client model, control of the relationship ultimately rests with the client. Clients are supposed to pursue their welfare selfishly, monitor the behavior and prescriptions of their service providers, refuse treatment if it is in their interest, and take their business elsewhere if they think they are being harmed. The professional, in turn, must safeguard the client's interest and see that no harm comes to him or her.

The professional/client relationship is fundamentally dyadic, but in schools, the paramount relationship is that of bureaucratic superior to student group. The class is the unit of instruction, the band or the team are units of performance, the age group is the unit of processing. Schools are batch-processing institutions. They run into intractable problems when they try to individualize schooling. Nonetheless, there are irresistible pressures to individualize schooling. In most fields, professionals can help one client without harming others, but many school outcomes are zero sum. Schools are graded performance arenas with prizes and punishments of some consequence to bestow. Schools are the major drivers of the status attainment process in American society. The machinery that is set up to differentiate kids cannot be adapted to helping every child win. School structure is not capable of supporting true professional/client relationships.

The particular professional model that is becoming dominant in education is the therapeutic model, which requires a teacher to be the child's advisor, advocate, confidante, and analyst, while trying to instruct him or her and control behavior. The therapeutic model presents grave problems for teachers. The model's role demands conflict with demands of the existing teacher's role. Teachers are not trained to be therapists; they work under conditions that do not facilitate therapeutic relationships with students, and staff are not selected for traits therapists should possess: analytic ability, empathy, capacity to put one's agendas aside for another.

Staff Differentiation

School staff face another problem: unending differentiation and elaboration of staff structure. Part-timers, volunteers, teacher aids, and other categories of new workers pour into schools. As in other asylumlike institutions, the need for more staff is compelling, whereas capacity to pay meaningful salaries to an adequate number of trained workers declines. Free and cheaper labor replaces higher priced labor. This results in more elaborately differentiated staff structures with divided responsibility and skill levels. School governance becomes more complex. Because friendships and social ties tend to follow status boundaries, role relationships become less personal and more formal. Bureaucratic control intensifies, and staff lose some of their autonomy. Teachers gain prestige by having subordinates but pay for it with a loss of sodality as differentiation proceeds. Staff differentiation also adds to workloads. Teachers are not trained to manage work teams and thus have to use instructional and class time to figure how to fit personnel to work that needs doing. Often they train low-skilled workers to do needed tasks, only to find assistants reassigned, dismissed, or leaving for better jobs.

District and building managers are aware of these problems but are forced to shift categories of staff from school to school to meet emergent needs. School staffing is sensitive to state funding formulas, local demography, and parent reactions to changing school policy. State funding is tied to actual enrollments, and enrollment projections at the district, school, or program level are volatile and reliable. At the start of each year, districts try to predict staffing needs and stretch personnel dollars as far as these will go. As the school year progresses, changes are made on the fly and school personnel are shuttled from school to school like pizza deliverers. This not only weakens staff members' solidarity and attachment to their particular school; it also jeopardizes teachers' vulnerable professional identity by confirming their suspicion that staff are merely interchangeable parts in assembly line education.

Constituencies and the Search for Reforms

Besides devising new categories of staff and moving personnel and students from building to building, districts respond to pressure for change by creating new programs. Program differentiation always increases staff differentiation, but program differentiation has a larger effect: It differentiates the educational system as a whole by multiplying constituencies and generating advocates for particular programs. Adoption of bilingual/bicultural programs, special education, magnet, alternative education, science, arts, or early childhood programs, for example, produces syndicates of parents and staff members who are committed to the perpetuation of these programs at any price. Districts find themselves in a trap. Pressure to change schools is unrelenting, but resources needed for the next round of change are committed to existing programs that districts are not allowed to abandon.

A majority of school reforms necessitate new role prescriptions that may not be accepted by staff. Districts seldom formally abandon old expectations and role requirements or see that new and old prescriptions are prudently integrated. Instead, new elements are shoved into the teachers' crowded role set and left to coexist or conflict with existing elements. Occupations become crazy-making when formal role and expectation sets have large numbers of discordant elements. In most occupations, functional mechanisms take care of integrating and rationalizing elements of role prescriptions. New technical demands that necessitate the reorganization of work come along slowly, and only a few highly qualified people are allowed to tamper with workers' role prescriptions. In education, things are different. Disturbing the role set of school people is a popular craze. Public education is highly politicized, and critics are legion. Each year, some blitzkrieging storm troopers get through the defenses of districts and shake up role prescriptions for teachers.

Restructuring

The current (1989) "ultimate" reform, "restructuring," requires teachers to take control of their schools and collectively transform them. A problem for the scheme is that teachers are not trained in organizational analysis and social engineering and have little sense of how to tease out problems or solve them. Teachers are not specially prepared for collective governance, and most seem ill prepared to become informed managers of school change. Continuing education efforts presently are not adequate to prepare teachers to restructure schools. Given their other job demands, one also wonders how teachers can find time to take care of the immense amount of work that restructuring demands.

Restructuring requires teachers to achieve, by themselves, what myriad well-prepared consultants, academics, and professional administrators failed to achieve: the transformation of the schools. Requiring this job of teachers is symptomatic of much that is wrong with the schools in America. Overloaded and underprepared staff should not be expected to do the restructuring that would be done by outside consultants and professionals in any other large organization. For that matter, we do not know that any agency can restructure schools in the country's highly charged, demanding environment. Organizations that succeed at self-renewal are un-politicized, tightly coupled, and have economic incentives and a clear mandate for change. Their managers are powerful and can force reorganization if there is no consensus, while keeping outsiders from meddling. Except for the mandate to change, public school staff have none of these.

The call for staff to "restructure" their schools is mostly rhetoric. State superintendents, federal agencies, school boards and districts, legislators, and the press corps are still deeply involved with school policy. Control of the nation's schools remains contested and divided. Even if staff were fully in charge, most of the problem reformers want licked lie beyond school walls where teachers cannot do much about them. The call to restructure the nation's schools seems to be just one more vague and sentimental prescription to which weary staff must respond.

INTERVENTIONS FOR TEACHERS

It now seems clear that no national agency or body has enough power to reconstitute America's public school system. New prescriptions and proposals for global reform just add to the general confusion. School problems are intractable because elements of the problem set are incommensurable. Statements of what is wrong are too divergent, demands put on schools too numerous, the outcomes sought too inconsistent, for national consensus on goals and strategies. Clinical sociologists can help individuals and, perhaps, individual schools but must realize that solving the problems of school personnel is not equivalent to solving the problems of schools in general. The best strategy for clinical sociologists is to work at the local level to deescalate expectations for schooling outcomes, bank down the attractiveness of schools to hysterical reformers, and try to insulate schools against the buffeting of a too-caring public. Education is one field of clinical sociology that rewards low aspirations. It is consoling to remember the words of Francis Crick's[11] ancient Persian sage who asks: Is no man so lost as the man who tries to go ahead when there is no way ahead? Progress can be made only in small steps, in work with teachers and other building personnel and, tentatively, with whole schools. Drastic change in the system of schools is beyond the expertise of the clinical sociologist.

I have tried to convey a sense of what public school teachers face so that we will know what we are dealing with when we see teachers in a clinical setting. The congeries of problems I set out (politicized environment, increasing staff and program differentiation, rapid turnover of personnel and students, invisibility, powerlessness, insufficient authority, poorly rationalized role prescriptions, emotional pain, and all the rest) are familiar to most teachers. Not all teachers experience these conditions as problems or are overwhelmed by them. Nevertheless, these issues lurk in the background of most public school teachers' lives, and one expects them to be peripherally implicated in any problem brought to clinical sociology by school personnel. The long-understood connection between career and "personality"[12-14] warns us that the character of institutions affects the feelings, concepts, and personalities of those who work in and pass through them. Contradictions in structure will emerge as contradictions within roles and contradictions between actors. Structural role strain and role conflict have lasting effects on "personalities."

In each situation, we need to do a full clinical assessment to find out what is wrong.[15] We must determine the extent to which workplace issues are tied up with the presented problem. Knowledge of workplace issues gives us a starting point for our assessment and guides the comparative workup. Some problems involving school staff turn out to be simple technical or instrumental matters that can be solved in a straightforward way by providing staff with training or information. Behaviorist models dominate the training and staff development fields, for example, Argyris and Schon's widely used model,[16,17] and behaviorist models are perfectly serviceable when a problem can be solved by providing staff with information or new skills. Marsick[18] gives us criteria for determining which problems can be solved by prescribing workplace learning. We must be able to specify the desired outcomes, and these must be observable and performance related. It must be possible to separate personal and work-related needs for development. The organization must be functioning well, with clear, hierarchical lines of authority, jobs that do not overlap, and rational systems of delegation and control. Most knotty problems in clinical educational sociology will not meet these criteria. This is not surprising because the deep problems of schools do not stem from simple technical deficits of workers.

Tough problems in clinical educational sociology do not have clear-cut answers; we can specify what needs to be done only in very general terms (e.g., team building, changes in institutional governance, more adaptive ways of responding to the organization's environment). Overspecification, as we have seen, is itself the gravest problem for schools. Behaviorist interventions that require staff to be little more than passive learners are almost certain to fail in schools. Deep organizational problems, which schools have in abundance, can only be solved by abandoning the behaviorist paradigm and moving to less mechanistic models that empower staff and liberate their creativity.[19] Many such models are available, for example, those of Carr and Kemmis[20] or Kolb,[21] and these have, in common, attempts to develop autonomy, reflectiveness, and critical awareness in organization members. Staff who are going to be involved with redefining their organization need an intervention that motivates them, moves them to activity, and fuses their discovery of new job skills with knowledge about the organization and themselves.

In my practice, I work with school staff in small ongoing groups, brought together outside work hours for support and professional development. In the beginning, support is the main reason for us to come together. Later in a group's history, professional development becomes a group's major focus. My techniques draw upon the formative work of two adult educators with sociological imaginations: Paulo Freire and Jack Mezirow. Freire's work[22] stresses the linkages between actors' objective conditions, awareness, and freedom to act. Freire teaches us how to help adults learn to look critically at the social situations in which they find themselves and act to transform their circumstances. In Freire's method, the world is not static but a problem to be worked on and solved. In dialogical encounters with others, persons learn to look at their world critically and perceive its contradictions. They become aware that ignorance of their own circumstances renders them powerless to solve the problems they face.

School staff tend to be silent and fatalistic. They do not routinely talk with one another about what it is like to work in schools. When pressed about their compliant acceptance of working conditions that border on the intolerable, they say, "What can we do? We are only teachers." For many teachers, conditions of teaching are givens, unalterable facts of life. School staff feel ignorant, resentful, impotent, and used. They do not see themselves as persons who design institutions but as passive acceptors of institutions designed by others. Because school staff do not consciously and cooperatively study why their schools are vulnerable to an environment that causes them trouble, they do not see how they can protect themselves. School personnel are so often depreciated that they internalize negative evaluations and depreciate themselves. They do not value what they have learned while working in schools. They believe their practical knowledge of how to educate children is inferior to the "scientific" and formal knowledge of the "experts" who research and write about schools. Teachers both turn to and mistrust "experts" who come into their schools professing academic knowledge. They have learned that experts are better at creating new problems than solving old problems. Academic knowledge is obtuse, hard to apply, and has hidden traps for staff. Teachers want help in straightening out things that are not working for them, but the help they get often frustrates and alienates them.

Trying to help people who are suspicious and alienated from their jobs is delicate work. We cannot change teachers by lecturing to them or prescribing for them. Taking an authoritative stance makes group members angry or brings out their submissiveness. Schooling them does not work either. Teachers are good students; in learning situations, they pay attention and parrot back what they are told. They participate enthusiastically in simulations and exercises, but once back in their schools, they will not act.

To make changes, staff must be motivated to study their schools and discover for themselves what is wrong and what they can do about it. They must see that their fatalism is itself a problem to be solved. I motivate teachers by getting them together to talk about their school-related problems. Issues that surface in dialogue are presented to the group as problems for everyone to consider and solve. I begin with simple questions that flow naturally from our conversation. Do teachers like their jobs? Who knows the most about education? Why do so many people criticize what teachers do? Is there anything teachers want to do that they cannot do in their schools? How are public schools different from private schools? Why do teachers have so much to do? The struggle to find answers we can agree on generates insightful discoveries and new questions. Our focus broadens and becomes sharper as we work together. We try to help individuals who have hurts and particular problems. As we move along, underlying patterns start to emerge from the group's individual problems in a manner reminiscent of the way in which patterns and particulars mutually determine one another in Garfinkel's[23] method of documentary interpretation. The particulars that the staff discuss are contextual (*indexical particulars* in Garfinkel's terms), and discussion of these begins to force a revision in their perception of the situation in their schools.

As a group leader, my role is to help participants search for what Freire calls *generative themes*—significant dimensions of contextual reality whose investigation leads to advances in critical thinking and new understanding of the world of schools. *Power, authority, discipline, control,* and *method* are some generative themes in teachers' lives. School staff know these words but have not considered them as powerful themes in their lives. My task is to keep participants looking for their own generative themes and talking about what they have found. As new themes emerge, I turn these around and "re-present" them as new problems. What I want the group to find are the principal contradictions of their lives in the schools. The groupwork aims to help teachers bring their own reality into full consciousness and to be able to describe their own reality in words that are contextual for them, not simply the parroted academic jargon they learned in college. Initially, I want them to explore their worlds of teaching without reducing the concrete to abstractions or generalizing. Later, I want them to acquire the habit of reducing the world they experience to propositions they can believe in, propositions that lead to action.

Groupwork teaches participants to critique their experiences and builds critical awareness. The common awareness that emerges in a supportive setting chips away individual teachers' alienation. As participants become more aware and accustomed to perceiving their school situation as a set of problems to be solved, rather than as an obdurate reality, their enthusiasm for working on the problem of how to make changes grows. When my work is done well, staff change from passive receivers of school life to persons with deep personal knowledge of their schools, who perceive themselves as actors, givers of culture and organization, rather than as passive recipients of someone else's action. If we get this far, and in some groups we do, the battle is won.

Groupwork is educative: at the end of the process, the learners come away with a fundamental shift in their perspectives, in the way they see themselves and their relationships to schools. They begin to think of themselves as having options for controlling their lives and dealing with constraints that had seemed beyond their control. Mezirow[24] calls this result *perspective transformation,* a major reordering of reality and one's own possibilities. Personal problems are now seen to have their causes in public issues. Although the group's new awareness does not solve any problems, it opens the way for individual and collective action that may solve them. In America, the womens, civil rights, and gay peoples movements transformed perspectives of participants and opened the way to change. So far, there has not been a comparable grassroots transformation of teachers' perspectives.

At this point, staff have moved beyond sentiment to knowledge they can trust, but all their problems are still before them, waiting to be dealt with. The next step is to find and mount attacks on the particular issues that staff have identified as problems for them in their schools. In this part of the intervention, the clinical sociologist can take a more active role in formulating a campaign and bringing knowledge of educational sociology to bear. Still working outside of school hours, the group begins to plan its moves. The academic literature loses its terror, and group members explore it eagerly for ideas. It is a bit like a war; the group has to formulate objectives, scout the opposition, recruit allies and court neutrals, and learn to think both tactically and strategically about school reform.

Not surprisingly, the problems staff set out to solve tend to center around the generative themes of teaching. Teachers are at least as good as sociologists at smelling out contradictions in public schools, though they may use different vocabularies to describe what they find. The issues I identified in the first two sections of this chapter turn up time and again in one guise or another. School staff with transformed perspectives are ingenious at finding solutions to these problems that vary from setting to setting but have common elements. Among the commonalities are the following:

Empowerment: Giving teachers the technical means to reach personal and professional goals. Empowerment is sought in institutional governance, in relations with superiors and the district, in the classroom, in meetings with parents and outsiders, in a new willingness to seek further education for instrumental reasons.

Solidarity: Breaking down the jealousies, mutual indifference, and isolation that public schooling breeds. Teachers learn to communicate across role, status, and discipline boundaries and see one another as similarly troubled persons.

Development of insight: Staff come to see that the study of education and of their own school is a legitimate and necessary part of their teaching roles. They become more sensitive to the need for self-study and appraisal of their achievements.

Developing agendas: Staff realize that others will plan their work for them if they are not preempted by staff's own plans for conducting education.

Defining what is legitimate work and learning how to refuse work that is not legitimate: Transformed staff become very sensitive about work issues. They learn to guard instructional time and reduce time wasted in unfruitful activity.

Asking for and getting support: School people are submerged in a culture of silence; as they become critically aware, they cry out to others for help with their problems. Transformed staff go to school board meetings. They write letters to newspapers and seek opportunities to win the public to their side. They fight for greater control over what goes on in schools. They see unions and professional associations as machinery that can be mobilized to help them in their struggles.

Healing emotional wounds created by role strains in the workplace: Transformed staff are more nurturing, more sensitive to role conflicts and role strains, good at helping one another cope with the stresses of teaching. Transformed staff try to put out emotional fires before they spread. They learn ways to arm themselves against the hurts of teaching, and they console others who are wounded.

Increasing control: Critically aware staff are not afraid to increase their power. They want to exert more control over students, the curriculum, and the way education is conducted in their buildings, and they are willing to fight to lessen the power of outsiders.

In the problem-solving stage, staff readily learn ways to rationalize role re-sponsibilities. Some of them recognize a need for help and training in bureaucratic infighting. Others want help with methods for increasing their share of resources and want to be shown how to lobby, write grants, and participate in development and fund raising. Some staff become experts at using (and deflating) outside experts who are brought to their schools as consultants. Other staff people try to improve communication with parents and the community and help laypeople get a better understanding of what schools as institutions can and cannot be expected to achieve. One of the things staff usually wrestle with in groupwork is the meaning and limits of accountability. Aware staff want greater access to the sophisticated educational literature and help with interpreting and applying it. They want to experiment with new teaching methodologies, new modes of classroom organization, new curricula, new ways of grouping students. They want to be in control, they do not want assistance unless they ask for it; they want procedures that work, not speculations, and they do not want their schools damaged in the process. Because public schools are highly politicized, transformed staff necessarily learn to be skillful at the politics of education, from the national level to the classroom.

Transforming teachers in the way I have described does not solve any of the social problems that have been heaped on schools. This is immaterial; schools cannot possibly solve these problems. Perspective transformation for teachers does help teachers build walls around their work, focus on their work, study and understand it, and struggle to keep it from being undone by persons who would bury schools in controversy. Helping teachers to develop critical awareness is the most important step in enabling them to manage their complex professional role and get back to doing what they do best, educating children.

REFERENCES

1. Grant, G. (1988). *The world we created at Hamilton High*. Cambridge: Harvard University Press.
2. Grubb, W., & Lazerson, N. (1982). *Broken promises: How Americans fail their children*. New York: Basic Books.
3. Riesman, D. (1973). *The lonely crowd* (pp. 213–224). New Haven: Yale University Press.
4. Corwin, R. G. (1965). *A sociology of education* (pp. 217–265). New York: Appleton-Century-Crofts.
5. Bourdieu, P. (1977). Cultural reproduction and social reproduction. In J. Karabel & A. H. Halsey (Eds.), *Power and ideology in education* (pp. 487–511). New York: Oxford University Press.
6. Jackson, P. W. (1968). *Life in classrooms*. New York: Holt, Rinehart & Winston.
7. Coleman, J. S., Campbell, E. Q. *et al.* (1966). *Equality of educational opportunity*. Washington: U.S. Government Printing Office.
8. Jencks, C., Bartlett, S., *et al.* (1979). *Who gets ahead? The determinants of economic success in America*. New York: Basic Books.
9. Hurn, C. J. (1985). *The limits and possibilities of schooling: An introduction to the sociology of education* (2nd ed.). Boston: Allyn & Bacon.
10. Hughes, E. C. (1964). Good people and dirty work. In H. S. Becker (Ed.), *The other side: Perspectives on deviance* (pp. 23–36). New York: Basic Books.
11. Crick, F. (1988). *What mad pursuit: A personal view of science* (p. 96). New York: Basic Books.
12. Hughes, E. C. (1937). Institutional office and the person. *American Journal of Sociology, 43*, 404–407.
13. Merton, R. K. (1957). Bureaucratic structure and personality. In R. K. Merton, *Social theory and social structure* (p. 195). Glencoe, IL: Free Press.
14. Strauss, A. (1959). *Mirrors and masks: The search for identity* (p. 92). Glencoe, IL: Free Press.
15. Saunders, B. (1990). Assessment in clinical sociology. In J. G. Bruhn & H. M. Rebach (Eds.), *Handbook of clinical sociology*. New York: Plenum Press.
16. Argyris, C., & Schon, D. (1974). *Theory in practice: Increasing professional effectiveness*. San Francisco: Jossey-Bass.
17. Argyris, C., & Schon, D. (1978). *Organizational learning: A theory of action perspective*. Reading, MA: Addison-Wesley.
18. Marsick, V. J. (1988). Learning in the workplace: The case for reflectivity and critical reflectivity. *Adult Education Quarterly, 38*, 187–198.
19. Lincoln, Y. S. (1985). *Organizational theory and inquiry: The paradigm revolution*. Beverly Hills: Sage.

20. Carr, W., & Kemmis, S. (1983). *Becoming critical: Knowing through action research*. Victoria, Australia: Deakin University Press.
21. Kolb, D. (1984). *Experiential learning: Experience as the source of learning and development*. Englewood Cliffs, NJ: Prentice-Hall.
22. Freire, P. (1972). *Pedagogy of the oppressed*. New York: Herder and Herder.
23. Garfinkel, H. (1962). Common sense knowledge of social structures: The documentary method of interpretation in law and professional fact findings. In J. M. Scher (Ed.), *Theories of the mind* (pp. 689–712). New York: Free Press.
24. Mezirow, J. (1978). Perspective transformation. *Adult Education, 28*(2), 100–110.

PART IV

WORK WITH SPECIAL POPULATIONS

CHAPTER 19

Culture Adaptive Therapy

A Role for the Clinical Sociologist in a Mental Health Setting

JULIA A. MAYO

For the past several decades, American awareness of cultural diversity has increased, aided by the high visibility of many of the new ethnic groups. High visibility often defines ethnic difference. Skin color, hair texture, accented English, religion, and specialized food practices are among the more observable objective signs of cultural difference. The push to the "mainland" by the Puerto Ricans and the West Indians in the 1950s, the Black Liberation movement of the 1960s, the Vietnam War, the influx of Cuban, Korean, and Cambodian refugees during the 1970s, the sharp rise in college enrollment of Asian students in the 1980s, all have impacted on raising American consciousness of the diverse ways in which individuals and families may share the same geographic space yet maintain different social and cultural lifestyles. Incidents achieving nationwide television and newspaper attention within the past 2 years include the Howard Beach attack (a black youth killed by a white mob), and Bensonhurst (two Puerto Rican youths attacked in an Italian neighborhood). Both incidents occurred in New York City where "turf" is sharply delineated by ethnic not geographic boundaries. Spike Lee's 1989 movie, *Do the Right Thing* graphically portrays ethnic, racial, and cultural conflicts of blacks, Italians, and Asians sharing the same space.

I hope, in this chapter, to heighten awareness, influence attitudes, and to sharpen skills in professional practice with the diversity of cultural groups who turn to us for social and health care needs. Wohl[1] makes the accusation that "major works on the subject of cross-cultural psychotherapy and counseling, although they are

JULIA A. MAYO • Department of Psychiatry, St. Vincent's Hospital and Medical Center of New York, New York, New York 10011.

cornucopias of information about dealing with differences, fail to integrate their messages on cultural differences in psychotherapy with basic psychotherapy and therapy theory and practice" (p. 344). According to Wohl:

> There are special problems in doing cross-sub-cultural psychotherapy in the United States that are derivative of the tradition of racial, religious, ethnic and class prejudices and bigotry in the American society. Dealing clinically with people who are significantly different, can be difficult enough, but where difference between the groups represented in the therapeutic interaction include a history of mistrust, resentment, chauvinism conflict or hatred, a far more complicated and difficult situation prevails. (pp. 351–352).

The majority of individuals who utilize public mental health care services on an ambulatory basis can be found among the poor, the working class, and minorities of color. To understand dysfunctional behavior, one must understand the significance of the sociocultural contexts in which these people developed and live.[2–7]

This chapter presents a concept of psychosocial intervention techniques that are anchored in the sociocultural context of the patient. What I refer to as culture adaptive therapy accepts the premise that ethnic status of color and gender in America carries with it an inherent stress associated with the process of acculturation. The issue of unresolved conflict regarding the degree to which ethnic identity is or is not syntonic with self-identity is critical to the outcome of the therapeutic process.

Acculturation, or the process of becoming bicultural has to do with establishing an operative balance between how much of one's own culture one wishes to keep and the extent to which positive relations with the dominant culture are sought and supported. Integration on the other hand, although acknowledging value of minority status, accepts the reality of the dominant culture by seeking to meld with it.[8–11]

A major shortcoming of traditional clinical interventions based on medical and/or psychological models is failure to consider the acculturation pattern of the family of the ill person. Coping patterns in cultural groups have identifiable phases that reflect the course of illness, ascribed role, gender status, and specific attitudes toward money, work, food, sex, and nongroup individuals beyond their ethnic boundary. The work of McGoldrick et al.[12] stands as a classic in describing familial differences among ethnic groups.

Traditionally oriented health and welfare services in major urban areas are neither sufficient nor effective in the face of rapid social changes. The emotional disturbance of individuals creates social problems for them and their environment. Considerable skill is needed to differentiate between symptoms that reflect biopsychopathological processes needing medication—for example, schizophrenia or organic brain syndromes—and symptoms of psychosocial origin requiring interventions that include sociological concepts.[13–17]

The medical model of health care as a sole approach will not fit the needs of diverse populations. An understanding of the basic distrust of the medical system on the part of many immigrant groups is important. The culture adaptive model, an interventive approach that interprets signs and symptoms of illness within the patient's cultural context, may be a more effective and appropriate model. This approach will be described in more detail in the following pages.

A GENERAL VIEW OF THE PROBLEM

Goffman[25–27] wrote convincingly that sound explanations of social behavior are to be found in the social processes of culture, environment, norms, values, and statuses that comprise the basis of human group life. The way people respond to psychosocial influences has much to do with whether or not they become "sick" and the form, duration, and intensity of the dysfunction. The work of Kleinman[8] and Lin[9] in particular implicate social influences as associative if not causal variables in the epidemiology of psychiatric disorders. Disorders of role performance stem from the individual's role in the sociocultural system. Such disorder is best understood in the context of relationships with others who make up this person's life space and the social role to which the person is assigned.

Rosenhan[28] stated that "the risk of distorted perceptions is always present, since we are much more sensitive to an individual's behaviors and verbalizations than we are to the subtle contextual stimuli that often promote them" (p. 257).

Geertz[29] asserted that the definition of a situation resides in symbolic meaning and collective interpretation made by specific others within a cultural setting (pp. 412–452). Recent research on stress and its effects has shown ethnic variation in the perception of life stress. Ethnic groups such as Asians, Puerto Ricans, and Afro-Americans are populations at high risk for medical and psychiatric illnesses associated with stress. The influx of minority groups of color over the past 20 years has led to a marked need to understand how lifestyles and belief systems affect mental health status. Anxiety, a ubiquitous human experience, may be expressed as panic in a Caucasian, somatization in a West Indian, a nervous *ataque* in a Puerto Rican. Seeking psychiatric help is perceived as a stigma to many minority groups and many may turn to non-Western, nontraditional folk healing practices where the language of distress is culturally syntonic.[30–33]

When self-care fails, many working- and lower-class blacks, Hispanics, and Asians will seek out the local spiritualist, herbalist, faith healer, or minister for relief from unexplained pain, loss of appetite, fatigue, dizziness, insomnia, fears, and strange bodily sensations. This is often the second phase in a prolonged search for relief from psychiatric symptoms. The third phase is one of waiting to get well. This may be an extended period during which marked clinical deterioration occurs. Usually it is at this point that a relative may bring the individual to an emergency room of a hospital for the first medical evaluation. Hospitalization frequently is necessary. Hospitalization reinforces the patient's belief that he or she cannot be helped, is "bad" and/or has brought some shame to the family and must be locked away.[21–23]

Lower-class men who are black, Hispanic, or Asian, particularly those on a low hourly wage without health care benefits, adopt a "macho" attitude that it is a sign of weakness to go to a doctor for physical complaints. And it is unmanly to seek medical help for emotional pain. Many instead turn to drugs and/or alcohol and find entry into the health care system via substance abuse programs when they can function no longer.

This late admission to treatment may confound making a correct assessment, particularly if depression is masked by substance abuse. Duration and type of treatment may be prolonged because of the severity and chronicity of the illness by the time the person presents for treatment. If hospitalization is required, jobs may be lost or families separated especially if the mother is the one hospitalized.

Psychiatry places itself at major risk for failure when it tries to treat patients of diverse cultures with only its concept of Western medicine. Recent decades have seen religious and cultural oppression, ethnic wars, mass population displacements, and poverty among culturally diverse peoples in the world. These challenge mental health professionals in this country to develop a programmatic therapeutic approach that recognizes origins of psychopathology as rooted in the psychosocial problems of groups that are culturally divergent.

Third World and developing countries have experienced rapid technological changes that have left vast populations without skills to earn a living and consequently to maintain a sense of self-worth. Many newly arrived refugees from nonwhite countries bring with them culture-bound disorders. These disorders are unique to the specific culture such as being "possessed or hexed" for West Indians; El Susto, weakness, fatigue, loss of appetite for Mexicans; koro, impotence, panic, or fear that the penis in retracting for some rural Chinese; latah, an exaggerated startle reaction for South Sea island groups as well as problems of physical and mental health. The meaning of life experiences such as shame, rape, loss, stigma, suicide, and violence must be understood within the social context of the families and their explanatory models of reality. Attempts must be made to place the degree to which each family or individual claims an ethnic identity on a continuum. We must also recognize that many factors contribute to why some individuals feel less or more intense about their cultural identity.

In culture adaptive therapy, the goal is to help people make sense of role conflicts brought on by discrepancies between their ethnic subculture and the dominant culture. The definition of this situation must be reworked to enable individuals to create a boundary that reframes *their* culture to embrace that of the dominant sociopolitical structure without doing violence to either self or other. The sociological practitioner in a health care setting assists the minority persons to learn new interpersonal coping skills and skills in presentation of the self that enable them to navigate the social system with a feeling of integrity and competence. Development of cultural sensitivity is neglected in the area of training of practicing professionals. Even minority staff, including minority physicians, have had their sense of self-esteem damaged as a result of cultural insensitivity within the health care system.

SOCIAL ORIGINS OF DEPRESSION

A substantial number of depressed minority women are seen by nonmental health professionals and/or tend to make multiple visits to nonpsychiatric physicians for symptomatic complaints that are not identified or related to emotional or psychiatric conditions. Depression as a psychosocial state is intertwined with the values and aspirations that people acquire and with the nature of the situation in which they perform major social roles. Chronic depression may be related to a cognitive-cultural schema, a negative view of the self, the world, and the future. For minority women, it may be derived from early incorporation into the self of the experience of double inferior status—gender plus color. Although the psychobiological factors of depression remain the same, regardless of race or sex, sociocultural factors may require modifications of standard treatment approaches.

Schwartz and Wiggins[34] argue that the structure of psychosocial systems are being anchored in the meanings that regulate human behavior. They submit that structures serve a dual purpose: "They maintain the difference between the events internal to the system and the events external to the system, and they establish a correspondence between the events internal to the system and the events external to it." Meanings then become the schema by which present experiences can be related to the past with a degree of predictability. It is through the process of socialization that differentiation occurs. For Schwartz and Wiggins, the family system regulates and guides the experiences and activities of family members. Children are socialized into the family structure so that they to respond to cues of the parents and not to others.

> Structures establish and stabilize a correspondence between various psychological and social systems, thereby regulating the interactions among these systems. These can be person, family, community, culture, sub-culture, and society-nation systems, each of which interacts with the other systems in a continuous process. When system demands are not met, the system is in jeopardy of structural change and/or damage. The skillful physician will seek knowledge of the patient's family, community, cultural and social systems. The understanding gained from observing and learning together with the patient must be based on evidence presented by the patient and not inferred on the basis of prior assumptions.

Loss, separation, marital dispute, and physical illness among other significant events have been widely acknowledged to be associated with depression.[35–37] Clinical depression occurs with twice the frequency among females as among males. As a group, black females tend to score high on most life change events contributing to depressive syndromes. A patient's subjective meaning to life experience is significant for the course and outcome of psychiatric illness. For minority females, cognitive style, life event stressors, and ethnic sex role status place them at high risk for development and persistence of depressive disorders. Relatively few, however, are hospitalized specifically for depression. Fewer still are found in outpatient clinics for psychological management of their depression despite the availability of third-party payment for treatment and a broad and flexible fee scale in clinics today. Community surveys have found a high prevalence of patients with chronic depressive conditions not severe enough to require hospitalization but producing personal distress and impairments of interpersonal functioning.[38]

THE CLINICAL SOCIOLOGIST AS MICRO CHANGE AGENT

This section focuses on the distinctive contribution of the clinical sociologist as an interventionist in the assessment and treatment of individuals and families where depression, depressive equivalents, and/or minority status play a role. Attention is aimed at recognition of the distinctive psychosocial spectrum manifested by depressed minority females, and a consideration of ethnicity is relevant to increased understanding of the cognitive style of depressed minority persons. If the content of depression among individuals manifests itself according to their ethnic experience and subcultural characteristics, the ethnically depressed person may present a language of depression in body and behavior as well as in speech. They may not be immediately interpreted as depressive symptoms as shown by members of the dominant culture. Problems may arise in recognition of depressive equivalents. Also treatment problems may emerge resulting from a persistent focus on the daily psychopathologies of current life status by the depressed minority individual.

I would like to pause here to make it clear that the minority female is only one specific illustration of how culture adaptive therapy (CAT) can be applied. This approach is valid one for any individual whose cultural context is at variance with his/her inner or outer reality. Case vignettes are presented to illustrate the use of CAT. The section following discusses process and interventive techniques.

Case 1

Mrs. C. is 54 years old, black, married, and the mother of three. She was hospitalized for the third time over the past decade for unipolar depression with delusions. At the time of her last admission, she was acutely depressed. For several days prior to admission, she had shown symptoms of anxiety, withdrawal, and agoraphobia. The family reported she refused to eat, had major sleep disturbance, and expressed irrational fears regarding the safety of herself and family. She responded well to antidepressant medication and the therapeutic milieu of the inpatient psychiatric service. She was referred on discharge to a private psychiatrist for antidepressant medication and clinical management. She was referred to me some months later for individual therapy.

Personal and medical histories are significant. Mrs. C. had a radical mastectomy that required further surgery and chemotherapy secondary to further lymph node involvement. At the present time, she is no longer on chemotherapy but undergoes regular periodic checkups.

Mrs. C. was the third of eight siblings born to West Indian parents. The father was a minister of an Orthodox African Methodist Episcopal Church. Strong adherence to values of obedience, abstinence, strict sex role adherence, and duty were encouraged both by her culture and her family. After 2 years of college, Mrs. C. married her present husband 26 years ago when he returned from duty in the navy. The husband, a blue-collar worker and a good provider, is "not given much to talk with women." He enjoys a beer with the boys on the weekend. He doesn't understand his wife's depression. He says for a black man, he has done well. He has bought his own home, sent his three children to college, and supported his wife at home while his children grew up. He appeared hurt, angry, and confused by his wife's illness. Although overtly cooperative and verbally supportive in the treatment plans, he made it clear he thought therapy was "so much nonsense." He attended two sessions but generally refused to participate in joint sessions, stressing that his wife was the patient, not him.

Also significant at the time of beginning therapy were the following: the last and youngest child was leaving home permanently, emptying the nest and leaving Mrs. C. alone with her husband who was less than empathetic. In addition, Mrs. C. had been mugged in the past 6 months in her neighborhood, and the house had been broken into the year before. It had been up for sale for almost a year, and Mrs. C. feared that it would never be sold. Over the past decade the neighborhood had deteriorated to a slum with many transients. Most of her friends had moved away, and two had died over the past year. Other than part-time work as a teacher's aide, Mrs. C. had little to fill her day.

Treatment

Mrs. C. was seen weekly for individual sessions for a year. She arrived early, never missed a session, dressed meticulously, at first in earth tone appearing much like a little wren. There was a ritual in her manner in which she took off her coat, gloves, scarf, folded them neatly on the chair opposite, and sat with both feet on the floor and hands folded in her lap.

For several sessions, she focused on somatic complaints, fears of being trapped and dying in a house and neighborhood she had come to hate. She saw her future as a hopeless wait in which there was nothing left for her. Efforts to redirect her attention to simple but positive steps to redress the situation met with increased resistance. She had a strong need to convince me that she was hopeless. I did not argue the point but directed her attention to her formative years. I remarked what effort it must have taken to be so well groomed when she felt so bad. Mild but positive comments about certain personality traits such her perfectionistic tendencies, her rigid sense of duty, and her capacity to internalize feelings evoked a spontaneous running commentary about her early childhood. The next several sessions were used (1) to interrupt the obsessive litany of self-destructive thoughts, (2) to provide a vehicle for stimulating positive emotional flow through the reimaging of significant events of the past, (3) to gain insight into how to present values of her belief system was programmed. It was revealed that Mrs. C. was an excellent dressmaker. She was also an organizer who had been active in many school, community, and church affairs. She liked parties, roller skating, theater, and travel. She also believed she could do these things only while her children were young or currently with her husband's approval. There had been no sexual contact between her and her husband for months, feeding her belief that, as a woman, she was unattractive and because of the mastectomy, was even repulsive.

Increasingly, she expressed her feelings about being a black female. To her, this was the equivalent of being utterly powerless. The illogic went as follows: She had outlived her usefulness as a mother. Her husband used her for a housekeeper not a wife or partner. She had never supported herself and feared the competitive market. She had no money of her own and nothing in her own name. She projected anger and frustration against men (father and husband) for authoritative edicts that excluded her from the decision-making process and hence power. She railed against the double standard system that supported sex and race discrimination that prevented her from pursuing fulfillment of covert but sharply felt needs to be an individual in her own right.

For a period of time, no effort was made to correct this faulty thinking. Affective expression was encouraged. She began to verbalize her deep negative feelings toward significant others. This generated an angry phone call from her husband accusing me of stirring up trouble. These accusations were accepted as expressed. Mrs. C.'s background as a product of a minister's family was used to rekindle church activities and to help her to recall folk wisdom in coping with a number of life events and adversities. Here the interjection of humor, the use of imagery to evoke laughter at oneself, and the recollection of past ploys to outwit or outfox one's oppressor, be it father, husband, or "the system," were used to good advantage. As Mrs. C. was able to hear the way she created a faulty premise in her style of thinking, she began to test alternative ways to view herself and others with positive results.

Increasingly she was able to use people other than her husband and family as a basis for reality testing. Content of dreams shifted gradually to successful outcomes and a hope for the future.

Treatment terminated when Mr. and Mrs. C. sold their house. Mr. C. retired. Mrs. C. took driving lessons and got a license, an achievement she was proud of. The car was purchased in her name. The couple moved south to purchase a new home among old friends and relatives. On ending, she was able to state she could now understand that while her depressions, her sex, and her color were biologically determined, what she did with each of them was determined by herself.

The sociocultural context of many black females born prior to the generation of present-day "womens libbers" contained a heavy program of learned helplessness. The socially sanctional role ascribed to women in general was one of obedience and submission to father or husband. Where women are programmed to believe they cannot make major life change decisions in areas such as work/career, money, dress, or place of residence, it does not *occur* to these individuals that the "program" is wrong. Instead, they place the fault not within the system but victimlike, within themselves. Working-class and middle-class black women in particular were taught to believe they were fortunate to be protected from a racist world by a husband who provided for them at home, believed themselves incapable of independent action, denied and/or repressed anger and frustration, and became depressed. This case shows that culture adaptive therapy helps to clarify needs and rights of the individual in such a way as to become ego syntonic within the cultural context of the individual.

Case 2

Mrs. T. is a 33-year-old Japanese ballet dancer married to G., a white performer in a well-known dance troupe. She has been married 12 years living and working in the United States as a featured performer. She speaks English reasonably well.

Her husband G. was recently hospitalized for a manic episode aggravated by alcoholism. The couple most often worked together in the same troupe though not specifically as partners. G.'s current depression and bouts of alcohol had put his career in jeopardy. Ms. T., who used her maiden name professionally, sought help to understand her husband's illness and to cope with the stress and uncertainty of her own life that his illness created. Ms. T. reported she was seen by a male psychiatrist who was Filipino. She stopped because she did "not feel comfortable with him." She had heard about me from other families on the ward where her husband was hospitalized. On initial presentation, Ms. T. was somewhat ingratiating. She repeated over and over how thankful she was I agreed to see her. She presented as a small, lithe, attractive, simply dressed young woman whose figure and bearing connoted a dancer. Her low, soft-spoken tone made it difficult to hear her. She was anxious and apologetic. She didn't know what to do about her husband, his condition, herself—what did it all mean?

It had been raining, and Ms. T. sat there on the edge of the chair, wet and clutching her purse and umbrella. She spoke quickly as if not to waste my time. I spent the first part of the session assuring Ms. T. that I was pleased to meet with her and trying to get her comfortably situated so she could tell me her concerns. She made the interesting comment that she resented being referred to an Filipino physician. She found him cold, hostile, and condescending. I remarked it was unfortunate that it was assumed that because both were Asian, the referral would work out. Ms. T. alluded briefly to the problems of being Japanese and a woman in a world where all Japanese were blamed for the "war." The Philippines were occupied by Japan during World War II, and a great hostility continues to exist on the part of many Filipinos toward the Japanese. For her a referral to the Filipino psychiatrist was not a viable option.

The first few sessions were spent obtaining information about the current crisis, G.'s illness and how Ms. T. had been coping with it. G. Had a history of manic-depressive episodes that were precipitated by stopping his medication and abusing alcohol. Ms. T. was not aware of his history when she married him. She was doubly upset because she had alienated herself from her family by marrying G. and by pursuing a career as a dancer. G., who was British, had no family, except for a brother with whom he did not get along, and had no reliable friends. Both had used the dance troupe as a family. Ms. T. was frightened by "this kind of sickness." She "did not understand it." For long periods, G. would be well, then he would have either severe depression during which he would withdraw, could not dance, spoke of wanting to kill himself, and stayed alone in a dark room. In the spring, he would become extremely energetic, loud, argumentative, sleep 3 or 4 hours at night, spend more money than he had, and run up large charge account bills. Use of alcohol escalated, and he became verbally and physically abusive. He had been taken to the hospital by police because he had gotten into a fight in a bar. G. had told her did not want to take his lithium that controlled his episodes because it caused him put on a great deal of weight. He used alcohol and marijuana to calm himself down.

Some time was spent providing Ms. T. with information about manic-depressive illness and the kind of lifestyle needed to maintain a stable condition. During these early sessions, it became apparent that over and above the problem of G.'s illness, Ms. T. had some conflicts of her own and was in acute emotional distress. I suggested we spend a few sessions focusing on herself. She reported she was born in Tokyo. Her father died in the war, and she was raised by her maternal grandmother. Although loved and given good care, the grandmother had strong traditional values that included loyalty to family and "bringing no shame to family by unbecoming behavior." To marry a non-Japanese, to leave one's home as an unmarried woman, or to pursue a career as a dancer, all were behaviors that violated the code of honor and respect due one's family. To have married a man who abused alcohol and drugs and had a "mental problem" caused Ms. T. the kind of anguish she had never known possible. She cried that her whole life had blown up in her face. She felt she had made terrible mistakes, was being punished for defying her family. She felt she could never trust her judgment again. She felt she could not abandon him while he was ill. At the same time she felt she could no longer live with him.

Ms. T. came for sessions weekly. Over the next few months, we worked on issues of her feeling demoralized, powerless, ashamed, and sad. She complained of feeling confused about "Who I am, who I have become." Her most important beliefs had been challenged. Issues of ethnicity, sex, work, independence, sickness, duty, competence, and self-esteem were all discussed. Ms. T. thought she had become "Westernized." She thought she had acculturated to Western society enough that being Japanese would not be a problem. Under stress, however, she stated she felt very Japanese, very alienated from Western ways. The first physician she saw rejected her because of her race and sex. Her husband's sickness brought her shame and sadness. At the same time, her sense of loyalty and duty required she stand by him. She knew only dancing as a career and felt she must continue with this even if it meant leaving G. behind.

Ms. T. continued to see me on a weekly basis for almost a year. At the termination of therapy, she had arranged a legal separation from G. She continued to befriend him and was a major factor in helping him get continued medical care and housing. When G. lost his job with the dance troupe, she helped him set a studio to teach dance. Ms. T. herself went on to gain international recognition as a solo performer in the dance troupe. She began to reestablish contacts with her family in Japan and extended her circle of Japanese friends in the States. Ms. T. would return to see me after international tours. She reported the last time I saw her that she felt at "peace with who I am, free to be me as a dancer and comfortable with my Japanese ways of thinking."

In the case of Ms. T., under stress the value system incorporated at the earliest development period, that is, childhood, became manifest. She suffered under the belief that one has a duty not to bring "shame" to one's race by association with those who are "different" and/or "crazy." She felt guilty because she wanted to pursue her career independently and not serve as a caretaker for an ill spouse. Furthermore, it never occurred to Ms. T. that she was entitled to help in her own right, that her needs and feelings merited attention for herself as a person of unique identity. Culture adaptive techniques of empowering the individual to make self-choices and of redefining ego boundaries so as to embrace both cultures in a positive fashion were critical to the successful outcome of Ms. T.'s therapy.

THE SOCIOCULTURAL HYPOTHESIS

The choice of what treatment for which patient is a clinical decision of the utmost importance. All persons who present for treatment with problems of emotional pain want relief of pain and distress. The paths to that goal are many. Culture adaptive therapy is one that promises to be of special value to individuals with problems of acculturation.

From a clinical point of view, ethnicity is more than distinctiveness defined by race, religion, or national origin. Conscious and unconscious processes that fill a deep psychological need for security, identity, and continuity are involved. This process is transmitted in an emotional language within the family and finds support in like units within the community. McGoldrick displays an unusual sensitivity to issues of culture and ethnicity and their relevance to treatment in health care settings. She writes:

> Appreciation of cultural variability leads to a radically new conceptual model of clinical intervention.—Defining what response is adaptive in a given situation is not an easy task. It involves appreciation of the total context in which the behavior occurs. The therapist's role in such situations, as in all therapy, will be that of culture broker, helping family members to recognize their own ethnic values and to resolve the conflicts that involve out of different perceptions and experiences.[11] (p. 23)

In cultures (such as black, chicano, Puerto Rican) where value is placed on group identity and where the individual has been socialized for group cooperative tasks consistent with strong kinship ties, demonstrating a lack of competitiveness may be misinterpreted as passivity and/or dependence by a culturally naive therapist.

No individual is "culture free." A sensitive and well-trained clinician can be helpful to a person seeking change with problems relating to one's self. Culture adaptive therapy offers a deliberate effort to understand how the person's cultural and ethnic identity relates to problems in current psychosocial functioning. CAT provides an important piece that has been neglected in comprehensive diagnostic assessment and treatment.

EVALUATION OF THE CAT PATIENT

Criteria for selection should include the following: An assessment of

1. Motivation for change in one's self and/or environment.
2. Cultural adaptive mindedness—i.e., the ability to see a cultural relationship between internal distress and external problems.
3. The patient should be able to make himself/herself understood in English.
4. An "intact ego"—i.e., well grounded in reality, not psychotic, He/she should be able to tolerate some anxiety and some degree of frustration.
5. He/she should give evidence of the ability to maintain at least one consistent positive relationship over time. Individuals with major drug/alcohol abuse or antisocial behavior are not appropriate for culture adaptive therapy.
6. Some determination should be made regarding practical aspects of the treatment such as fees, work requirements, family attitudes, travel time for treatment, and other things that may impede the course of treatment.

The life history or case study method lends itself well to culture adaptive therapy. Complete data are rarely secured in one session and may be spread over several interviews. Data for later interpretation should be organized around the information the patient provides. A first step in making sense of this information is to formulate a tentative maladaptive, cultural schemata.

Schemata are broad, basic themes regarding oneself and one's relationships with others. These themes are formulated early in childhood based on parental messages regarding self and behavior. They form the *modus operandi* of one's life. The cognitive schemata may focus on issues within the culture related to role/identity; dependence/independence; separation/attachment, competition/control; self-esteem/inadequacy, or they may be situational/environmental in nature. Maladaptive schemata show as repetitive themes. The person returns over and over again to beliefs about self/other that interfere with healthy pleasurable functioning.

Stressful life events and environmental stress, although not specific for depression, have been greatest in lower-class minority females. Many factors place an individual at risk for depression, including absence of spouse. An intimate confiding relationship with a spouse has been found to be the most important protection against depression in the face of life stress. The female living alone in poverty is at high risk for a depressive reaction associated with loneliness, isolation, grief, loss of status, and loss of role. It is not difficult to understand how growing up black and female in America, a child would attempt to emulate white cultural standards projected as the "norm" by society. Unless specific effort is made to clarify this "norm," the child and later the adult would incorporate the negative self-concepts that could lead to chronically low self-esteem, decreased ability to cope with stress, and increased susceptibility to depression.

Once the particular maladaptive schemata have been identified and accepted by the person as being true for him/her, the intervention using cultural adaptive techniques may be applied. As with any well-trained therapist, the therapist must possess a knowledge of dyadic dynamics, psychodynamics, and systems theory as well as basic training in one's own discipline, that is, psychiatry, psychology, social work, clinical sociology, nursing. The therapist should be a mature person with sufficient healthy life experience of success, loss, intimacy, congruence, and conflict resolution in object relationships. The following points are relevant:

- Empathic listening. The therapist "witnesses" with the patient as the story unfolds.
- Make the therapeutic alliance a "we" experience. Encourage the person to share his/her sense of things.
- Make therapy an educational experience by giving new information and correcting old myths.
- Ignore material that is not relevant to the issue by reframing questions and making interpretations of the focal problem.
- Create a threshold of tolerance within the session that allows the patient to deal with painful material.
- Make an effective connection through culturally syntonic projection of sincerity, respect, nuance, gesture, and body language.
- Pay attention to potential countertransference issues stemming from the therapist's need to deny ethnicity, overcomply with requests, deny feelings of hostility or ambivalence, or succumb to feelings of pity or guilt.
- When the therapist is not familiar with the content of a specific culture, information must be freely sought and the meaning of the information to the patient clarified. It is around a clarification of cultural content that ethnocultural coalescence occurs.

TERMINATION OF THERAPY

Several sessions before a predetermined time for ending, the therapist and patient should review the reasons for the patient coming to therapy. The patient should be relatively free of clinical symptoms of stress or depression. He/she should be able to identify his/her basic recurrent conflict in terms of a sociocultural framework that the patient accepts as true for himself/herself. Some problem solving and conflict resolution techniques learned during the course of therapy should be reinforced. The patient should be able to identify factors in his/her real-life situation and within himself/herself that place him/her at risk for relapse. The patient should be able to leave the therapy with a heightened sense of self-esteem, a regained sense of inner control, and some confidence in his/her ability to function adequately in the world in which he lives.

CONCLUSIONS

Cross-cultural research has established that psychopathology is universal but that its manifestation differs from culture to culture. There are two basic ways to understand case definition and signs and symptoms of psychiatric disorder. One is the (etic) view that sees psychopathology as universal disease phenomena and sociocultural factors as pathoplastic. The alternative view and the one to which I subscribe is (emic) culture-specific and focuses on differences between cultures.

I submit that major problems exist in health care delivery systems where Western-oriented diagnostic labels and psychoanalytic techniques based on a white middle-class value system are applied to subcultures with the dominant group without adjusting for sociocultural differences in help-seeking behavior, illness behavior, and treatment response.

This chapter examines the role of the clinical sociologist in a mental health care setting. I suggest the problem of appropriate treatment for the minority individual results not so much from inappropriate goals of treatment but from inappropriate and/or inadequate methods related to failure to consider the sociocultural context within which the illness developed.

Sociologists offer a major contribution by providing a specific body of knowledge and expertise in understanding man as a unique social being within a distinctive social order. Whether or not a helping process is psychotherapeutic is less important than the sociocultural context within which interventions are made. Although it may seem self-evident that context as well as content must be evaluated, such a consideration is often the exception rather than the rule. Culture adaptive therapy does not change the basic definition of psychotherapy as a dyadic process of working through conflicts based on transference. What changes is the understanding of the sociocultural meaning of life experience within the clinical setting from a sociological perspective. In working with a person in whatever way he/she presents himself/herself, it may be essential for a positive outcome to use culture adaptive interventions I have described in the therapeutic process. Clinical sociology provides evidence for a valid practice where culture adaptive therapy allows a rational and different conceptualization of transference that makes possible effective treatment of culturally diverse individuals.

REFERENCES

1. Wohl, J. (1989). Integration of cultural awareness into psychotherapy. *American Journal of Psychotherapy, 3,* 343–355.
2. Bell Norman, W., & Spiegel, J. P. (1986). Social psychiatry: Vagries of a term. *Archives of General Psychiatry, 14,* 337–345.
3. Brown, G., & Harris, T. (1978). *Social origins of depression: A study of psychiatric disorders in women.* London: Tavistock.
4. Finlay-Jones, R., Brown, G. W., & Duncan-Jones, P. *et al.* (1980). Depression and anxiety in the community: Replicating the diagnosis of a case. *Psychological Medicine, 10,* 445–454.
5. Black, C. M., & Enos, R. (1980). Sociological precedents and contributions to the understanding and facilitation of individual behavior change: The case for counseling sociology. *Journal of Sociology and Social Welfare, 7,* 648–664.
6. Foulks, E. (1980). The concept of culture in psychiatric residency education. *American Journal of Psychiatry, 137,* 7.
7. Griffith, E. E. H. (1988). Psychiatry and culture. In J. Talbot, R. Hales, & S. Yudofsky (Eds.), *American psychiatric press, textbook of psychiatry.* Washington, DC: APA Press.

8. Kleinman, A., Eisenberg, L., & Good, B. (1978). Culture, illness and cure. *Annals of Internal Medicine, 88*, 251–258.
9. Lin, K. M. (1986). Ethnicity and psychopharmacology. *Culture, Medicine and Psychiatry, 10*, 151–165.
10. Moffic, H., Kendrick, E. *et al.* (1987). Education in cultural psychiatry in the United States. *Transcultural Psychiatric Research Review, 24*, 167–187.
11. McGoldrick, M., Pearce, J., & Giordano, J. (1982). *Ethnicity and family therapy.* New York: The Guilford Press.
12. O'Connell, R. A., Mayo, J. A., Eng, L. K. *et al.* (1985). Social support and long-term lithium outcome. *British Journal of Psychiatry, 147*, 272–275.
13. Mayo, J. A. (1966). What is the social in social psychiatry? *Archives of General Psychiatry, 14*, 449–455.
14. Mayo, J. A. (1979). Marital therapy with manic-depressive patients treated with lithium. *Comprehensive Psychiatry, 20*, 419–426.
15. Adebimpe, V. R. (1984). Overview: American blacks and psychiatry. *Transcultural Psychiatric Research Review, 21*, 81–138, 279–285.
16. Adebimpe, V. R., Hedlund, J. L., Cho, D. W., & Wood, J. B. (1982). Symptomatology of depression in black and white patients. *Journal of the National Medical Association, 74*, 185–190.
17. Blumer, H. (1969). *Symbolic interaction, perspective and method.* Englewood Cliffs, NJ: Prentice-Hall.
18. Ritzer, G. (1988). *Contemporary sociological theory* (2nd ed.). New York: Knopf.
19. Rochbertq-Halton, E. (1986). *Meaning and modernity: Social theory in the pragmatic attitude.* Chicago: University of Chicago Press.
20. Kaptchuck, T., & Croucher, M. (1987). *The healing arts.* New York: Summit Books.
21. Kleinman, A. (1983). The cultural meanings and social use of illness. *Journal of Family Practice, 16*, 539–545.
22. Eisenberg, L. (1977). Disease and illness: Distinctions between professional and popular ideas of sickness. *Culture, Medicine and Psychiatry, 1*, 1–23.
23. Tseng, W-S., & McDermott, J. F. (1981). *Culture, mind and therapy, An introduction to cultural Psychiatry.* New York: Brunner/Mazel.
24. Goffman, E. (1959). *The presentation of self in every day life.* Garden City, NY: Doubleday Anchor.
25. Goffman, E. (1961). *Asylums.* Garden City, NY: Doubleday Anchor.
26. Goffman, E. (1963). *Stigma: Notes on and management of spoiled identity.* Englewood Cliffs, NJ: Prentice-Hall.
27. Rosenhan, D. (1979). On being sane in an insane place. *Science, 197*, 250.
28. Geertz, C. (1973). *The interpretation of cultures.* New York: Basic Books (pp. 412–453).
29. Falicov, C. J. (1982). Mexican families. In M. McGoldrick, J. Pearce, & J. Giordano (Eds.), *Ethnicity and family therapy* (pp. 134–163). New York: The Guilford Press.
30. Rubenstein, H., & Block, M. H. (1982). *Things that matter: Influences on helping relationships.* New York: Macmillan.
31. Toombs, S. K. (1987). The meaning of illness: A phenomenological approach to the physician–patient relationship. *Journal of Medical Philosophy, 12*, 219–240.
32. Mechanic, D. (1978). Effects of psychological distress on perceptions of physical health and utilization of medical and psychiatric facilities. *Journal of Human Stress, 4*, 26–32.
33. Schwartz, M. A., Wiggins, O. P. (1986). Systems and the structuring of meaning: Contributions to a biopsychosocial medicine. *American Journal of Psychiatry, 143*, 1213–1221.
34. Lloyd, C. (1980). Life events and depressive disorder reviewed. Events as predisposing factors. *Archives of General Psychiatry, 37*, 529–535.
35. Beck, A., Bush, A., Shaw, B., & Emery, G. (1979). *Cognitive therapy of depression.* New York: The Guilford Press.
36. Ellis, A. (1979). Rational-emotive therapy. In. I. Corsini (Ed.), *Current psychotherapies* (2nd ed.). Itasca, IL: F. E. Peacock.
37. Karasu, B. (1984). Outcome research in psychosocial therapy. *The Psychiatric therapies* (American Psychiatric Association Commission on Psychiatric Therapies). Washington, DC: American Psychiatric Association.
38. Laborsky, L. (1984). *The Principles of psychoanalytic therapy.* New York: Basic Books.

CHAPTER 20

Empowering Women

A Clinical Sociology Model for Working with Women in Groups

JANET MANCINI BILLSON AND ESTELLE DISCH

OVERVIEW

In this chapter, we present ways of using clinical sociology and feminism to help women find support, sanity, growth, and empowerment through participation in groups. We examine the ways in which a sociologically oriented group process functions to help group members see personal problems as reflections of social/ structural issues, leading women to insight, empowerment, and personal growth.

Cultural, psychological, and physiological characteristics that make working with women distinct from working with men are explored. Strategies for facilitating women's groups are outlined for trained group leaders who want to create a positive therapeutic and growth environment for women. Finally, client rights and professional ethics relating to sociological practice with women are discussed.

This model and the clinical materials presented emerge from our work in a variety of groups: women's support and personal growth groups; a 2-year health group for women; a short-term group for women with breast cancer; and 1-day workshops for women who have health problems, or who have been sexually abused by their psychotherapists.*

* We use the term *therapeutic groups* or *women's groups* interchangeably and to include what are commonly called support groups, personal growth groups, or therapy groups. Not all groups are "group therapy," which implies a psychological or psychoanalytical approach; but we assume that well-facilitated groups are therapeutic. We are two white, professional women who have facilitated groups for the past 15 years. Our experience has primarily been with homogeneous groups of white, middle-income women,

JANET MANCINI BILLSON • Department of Sociology and Women's Studies, Rhode Island College, Providence, Rhode Island 02908. **ESTELLE DISCH** • Department of Sociology, University of Massachusetts, Boston, Massachusetts 02125-3993.

A TERRIBLE AND MAGNIFICENT LESSON

C. Wright Mills[1] argued that we become aware of our "own chances in life only by becoming aware of those of all individuals in [our] circumstances" (p. 5). This is the sociological logic for the existence of therapeutic groups, consciousness-raising groups, or social movements. Mills warned that expanding awareness beyond our own lives can be both a terrible and a magnificent lesson. Yet the broad range of human behaviors and emotions we encounter is counterbalanced by the opportunity for ameliorating many problems facing women today.

Because we believe that good therapy leads to empowerment and liberation from social structural constraints, we emphasize the intricate relationship between woman as individual and woman as member of society. Mills eloquently described the intersection of individual and society:

> In the welter of their daily experience . . . the framework of modern society is sought, and within the framework the psychologies of a variety of men and women are formulated. By such means, the personal uneasiness of individuals is focused upon explicit troubles and the indifference of publics is transformed into involvement with public issues.* (p. 5)

Mills urged that the individual be analyzed within the context of a particular societal structure, social order, or historical place, and that we ask specifically:

> What varieties of men and women now prevail in this society and in this period? . . . In what ways are they selected and formed, liberated and repressed, made sensitive and blunted? (p. 7)

By asking these questions for ourselves and with our clients, we come closer to grasping the meaning of our experiences as individuals located within a socio-cultural and historical context. The task of social science is to analyze the interplay between private troubles and public issues, Mills concludes. Similarly, we believe the task of the practicing sociologist is to bring that sociological analysis and theoretical framework into direct work with individuals in therapeutic settings.† We pay

---

including lesbian women. We are not prepared to generalize our conclusions beyond the white contexts in which we have done most of our clinical work. The same central issues and principles of group facilitation have applied when women of color have participated in the groups. However, groups comprised mainly of women of color might respond more positively to variations in facilitation or emphasize some issues more than others.

    Although we have not co-led a women's group, we have compared notes and have co-led in other contexts.

* Mills observed: "Perhaps the most fruitful distinction with which the sociological imagination works is between the 'personal troubles of milieu' and the 'public issues of social structure.' *Troubles* occur within the character of the individual and within the range of his immediate relations with others; they have to do with his self and with those limited areas of social life of which he is directly and personally aware. . . A trouble is a private matter: values cherished by an individual are felt by him to be threatened (p. 8).

    "*Issues* have to do with matters that transcend these local environments of the individual and the range of his inner life. . . . An issue is a public matter: some value cherished by publics is felt to be threatened" (p. 8).

† Our emphasis here is on working with women in groups, but the framework applies to working with men and with women individually.

special attention to the incorporation of sociological concepts into the therapeutic process: lifestyle, status, role expectations, role conflict, definition of the situation, stereotyping and labeling, deviance, isolation, scapegoating, victimization, and self-concept, to mention just a few.

MICROCOSM: THE HEALING CAPACITY OF THE GROUP

How does a women's group work for its members? The group is a microcosm of the society in which each participant lives, as Slater[2] has suggested. The scars of such socialization errors as gender stereotyping, the constraints on opportunity and creativity built into a particular social system, the faulty logic that strips women of their ability to establish meaningful, prosperous lives, the victimization and abuse that women suffer as children and adults, the frustrations of failed relationships—all are brought into the group setting. Here they can be discussed, analyzed, felt, shared—"processed"—in a relatively safe, comfortable, nonjudgmental, and warm environment. Participants learn that others wear similar scars and that they are not entirely alone. Together they work toward possible solutions and fresh insights; together they celebrate strengths.[3] As women realize they are not alone or "crazy" for feeling distressed, they learn not to blame themselves for injustices and abuses they have suffered.

The support or personal growth group serves many functions that contribute to the healing capacity of the group. For example, a group:

- Helps women reconceptualize issues and collectively address the oppression of women as it affects group members
- Serves as an information source for women who share a common problem
- Engenders hope and reduces a sense of isolation
- Affords opportunities to develop a more realistic sense of strengths and resources, outside of the context of dependency role relationships
- Enables women to broaden their repertoire of coping skills
- Provides a place to practice or rehearse new skills or behaviors
- Provides an opportunity for women to ventilate feelings
- Supports women during attitude, value, or behavioral change
- Helps women learn how to utilize effectively other support systems including those that are sensitive to women's issues
- Facilitates the development of new friendships and meaningful bonds with other women
- Affords opportunities to express feelings that are difficult to explore with significant others
- Offers both positive and negative models of behavior, which women can evaluate in light of their own needs, personality, etc.
- Enables women to receive constructive, nonthreatening feedback about their interaction style in groups.

These functions contribute to linking women to other women so that they become more aware of how their own troubles are enmeshed in social contexts. They also help women move from analysis and abstraction to behavioral changes. Women often experience impressive gains in confidence and self-esteem in a group setting where they are not tied into dependency role relationships that define them as inferior. By working through difficult feelings toward (and with) other group members and the therapist, women begin to feel stronger and more authentic.

But, because these functions are present in well-facilitated groups for either gender, it is important to examine how working with *women* in groups is different from working with men.

BLUEPRINTS AND IMPRINTS: THE SOCIOLOGICAL DIMENSION

Social architectures are blueprinted differently for females and males. Working successfully with women in groups requires that we attend to the uniqueness of women generated by these blueprints.[4] Cross-cultural differences are just as important as within-cultural variations; we include selected cross-cultural references in the bibliography for this reason.

Status

In most societies, women have traditionally been lower in status than men; this has left a legacy of assumptions that men are superior to women, more powerful, more knowledgeable, and therefore should have more rights.[5] These beliefs have been held both by women and men. The female history of gender oppression, exploitation, and victimization leaves a cultural imprint of low self-esteem and lack of confidence: a cultural inferiority complex.[6]

The literature on reactions to minority status and oppression indicates that women share, to some extent, reactions seen among other oppressed/enslaved groups: passivity, submission, passive aggression, withdrawal, escapism, depression, and, less frequently, rebellion.[7,8] Women with multiple low statuses are in multiple jeopardy; examples include lesbian women, poor black women, and members of certain religious minorities.[9]

Roles

Women have been homebound and childbound in most societies.[10-15] This has left a legacy of assumptions about the "proper place" of women: the domestic sphere.[16-19] Men are defined as "naturally" and legitimately belonging in the public sphere of interesting or well-paying work outside the home. Women who venture outside the domestic sphere are viewed as interlopers, intruders, or masculinized upstarts.[20,21] (Black women, who have a long history of working outside the home, have often been employed in white people's homes.) This dichotomy is most striking in industrial and postindustrial societies. Although the pattern is changing, the history of economic discrimination in the workplace reinforces the concept of woman as homemaker/mother, not woman as professional.[22-24]

The rigidity of stereotypical roles depicting women as legitimately functioning only in domestic production roles has left a cultural imprint of guilt, confusion, role conflict and strain, shaky confidence, fear of success, and fear of failure.[25,26] Women set their sights too low, waiver on making decisions, and internalize the barriers to success and achievement that societal blueprints have delineated for them.[27]

Values

Women traditionally have been raised to value nurturance, kindness, patience, being "nice," not making waves, being attractive, supportive, caring, understanding, tolerant, and responsible to and for others. This socialization blueprint can make it difficult for women to be confrontive or demanding; to feel comfortable in choosing to take care of self first; or to be honest and forthright.[28]

The veneer of sociability and "niceness" leaves women open to slipping too easily into the role of victim in response to physical or verbal abuse. Caretaking values inculcated through a complex socialization process justify understanding and forgiveness rather than personal rights and dignity. The female imperative leaves a cultural imprint of inauthenticity. The people-pleasing mandate often twists into aggressive behavior when a woman is understanding and patient too long in the face of abusive behavior, then suddenly displays an outburst of temper, "bitchiness," or violence—and feels guilty.[29]

The differential socialization of women has implications for group work. The therapist should take care not to overwhelm clients with her own status (degrees, etc.); be cognizant that she serves as a role model for other women; support assertive and confrontive behavior; support breaking the veneer of niceness; be authentic herself; and expand each client's options through referrals to other professionals as warranted.

A CELEBRATION OF DIFFERENCE: THE PSYCHOLOGICAL DIMENSION

Historically, women and men have been perceived in all cultures as having certain fundamentally different traits, needs, and skills. Unfortunately for women, their unique characteristics and talents have often been devalued or defined negatively. Traditional psychology and psychiatry reflected the biases of male-dominated patriarchal society in defining mental health: "Male" characteristics such as autonomy, independence, emotional control, objectivity, self-reliance, and logic were the key constituents of good mental health.[30] Opposite "female" traits such as dependency, emotional expressiveness, and intuitiveness were defined as signs of mental weakness or even disorder.[31,32] Robb cites Irene Stiver:

> According to the theory by which they were supposed to practice, autonomy and separation were the acme of human development, and psychotherapists were supposed to help their patients ascend a pinnacle of self-reliance.[33]

The last two decades have seen a paradigmatic shift away from the male-oriented psychology of self toward a more balanced psychology of relationship and connection.[33–35] This shift has been spurred by the writings of Jean Baker Miller,[36] Nancy Chodorow,[37] Carol Gilligan,[38] Belenky *et al.*,[39] and other feminist theorists who do not equate male/female differences with male superiority/female inferiority. The "new psychology of women" contends that women are "quite validly seeking something more complete than autonomy as it is defined for men, a fuller not lesser ability to encompass relationships to others, simultaneously with the fullest development of oneself."[33,36,40] Connection, caring, relationship, cooperation, collaboration, and bonding are concepts that figure prominently in a normal woman's identity. Whereas in the past, these same concepts would have been expressed in male psychiatric terminology as dependency needs, merging, manipulation, fusion, identify diffusion, or weak ego boundaries, now they are defined as constructive, healthy elements of the human psyche for both women and men.

Freudian theories of female identity formation that centered on penis envy and genital deficiency have been replaced with new models that emphasize differential socialization, the complexity of mother–daughter relationships, and the female capacity for empathy. Girls and women thrive in relationships: "for women the apex of development is to weave themselves zestfully into a web of strong relationships that they experience as empowering, activating, honest, and close."[33] At the heart of the psychology of women now lie "intersubjectivity" and "mutual empathy," rather than the double damnations of deficiency and dependency.

The dynamics of women's groups thrive because of these belatedly celebrated female capacities for nurturance, cooperation, and empathy. Young-Eisendrath and Wiedemann[41] refer to this as the "cooperative assumption" that dominates women's interaction.

A DOUBLE-EDGED SWORD: THE PHYSIOLOGICAL DIMENSION

The physiological functions that are the hallmark of femaleness—menses, childbearing, lactation—constitute a double-edged sword that helps determine a woman's life chances, her sexuality, and her identity.[42] Both pain and pleasure emanate from a complex physical self that we sometimes cannot trust.

The Biological Clock

Female physiology places pressure on women to have children and to have them sooner than is essential for men. In an era of technologically feasible reproductive choice, the ability to conceive and bear children often creates role conflict and identify confusion. "Marriage and family" compete with educational and occupational advancement, especially for middle-class women with significant career options. For lower-income women, especially urban women of color, early pregnancy often forecloses opportunities for both emotional and educational/career growth.

Because women traditionally have borne the cultural responsibility for perpetuating the species, socializing children, and caring for the sick and elderly, resistance to that pressure can alienate women from family and friends. Yet, employers hold back on promotion, comparable pay, and unique opportunities for growth because as women move into careers in their 20s and 30s, it is anticipated that they will also be more likely than men to move out of them. This double bind creates excruciating conflict and blocked opportunities for some women.

Cyclical Nature of Female Physiology

Men do not exhibit the same identifiable and regular cycle of menstruation (and menopause) that contributes to self and cultural perception of women as flighty, erratic, bitchy, or unreliable. If a man is perceived as being emotional or out of control, it is defined as an individual aberration, rather than as a hormonal/gender-specific "curse."

Beyond the social impact of menstruation are the physical symptoms of pain or discomfort that can become debilitating for some women. Some experience depression and irritability prior to menstruation, a pattern now identified as PMS (Premenstrual Syndrome). These physical and emotional symptoms can affect a woman's general sense of well-being, relationships with others, energy level, and ability to concentrate. Many PMS patients report that their doctors fail to take their complaints seriously.

Reproductive Disorders

Women suffer more than men through their 20s, 30s, 40s, and 50s from both minor and serious difficulties with the reproductive system. This is a biological penalty for the privilege of being the sex that is capable of bearing children. Among women who come to support groups, we find a high incidence of histories of breast lumps, irregular cycles, ovarian tumors or cysts, fibroids, PMS, hysterectomy, mismanagement of estrogen replacement therapy, and other gynecological problems. Women also suffer more than men from hypoglycemia, anemia, and thyroid disorder, which are often undiagnosed.

Older women often experience embarrassing symptoms of menopause, such as hot flashes or sweats (which lower their public confidence) or depression. This occurs early for women who have hysterectomies resulting in "surgical menopause." The cessation of ability to have children, along with reproductive disorders that result in infertility, can have enormous repercussions for a woman's identity and self-image in a society that defines being female in terms of being a mother.

Reproductive Freedom

The absence of safe, noninterfering birth control without threat of serious side effects restricts women's choices regarding the timing and number of children they will have, if any, and the nature of heterosexual encounters. Gynecological problems like minor infections also interfere with free sexual expression and gratification.

SOCIODIAGNOSIS: THE FOCUS OF GROUP WORK

Now that we have examined briefly the general way therapeutic groups work and how working with women implies attending to certain characteristics that tend to distinguish them from men, we can discuss the kinds of specific issues women bring to the groups we facilitate. The therapist or group leader who is operating from a sociological *perspective learns to recognize the personal troubles that women bring to the group as part of a broader context of issues facing all women. The most common are:

Transitional issues
  Separation, divorce, marriage
  Illness
  Moving
  Death of loved one
  Children leaving home
  Educational, career change

Interpersonal issues
  Discord in adult intimate relationships
  Discord with children
  Discord with parents
  Discord in workplace

Social isolation issues
  Rejection
  Inability to connect with intimates
  Lack or loss of friends
  Severed ties with family
  Lack of integration into community
  Adjusting to change in employment status
  Religious shifts

Social structural issues
  Restrictive gender roles
  Gender stereotypes
  Homophobia
  Poverty, inadequate housing
  Literacy, education deficits
  Language barriers
  Lack of skills
  Various discriminations
  Unemployment, underemployment

Identity issues
  Role conflict
  Identity confusion
  Gender exploration
  Sexual identity
  Coming out as a lesbian
  Adaptation to role shifts
  Professional self-concept
  Head of household
  Severe dependency on others
  Love/sex addiction
  Labeling by self and others

Abuse issues
  Incest
  Rape (including marital and date rape)
  Molestation
  Other physical assault
  Verbal abuse
  Sexual harassment
  Medical malpractice and inattention
  Sexual malpractice by therapist, other
    professionals

Health issues
  Pregnancy, childbirth
  Miscarriage, abortion
  Menarche, menopause
  Gynecological disease and surgery
  Sexually transmitted disease, including
    AIDS and high AIDS risk

  Cancer
  PMS
  Alcohol abuse
  Substance abuse
  Other health problems

These lists of issues are not exhaustive, but they can be used as checklists for new clients: Does the woman have issues under several categories, or several issues in one category? What private troubles are present in her life? What social issues are reflected? Which therapeutic issues and strategies will be relevant for her growth?

Women sometimes share more public issues, such as discrimination, before they talk about more personal issues, such as abortion or incest. It is useful to engage group members in identifying the issues they share in common and how they intertwine. Rejection by significant others, either as children or adults, contributes to low self-esteem and even self-hatred. Feelings of anger, inadequacy, failure, and guilt run pervasively through all these issues. Guiding each client toward improved self-esteem is a key to their successful resolution.

FROM DIAGNOSIS TO PRESCRIPTION: SOME GUIDING PRINCIPLES

What basic principles guide sociological practice with women? Some of the issues women bring to groups cannot be changed, and must, instead, be grieved: a childhood incest experience, the death of a spouse or parent, for example. Other issues are somewhat amenable to change through participation in a group: Discord with significant others might be lessened by modifications in a woman's perceptions and behaviors that occur as a result of her work in the group.* In either case, if the facilitator proceeds with the following principles in mind, the woman's ability to *cope* with her issues will be enhanced. Her self-esteem, sense of personal power, flexibility, and creativity in handling issues will grow. These principles emerge from our discussion of the ways in which women are unique.

Empowerment

It is critical for women to become aware of the power available to them and to expand their perception and practice of power. Rape, incest, prejudice, verbal abuse, isolation, poverty, etc., all contribute to a woman's definition of self as powerless.[43] In order to become empowered, women must experience at least the following liberations.

Liberation from Dependency

Most of our clients have been socialized into economic and/or emotional dependency on men. By moving directly from dependency on father to dependency on "Mr. Right," they miss the opportunity to become autonomous persons. If they

---

* We find that a woman may join a support group because of stressful family dynamics resulting from problematic behavior of her partner (alcohol or substance abuse, for example) or her child (school failure or delinquency, for example). In such cases, the woman clearly cannot "fix" the problem experienced by a significant other; the group offers support, and we make referrals for family therapy or individual treatment for others as appropriate.

do not feel independent or are not economically independent of males, they are more susceptible to abusive relationships. (Even a son can take on the role of the abusive, dominant male upon whom his mother depends).

The decision to remain single flies in the face of societal expectations.[44–46] Some women spend large portions of their lives in abusive or dissatisfying relationships because of their fear of being alone or because of limited economic resources, or both. And some lesbians, allegedly "free" of men, transfer their deep dependency needs to women partners and find themselves equally "hooked" on relationships that do not meet their needs.

EXAMPLE: Judy has been living with Steve for several years. She is in school; he contributes to her support. Every Friday she gets sick, spending the weekend in bed. Eventually she realizes that her illness is a way to avoid having contact with Steve; she is tired of his constant demands for sex and his lack of sensitivity to her needs. With the support of the group she breaks away and finds a group living situation with other women. As soon as she moves out, her weekend sickness disappears. Shortly thereafter, she realizes she is more attracted to women than to men and she starts to come out as a lesbian.

Liberation from Full-Time Nurturing Roles

The vast majority of our clients have been socialized into nurturance of others, which includes caretaking, providing a buffer between other people, protecting people's feelings, protecting children from male abuse and violence, mediating conflict, and so forth. This can rob others of authentic relationships and sets the woman up to be the one who gives rather than receives nurturance. Women are keepers of the culture and keepers of the peace, which contributes to high levels of burnout and stress. Some feel responsible for solving major social problems, not realizing that this aspiration, like solving conflict in the home, is incredibly stressful.

EXAMPLE: Anna had a sexual relationship with her therapist for several years during so-called psychotherapy. She always thought that the therapist would leave his wife and marry her. One day he told her that he could not do that and would not see her anymore. With the support of a workshop for survivors of sexual malpractice, Anna was helped to see that she had not only been badly hurt but deserved some justice. Her stance was to blame herself for "letting it happen," rather than to blame the therapist for unethical practice. Although still ambivalent about "hurting" him and making a "mess" of his life, she began to see that her impulse to protect him meant she was placing his needs above hers. After a few months of postworkshop support, she decided to file a complaint against him.

Liberation from Passivity and Inertia

Women have been taught that they should be patient, calm, loving, kind, tolerant, receptive to other's ideas, and accepting. Other people (usually older, male, or in authority) make things happen. If a woman attempts to be assertive, her lack of passivity may alienate or frustrate those around her. She is impertinent, uppity, weird, or even "sick." She is assumed to be naturally passive—deviations from that role are met with abuse, criticism, or disdain.

In order to become empowered, a woman must be able to perceive herself as the one who can make things happen, at both the personal level and at the social system level. She needs help in becoming unique and self-determining. Politicization is integral to this process.

Most of our clients have had to overcome major tendencies toward letting others take charge. Our work with women focuses on helping them identify actions they might like to take and muster the courage to do so.

EXAMPLE: Donna had wanted to go to art school for years. Her father thought it was "a crazy idea" because art is not a lucrative career. Her mother had no opinion but tried to keep Donna and her father from fighting over the subject. Donna's internalization of her parents' attitudes left her immobilized. With the support of a group, she became aware of how much she really wanted to be an artist. Gradually she confronted her fear of her father and grieved the reality that he would not support her choice. She found a way to go to school and work part-time, overcoming the inertia created by her need to make her parents happy.

Liberation from Victimization

Liberation from victimization implies being able to feel actively in control of one's life and free from the paralyzing fear associated with various forms of abuse. Force or the threat of force is especially debilitating for women who live in relationships marked by domestic violence, but verbal and psychological abuse are also disempowering. Women who suffered abuse as children may find it difficult to avoid abusive relationships as adults.

EXAMPLE: Mary was a victim of incest with her grandfather and emotional and physical abuse from her parents as a child. When she was a toddler, Mary's father stuck her head in the toilet and flushed it. Her mother threatened to drown Mary and her siblings for disobedience. After 20 years of marriage to a violent and angry man who rejected and beat her, Mary joined a religious group that offered marital harmony. The group preached submission and compliance with her husband's wishes. Mary became suicidal, sought counseling, and decided to divorce her abusive husband. The church officially shunned her, put her on trial, and forbade her daughters to look on their mother's face: She was a "sinner," their father a "saint." Her only path out of victimization was to give up her marriage, children, religion, and community. Mary joined a support group during the transitional period for help with grieving and rebuilding a meaningful network of nonabusive relationships. Her goal, to "become a human being," clearly expressed the extent to which victimization had stripped her of a clear and positive sense of identity.

Connecting/Reconnecting

Positive affiliations and connectedness are critical to well-being for all humans. Women have often established destructive and alienating relationships with men because of unresolved issues that led them to seek men who will punish them.[47] Connections to other women may be attenuated or guilt-ridden.[48] It is important for women to reassess relationships with significant others and reconstruct them in ways that do not involve abuse and overdependency—or to create new positive relationships. Social isolation on all levels must be addressed. The practicing sociologist is aware of the importance of integration into social networks for the maintenance of good mental health.

EXAMPLE: Marge was sexually abused by her father as a child and oriented all her energy toward abusive men as an adult. Her mother was also abused and offered little support or protection to Marge and her siblings. Marge's image of herself as a "sex object" was so pervasive that she could barely imagine other possibilities for herself. She had few women friends and trusted none to know what she was feeling. She was single-parenting a male child who hit her. On the recommendation of her son's guidance counselor, Marge skeptically joined a women's support and therapy group. The group leader helped her realize that she deflected all support, making very little contact with the other women. She generally seemed to devalue herself and others in the group. As she slowly discovered the pain she suffered as a child, she began to make better bonds with women in the group and to accept their support (several others had been abused as well). Slowly she developed friendships in the group and started to value herself more, realizing that women are important and worth caring about after all. The group encouraged her to join Love and Sex Addicts Anonymous. Her self-esteem increased as she began to believe that group members liked her and that society's values about women are unfair and inaccurate.

Building Self-Esteem and Self-Confidence

These depend on resolution of past issues and are essential to new growth. Women often plateau in their climb toward greater self-esteem. They have to go back and work on the unfinished business of childhood (incest, abuse, violence, alcoholism, neglect) in order to be ready for more growth.[49] It is necessary to help women see how societal values and attitudes toward women have worked through individuals to diminish or destroy their self-esteem. They need to rebuild (or build) confidence in themselves and a sense of trust in their own abilities.[50,51]

EXAMPLE: In working with Marge, the group leader offered substantial "teaching" about women's roles in the social order, images of women as sex objects in the media, and the effect of the self-fulfilling prophecy on many girls who, sexually abused as children, begin to define their role as an object of sexual use and abuse for men. Because most women in this society share some degree of this socialization, the leader worked with the group to help identify times when members had felt oppressed by men and to examine how that oppression had affected their self-images. As a group, the women grappled with understanding how external messages had beaten down their self-esteem and confidence. Many were able to identify ways in which they had been programmed for self-hatred and failure and to transfer that awareness into anger at the social order.

This anger is healing: It helps women feel less to blame for their self-hatred; it helps them feel less alone; and it helps them feel empowered to struggle against what hurts them in everyday life.

EXAMPLE: Another group member, Eve, was a sensitive, serious psychiatric nurse who worked at a state hospital. A distraught and violent patient, whom she had requested psychiatrists to remove from her ward, hanged himself on Eve's shift. She was charged with negligence and suspended even though she had responsibility for two wards at the same time, was understaffed, and had called for more help. Her confidence was shattered. She came to a support group complaining of anxiety and depression. She believed her union and friends did not support her appropriately; she also felt that if it had happened to someone else, reactions would have been more supportive. This blow to her self-esteem compounded the threat of losing her license. Eve received support from the group during a long wait for the state nursing board to review the case. After her license was suspended for a year, she became extremely depressed. A psychiatrist advised her to use her depression to get Workmen's Compensation. The group enabled her to see herself as strong and healthy, rather than label herself as *sick*. With their encouragement, she appealed the board's decision, won the case, and took a university course to improve her managerial skills. She worked on the issue of defining her self for herself, rather than accepting definitions placed on her by others.

Enhancing Self-Awareness

Women have so often heard that they are too emotional, that they have learned to repress or hide their feelings. Some have also been told that they do not have an idea worth discussing, or their solutions to problems are inappropriate. The 1988 movie, *Working Girl*, is an example of this. Women need help in noticing and respecting all their feelings, ideas, and wishes—even those that contradict each other or are difficult to accept. Attending to feelings and ideas is linked to a woman's acceptance of herself as she really is and taking responsibility for herself in all respects. Authenticity flourishes as the veneer of the female imperative is slowly peeled away.

EXAMPLE: Anna seemed withdrawn for a few sessions so the group leader asked her what was happening. Anna said "nothing," but the leader pointed out that Anna looked upset and said she would like to know what Anna was feeling. The leader reiterated the importance of honesty, even if what one has to say is unpleasant. She talked about how women are socialized to please others and not make waves. She pointed out that Anna already knew well how to sit on her feelings, but the purpose of the group was to take risks and push past barriers women have been socialized to live with. Anna revealed that she was hurt by something that had happened in the group 3 weeks earlier; she was afraid that if she told the truth about her reaction, other members would dislike her. It turned out that others had shared her analysis of the situation; her feelings were validated. She was able to resolve the conflict with the other group member, who had intended no harm. When one person after another takes a risk of this sort, the group as a whole becomes more self-aware and open.

Making Peace

Self-acceptance leads to the expectation that significant others should accept and respect one. The group helps each woman discover that a healthy woman is a healthy person, that being a woman does not have to carry a hidden stigma or handicap, that love relationships do not have to be cloaked in pain and fear. Resolving role conflicts without using denial, without hiding, and without accepting negative self-definitions is the ultimate product of making peace with oneself.

EXAMPLE: Martha felt physically unattractive most of her life. One night in the group she started yelling at the group leader, claiming that the leader "had it made" because she was "pretty" and complaining that boys and men never liked her because of her looks. The leader was able to help her realize that her anger was a response to a number of factors: her loneliness; her perception that the leader had a happy life; and her rage at a social order that sets narrow standards of beauty, leading large numbers of women to despise themselves. In focusing her anger outside herself onto the wider society, Martha was able to find relief and self-acceptance. In owning her loneliness, she was able to get support from other group members who also felt lonely. In hearing about the group leader's experience as a "pretty" woman in this society, she realized that being attractive is not necessarily an answer to the multiple needs women have.

Consolidation

If a women's group is to be successful, insights must be translated into behavioral changes. Making decisions, taking control, getting needs met, and letting go of old habits are positive signs of consolidation. A definite advantage of the group setting is the availability of support and encouragement during a period of transition. Consolidation relies on continuing reinforcement of growth.[52] Role-playing and assertiveness training are good techniques for promoting consolidation.[53]

EXAMPLE: Linda had been upset by her sister's drinking for years. She was afraid to deal with the issue because she was afraid of losing her sister, but she found herself in a rage much of the time. With the help of the group, Linda faced her anger and realized that she had to confront her sister, no matter what the outcome. The group supported her in owning the power that would come when she embraced her integrity. Linda made a decision to refuse to spend time with her sister if she was drinking and told her sister so. In becoming aware of and accepting her own boundaries, Linda reinforced her self-respect, even though she did, in fact, lose contact with her sister for a substantial period.

Autonomy within the Group

It is important for women that facilitators establish clear boundaries; legitimize individual differences; and support each member's right to say no to certain exercises, pass on a particular topic, work at her own pace, and have complete control over what kind of touch is received by her. The norm of autonomy inside the group transfers to her relationships in other groups. Leaders refrain from socializing with group members in order to strengthen bonds among the members and to remove the possibility of boundary confusion caused by dual relationships.

GUIDELINES FOR GROUP FACILITATION: THE PRINCIPLES APPLIED

Demeanor of Facilitator/Therapist

Our experience, which is borne out by research on therapeutic styles, indicates that warmth, lack of judgmental attitudes or criticism, and positive regard for each woman are crucial for successful group facilitation and the liberation and empowerment of each member.

Therapeutic group facilitation is an art rather than a science. There is no formula that works for every leader or every group. However, we can offer these very simple but critical elements of style that will help ensure a positive demeanor: Avoid put-downs; always be present shortly before and after each session to indicate its importance to you; never play favorites; avoid male bashing; offer interpretations— don't impose them; avoid criticism; leave your need to be right at the door; remember that we are all learning together.

It is essential to engage with a supportive colleague in a regular self-reflective evaluation of our roles as therapists.

Individual versus Group Sessions

Identification of key personal troubles and public issues should be made during an intake session with each client who joins an ongoing group. Some clients, by mutual agreement, need a number of individual sessions prior to joining a group. Taking a careful history prior to a client's entrance in a group is an important process for both therapist and client. It is important for each woman to be ready to enter a group (and for it to be prepared for her entrance). The vitality of the group depends on conscientious screening and preparation of group members.

Establishing Ground Rules

Prior to entering a group, each woman is engaged in a dialogue regarding essential group ground rules: confidentiality, respect for individual differences, owning one's own feelings and interpretations. Every group should also be given the opportunity to develop ground rules regarding, for example, punctuality, regular attendance, smoking, interrupting, touching, and extragroup contact. The facilitator also should be frank about her expectations. If members are expected to attend regularly, and to pay for missed sessions, be clear about that at the outset.

Groups tend to have an elasticity that enables them to withstand a certain amount of ground rule violation, but it is important for the facilitator to check out how members are feeling about that elasticity.

Breaking the Ice

In the early life of a new group and at the beginning of every session, it is important to help members lower their everyday masks, feel comfortable, and shift from less intimate roles. Ice breakers mark the group as a different place with its own boundaries, ground rules, and opportunities. Ice breakers can be elaborate while members get to know each other better.[54,55] Exercises that help members learn each other's names are fine. Experiences that derive from some commonality are also useful for stimulating interaction and building trust. For example, women in a heterogeneous group can be invited to write briefly on how they feel about the first night of the group, an experience they all share regardless of age, marital, or job status. Or they can be invited to tell one other person why they joined the group, then share feelings with the whole group. Women in a homogeneous group, focusing perhaps on life after divorce, can be invited to begin with some information about themselves: how long they were married, separated, and divorced; children; work; residence. Sharing verbally in pairs first lessens anxiety about sharing with the whole group.

We often use a simple ice breaker at the beginning of each session that serves as a "checking-in" process: "In a minute or two, say how you are feeling about yourself or your life this week"; or, more directly, we give each member a minute to state whether she has something specific to work on this session. This ensures that the facilitator is aware of any severe problems, changes, traumata, or time-limited issues.

Once a group is breaking down typical social barriers to interaction, the ice breakers can become more specific to issues that emerge as common bonds. Guided imagery and guided fantasies can help women start talking about painful or forgotten feelings surrounding, for instance, incest, abuse, rape, or failure.

Building Trust and Common Bonds

As the group begins to build trust through increasing levels of self-disclosure and expressions of mutual interest and support, it is the facilitator's role to help women see that they share some basic issues and common bonds. The healing capacity of the group depends on each member coming to realize that she is not alone. Stressing the similarities, while acknowledging individual differences, helps women feel less isolated and more connected.[30] The facilitator constantly works to make the group process "visible" to members because how they interact with each other and the facilitator is often reflective of other relationships. Helping women react to each other more honestly and directly contributes to emerging authenticity and confidence and helps counteract the dishonest relationships most have experienced.

The facilitator, with the group's assistance, establishes the norm of not avoiding feelings or overintellectualizing. The group moves forward quickly as private troubles, personal opinions, and individual feelings are reflected back to the group in analytical statements highlighting shared experiences. The group then becomes increasingly adept at making its own connections in a spirited analysis of issues that affect their lives.

Promoting Equality within the Group

Equality within the group rests on a simple principle: The outcome of the group is the responsibility of each member. A key task of the facilitator is to gatekeep group interaction so that more participatory members are helped to learn how not to dominate quieter or less participatory women. It is useful to establish norms early regarding interrupting, simultaneous talking, and keeping focused. It is preferable for the group to maintain these norms, but the facilitator must use verbal and nonverbal cues to gatekeep toward equality of interaction opportunity in the group. If this does not occur, women having difficulty finding a place in the group will perceive it (rightly so) as an unsafe place for them. Trust levels cannot intensify if a subgroup dominates. Absenteeism or attempts to leave the group are signs that gatekeeping may be ineffective.

Politicization

Because we work from a sociological perspective, we find it appropriate and helpful to bring in newspaper or magazine articles relevant to issues emerging in the group, to suggest readings, or to cite research findings from the literature about women. This expedites the process of making intellectual and emotional linkages between personal troubles and social issues, further empowering group members.[57]

Closure and Termination

Just as ice breaking is important to open group members up to each other, closing the boundaries is necessary at the end of each session and upon completion of the group's life.

Closure includes summing-up statements that reward both group and individual progress, positing questions for further exploration, and recognizing unresolved issues. As with all group process, closure is modeled initially by the facilitator. The members become increasingly proficient at bringing sessions to closure. Interpreting feelings, sharing insights, and voicing frustrations aid women in leaving the group.

When a group terminates or a member leaves the group permanently, we engage in a mutual assessment of progress and look toward future growth and sources of support. This might include encouragement for the group to continue to meet as a leaderless group, an idea that often originates with members. Some analysts argue that this is a way of dealing with the anxiety of separating from the therapist; we believe that it makes sense for women who have worked intensively together to establish intimacy, equality, support, bonding, and cooperative learning to continue to work for each other's personal growth and health, if they so choose.

PROFESSIONAL CONCERNS

Expanding the Web: Referrals

Professional maturity dictates that we are able to make a frank assessment of our own strengths and limitations. Every therapist or facilitator should develop an extensive list of referrals to other professionals and agencies that offer services not available from her or in the group. Expanding the awareness of women regarding community services or action groups can also contribute to politicization.

Logistics

Every group requires a private, protected space in which to work. Comfortable chairs or cushions arranged in a closed circle so that each member can easily see every one else's face creates a conducive environment for group interaction. Women need to be protected from the interruptions of telephones, children, or colleagues.

We keep notes on each member, commenting on goals, progress, issues, essential history, telephone number, and address. If third-party payments are possible, record keeping may have to follow insurance company guidelines. For income tax purposes, we keep careful records of receipts and expenses.

Management of Schedules, Fees

We generally run groups in weekly sessions of 90 to 120 minutes. We ask for a renewable 3-month commitment in ongoing groups. If we work with more than one group in an evening, we allow at least 30 minutes between them for private time and note keeping.

Fees depend on the clientele and on how you see your role as facilitator/ therapist. We set fees according to a sliding scale that accommodates women who work in low-paying jobs, so the group can be open to a wide range of potential members. Generally, we prefer to keep fees fairly low, paid weekly or in advance.

Advertising

Doctor's offices are good places to leave cards, brochures, and rate cards. A personal introduction may generate referrals. Notices on supermarket billboards or on community-access cable television widen exposure. Networking through local professional associations and community groups can elicit referrals. We find that word-of-mouth referrals from past clients are the largest source of group members; next are those who respond to ads in community newspapers.

Training and Certification

People interested in working with women in groups should complete an extensive training program in group facilitation and group dynamics; in addition, familiarity with the literature on girls and women is essential to effective therapeutic intervention. Group theory and skills are available through clinical training programs or continuing education courses offered by graduate departments of social work, counseling, sociology, or psychology. Information regarding institutions that offer doctoral work in clinical sociology is available from the Sociological Practice Association.

Clinical sociologists are certified through the Sociological Practice Association after completing a specified sequence of doctoral-level education in sociology, clinical training, supervised hours of practice, and demonstration of skills at an annual SPA meeting. Certification must be renewed annually. Conferences sponsored by SPA provide opportunities for further training and professional contacts. Clinical experience can sometimes be arranged through internships or apprenticeships with certified clinical sociologists. The *Clinical Sociology Review* and *Sociological Practice* are related professional journals. Insurance is available through SPA, which also has a complete listing of graduate programs and certification standards.

Ethics

The Sociological Practice Association expects that all members, and especially Certified Clinical Sociologists, will adhere to its Code of Ethics. We cannot emphasize strongly enough the importance of clear, professional boundaries in all group work, especially with women. Women's boundaries are violated so frequently that they often do not notice when a therapist has violated them (one in three girls is sexually abused; one in three women will be raped in her lifetime).[58–60] Boundaries are limits on behavior and statements from each woman as to what she can tolerate without feeling violated. Boundary violations are often thought of as physical but can be emotional or intellectual as well (for example, telling a person what she thinks or feels; emotional enmeshment; role reversal between clients and therapists).

Clear boundaries in clinical work include sessions that occur at prearranged times (except in emergencies) and that start and end on schedule; a clear fee arrangement; clear and renegotiable treatment goals; group time focused on members, and in which client welfare is of foremost importance (i.e., the therapist does not use the time to discuss her own problems); clarity on the part of the therapist as to how her values impact on group process and content; a clear contract about confidentiality and its legal limits, so that each member knows who else might be aware of her case (e.g., supervisors), and under what circumstances the therapist would have to break confidentiality (e.g., the client reports that she is abusing her children); and no dual relationships such as sexual or social involvement (the latter may be inevitable because of shared social/political circles in small communities, in which case the outside contact should be carefully monitored).

If the therapist's boundaries are clear, the client can be free to express whatever she experiences without fear of being invaded or fear that her own behavior might violate the boundaries of appropriate therapy. Unclear boundaries can lead to boundary violations or to censorship on the part of the client, who knows at some level that the therapist is not trustworthy. Therapists who notice that they are not competent to handle certain feelings or issues should make appropriate referrals. A supervision system (either peer or paid) is very important to help practitioners sort out their areas of competence and weakness.

THE IMPACT ON US OF WORKING WITH WOMEN IN GROUPS

Working with women in groups has been immensely satisfying and inspiring. When we welcome members to a new group and listen to them tell their stories, identify their feelings, build alliances with other members, and assert themselves in their lives outside the group, we feel we are making an important contribution to a world that badly needs the female half of its population to stop taking abuse and contribute constructively to a more positive social order. The empowerment of women is greatly facilitated by our perspectives as sociologists. As we watch a group of women develop a sociological imagination, we are reinspired by Mills's idea and more deeply committed to the sociological vision as a healing force in society.

CONCLUSION

A therapeutic group for women, as a microcosm of society, is an opportunity for discovery, growth, and renewal. Each woman can work through her personal troubles with the support and reflective analysis that emerges from group interaction. Facilitation of the group must avoid the typical oppressions and devaluations that women face in society at large. The group should be led toward achievement of the personal goals of empowerment, liberation, self-awareness, and positive connections to others.

The clinical sociology model of working with women in groups implies a critical awareness of the research and theory regarding the unique status and role of women; emphasis on the sociogenesis of personal problems; and creation of a group setting that takes advantage of the special strengths of women.

REFERENCES

1. Mills, C. W. (1959). *The sociological imagination.* New York: Oxford University Press.
2. Slater, P. (1966). *Microcosm: Structural, psychological, and religious evolution in groups.* New York: Wiley.
3. Sheehan, V. H. (1973). *Unmasking: Ten women in metamorphosis.* Chicago: Swallow.
4. Lott, B. (1987). *Women's lives: Themes and variations in women's learning.* Monterey, CA: Brooks-Cole.
5. Firestone, S. (1970). *The dialectic of sex: The case for a feminist revolution.* New York: William Morrow.
6. Lengermann, P. M., Wallace, R. A. (1985). *Gender in America: Social control and social change.* Englewood Cliffs, NJ: Prentice-Hall.
7. Hacker, H. M. (1951). Women as a minority group. *Social Forces, 30,* 60–69.
8. Chafe, W. (1988). Sex and race: The analogy of social control. In Paula S. Rothenberg (Ed.), *Racism and Sexism: An integrated study* (pp. 334–349). New York: St. Martin's Press.
9. Hooks, B. (1984). *Feminist theory from margin to center.* Boston: South End Press.
10. Epstein, C. V. (1970). *Woman's place: Options and limits in professional careers.* Berkeley: University of California Press.
11. Basow, S. A. (1980). *Sex role stereotypes: Traditions and alternatives.* Monterey, CA: Brooks/Cole.
12. Richardson, L. (1981). *The dynamics of sex and gender.* Boston: Houghton-Mifflin.
13. Anker, R., Buvinic, M., & Youssef, N. H. (Eds.). (1982). *Women's roles and population trends in the Third World.* London: Croom Helm.
14. Richmond-Abbott, M. (1983). *Masculine and feminine: Sex roles over the life cycle.* Reading, MA: Addison-Wesley.
15. Roberts, E. (1984). *A woman's place.* Oxford: Basil Backwell.
16. Rosaldo, M. Z., & Lamphere, L. (Eds.). (1974). *Women, culture, and society,* Palo Alto, CA: Stanford University Press.
17. Jaggar, A. M., & Struhl, P. R. (1978). *Feminist frameworks: Alternative theoretical accounts of the relations between men and women.* New York: McGraw-Hill.
18. Hartsock, N. C. M. (1983). *Money, sex, and power.* Boston: Northeastern University Press.
19. Hartmann, H. (1986). *Women's work, men's work.* Washington, DC: National Academy Press.
20. Kanter, R. M. (1977). *Men and women of the corporation.* New York: Basic Books.
21. Kahn-Hut, R., Daniels, A. K., & Colvard, R. (1982). *Women and work: Problems and perspectives.* New York: Oxford University Press.
22. Chafetz, J. S. (1974). *Masculine/feminine or human? An overview of the sociology of sex roles.* Itasca, IL: F. E. Peacock.
23. Chafetz, J. S. (1983). *The changing position of women in the family: A cross-national comparison.* Leiden: E. J. Brill.
24. Chafetz, J. S., & Dworkin, A. G. (1986). *Female revolt: Women's movements in world perspective and historical perspective.* Totowa, NJ: Rowman and Littlefield.

25. Smith, D. E. (1977). Women, the family, and corporate capitalism. In M. Stevenson (Ed.), *Women in Canada* (pp. 14–48). Don Mills: General Publishing.

26. O'Brien, M. (1981). *The politics of reproduction.* London: Routledge & Kegan Paul.

27. Machlowitz, M. (1985). What worries you most? *New Woman,* Sept., pp. 124–129.

28. Andersen, M. L. (1988). *Thinking about women: Sociological perspectives on sex and gender.* (2nd ed.). New York: Macmillan.

29. Straus, M., Gelles, R., & Steinmetz, S. (1980). *Behind closed doors: Violence in the American family.* Garden City, NY: Anchor/Doubleday.

30. Wyckoff, H. (1977). *Solving women's problems: Through awareness, action and contact.* New York: Grove Press.

31. Broverman, I. K. *et al.* (1970). Sex-role stereotypes and clinical judgments of mental health. *Journal of Consulting and Clinical Psychology, 34*(1), 1–7.

32. Sapiro, V. (1986). *Women in American society: An introduction to women's studies.* Palo Alto, CA: Mayfield.

33. Robb, C. (1988). A theory of empathy. *Boston Globe Magazine,* Sunday, October 16, 1977.

34. Smith, D., & David, S. (1975). *Women look at psychiatry.* Vancouver: Press Gang Publishers.

35. Robbins, J. H., & Siegel, R. J. (Eds.). (1985). *Women changing therapy: New assessments, values, and strategies in feminist therapy.* New York: Harrington Park Press.

36. Miller, J. B. (1986). *Toward a new psychology of women* (2nd ed.). Boston: Beacon Press.

37. Chodorow, N. (1978). *The reproduction of mothering: Psychoanalysis and the sociology of gender.* Berkeley: University of California Press.

38. Gilligan, C. (1982). *In a different voice: psychological theory and women's development.* Cambridge: Harvard University Press.

39. Belenky, M. F. *et al.* (1986). *Women's ways of knowing.* New York: Basic Books.

40. Mowbray, C. T., Lanir, S., & Hulce, M. (Eds.). (1984). *Women and mental health: New directions for change.* New York: Haworth.

41. Young-Eisendrath, P., & Wiedemann, F. L. (1987). *Female authority: Empowering women through psychotherapy.* New York: Guilford.

42. Laws, J. L., & Schwartz, P. (1977). *Sexual scripts: The social construction of female sexuality.* Hinsdale, IL: Dryden.

43. Allen, C. V. (1980). *Daddy's girl.* Toronto: McLelland and Stewart.

44. Bernard, J. S. (1973). *The future of marriage.* New York: Bantam Books.

45. Bernard, J. S. (1975). *Women, wives, mothers: Values and options.* Chicago: Aldine.

46. Bequaert, L. H. (1976). *Single women: Alone and together.* Boston: Beacon Press.

47. Norwood, R. (1985). *Women who love too much.* Los Angeles: J. P. Tarcher.

48. Rich, A. C. (1981). *Compulsory heterosexuality and lesbian existence.* London: Onlywomen press.

49. Chapman, J. R. (1987). *Response to the victimization of women and children, 10,* 1–4. New York: Guilford.

50. Manis, L. G. (1977). *Womanpower: A manual for workshops in personal effectiveness.* Cranston, RI: The Carroll Press.

51. Brown, L. (1985). Power, responsibility, boundaries: Ethical concerns for the lesbian feminist therapist. *Lesbian Ethics, 1,* 3, 30–45.

52. Leiberman, M., Yalcolm, I., & Miles, M. (1973). *Encounter groups: First facts.* New York: Basic Books.

53. Osborn, S. M., & Harris, G. G. (1975). *Assertive training for women.* Springfield, IL: Charles C Thomas.

54. Eberhardt, L. Y. (1976). *A woman's journey: Experiences for women, with women.* Columbia, MD: New Community Press.

55. Carney, C. G., & McMahon, S. L. (Eds.). (1977). *Exploring contemporary male/female roles: A facilitator's guide.* La Jolla, CA: University Associates.

56. Johnson, D. W., & Johnson, F. P. (1982). *Joining together: Group theory and group skills.* Englewood Cliffs, NJ: Prentice-Hall.

57. Bruley, S. (1976). *Women awake: The experience of consciousness raising.* London: Author.

58. Disch, E. (1989a). Sexual abuse by psychotherapists. *Sojourner, 14*(9) (April), 20–21.

59. Disch, E. (1989b). When intimacy goes awry: Sexual involvement between therapists and clients. *Woman of Power,* [13, Spring, pp. 54–57].

60. Bates, C. M., & Brodsky, A. M. (1989). *Sex in the therapy hour.* New York: Guilford.

CHAPTER 21

Gerontology and Clinical Sociology

RAE BANKS ADAMS

INTRODUCTION

If you had been born in 1900, your life expectancy would have been 47 years. Those born in 1990 can expect to live about 75 years. If they survive the volatile teen years, they will likely live an additional 5 to 10 years, or more. In fact, persons aged 85 and older make up the fastest growing age group in the United States. Although other indicators of aging should be included in defining those who are old, age 65 or older is the most frequently used, especially for entitlement programs. For the first time in the United States, persons 65 and older outnumber those under 25. As a result of the rapid increase of the older population, many social changes are occurring; society is charting a new course for a "new" age group.

In the past, the elderly made up a small part of the population. Few traditions emerged on which to base social norms for this age group. Although some would argue that the lack of social norms is beneficial, most sociologists agree that, with an absence of norms, social disorganization and anomie result. Today, many of the older group live on the fringe of society, in part because of the lack of clearly defined roles for the elderly. Caught in this situation, many older persons, their families, and others in their social network need assistance. The clinical sociologist can offer valuable insight and service to this category of people. The clinician who is or will likely be working with older adults should make a thorough study of the field of gerontology. This chapter provides an overview of the developmental features of later life, provides examples of intervention, and concludes by identifying areas where clinical sociologists can make contributions to sociological research in gerontology.

RAE BANKS ADAMS • Department of Sociology, Abilene Christian University, Abilene, Texas 79699.

SOCIAL GERONTOLOGY

The field of social gerontology is a direct outgrowth of sociological studies of demographic changes in populations. As a result of these studies and the impact the aging population had on major social institutions, aging emerged as a social issue. As research developed, the study of older adults in their social settings became what is currently known as social gerontology. A coursed called social gerontology usually serves as the foundation course for beginning students in gerontology. Theories or frameworks have emerged that are unique to understanding the aging process from a sociological perspective. The clinical sociologist brings to the discipline the ability to apply traditional research and theory in a clinical and therapeutic setting.

Hendricks and Hendricks[1] categorize social gerontology theories as the "early theories," "second generation theories," and "emergent theories." The clinical sociologist who works with older adults or organizations designed to serve older persons should have some understanding of these theories. Here they can be mentioned only briefly.

THEORIES

Earliest Theories

The *activity theory* posits that in order to age successfully, persons either continues their normal activities and roles or, when a role is changed, such as at retirement, persons should offset the losses of old activities with new activities. *Disengagement theory*, the opposite of activity theory, views the diminishing or change of roles in later life as mutually functional for both the individual and society. For example, when older people give up formerly held work roles, it allows young people to move into these positions permitting an equilibrium within the system. This theory has met with a great deal of criticism among gerontologists. *Continuity theory* is built on the premise that "in the course of growing older, the individual is predisposed toward maintaining stability in the habits, association, preferences, and lifestyles that he or she has developed over the years."[2] Sociologically oriented theorists hold that continuity is maintained as a result of the normal socialization process. Anticipatory socialization will prepare the older adult for an orderly transition from one stage of life to another.

Psychologically oriented theorists generally deal with continuity by examining how, or if, personality continues to develop during the later stages of life. However, there is considerable controversy over whether, and how much, one's personality changes as he or she grows old. Neugarten, Havighurst, and Tobin[3] stated that "there is considerable evidence that in normal men and women there is no sharp discontinuity of personality with age but instead is increasing consistency."

In explaining *subculture theory*, Rose[4] suggested that, as greater numbers of people in the population age, they will most likely adapt better by forming networks within a subculture. Rose maintained that because one's self-concept is derived from interpersonal relationships, older persons will have a better self-image by interacting with persons of their own age rather than with other age groups. An outgrowth of such thinking has been the clustering of housing developments for the aged and the building of retirement communities restricted to older residents.

Second Generation Theories

Age stratification theory proposes that the various strata in societies are a result of different age groups being viewed and treated differently within the society. There is need for empirical studies related to this theory as some critics of the theory argue that a number of variables other than age can account for social stratification. However, the theory is one current explanation of agism that is found in most societies. *Modernization theory* is an attempt to explain how aging differs by examining cross-cultural comparisons of the elderly and the social structural arrangements in their daily lives. *Exchange theory* suggests that those who adapt best to aging are those who are able to negotiate satisfactory exchange in a reciprocal process with other actors, old and/or young.

Emergent Theories

Social environmental theories focus on the interdependence between the person and the environment. *Political economic theories* analyze older person's location within the macrosocial structure in order to determine if there is a correlation between such things as one's life satisfaction and one's access to goods and services within the system.

PERSPECTIVES ON THE LATER STAGES OF LIFE

Three broad perspectives have emerged to examine and explain the aging process: the physical or biological, the psychological, and the sociological. No one orientation is adequate to explain the aging process. Most working in the field of gerontology agree that it is best to use an interdisciplinary approach. Atchley[5] stated that multiple approaches may appear contradictory and confusing, but each serves a purpose. Riley[6] and Foner[7] suggested that, rather than trying to synthesize specific descriptive theories of aging, a broader frame of reference, such as the age stratification perspective, is needed. In this section biological and psychological concerns are briefly sketched with greater attention given to sociological perspectives.

Biological Perspectives

A few decades ago, it was generally assumed that as one grew older, the body aged due to increased vulnerability to disease and reduced viability of the physical system. However, in the past few years, a variety of more specific biological explanations for aging have been proposed. Atchley[8] categorized these:

1. A hereditary genetic program sets limits on growth, aging longevity.
2. Age-related declines are the functioning of the genetic program that causes newly formed cells to be less effective than their predecessors.
3. Age-related lowered efficiency of the immune system in identifying and destroying potentially harmful germs, viruses, or mutated cells such as cancer cells.
4. A decrease with age in the capacity of the endocrine system to control various vital functions such as respiration rate, temperature, or blood pressure.
5. Age-related decline in the capacity of the nervous system to speedily and efficiently maintain bodily integration and prevent bodily deterioration.

Familiarity with biological explanations of aging is especially useful to the clinical sociologist working with a medical team. Even more important, the clinician should be sensitive to possible biological/physical factors that could be contributing to the client's problem(s). Therefore, it is important for the clinician to determine that the client's medical history is current.

Psychological Perspectives

The psychological approach to understanding aging is multifaceted and, in some areas, fringes both biological and sociological approaches. For example, some psychologists have made important contributions to understanding stages of development and of personality characteristics of older adults over the life cycle. The life-span approach will be dealt with as a separate perspective later in this chapter.

Psychological issues include sensory and cognitive functioning and the impact that life's experiences have upon them. The perspective examines how age relates to learning and memory loss; time and psychomotor responses; loss of hearing and vision; disappointment in life goals; grief, and so forth. In addition, the clinical sociologist needs to be aware of psychological disorders. These include the affective disorders, anxiety disorders, and psychotic disorders, as well as organic disorders such as Alzheimer's disease. Again, familiarity with the psychological perspectives to understanding aging is vital in clinical work.

Sociological Perspectives

The sociologist is trained to analyze the interactions of individuals or groups within a particular social structure. In the field of aging, just as in other units of society, to understand and explain this interaction, the three broad, major theoretical perspectives of sociology are utilized: functionalism, conflict, and symbolic interaction.

The functionalist focuses primarily on how the older person or age cohort would fit into the larger group; what parts they play: whether their roles were functional or dysfunctional, and so forth. For example, what is the role for the older cohort group in the workplace? Or, what statuses do older persons occupy in contemporary family units?

The conflict theorist examines the role of older people related to the conflicts that occur as a result of their competing for scarce resources. For example, what conflicts might occur in the workplace between younger and older employees? Or what is the potential for conflict as a result of the dependency ratio? The dependency ratio is the ratio of those in the work force who produce goods and services to those out of the workforce.

The symbolic interaction perspective can be utilized to understand how the person's socialization process is internalized by the meanings that the individual has given to actions with other individuals or groups. For example, as people grow older, they perceive themselves in their environment and place meaning on how others in their group(s) are perceived as viewing them as they grow older. Through this process, older persons may determine how to behave as they interpret their perception of what significant others expect of them. The *labeling theory*, an outgrowth of symbolic interaction, will be utilized as an example of clinical work later in this chapter.

LIFE CYCLE/HUMAN DEVELOPMENT/STAGE THEORIES AND PERSPECTIVES

Kalish[9] believed that anyone concerned with maintaining human dignity must be concerned with understanding the entire life cycle, including later years. Perhaps this statement explains why almost all of the perspectives (biological, psychological, and sociological) deal with the socialization and development of the individual or cohort group in an attempt to explain the aging process. Among the frequently cited theorists who have made contributions within developmental theories are Erik Erikson, Abraham Maslow, Robert Havighurst, and Bernice Neugarten. However, among these, only Neugarten's work focuses entirely on the middle age and older stages of the life cycle.

Generally, the life cycle, stage, or developmental perspective implies age-graded norms. Those who age successfully will have internalized the appropriate norms for a particular stage, or age, in life. However, as pointed out earlier, some would suggest that identifying the "appropriate" norms for mature adults is restrictive and is an attempt to make all older people fit into one category or type. At any rate, the developmental or stage approach to explaining successful aging is a popular model of which the clinician should be aware. But before suggesting the use of the life-cycle models as a basis for clinical work, the clinician should be made aware of some concerns regarding the application of these theories or frameworks. Schulz and Ewen[10] included the following statement in their critique of life-cycle or stage theories:

> Stage theories have a certain appeal: they cover a broad range of people and ages, and they are simple enough for the general public to comprehend and use as a developmental yardstick. They are also attractive because they propose that individuals continue to grow and develop throughout their lives, thereby providing hope for those whose current lives are far from satisfactory. (pp. 205–206)

Of greatest concern may be the tendency for some to lump all older people into one category and expect them to develop in such a way that they will be and act alike. Schulz and Ewen addressed this concern when they stated:

> Even though the stage theorists undoubtedly intend their age ranges as general guidelines, rather than as inflexible boundaries, it still seems highly unlikely that all (or even many) adults will encounter the same stage at similar ages. Even when specific ages are not emphasized (as in Erikson's theory) differences among adults are probably too great for a stage model to have widespread applicability. (206)

Keeping these limitations in mind, the clinician may find stage theory models useful in certain situations. For example, knowing Havighurst's[11] developmental tasks for those who are 50 to 60 and 60 to 70 may be helpful in identifying goals that could serve as appropriate behavior when a client appears to be having trouble adapting to acceptable social norms. According to Havighurst, appropriate tasks for those 50 to 60 include: accepting physical changes; dealing with parents; and experimentation with new careers, marriage relations, and activities. For those 60 to 70: adjustment to declining health; adjustment to retirement and lower income; death of spouses; and establishment of satisfying living arrangements; and wisdom, acceptance of life.

Due to varying factors, such as health, economic conditions, and the like, specific age-graded boundaries will not likely be applicable to all older persons. However, when used as general guidelines, these developmental tasks, for example, might be useful in aiding the client and/or their family gain a better insight into some adjustment patterns that many consider to be "normal" for those reaching old age.

Someone has suggested that the best definition of successful aging is the ability to adapt. If this is true, those in old age have a golden opportunity to practice, for the losses of the old are very real: loss (or at least changes) in health, wealth, family and friend networks, physical appearance, and so forth. This is not to imply that the last stage of life cannot be a time of fulfillment and happiness; however, few will deny that a great many changes are inevitable. As a result of experiencing life over many years, it is generally expected that the older, mature person who ages successfully will have gained a great deal of insight and knowledge, and as a result, will have obtained wisdom in their old age. Erikson[12] who identified eight stages of development in the life cycle holds this expectation for those in the last stage.

Most of Erikson's work dealt with early life stages of development. Only the last two stages address middle age and old age. Erikson's seventh stage involves conflict between generativity and stagnation that extends from young adulthood into old age. If a sense of individual achievement and fulfillment in life is not achieved in this stage, the result will likely be a personality that exhibits stagnation and bitterness.

The eighth and final stage of life, Erikson labels *integrity vs. despair*. The healthy personality approaches the end of life with a feeling of fulfillment of the previous seven stages. The person is not overly concerned with pending death but feels a continuity of life between oneself and the younger generation. Reflections of one's experiences result in wisdom that can only be found in later life. Failure to cope with life appropriately at this stage results in feelings of meaninglessness, despair, and a sense of uselessness in life. Hall and Lindzey[13] summarize Erickson's eighth stage as follows:

> The last ages of the epigenetic process of development is labeled integrity. It can best be described as a state one reaches after having taken care of things and people, products and ideas, and having adapted to the successes and failures of existence. Through such accomplishments, individuals may reap the benefits of the first seven stages of life, and perceive that their life has some "*order and meaning within a larger order*." Although one who has reached a state of integrity is aware of various life styles of others, he or she preserves with dignity their own style of life and defends it from potential threats. This style of life and the integrity of culture thus becomes the "patrimony of the soul." (p. 99)

The clinician should keep in mind that the term *wisdom* and its identifying characteristics are ambiguous. For example, from an aging parent's vantage point, the parent may perceive the he or she is acting wisely and with integrity, whereas their adult child or children may totally disagree. Because the desired outcome or goals may be different for each of these, it may be difficult (or not appropriate) for the clinician to make judgments regarding who is acting wisely. The clinician's role is not that of playing judge but to assist the client(s) in reaching acceptable relationships or situations.

On the other hand, Erikson's explanation of wisdom and Havighurst's developmental stage of wisdom might be extremely useful when the clinician is confronted with an older client who is exhibiting deep depression and/or despair. When this is the case, it might be useful to examine the client's life history in order to determine if life expectations have, or have not, been met, and/or are they in fact accepting their age and its limitations as well as opportunities to continue to grow.

Several techniques may be useful in obtaining a life history and may be conducted in either individual or group settings. Butler[14] pioneered the use of life review and reminiscing therapy as beneficial behavior and necessary tasks of old age. Some techniques for using life review and reminiscing include group discussions of the past, storytelling, and role playing.

King[15] pointed out the value and possible purposes of reminiscence therapy and how it can serve in clinical work:

1. The feelings associated with current struggles may be reflected in the affect attached to reminiscences.
2. The remembered past may be pleasurable.
3. Memories may provide the basis for problem solving.
4. The older person can reminisce socially and thereby receive validation or support when needed.
5. The reminiscer has the opportunity to analyze past events of which he is not proud, and through the life review, resolve these old conflicts.
6. The natural mourning process, including taking time to reflect upon shared past history, can be accomplished through reminiscing. (272–286)

Frequently a "life satisfaction" instrument is used to measure one's fullness of life. Perhaps the most frequently used scale is the Life Satisfaction Index A (LSIA) that was originally developed by Neugarten, Havighurst, and Tobin.[16] The scale consists of 20 items that relate to apathy, self-concept, optimism vs. pessimism, and others. Also, George[17] has developed an integrated model of transition for middle and later life. Variables associated with perceived well-being include such things as association with family finances, resources, and so forth.

For whatever reason, as stated earlier, failure to attain a good self-image and acceptance of the normal aging process and what Erikson and Havighurst refer to as "wisdom" can result in depression and despair. For example, failure to come to terms with changes that are necessary after retirement may lead to feelings of uselessness and meaninglessness, of no longer belonging to a vital part of society, and ultimately to low self-esteem. Further, when there has been little or no socialization to prepare for later life and norms are weak to indicate expected behavior, ambiguous feelings about what one is supposed to do or be may occur. As stated earlier in this chapter, such an absence of norms may result in a situation of anomie.

ANOMIE AND THE OLD

When persons believe that they have few choices in life and that there are no clearly identifiable roles, and no goals to look forward to, feelings of alienation can often lead to an anomic situation. Although space does not permit a full discussion of anomie theories, the clinician should be aware of the theories and of the indicators of anomie and should be prepared to deal with anomic situations in the clinical setting.

Although more recent work has been done in the field of anomie, at least knowledge of Merton's[18] typology of deviance in response to anomie can be valuable. In many cases, simply explaining Merton's responses to anomie to clients brings about awareness and then change in their attitude and behavior. Interestingly, many of the older persons would not refer to themselves as deviant, yet they could be properly classified by Merton's typology as the "ritualist" deviant. That is, their goals have not purposefully been abandoned, but there was no perception of goals or they were not well defined. Yet, just as the ritualist, many older people become somewhat obsessed with seeking ways to continue to live out their lives as fully as possible yet fail to be a part of the whole because they become absorbed with daily routines that are meaningless. The isolate who is obsessed with TV watching is a good example.

Other categories of deviance can also be observed among the anomic old. The person who takes extreme measures in order to remain young looking may be classified as an "innovator." The "rebel" may be the person who joins a group such as the Gray Panthers, a somewhat radical group whose goal is to change the image of the aged in society and to establish a rightful place for them. Or, it may be the "conformist" who rarely admits that there are any problems associated with aging, when in fact, he or she may be experiencing real problems but deny them or hide them from others.

None of these older persons are appropriately adapting to becoming old. And because anomic individuals tend to be dysfunctional in any social system, these persons are the ones who are likely to be in therapy, along with their families or those in their support system.

It should be pointed out that it is not my intent to label all of the old as deviant.

In fact, the tendency to label issues related to the aging population as "social problems" should be viewed as dangerous. It should be the goal of every person to stop this tendency. After all, because most of us will reach old age in the future, it can be self-serving.

A FRAME OF REFERENCE

A specific framework or model for working with the older population that would be appropriate and could be utilized by the clinical sociologist in every circumstance would be difficult to formulate due to the multifaceted opportunities for applications. Different approaches and techniques are needed when working with larger units, such as with agencies, as opposed to working with smaller units, such as individuals, family relationships, or in other small groups. It has been this author's experience that an eclectic approach to the application of theories and frameworks has been necessary. However, some general questions should be answered by the clinician prior to his or her commitment to working with older persons.

Of primary concern would be the clinician's objectivity toward the aging population in general. Questions that might help clinician's clarify their own attitudes are:

- Do I hold stereotypes toward the old that reflect bias or ageism?
- Do I personally fear growing old and could that affect my judgment toward the client?
- Do I perceive certain roles as appropriate for people classified as "old"?
- How do I place worth on the old compared to the worth I place on youth?

Any bias toward those perceived to be old must be resolved before objectivity can be obtained.

Another factor that should be considered is the clinician's amount of knowledge about the field of aging. Some areas for knowledge have already been mentioned. In addition, it is imperative to know the many programs and sources for services that are available for older adults. In many cases, linking the client to the network of services available can be a valuable part of a solution to a problem. Knowledge about the many programs can be obtained through such offices or agencies as Area Agency on Aging, state and city agencies on aging, the Department of Human Services, local information and referral offices, organizations such as the American Association of Retired Persons (AARP), and many others including local churches or synagogues. The importance of knowing about these resources cannot be overemphasized.

Further, in therapeutic settings, clinicians need to assess their own training (or lack of training) for working with older adults. Although courses in gerontology are more frequently being included in university curricula, most of those who studied prior to the past decade probably received little or no training regarding the skills needed to work with older persons. Focus has almost entirely been on the young through middle age. Working with older adults, especially the advanced old, is drastically different from working with youth. For example, hopes for high productivity and a seemingly endless future is usually the focus for change among the young. Also goals often include gaining independence and maturity. Although this is not to say that the old have no future, the reality is that their future is diminishing; life is, in effect, coming to a close. *Dependence* is a real threat when most are struggling to maintain *independence*. Physical limitations often hinder behavior change, and progress or improvement can be slow, especially when working with clients who suffer some form of dementia. With the exception of grief therapy, few counselors or clinical workers in any discipline have been trained to work in situations related to older persons. There is a great need for the training of clinical sociologists, social workers, psychologists, and other types of professional helpers in order that they can work more productively with older persons.

Schmidt[19] has provided a list of important issues to be considered by those counseling older adults. The questions are:

1. Why do we wish to provide counseling for older persons?
2. On what should counseling of older people be based?
3. What might be achieved from counseling older people?
4. How might the costs be managed?
5. When and where might counseling be provided?
6. Who might provide the counseling?
7. What approaches or procedures may be appropriate?
8. Should such counseling be evaluated?

Schmidt also lists possible achievements of counseling older people:

1. Improved problem solving by cognitive, self-instruction training.
2. Improved decision making and life planning.
3. Coping with loneliness and reduced social contacts.
4. More effective accomplishment of various tasks of daily living.
5. More satisfactory management of when and how to die.
6. More effective use of all psychosocial services in a community.

Not all clinical sociologists will be attracted to working with older adults for a number of reasons. However, the rewards for those who choose to work in this area can be many. In the remainder of this chapter, some case studies, further assessment techniques, and applications of theories are presented. The primary purpose is not to imply that success is always the result but to show how general sociological knowledge can be utilized in gerontological settings. These are actual cases with names changed.

CASES, TECHNIQUES, AND THEORY APPLICATION

Crisis Intervention and the Clinical Sociologist

Crisis intervention is defined by Byers[20] as "a practice oriented set of procedures designed to offer emotional first aid to someone experiencing incapacitating stress." Clinicians other than sociologists are generally thought to be involved in such practice. However, Chaplan is quoted by Glassner and Freedman[21] as stating that "the work of crisis interventionists can be quite instructive for the clinical sociologist in that clinicians need to be made aware of which events in the life cycle tend to produce crises for group members." According to Chaplan, the major hazardous circumstances affecting older adults are moving to a new community, undertaking new social or occupational responsibilities, or relinquishing job responsibilities through retirement.

It is not unusual to think primarily of the social worker as the appropriate interventionist who becomes involved in crisis intervention. For example, it is quite normal to find social workers leading self-help groups in drug intervention, family survivors of suicide victims, and the like. Glassner and Freedman,[22] however, make a clear distinction between the social worker's role and the role of the clinical sociologist. "Social workers differ from clinical sociologists in that social workers are trained primarily in psychological traditions, usually defer their own critical judgment to that of the agency or client, and tend to be unable to vary the methods in which they are trained in order to meet the needs of the person, group, or situation." Of primary importance to this author is that the social work profession is not grounded in a framework based on theoretical orientations. Therefore, it may be that the major contribution that a clinical sociologist can make in crisis intervention is to offer varied theoretical perspectives upon which to base assessment techniques and methodological approaches. This contribution would justify the involvement of the clinical sociologist in crisis intervention therapy.

The Use of Labeling Theories in Clinical Work

The self-fulfilling prophecy, which is associated with labeling, can creep, unintentionally, into a family system through what seems like harmless actions and words. For example, the term *senility* is frequently given as a response by college students when asked to describe old age. Further, it is generally reported that as one grows older, he or she becomes somewhat fearful of the disease of senility. And, although only a small percentage of the aged suffer from the disease, it becomes somewhat easier to apply the label especially when society views many of the old as senile and when it is encouraged by labeling (whether inadvertently or not) by significant others.

Several labeling frameworks might have been successfully used in the case, but for this particular situation, a model by Hammond, Goodman, Green, Hall, and Taylor[23] was utilized. The steps of the model and the application to the case follow.

The Case of Mother Wilson

1. The individual is found to have committed a deviant act, or is thought to have committed such an act. *Application*: One day Mother Wilson goes out of her home to visit her daughter, forgetting that she has a chicken cooking in a pot on the stove.
2. The person then is thought to be a particular "kind of person"; the kind of person who commits such acts. Stereotyping occurs because the deviant act was perceived

as no accident but part of a pattern. *Application*: Upon returning to her home with her daughter, they find the house filled with smoke. Mary, the daughter, says, "Mama, you must be out of your mind—you're getting as forgetful as Old Lady Smith and those other biddies you call friends."

3. People tend to redefine the past acts of the labeled deviant in a way that demonstrates that the person has always been a deviant; that is, the pattern is filled in. *Application*: Mary goes home and tells her husband, John, about the incident. John says, "You know, I've noticed lately that your mother keeps forgetting names, and last week she even forgot to wear her coat home after she had been here for the day."

4. Furthermore, people expect that the person will continue to be a deviant. They watch for and expect further deviant behavior. *Application*: Mary and John talk it over. They decide that Mary's mother is getting old and perhaps a little senile. They agree that they had better watch her closely. She might burn the house down or even get so bad that she could not live alone.

5. Equally important is the change in self-conception that is likely to occur in the person who is being labeled. People who are labeled as deviant and from whom further deviance is expected often come to expect deviance of themselves. Because of these expectations, a profound reorganization of the individual's self-conception, and then of his or her personality can occur. *Application*: In conversations with Mother Wilson, Mary's and John's ideas surface, and Mother Wilson begins to understand that they are worried about her. She begins to monitor her own behavior, and the next week when she forgets her handbag at the grocery check-out stand, after she has placed it on the counter to put on her coat, she mentally concludes that they are probably right. She must accept the fact that she is getting old and may even be getting senile like Old Lady Jones who lives in "that home."

Such interaction by the actors should be clearly pointed out by the clinician and new ways found to handle fears of future limitations or illnesses. Damaged identity, or a "spoiled identity," as described by Goffman[24] can and does occur in families and in other social groups, although unintentional on the part of the labeler.

After explaining the way labeling works to the clients, by using storytelling techniques and fictitious names and occurrences, the actors in the situation were able to identify themselves. After being made aware of the danger and shown ways to interact in more appropriate ways, the attitudes and behaviors were changed. Mrs. Wilson shed the label, and her self-image improved. In this case, Mrs. Wilson was not "becoming senile" but had that been the case, the family members should have been made aware of the fact that actual senility can be reinforced simply by applying labels.

The Use of Assessment Techniques

Assessment techniques are unlimited for the imaginative clinical sociologist. Caution should be taken, however, to validate techniques that have not been tried and tested by previous use. A review of validity and reliability for measurement techniques is suggested. By controlling for validity, not only can the clinician know the accurateness of his or her own methods, but the reporting of his or her successes and failures with particular techniques can be validated. The valid adaptation of techniques designed for other age groups is not only useful in gerontological settings, but in many cases it is necessary in that there are limited gerontological resources specifically designed for intervention. An example of adaptation is the assessment of family functioning from a cultural perspective, which has been developed by Hepworth and Larsen.[25] But whatever the source, most family therapy techniques include the assessment of power within a family by asking questions such as Who does what and who comments on it? Who speaks for whom? Who agrees with whom? Who holds the ultimate authority in decision making? Is the family's power structure stable? Are members of the family content with the relative distribution of power?

In order to demonstrate how the clinician may make use of these types of questions, the following case, with comments on technique and application of social theory, may be helpful.

The Case of the Loving Extended Family

The daughter asked for an initial visit to discuss her mother and father (both in their early 80s) and the daughter's own children; a daughter and a son-in-law (both in their late 20s). From the initial visit, the following was determined:

Gran and Gramps lived in a small college town where he had retired from a long and successful career as dean of students. In order to supplement his retirement income, over the years they had purchased several pieces of rental property. Their daughter had married, and she and her husband continued living in the town near her parents. As grandchildren were born, Gran developed a special affection for one particular granddaughter.

Although Gran had had no active role with the college, she had received a great deal of social status due to the dean's success. Also, she had established status in the family due to inherited family money that allowed the couple to live beyond the typical small college administrator's salary. Over the years, especially after the dean's retirement, the dean had developed a rather severe hearing loss, and Gran had taken on the role of the "explainer." And, if she had not always had the role, she had, over the past few years, assumed the dominant role of primary decision maker in the family. She still had a great deal of control over the daughter and son-in-law in that she was pleasant to be with. The daughter and her husband also had strong familial ties based on feelings of responsibilities to older, caring parents.

When the favored granddaughter realized than Gran and Gramps were getting old and not likely to live many more years, the granddaughter, who had moved away and married, convinced her husband (without coercion) that they should move back to the college town and be near Gran and Gramps so that they might enjoy the last few years of the grandparent's lives. The grandparents were overjoyed with the news and suggested that because the grandson-in-law had no specific job lined up, the couple move into one of their rental properties and take over the management of their affairs. The younger couple's motives were unselfish, and the opportunity to receive financial assistance in the form of job and housing was welcomed and approved of by all the extended family members. As might be expected, the years of being separated, except for holidays, had not prepared the young couple for the day-to-day interaction with the older couple. After a few short months, and as Gran began to show some signs of acute memory loss, agitation, and mild neurosis, the grandchildren became disenchanted with the arrangements. Gran's daughter, mother of the favored granddaughter, tried ways to intercede in the potential problems to protect the grandchildren. However, Gran was not cooperative with the daughter and blamed her for many of the problems. As Gran's health deteriorated, the daughter became the focus of Gran's verbal abuse. The daughter's husband tried to intervene, only to retreat quickly so as not to lose the status he had established with the older couple over the years. The grandson-in-law was bewildered (as the outsider), and when increasing demands were made on him for services by the older couple, he felt caught in the middle. The granddaughter remained the "apple of Gran's eye," but she too felt the pressure by other family members to control Gran. Controlling Gran was not her perceived role, however, for she had taken on the role of the placator to Gran.

After gathering the history, it was decided that intervention based upon Homan's[26] exchange theory, in which five theoretical propositions of exchange are described, would be appropriate for application. By explaining the propositions to the family, it was believed that the actors might best be able to understand the situation if the scenario could be "played back" for them in a simple framework showing how power and reciprocity is a part of daily symbolic interaction. Further, it was decided that due to the physical condition of Gran, her behavior would not likely change, although some change might be possible for Gramps. The following intervention was undertaken.

1. After the daughter's initial visit, a session with the younger couple was requested. The therapist knew the older couple, but if that had not been the case, a visit to their home would have been appropriate. Or, if Gran's condition permitted, a visit by the older couple to the office would have been arranged.

2. It was requested that Gramps and Gran have a medical checkup. It was found that Gran did have biological problems that could have been a contributing factor to some of the irrational behavior.

3. With all four of the younger family members present, a technique requiring each person to give their perception of their own and other's roles was explained. A sociogram was developed on paper for them to see. After a short period of time, "labels of roles were agreed upon for each member, with the labeled member's approval that the label was, for the most part, accurate. For example, the granddaughter was labeled as the instrumental and expressive leader of the group. The daughter was labeled the scapegoat.

4. A scenario of a family problem was acted out in a type of sociodrama at which point the actors were to answer the following questions with the consensus (if possible) that the answers were accurate. If consensus was not possible, a record of the dissenters was to be kept: Who does what, and who comments on it? Who tells, or speaks, for whom? Who agrees with whom? When a decision must be made, who gives in, and who makes the decision?

5. After a couple of sessions and analyzing another scenario, it was determined that the propositions of the exchange theory could be given to each actor on a sheet of paper. As a group, they were asked to see if the framework might fit their group regarding power and reciprocal relations. Each was able to see the possibility of counterproductive interactions based upon inappropriate exchange and power.

6. Each was asked if he or she wanted to change the power structure; that is, were they willing to pay the price for removing the power from Gran? It was pointed out, that due to her traditional status and role, some of the family members might react with feelings of guilt. After it was decided, by the family, that transfer of power was desirable, specific assignments were given to each actor so that slowly (and hopefully less painfully) the long-established power base could be shifted. It was determined that the easiest transfer of power for Gran would be to the granddaughter. This was acceptable to the other family members.

7. When each had a clearly defined role to play and an acceptable status, so far as their relationship with Gran, the family was able to function smoothly for the several more

months of Gran's life. Later, after her death, no feelings of guilt on the part of the survivors were expressed. In fact, each felt that his or her behavior was appropriate for the situation.

The clinician worked within a sociological framework. By applying sociological theory with a focus upon the group interaction rather than the individual, the family structure was altered. Social roles and patterns of interactions were identified, and planned exchanges of roles were defined and brought about. A systemic approach was utilized with the primary focus being upon exchange theory. Knowledge of role theory was also used but was not explained to the clients as a part of the method of intervention.

A situation was explained by Glasser and Freedman[27] about a 74-year-old black woman who participated in a day care center program for older adults. Because she was unwilling to take an active part in the therapeutic activities designed for the group, her case was presented to a staff of behavioral experts, which included a clinical sociologist. After some questioning of the client, the sociologist asked the woman about her religious preference. The client responded that she was Pentecostal and held deep religious convictions, even more zealous than most Pentecostals. One of her strongly held objections to the day care program was the use of "sinful" audiovisual aids. The audio appeared to be mumblings that she interpreted as "speaking in tongues." She stated that the Bible made no mention of audiovisual devices as an appropriate medium that had been gifted with this particular talent. After the insight into the cultural influences upon the woman's behavior, other therapeutic activities were planned in which the woman was willing to participate. The ability to focus upon the behavioral consequences, brought about by particular culturally held values, allowed the clinical sociologist to make a valuable contribution to the case.

The Case of the Adult Day Care Center

It is not unusual for the clinical sociologist, working in the field of aging, to be called upon as a consultant or to serve on boards for such organizations as senior citizens centers, nursing homes, or adult day care centers. The following case shows how knowledge of social structures and the ability to apply social theory were useful in a case involving an adult day care center.

The center had initially been privately funded with a small matching grant from the local city government. About two-thirds of the daily clients qualified for payment to the center through medicaid. The other clients were private pay. The facility was licensed for 60 clients and averaged about 45 in daily attendance. In order to break even, the center needed at least 85% daily attendance, so money was always a problem. A law was passed requiring state mental health and mental retardation (MHMR) facilities, to reduce the number of clients housed in institutions. An MHMR facility was located in the same town as the center, and began to refer some mentally impaired adults to the center for day care, then return them to a foster care home at night. The center quickly filled to capacity and, in fact, was overcrowded. A clinical sociologist was serving on the advisory board for the center and was asked to make recommendations regarding a rapidly deteriorating situation involving behavioral problems. Although funds furnished by the government to pay for the MHMR clients were welcomed, the two groups of clients (those from MHMR and the former older-aged clients) were not interacting satisfactorily, even though many were cohorts of the same age. The center also felt pressure to serve the MHMR clients due to the fact that of the original clients, two-thirds were receiving government financial aid, and, if the MHMR clients were not served, the agency might remove all clients who received government funds from the facility on the basis of discrimination.

The director of the center requested that the clinical sociologist find a legal way to refuse the MHMR clients because he believed that putting the two groups together was dysfunctional. To the clinical sociologist, it seemed that the opportunity to try to find ways to combine the two groups satisfactorily was more functional in that the center badly needed the financial resources that could be gained by the additional MHMR clients. Most of the original clients were over the age of 65 and were mentally functional. How could they be resocialized to accept the MHMR clients, many of whom were under the age of 65? A plan was devised by which the older clients and their families were asked to cooperate in experimenting with putting the two groups together. Most were willing. A few stopped attending the center. The plan called for a limited type of "buddy" system between an older adult and a MHMR client. Certain goals were set for the older adult. When a MHMR client became behaviorally uncontrollable, a nurse practitioner was there to assist. Plans were drawn to build on additional space to the facility that was to be designed primarily for the MHMR client; however, no barriers would be placed to stop interaction between the two groups. Group activities were planned that were designed to educate the older client so that old stereotypes of the mentally handicapped could be replaced with new concepts of the value of the handicapped person. At first, limited interaction was requested but encouraged. The plan was successful, and presently the center is operating at maximum capacity, and funds for the additional space have been found and an additional building started.

The situation was addressed from a functional perspective rather than conflict. There was a group problem, not an individual problem, even though it was an individual's behavior that was labeled as deviant that was the precipitating incident that brought the problem to the clinical sociologist.

Some Suggested Resources

A book by Weiner, Brok and Snadowsky,[28] *Working with the Aged*, has proven useful when working in institutions and with communities. Another recommendation is *Gerontological Practice: Issues and Perspectives*, by Boyd and McConatha.[29] Or for the clinician who is working in an institutional setting with other professionals, a text edited by Burnside[30] can be most helpful, especially for the sociologist who needs to become familiar with various techniques used by psychologically oriented therapists.

RESEARCH

At the present time, little research has been reported as a direct result of clinical sociologists gathering and reporting data related to older cohort groups or from data regarding the organizations that serve them. As multidisciplinary approaches continue to be utilized to study the aging process, it becomes increasingly important that clinical sociologists make contributions to the field of gerontology. An excellent way for the clinician to contribute is by carefully keeping records and collecting data regarding their practice, thereby adding valuable data to data banks being compiled on this age group. Although it may not be the clinician's primary role to conduct research, it is every sociologist's responsibility to insure that appropriate social data are utilized as social science becomes increasingly involved in exploring, describing, and explaining the phenomenon associated with this "new age" or the newly emerging "third stage" of life.

THE CHALLENGE

There is no doubt that one of the most challenging groups with which to work at the present time is the rapidly growing and changing group that has been labeled as old. One challenge comes from the fact that the clinical sociologist is likely working in new areas in which there is little tradition upon which to base intervention. Another challenge comes from the fact that this older age group often views psychological therapy with skepticism. The advantage for the clinical sociologist is that sociologists have not been traditionally labeled as therapists or counselors; therefore, the older client may be more willing to discuss personal issues with the sociologist rather than with a therapist from another discipline.

In addition, there is the challenge of working with teams from other disciplines, particularly from psychology and the field of medicine. Great rewards, both personal and professional, can be experienced by the clinical sociologists as they attempt to meet these challenges.

REFERENCES

1. Hendricks, J. H., & Davis, C. D. (1986). *Aging in mass society* (3rd ed.). Boston: Little, Brown.
2. Cox, H. G. *Later life: The realities of aging* (2nd ed.) (p. 35). Englewood Cliffs, NJ: Prentice-Hall.
3. Neugarten, B. L., Havighurst, R. J., & Tobin, S. S. (1968). Personality and patterns of aging. In B. L. Neugarten (Ed.), *Middle age and aging* (pp. 173–177). Chicago: University of Chicago Press.
4. Rose, A. M. (1965). The subculture of the aging: A framework in social gerontology. In A. M. Rose & S. S. Robin (Eds.), *Older people and their social worlds* (pp. 3–16). Philadelphia: F. A. Davis Company.
5. Atchley, R. C. (1983). *Aging: Continuity and change* (2nd ed.). (Pp. 17–39). Belmont, CA: Wadsworth.
6. Riley, M. W. (1971). Social gerontology and the age stratification of society. *The Gerontologist 11*(1 Pt. 1), 79–87.
7. Foner, A. (1986). *Aging and old age.* (Pp. 8–11). Englewood Cliffs, NJ: Prentice-Hall.
8. Atchley, R. C. (1983). *Aging, Continuity and change* (2nd ed.). (Pp. 18–19). Belmont, CA: Wadsworth.
9. Kalish, R. *Late adulthood: Perspectives on the human development* (p. 14). Monterey, CA: Brooks/Cole.
10. Schulz, R., & Ewen, R. B. (1988). *Adult development and aging* (pp. 205–206). New York: Macmillan.
11. Havighurst, R. J. (1953). *Human development and education.* New York: Longman.
12. Erickson, E. H. (1963). *Childhood and society* (2nd ed.). New York: Norton.
13. Hall, C. J., & Lindzey, G. (1978). *Theories of personality* (3rd ed.). New York: John Wiley & Sons.
14. Butler, R. N. (1963). The life review: An interpretation of reminiscence in the aged. *Psychiatry, 26*(65) 76.
15. King, K. S. (1984). Reminiscing, dying, and counseling: A contextual approach. In I. Burnside (Ed.), *Working with the elderly* (2nd ed.; pp. 272–286). Monterey, CA: Wadsworth Health Sciences.
16. Neugarten, B., Havighurst, R. J., & Tobin, S. (1961). The measurement of life satisfaction. *Gerontology, 16,* 134–143.
17. George, L. K. (1985–1986). Life satisfaction in later life. *Generations 10*(3), 5–8.
18. Merton, R. K. (1968). *Social theory and social structure* (2nd ed.). New York: Free Press.
19. Schmidt, L. D. (1976). Issues in counseling older people. *Educational Gerontology 1*(2), 187–192.
20. Byers, B. D. (1987). Use of clinical sociology in crisis intervention practice. *Clinical Sociology Review, 5,* 102–118.
21. Glassner, B., & Freedman, J. A. (1979a). *Clinical sociology* (p. 12). New York: Longman.
22. Glassner, B., & Freedman, J. A. (1979b). *Clinical sociology* (p. 15). New York: Longman.
23. Hammond, P. E., Goodman, L. W., Green, S., Hall, R. H., & Taylor, M. C. (1975). *The structure of human society* (p. 424). Lexington, MA: D. C. Heath and Company.

24. Goffman, E. (1963). *Stigma: Notes on the management of spoiled identity*. Englewood Cliffs, NJ: Prentice-Hall.
25. Hepworth, D. H., & Larsen, J. (1986). Direct social work practice theory and skills (2nd ed.; pp. 222–226). Chicago: The Dorsey Press.
26. Homans, G. C. (1974). *Social behavior: Its elementary forms* (revised ed.). New York: Harcourt Brace Jovanovich.
27. Glassner, B., & Freedman, J. A. (1979c). *Clinical sociology* (p. 27). New York: Longman.
28. Weiner, M. G., Brok, A. J., & Snadowsky, A. M. (1987). *Working with the aged* (2nd ed.). Norwalk, CT: Appleton-Century-Crofts.
29. Boyd, R. R., & McConatha, D. (Eds.). (1982). *Gerontological practice: Issues and perspectives*. Lanham, MD: University Press of America.
30. Burnside, I. (1984). *Working with the elderly* (2nd ed.). Monterey, CA: Wadsworth Health Science.

CHAPTER 22

Drug Abuse Prevention

Clinical Sociology in the Community

W. DAVID WATTS AND NINA B. WRIGHT

INTRODUCTION

Drug and alcohol abuse cost the nation billions of dollars a year in lost productivity and human suffering. Human service, medical and law enforcement professionals have been struggling to reduce demand, limit supply, and reconstruct lives. Sociologists, frequently in conjunction with other social scientists, are working to examine the following issues: the definition of drug use as socially deviant behavior;[1,2] the effects of culture on drug use;[3] the process of becoming a drug user;[4] and the evaluation of the success of various interventions.[5] Drawing on the authors' experience in one community, this chapter reports on the role of the sociologist in facilitating a community's action to reduce drug and alcohol abuse, particularly among adolescents.

Drug and alcohol abuse are problems that challenge the full scope and range of scientific knowledge and professional action. Sociologists have a great deal to offer in the struggle to control drug and alcohol abuse; however, the problem requires a cooperative, multidisciplinary approach rather than a narrowly defined, one-dimensional effort. Secondary intervention efforts, such as the treatment of persons with drug and alcohol problems, primarily have been the province of counselors, clinical psychologists, social workers, and psychiatrists. Recently, however, sociologists[6] have become more involved in the treatment of substance abuse and have been particularly successful in helping other professionals recognize that cultural factors contribute to or deter drug and alcohol problems in different populations. Sociologists[7] have contributed to an understanding of the relationship of alcohol and drug abuse to family violence, and they have helped to sensitize

W. DAVID WATTS • College of Arts and Sciences, Southeastern Louisiana University, Hammond, Louisiana 70402. **NINA B. WRIGHT** • High Risk Youth Prevention, San Marcos, Texas 78666.

citizens and policy decision makers to the multigenerational effects of severe family dysfunction. Sociologists working with law enforcement agencies have contributed to the reduction of drug availability in some areas.

Actions to improve the community, based in the theories and methods of sociology and widely shared, legitimate values, may be defined as clinical sociology. Applied sociology seeks only to apply sociological theories and methods to a client-defined problem; clinical sociology attempts to facilitate social change for the improvement of the group, organization, or society. The clinical sociologist is an activist, working in the community to accomplish some larger social good. Although there are no absolute standards guiding the sociologist in the selection of values to facilitate positive interventions, such values as democracy, social justice, self/group actualization, and treatment of others as ends in themselves are consistent with this definition of clinical sociology.

This chapter will outline and discuss some of the interventions that can be used by clinical sociologists working with communities, groups, and individuals to achieve positive social change when dealing with drug and alcohol abuse. On the basis of our experience in one city, we will discuss obstacles to change and suggest ways to eliminate them, using sociologically grounded strategies for community prevention and intervention.

There are three stages or levels of sociological intervention processes with drug abuse. The first stage, initial intervention, includes techniques for community access and definition of the drug abuse situation in the community. The second stage requires the development of community organization techniques for drug abuse prevention and includes networking with various groups, for example, police, schools, family, media, business, and religious groups. The third stage, peer prevention, is the most effective intervention process but depends on the success of the previous intervention strategies. An outline of each of these strategies follows.

Primary prevention efforts, which have been given little attention in the past, are now being addressed by numerous professionals including educators, social workers, psychologists, and sociologists.[8] Increasing the awareness of prevention as an option and precondition for community change is a difficult task; it requires awareness of and concern about drug abuse as a problem within the community. Overcoming community denial, resistance against the recognition that a problem exists, is frequently the first challenge the clinical sociologist faces.

The clinical sociologist can intervene with drug abuse at a number of social levels. Intervention can occur at the macro- (national/state), meso- (community/organization), or micro- (individual) levels. Boundaries between disciplines are indistinct when professionals of different training and experience work in each others' domains. However, sociologists can intervene with individual cases or with small groups in a treatment context.[6] Sociologists, by the nature of their discipline, are theoretically and methodologically prepared to intervene at the community or organizational level, including the national or state level.[9] Awareness of the organizational goals, structure, function, and leadership of a community or organization are key to the success or failure of the intervention. The sociologist must assess the formal and informal structure of the organization, the actual and prescribed distribution of authority and power, and the key figures in the organizational structure and operation. Clinical sociologists who attempt to intervene in organizations of their own professional authority may find themselves intervening in a vacuum.

INTERVENTIONS

A series of community interventions by clinical sociologists to facilitate social change and reduce substance abuse among youth begins with four steps: (1) access, (2) definition of situation and problem, (3) overcoming resistance and denial, and (4) getting the job. After having been identified by community leaders as a professional who can contribute to successful intervention against drug abuse, the sociologist can initiate and utilize a number of theoretically based and research supported second-stage interventions. These operate at four interdependent levels: community, organization, family, and peer.

Initial Interventions

Access

Access to the community and its network of institutions and organizations is a precondition to effective intervention by the clinical sociologist. Sociologists can bring to bear elements of both their personal and professional identities to facilitate access for drug and alcohol abuse interventions. The public image of sociologists as social researchers facilitates access to community decision makers. Community leaders recognize the professional legitimacy of sociologists' involvement with social problems, as researchers who gather data about and offer explanations of drug abuse. Much of the work by sociologists on drug abuse is grounded in professional goals and disciplinary issues; but when research is clinical in nature, focus, and purpose, it must be grounded in efforts to improve the community, as well as good sociology.

Everyone, including sociologists, has a legitimate, personal interest in drug and alcohol abuse. Many sociologists, like other professionals, are parents whose children are at risk. As parents, we had expressed concern to the superintendent of our district about rumors of high levels of drug abuse in the schools and about the steps being taken to control the problem. One of us sought permission to research the frequency, prevalence, and correlates of drug abuse and asked to survey high-school students as part of a study of delinquency. Our request corresponded with pressure from individual parents and groups. As a result, the superintendent of our district needed objective, reliable, and comparable data about drug abuse and recommendations for improvement of the problem. Combining our professional and personal identities, we gained access to the schools for drug abuse prevention.

Definition of the Situation/Recognition of the Problem

Unless the school or community is already motivated to do something about substance abuse, the second intervention of the clinical sociologist must be to help the community pull down the wall of denial that has been built up around drug and alcohol abuse. Just as families who live with a mentally ill member are reluctant to seek professional help or hospitalization, communities may be slow to recognize that they have a drug or alcohol abuse problem. Many believe that drug abuse exists in other cities, neighborhoods, or schools, but not in their own. Some parents or community leaders may acknowledge that adolescents drink and use drugs but deny that it is a serious problem requiring response. Some may fear that the reaction to drug abuse will produce more damaging delinquency and greater drug abuse. It is the task of the clinical sociologist to assist the community in recognizing that drug and alcohol abuse exists and that it deserves an active response.

The problem that the sociologist faces is one of definition of the situation. Communities ignore substance abuse because it has not been defined as a problem; the sociologist, acting as a moral entrepreneur,[10] can focus public awareness on correlates of drug and alcohol abuse, chipping away at the wall of denial. As Berger and Luckmann[11] argue, knowledge, properly grounded in the institutionalized symbols of a society, creates social reality. The clinical sociologist has powerful methodologies for bringing drug abuse and its consequences to the attention of the community and its leaders. Survey research has been used to gather data about drug abuse by America's high-school seniors[12,13] and by persons in other age groups.[14,15] Adaptation of existing instruments, such as the Monitoring the Future questionnaire, permits comparisons between the local community and state/national patterns of drug and alcohol use, assessing the relative severity of a community's drug problem. When combined with official statistics and the stories of parents or children who have used drugs or have been approached by others to use them, survey data can assist a community in recognizing the nature and extent of the drug problem among its children. Survey data can not only help a community overcome denial of the problem but can identify correlates of drug abuse that can be used to construct interventions. Many states have initiated a statewide drug and alcohol abuse survey that can include information on where, when, age of initiation, and knowledge/attitudes about drug abuse as well as other problem behaviors. Comparing state and national data with local survey findings assists with overcoming community denial and pinpointing targets for intervention.

Defining the Problem with Data

Data from the school district and community reported here were gathered intermittently over a number of years. We will discuss a selection of the data to show the process of establishing need for further intervention. Table 1 shows the prevalence and recent percentages of drug use for a local sample and a national sample of seniors for 1986, the year that data were first gathered in this high school. Comparing the local with national data for the same year shows that this community had higher than national rates of lifetime use for alcohol, marijuana, inhalants, cocaine, barbiturates, LSD, stimulants, and heroin. During the past month, seniors in this community reported higher rates of use for all drugs, including alcohol, marijuana, inhalants, cocaine, heroin and other narcotics, barbiturates, LSD, stimulants, and tranquilizers than did the national comparison group. The local sample use of

TABLE 1. Comparing Prevalence and Recency of Use of Drugs:
Local (L) 1986 (N = 205) and National (N) 1985 (Approximate N = 16000)[a]

	Ever used		Past month		Past year not past month		Not past year		Never used	
	L	N	L	N	L	N	L	N	L	N
Alcohol	98.4	92.2	78.4	65.9	15.2	19.7	4.4	6.6	1.5	7.8
Marijuana/hashish	59.1	54.2	26.3	25.7	19.3	14.9	13.5	13.6	40.9	45.8
Inhalants[b]	18.2	15.4	5.9	2.2	6.8	3.5	5.5	9.7	81.9	84.6
Cocaine	22.1	17.3	9.8	6.7	10.1	6.4	2.2	4.2	77.9	82.7
Barbiturates[c]	10.8	9.2	3.5	2.0	5.3	2.6	2.0	4.6	89.2	90.8
Tranquilizers[c]	6.4	11.9	3.0	2.1	1.4	4.0	2.0	5.8	93.6	88.1
LSD	13.7	7.5	6.9	1.6	4.8	2.8	2.0	3.1	93.6	92.5
Stimulants	28.3	26.2	10.3	6.8	12.6	9.0	5.4	10.4	71.7	73.8
Heroin and other narcotics	5.9	1.2	1.5	0.3	—	0.3	1.0	0.6	94.1	98.8

[a]National data obtained from Johnson, L. D., O'Malley, P. M., & Bachman, J. G. (1986). *Drug use among American high school students, college students, and other young adults: National trends through 1985.* Rockville, MD: National Institute on Drug Abuse.
[b]National data based on four questionnaire forms. National N is four-fifths of N indicated.
[c]Only drug use that was not under a doctor's orders is included here.

alcohol in the last 30 days was 12.5% higher than that for the national group. The data suggest that there is a core group of drug users in this community high school. This speculation is reinforced by the lower discontinuance rates for many drugs for the local sample than for the national sample, as shown in the columns labeled "not past year" and "past year not past month." By comparing the local and national samples on a range of drugs, we can more specifically identify the drugs that are problematic for this community. In this case, the stronger drugs, LSD, cocaine, inhalants, heroin, stimulants, and alcohol, are being abused at a higher rate locally than nationally.

In 1988, another survey of student drug use was conducted to establish new baseline data for a series of interventions, some that were in process and some that were to be initiated that year (detailed in later sections of this chapter). As shown in Table 2, the data are broken down by male and female, showing the percentage of change in drug use in the last year by seniors in the high school. For the most part, drug use by males and females declined. We shared these indications of change with school officials, teachers, and community leaders to show them that combatting drug abuse can be successful and to demonstrate that drug abuse still exists in the community. In 1990, we will compare our survey findings to assess our progress and determine where additional drug prevention efforts need to be focused.

When gathering drug abuse data, it is as important to measure the antecedents and consequences of drug abuse as it is to measure its frequency and prevalence. Drug abuse antecedents and consequences form the basis for theoretically based interventions. Sociological theory provides a foundation from which concepts can be derived and developed into associative measures. Theory frames not only the measurement of drug abuse but points to areas for practical intervention. In the

TABLE 2. Comparisons of Percentage Changes in Reported Alcohol and Drug Use in the Last Year among Senior High-School Students From 1986 to 1988 Surveys

	Males			Females		
	% 1986	% 1988	% change	% 1986	% 1988	% change
Alcohol	80.8	81.5	+1.5	87.4	84.9	−2.5
Marijuana	50.3	37.0	−12.7	41.1	35.8	−5.3
LSD	14.2	3.8	−10.4	7.0	5.7	−7.7
Coke	22.7	10.9	−11.8	13.4	5.7	−7.7
Amphetamines	21.4	5.8	−15.6	19.7	7.7	−12.0
Barbiturates	7.1	3.8	−3.3	6.3	1.9	−12.1
Heroin	3.9	0.0	−3.9	0.6	1.9	+1.3
Other narcotics	8.4	3.7	−4.7	3.2	5.7	+2.5
Inhalants	10.4	9.4	−1.0	12.7	9.4	−3.3

first survey of the high school, variables were included that operationalized two theoretical approaches to delinquency and deviance: control theory[16] and peer association theory.[17] Control theory was operationalized by using a few of the questions that Hirschi[16] developed, with particular emphasis on the quality of parental relationships. Being able to share with parents, reporting that parents understand, and that parents know where and with whom the adolescent is when away from home, were found to be the most effective family measures preventing multiple drug abuse. Each respondent also was asked to report how many of his or her friends used a particular drug.

Multiple drug abuse was measured with a combined variable, created by adding drug use for each time period for each respondent. A number of variables measured the quality of family life and control from the point of view of the adolescent. Whether or not parents understand the youngster; whether the adolescent feels comfortable sharing feelings and experiences with the parents; whether or not the youth reports that his or her parents know where he or she is and who he or she is with; and whether or not the parents physically hit the youth are the principal measures of family/youth relations. These measures reflect three dimensions of family life: intimacy and trust, parental control, and parent/child violence. Only one of the intimacy and trust measures, parental understanding, is correlated significantly with multidrug use in a lifetime ($.21, p<.05$), past year ($.18, p<.01$), and past month ($.14, p<.05$). This weak but significant relationship washes out when all family variables and friends' drug use are entered into a multiple regression equation.

Parents knowing where their adolescents are when away from home is significantly related to lifetime multidrug abuse ($.21, p<.01$), last year ($.31, p<.01$), and last month ($.29, p<.01$). This relationship holds when a multiple regression formula is used; the Beta for parents knowing where their children are (lifetime $.14, p<.05$; last year $.18, p<.01$; last month $.20, p<.01$) is significant. Adolescents believing that their parents know where they are is the only family measure that is significant in a multiple regression equation. Parents knowing who their children are with, along with sharing with parents and being understood by parents, were not significant in a multivariate regression equation. Parents hitting their adolescents was not correlated significantly with drug use in either bivariate or multivariate measures, although parental abuse along with drug abuse is significantly related to violent delinquency when the sample is broadened to include adjudicated delinquents.

These findings on family factors and drug use can be used by the clinical sociologist to intervene in the community by focusing parents and involved citizens on the empirically demonstrated relationships. Parent-training seminars and workshops can utilize this information to target curricula to maximum effectiveness for successful intervention.

Kandel and others found that peer involvement with drugs is more important than parental/family factors in explaining drug and alcohol abuse among adolescents. The findings from this community survey are no different. Friends' drug use was highly correlated with multidrug use over the lifetime (.64), past year (.64), and past month (.53). In a regression analysis, friends' drug use accounted for over 40% of the variance for lifetime and past year use and just under one-third of the variance for use in the past month. The clinical sociologist must use this data to design an effective prevention program. Friends' drug use, as a measure of a peer culture supporting drug abuse, should be confronted directly. Community interventions should be premised on this finding; otherwise, the project will fail to strike at the heart of the problem: the existence of a peer culture that supports and recruits users.

When control theory and peer association variables were entered into a regression equation with multiple drug use as the dependent variables, 44% of the variance was explained for lifetime multidrug use, 45% for drug use in the last year, and 33% in the last month. The overwhelmingly powerful variable was friends' drug use, accounting for almost all of the variance. The only other variable that significantly contributed to explaining the variance was parents knowing where their children are when away from home. These data are important for structuring the interventions that follow.

Another important finding, consistent with the literature,[18] is the moderate to strong correlation with other delinquent behaviors. For example, the Pearson product moment correlation for multidrug abuse and selling drugs was .54 ($p<.01$). Other delinquent behaviors also correlated significantly with multiple drug abuse: vandalism (.43), serious assault (.44, $p<.01$), theft (.36, $p<.01$), and shoplifting (.39, $p<.01$). Although some parents and community members may not be greatly concerned about drug abuse, many are concerned about theft, assault, and vandalism. These data reinforce the importance of investing time and money in the effort to suppress adolescent drug abuse.

Further evidence for the importance of reducing drug abuse among high-school students is the relationship between drug use and academic performance. In the 1988 survey of over 244 seniors in the local high school, it was found that students who used drugs other than alcohol at any time in their lifetime were significantly less likely (11.0% vs. 28.3% for nondrug users), to report their most common grade as A; drug users were more likely (29.2%) to make C's than nondrug users (19.6%; $\chi^2=14.06$, df$=7$, $p<.01$). Within the last year, 23.6% of nondrug users and only 10.9% of drug-using students reported making A's; similarly, only 19.5% of abstinent students made C's, whereas 33.9% of drug-using students reported C's ($\chi^2 = 10.6$, $df = 7$, $p < .01$). Information about drug abuse, delinquency, and academic success can help a community to acknowledge its drug problem. Parents, in particular, can become highly motivated to do something to protect their children.

Gathering and analysis of data are important, even if a community is aware that it suffers from the problems of drug and alcohol abuse. Newspaper accounts, television and radio discussion programs, and other media have educated the public to the dangers of drug and alcohol abuse and, most recently, the effects of crack cocaine and its attendant crime problems. The publication of survey findings in the newspaper and the discussion of the findings by researchers and public officials contribute to community awareness of drug and alcohol abuse as significant problems that require community action.

Community Organization for Drug Abuse Prevention

Although the gathering and analysis of data are critical first steps in helping community leaders to become aware that drug and alcohol abuse are not just a national urban problem but a local community problem, the clinical sociologist needs to promote community awareness of drug and alcohol abuse as issues that can be confronted and dealt with on a local level. Together with older professionals who are concerned with the antecedents and consequences of drug and alcohol abuse, the clinical sociologist can network with community leaders and involve them in the development and enforcement of direct interventions. A large number of institutions that can affect any youth problem, including drug and alcohol abuse, exist within every community.

Professional Networks

Every community has a wide range of helping professionals who are focused on some aspect of the community's problems, including drug and alcohol abuse. Although, at this time, there is no nationally recognized professional organization of drug and alcohol abuse prevention specialists, there are organizations with accreditation and certification standards for professionals treating drug and alcohol abuse. Treatment professionals who are committed to working on various facets of the drug and alcohol problems in their communities want to involve other qualified people but may not know how to assess the skills and contributions of sociologists. Sociologists, as they become integrated into the community of professionals involved in drug abuse intervention, may confront a number of problems. The sociologist may not be seen by other professionals as being properly trained. Sociologists who are interested in drug and alcohol abuse treatment should first determine whether or not their states have certification requirements. Meeting those requirements will enhance acceptance for sociologists among their professional counterparts. Sociologists also need to demonstrate to other drug and alcohol abuse professionals that they share the value orientation that drug and alcohol abuse is harmful. Most other professionals accept the disease model of drug and alcohol abuse and are aware that some of the harshest criticism of that model comes from sociologists. The sociologist, building on research skills, can not only gain access but can be sought after as a member of the drug and alcohol abuse community team.

Team building is essential to the success of a community drug abuse prevention and intervention program. Networking is a critical part of that team-building effort. Effective networking facilitates the sharing of information about successful strategies, the assessment of specific needs in the community, and the coordination of community response in order to prevent drug abuse. Without networking and sharing, professionals from different organizations are likely to conflict with one another, duplicate effort, and create a scattered and disorganized effort to prevent drug and alcohol abuse.

Networking involves facilitating communication between community organizations, interested individuals, and drug and alcohol abuse professionals with a common interest. Youth drug abuse involves police, families, and schools. These community organizations, and others, must be included in a prevention network. Their cooperation is essential. It is important to include other community groups, such as churches, businesses, and mass media, in a network that functions to prevent drug and alcohol abuse.

Police

Drug and alcohol abuse correlate with delinquency and other youth problems, such as dropping out of school, teen-age pregnancy, and poor school performance. State, local, and national police agencies use a number of strategies to reduce drug abuse. These include reducing the demand for drugs and limiting the supply. For example, the Border Patrol, which has statutory responsibility for controlling immigration and the flow of illegal drugs into the United States, recently became involved with school districts in an educational program for children at all levels, with particular emphasis on pre-elementary- and elementary-school children.

Local police departments are investing more time and effort in delinquency prevention, including drug abuse prevention. With the support and cooperation of school officials, police continue to fulfill their traditional role, investigating and arresting youthful drug users. An undercover operation, conducted without the knowledge of school officials, can result in "blown cover" for the undercover agent and increased resentment and hostility between police and school authorities. As Drug Abuse Resistance Education (DARE), developed by the Los Angeles Police Department and widely adopted throughout the United States demonstrates, police can play an important role in prevention. DARE trains police officers in communication techniques, drug abuse education, and public relations so that they can work full-time with schools to prevent drug abuse and increase trust between the police and the community. In addition, police can serve as resource officers in schools, either in uniform or out of uniform, working with youth on a daily basis to resolve problems, maintain order, and to represent legal authority in the schools.

Law enforcement agencies throughout the country use canine search techniques, better known as "drug dogs," to locate illegal drugs. In recent years, school districts increasingly have employed drug dogs to search school buildings and student vehicles. Use of drug dogs is justified by proponents on the basis of prevention. The argument is that students will be deterred from using or bringing drugs to school because they will be at risk of detection. However, because present legal interpretation prevents the dogs from searching students, users and sellers can simply carry the drugs with them. We assessed a drug dog program in our community's high school and found, on the one hand, that 10% of drug users said that drug dogs affected their behavior. On the other, 25% of users reported that drug dogs reduced the availability of drugs on campus and 30% believed that the program reduced the number of students bringing illegal drugs to school. Use of drug dogs affects the climate of drug tolerance in the schools and can help to build working relationships and trust between law enforcement, school officials, and clinical sociologists. Drug dogs may not stop students from bringing drugs to school or using them, but they can reinforce community cooperation and create an atmosphere in the schools of a committed effort to control drugs.

Schools

Facilitating police–school cooperation requires some intervention with schools, teachers, administrators, and parents. This may be more difficult for the clinical sociologist than working with police, because school districts are more participatory than law enforcement agencies. Defining and restricting the social and institutional context within which drug use occurs is a critical first step toward achievement of the goal of reduce drug use among adolescents. The clinical sociologist in the school district needs to work with teachers, administration, the school board, and parents.

As an elected body, the school board sets policy for the district, hires and fires the superintendent, and reflects the collective opinions of the active electorate. Policies that do not serve the needs and interests of the district, as defined by the electorate, can result in a change in school board members. The school board is critical in the support of drug abuse prevention; the clinical sociologist can assist the board with strategies and resources. Examples of such strategies include demonstrating the relationship between drug use and academic performance, seeking recognition for district drug abuse prevention efforts, and assisting with grassroots organizing about drug abuse.

The good will and approval of the school board is essential to the superintendent, whose support for drug and alcohol abuse prevention is vital. The superintendent of a school district can set the stage for drug and alcohol abuse prevention/intervention, or he or she can stop it from happening, usually by refusing to recognize that a problem exists. Whether giving permission to survey students about the extent of the problem or leading other administrators and teachers in planning active prevention of drug and alcohol abuse, the support of the superintendent is critical. Few school districts have adequate resources, and the clinical sociologist, with research, writing, and organizational expertise, may be able to bring additional money to the school district to assist with drug abuse prevention.

Parents, who are generally a passive force in education, are also voters whose children are being educated. What may be most challenging and difficult to the clinical sociologist, who is trying to mobilize a community to take part in substance abuse prevention and intervention, is the involvement of parents in the process. Publicity can help to increase parental awareness of drug and alcohol abuse. Newspapers are often eager for hard factual data. In our case, we summarized the data on the local use of drugs reported by the students and compared our findings with those of similar surveys undertaken in previous years. Publication in the local newspaper presented the data in a clear, difficult-to-deny context enhancing parental awareness of drug and alcohol abuse among schoolchildren. The sociologist can spread the word on drug use in the community in other ways as well, speaking to community groups, such as PTA meetings, teacher in-service workshops, and community service clubs.

Another activity that has been successful in a number of communities is a drug and alcohol awareness fair or symposium. These events, frequently held on public-school grounds, emphasize community awareness of the problems of youth, drugs, education, and families. Sociologists, who are sensitive to the need for a communitywide effort to prevent drug and alcohol abuse and skilled in working with all segments of communities can organize youth groups, service organizations, and health and educational institutions to participate together in a 1-day fair. The community fair provides an excellent opportunity for in-patient and out-patient treatment organizations to make contact with persons in need of their services, attracting them with displays that are flashy and professional. Self-help organizations, such as Alcoholics Anonymous, Narcotics Anonymous, and Al-Anon, appreciate the opportunity to expose other community members to their organization and philosophy. Police agencies can put on impressive displays of drug paraphernalia, weapons, and drug detection capability. Demonstrations of drug-sniffing dogs are always interesting and exciting for the participants. Many states, such as Texas, have drug-free bands, sponsored by law enforcement agencies. These groups, frequently tested to document their drug-free status, dress, act, sing, and look like any popular rock'n roll band. Teenagers are attracted to them and to the carnival-like atmosphere of the drug-free fair. A lot of education about the physical and social consequences of drug and alcohol abuse can occur within a short period of time. Drug-free fairs, alone, cannot educate parents or youth regarding drug and alcohol abuse, but they bring drugs and alcohol abuse to community consciousness and provide another base for community mobilization.

Family

Families are critical to the community's response to drug and alcohol abuse. The only variable in a multiple regression equation, beside friends' drug use, to significantly affect self-reports of drug use, is the adolescent's belief that parents know where he/she is. Commonsense notions of child rearing and the arguments of control theorists tell us that parental control can affect drug use.

There are other strategies beside research-based publicity about drug abuse that the sociologist can use to involve families in an effective drug abuse prevention strategy. Parenting skills training can help parents sharpen and improve interaction with their children. Recent research[19,20] reports that parents are the most critical significant other for preschool and elementary children. Parents diminish in importance as a referent for behavior as maturing children substitute peers. Workshops that seek to improve parenting skills provide a model that will enhance the self-esteem of young children. Oetting and Beauvais[19] propose that although self-esteem is not a critical variable affecting drug use among older adolescents, it is important for setting the stage for adolescent clusters of drug abuse. Children with low self-esteem seek out other children with similar problems and engage in a number of troubled behaviors that include drug abuse. Training for parents of young children is a preventive strategy that teaches skills to enhance child self-esteem.

Training can focus on parents of older children but with a different emphasis. Our experience is that parents are remarkably ignorant of the drugs in use, their biological and psychological effects, symptoms, and social consequences of use. A didactic workshop, teaching current scientific findings regarding the effects of drugs and alcohol, can awaken parents to danger to their children as well as to themselves. Within the last 20 years, drug and alcohol effects have been reexamined; but drugs like marijuana and cocaine have been used increasingly because they are perceived as harmless. Realistic information about drug effects can alter parent beliefs of harmlessness. It is our experience that parents who recognize the need to protect their children from drugs will be open to suggestion.

Parents cannot turn their homes into prisons or concentration camps for adolescents, but they can permit their adolescent children to go out without losing control. One strategy is to join a network of families that shares a commitment to drug- and alcohol-free adolescence and refuses to permit youth to consume drugs or alcohol in their homes. Teens, outside their own homes, often go to friends' houses, where alcohol and other drugs may be available. When parents join together in a network to prevent drug and alcohol abuse, teens become more aware that drug abuse is not condoned or supported by the adult community.

A parent network can also be the foundation for an institutionalized parent group with a clear purpose of preventing and intervening with drug abuse. PRIDE (Parents' Resource Institute for Drug Education, Inc.) is one well-known national organization that parents have formed to resist drugs. Another, the National Federation of Parents, sponsors an annual drug awareness week, Red Ribbon Week, in October, which provides a focal point for committed parents and youth to participate in drug and alcohol abuse prevention. Parent groups, whether chapters of national organizations or local efforts, can support police prevention and enforcement efforts, volunteer to work with the schools in prevention, and contribute time and energy to treatment as well as prevention efforts. By joining together in an organized fashion, parents work with others to publicly prevent and reduce drug use. As the fabric of prevention efforts is created in a community, parents are a critical component of the threads that bind the community into a cohesive whole.

Other Community Institutions: Church and Business

Religious participation by youth is generally associated with lower rates of drug use, although this relationship is mitigated by other factors such as ethnicity, income, and family attitudes. Churches and other religious organizations constitute a critical element of the community, providing solidarity and cohesiveness through shared beliefs, ritual participation, and other voluntary associations. Church involvement in a communitywide drug prevention effort is not novel but is necessary. Churches provide both legitimation and reinforcement for youth and other community members as they join a drug-free effort across denominational lines. Churches do not need to condemn or ban drinking and smoking, but they do need to educate their members about the health and social consequences of drug and alcohol abuse as well as the morality of substance abuse.

Churches almost invariably sponsor youth groups in addition to their religious education program. Although children who live in disorganized families are less likely to attend church, the involvement of churches in a drug abuse prevention program reinforces community, families, and youth in their resistance to drug and alcohol abuse. The clinical sociologist, working as community organizer, can facilitate active church participation with drug prevention activities.

Business, as the economic backbone of a community, helps to establish actual norms with regard to drug and alcohol consumption. Employers create and enforce workplace expectations for drinking and can limit drug use through a number of techniques. Few employers appear willing to undertake the cost or the legal liability of urine testing. By supporting drug abuse prevention efforts in the schools and on a communitywide basis, employers lower the risk of a community definition of drug and alcohol abuse as acceptable behavior, resulting in fewer employees who have drug problems. Lower liability and increased worker efficiency creates an incentive for business to become involved with drug prevention.

The clinical sociologist, as community organizer, needs to create and maintain working relationships with the business community and its professional organizations for legitimacy, support, and funds. The sociologist, working as educator and community organizer, needs to reach out to the business community to enlist their support and money for such activities as Red Ribbon Week or a drug-free fair.

Media

There is no question that mass media play an important role in defining what is real in the community. Newspapers, through the release of survey findings, can make a public issue of what is, for most families, a private problem. Publication of survey findings in our community produced tremendous interest in the prevention and treatment of drug and alcohol abuse problems. Information on self-help groups, such as Alcoholics Anonymous, is critical for the community recognition of existing alternatives to denial of drug and alcohol problems.

Television and other media like stories about drug problems. They have human interest value, containing the pathos of addiction and a clearly defined villain. The clarity of the conflict over youth, where drugs and alcohol are the principle object of conflict, makes drug prevention newsworthy. Prevention and treatment may not be as flashy as addiction, but clever events, like drug fairs, can be used to involve the media, providing greater publicity and promoting awareness in the community regarding prevention's needs.

Clinical sociologists can work with media to reinforce networking activities with schools, police, churches, and families. Media perform the important function of information dissemination, thereby helping to integrate the activities of the different groups. Media also provide a public forum for opposing views. Letters to the editor and radio talk shows provide an opportunity for public discussion of opposing views regarding drug use. While the outcome of public debate is never certain, community members often increase solidarity and support for the anti-drug abuse position. Mass media can contribute to community awareness, cohesiveness, and cooperation in meeting the drug abuse challenge.

Peer Prevention of Drug Abuse

The discussion of clinical intervention strategies to prevent drug abuse has focused principally on community organization and coordination. Specific strategies to reinforce community resistance to drug abuse have been discussed. Drug prevention education has not been presented as a principal intervention strategy. In the 1970s, drug education of schoolchildren was the principal prevention technique, resulting in increased knowledge about drugs; however, in too many cases, drug use continued to increase. Over time, programs that emphasize teaching students about drugs and appropriate attitudes to reject drugs increasingly have been challenged in the American public school curriculum.

Prevention Education: What Works?

When evaluating the success or failure of drug prevention efforts, five factors are frequently examined: knowledge, attitudes, skills, behavior, and use.[8] Knowledge and attitudes about drugs were thought to be critical to drug abuse prevention but have not proven to be so. Some prevention specialists have increased the skill levels of young people, focusing on refusal skills and social and life skills. The theory is that children who have been trained in socially comfortable ways to deflect invitations to drug use can resist peer pressure to use drugs. Behavior refers to the constellation of school and social behaviors, such as attendance, grades, and delinquency involvement. Drug use is, of course, what is intended to be prevented.

Tobler,[8] in a meta-analysis of 143 youth drug prevention programs, found only two types of programs to be successful. Programs, which contain no direct knowledge about drugs and emphasize competence of participants in productive, conforming activities, were particularly successful for at-risk youth on the behavior dimension. The most significant effected shift in drug use occurred in those programs that used peer prevention. Organized into peer groups that shared responsibility for drug education, including refusal skills as well as social and life skills, peer prevention programs were more than twice as successful in preventing kids from starting to use drugs as any other type of prevention program except the alternative activities model.

Perry[21] reports that peer-led groups, which identify functional meanings of drug use for their members and which develop shared strategies for alternative behaviors, are effective in delaying the onset of tobacco consumption and other drug-using behaviors. The peer prevention approach, which has been evaluated in numerous studies, has achieved significant reductions in smoking rates after almost 3 years. Other studies[22] have found that peer-led programs are more effective than no program or teacher-led programs, as measured by marijuana use, amount of alcohol consumed, and frequency of drunkenness. Peer groups are more effective in reducing inhalant and marijuana use than other program alternatives including parent effectiveness, support groups, problem-solving groups, or humanistic education.

Laying the Foundation

Based on our community experience, the first stage in facilitating peer prevention is developing support. Analysis of the survey data we collected in this community demonstrates that friends' drug use accounts for almost 40% of the explained variance. Friends who use drugs are highly dependent on one another to start and maintain their use in this community. Data from youth in the community can be compared with that from other locations, but local findings create a foundation upon which community support for peer prevention programs can be built.

The schools and the professional network must be persuaded of the importance, ease, and effectiveness of peer prevention. Some strategies for persuading school officials include visits to school districts that have implemented peer programs and workshops in which peer prevention is detailed. In our community, we organize trips to schools that had programs that had been identified by the state or the U.S. Department of Education as model drug prevention programs by a committee of teachers and administrators. Some of the 10 schools that we visited, notably L. D. Bell High School, in Euless, Texas, and McArthur High School, in Irving, Texas, had implemented peer prevention programs. Observance of the successful programs in these schools, the teachers and counselors involved with the programs, and the enthusiasm of the young participants helped to overcome the resistance and concerns of the school personnel who will be taking the initiative in our community.

Once school and community leaders have been introduced to the peer prevention concept and convinced of its effectiveness, it is important that they be given information and training in peer prevention. At the time of this writing, the Drug Free Schools and Communities Program provides funding to the states on a youth per capita basis to support local drug education and prevention activities. School districts can use some of their Drug Free Schools allocation to present workshops on peer prevention to teachers, counselors, and principals. Peer prevention experts are available (see[21,23]) to train others and develop a full peer prevention program within the community.

One factor that may increase the acceptance of peer prevention is its cost. Apart from the expense of hiring consultants to assist with the initiation and planning of a peer prevention project, costs for this type of program are low. Professional staff time is required for initiating, recruiting, training, and maintaining peer prevention groups, but these responsibilities frequently can be assigned to existing staff. Clinical sociologists who specialize in peer prevention and who have worked in and with schools may also be able to perform this function. As Tobler[8] documents, low-intensity peer prevention programs are very cost-effective, enhancing their attractiveness to communities.

Peer Prevention: How to Implement It

It is best not to be too ambitious when beginning a peer prevention program. Begin an effort at peer prevention in one school at a time or, at most, with students at a single grade level. A citywide or district effort to implement peer prevention in all grades is too ambitious a program to attempt during the first year. A number of communities have chosen to start peer prevention programs in the elementary school, before children are truly at risk. One elementary program, using an integrated, didactic curriculum beginning in kindergarten, includes peer prevention as the culminating experience for the child.

A children's club in the fifth or sixth grade helps elementary students to believe that they are making a worthwhile effort. One school district, Pleasanton, Texas, has adopted the CHICKEN Club concept from the Optimists. The CHICKEN Club is an elite organization, which only fifth or sixth graders are permitted to join. CHICKENS are granted special privileges in school and are asked to speak to children in the lower grades. CHICKENS sign a drug-free pledge, learn to recite the CHICKEN rap, and are expected to act as models for other youth. Turning a common epithet into something positive strengthens youth resistance to drug abuse. CHICKEN stands for: Cool, Honest, Intelligent, Clearheaded, Keen, Energetic, and Not Interested in Drugs. The CHICKEN rap is memorized and recited with all the zest of street raps:

> We are the chickens yes sir'ee
> And we've come to talk to you seriously.
> We don't take drugs cause they're bad for your body.
> We can do other things when we want to party.
> When people say "Come on. Let's get high." we just
> Turn around and say "Bye, bye."
> Chickens know drugs can mess up your head.
> Drugs can also make your best friend dead.
> So don't be a fool, drugs aren't cool.
> Keep your heart tickin' and just be a chicken.

Other communities have started their peer prevention programs in high-school, perhaps because this is the level where the greatest need exists. Peer prevention in high school is effective, catches on quickly, and the students are enthusiastic. If you are starting at the high-school level, be careful in choosing the students to be invited to join the group. Perry[21] suggests having peer leaders selected by class election; others have conducted formal or informal sociometric studies to insure that effective and instrumental leaders are selected from the group. Because high school students are so clique oriented, there is a danger that the new peer prevention group will be labeled "the goody two shoes" group or the "druggies." Some people who have started at this level recommend bringing in a mix of students from different cliques. A separate group should be established for recovering drug abusers; they have different needs than students who have never used drugs. Separation of the two groups prevents ex-drug abusers from being chosen for leadership positions and drug use being idealized. A support group for recovering abusers within the school, with connections to Narcotics Anonymous and Alcoholics Anonymous, can be very helpful in lowering recidivism and further integrate users into the community.

The peer prevention group needs to be carefully and fully taught the chemical, biological, psychological, and sociological facts associated with drug and alcohol abuse. It is a truism in the field that students who use drugs know more about them than their teachers. The purpose of this training is to ensure that the teachers in peer prevention programs are well trained and able to field a wide range of questions about drugs. The training is extensive;[21] peer prevention participants must give up weekends and afternoons for an extended period of time. Although this strengthens the commitment of the student, it strains the resolve of teachers who are responsible for peer training.

Build *esprit de corps* among peer prevention participants. Some popular techniques that sociologists can suggest and initiate include lock-ins, in which high school students and the peer prevention sponsor are "locked up" overnight at someone's house, the school gym, or a church basement. Group outings that require cooperation and the development of trust, such as Outward Bound or Ropes, can create solidarity and unity of purpose in the group. Visible symbols, such as jackets, T-shirts, and special greetings, can be developed by group members to enhance their commitment and cohesiveness.

Monitor the peer prevention group. A school counselor or the clinical sociologist working with the group needs to remain in close contact. All peer prevention presentations must be monitored, either by the group sponsor or by some teacher or other responsible adult. Peer prevention meetings and parties must be as carefully monitored as those outside the movement to avoid imputations of misconduct.

Peer prevention groups need to cooperate with other programs in the schools and the community. Staff members of drug and alcohol prevention councils or treatment facilities can serve as expert consultants on technical questions, improving training and making student leaders aware that other professionals can assist. Within the school, peer prevention activities should be coordinated with other school-based programs, such as student assistance and children of alcoholics. Student assistance programs have a core team of teachers and administrators who are trained in identifying children who are at risk of drug and alcohol abuse. These children, after consultation with their parents, are referred to alternative activities that are designed to enhance self-esteem, competence, and drug-free activities. Peer prevention groups are targeted to serve the student who is at ordinary risk, not the high-risk student.

Clinical sociologists are uniquely equipped to help develop peer prevention programs as part of the community effort against drug and alcohol abuse. Sociologists can collect and analyze data to be used as a basis for designing an appropriate series of interventions against substance abuse that involve major community institutions as well as peer groups. The evidence that was collected in our community and the progress that we are making in building community awareness and motivating interest in peer prevention suggest, on a case study basis, that the approach works as an organized set of interventions.

PROBLEMS IN COMMUNITY DRUG ABUSE PREVENTION

Although a strong consensus exists that drug abuse and alcoholism are serious problems that erode our society and attack the quality of life in present-day American society, the opinion is not universally shared. Within the last 25 years, many Americans between the ages of 18 and 45 experimented with illegal drugs. Some probably used selected drugs for significant periods in their lives; others may continue to use them. Like alcoholics, drug users do not readily or easily give up their drugs. Through organizations, such as NORML (National Organization for the Reform of Marijuana Laws) and through community pressure, groups and individuals passively and actively resist drug abuse prevention. Sociologists can rapidly find themselves to be controversial public figures, asserting what appeared, at first, to be a noncontroversial, high-consensus position. However, sociologists who are working closely with other community institutions, despite the discomforts of public pressure, will find themselves protected and supported by other public figures. Conflict, indeed, can be functional.

Another problem that confronts the clinical sociologist, or anyone working in drug abuse prevention, is a lack of resources. Most federal spending on drug abuse is invested in supply reduction through law enforcement. Prevention efforts receive less than $100 million a year, well below the amount needed to mobilize community support for drug prevention; local communities and many states believe they cannot afford drug abuse prevention programs. Sociologists can work to obtain resources to support drug abuse prevention programs at the local and national levels. It may be necessary to impress local authorities, particularly those in schools, that they cannot afford *not* to invest in drug abuse prevention. The constellation of problems that accompanies drug abuse can be so serious that it undermines effective learning and community life. Sociologists, at the national level, can work to obtain federal funds to support local projects. Grants allocating federal funds are highly competitive, but they can provide a significant boost to community activities that will reduce drug and alcohol abuse.

Clinical sociologists may meet with resistance from other professionals who have an interest in drug and alcohol abuse. They may question the treatment expertise sociologists bring to the area and the special skills sociologists have. The drug abuse professional community, principally made up of professionals with training in counseling, psychology, and social work, may not readily accept sociologists and their training. Sociologists have been doing a great deal to professionalize, discover their clinical roots, and develop clinical theory and practice, but recognition by other professionals has been slow in coming. Recognition will result from a demonstration of professional success.

REFERENCES

1. Duster, T. (1970). *The legislation of morality: Law, drugs, and moral judgement.* New York: Free Press.
2. Watts, W. D. (1971). *The psychedelic experience: A sociological study.* Beverly Hills, CA: Sage Publications.
3. Becker, H. S. (1967). History, culture, and subjective experience: An exploration of the social bases of drug-induced experiences. *Journal of Health and Social Behavior, 8,* 163–176.
4. Becker, H. S. (1963). *Outsiders: Studies in the sociology of deviance.* New York: Free Press.

5. Hanson, D. J. (1980). Drug education: Does it work? In Frank Scarpitti & S. K. Datesman (Eds.), *Drugs and the youth culture* (pp. 251–282). Beverly Hills, CA: Sage Publications.

6. Hoffman, F. (1987). An alcoholism program for Hispanics. *Clinical Sociology Review, 5*, 91–101.

7. Gelles, R. J., & Strauss, M. A. (1988). *Intimate violence.* New York: Simon and Schuster.

8. Tobler, N. (1986). Meta-analysis of 143 adolescent drug prevention programs: Quantitative outcome results of program participants compared to a control or a comparison group. *Journal of Drug Issues, Fall*, 537–567.

9. Etzioni, A. (1988). *The moral dimension: Toward a new economics.* New York: Free Press.

10. Watts, W. D. (1989). Reducing adolescent drug abuse: Sociological strategies for community practice. *Clinical Sociology Review, 7*, 152–171.

11. Berger, P. L., & Luckmann, T. (1966). *The social construction of reality.* New York: Anchor.

12. Johnston, L. (1972). *Drugs and American youth.* Ann Arbor, MI: University of Michigan.

13. Johnston, L. D., O'Malley, P. M., & Bachman, J. G. (1986). *Drug use among American high school students, college students, and other young adults: National trends through 1985.* Rockville, MD: National Institute on Drug Abuse.

14. Fishburne, P. M., Abelson, H. I., & Cisin, I. (1979). *National survey on drug abuse: Main findings.* Washington, DC: National Institute on Drug Abuse.

15. Fredlund, E. V., Spence, R. T., & Maxwell, J. (1989). *Substance abuse among students in Texas secondary schools—1988.* Austin, TX: Texas Commission on Alcohol and Drug Abuse.

16. Hirschi, T. (1969). *Causes of delinquency.* Berkeley, CA: University of California Press.

17. Kandel, D. (1973). Adolescent marijuana use: Role of parents and peers. *Science, 181*, 1067–1070.

18. Carpenter, C., Glassner, B., Johnson, B. D., & Loughlin, J. (1988). *Kids, crime and drugs.* Lexington, MA: D. C. Heath.

19. Oetting, E. R., & Beauvais, F. (1987). Common elements in youth drug abuse: Peer clusters and other psychosocial factors. *Journal of Drug Issues, 17*(2), 133–151.

20. Simmons, R. L., Conger, R. D., & Whitbeck, L. B. (1988). A multistage social learning model of the influence of family and peers upon adolescent substance abuse. *Journal of Drug Issues, 18*(3), 293–315.

21. Perry, C. L. (1987). Results of prevention programs with adolescence. *Drug and Alcohol Dependence, 20*, 13–19.

22. Sexter, J., Sullivan, A., Werner, S., & Denmark, R. (1984). Substance abuse: Assessment of the outcome of activities and activity clusters in school-based prevention. *International Journal of the Addictions, 19*, 79–92.

23. Scott, S. (1988). *Positive peer groups.* Amherst, MA: Human Resources Development Press.

Index